D0911503

The Good Neighbor Guidebook for Colorado

The Good Neighbor Guidebook for Colorado

Necessary Information and Good Advice for Living in and Enjoying Today's Colorado

Nancy S. Greif
Erin J. Johnson,
Editors

Foreword by
Charles Wilkinson

Johnson Books
BOULDER

Copyright © 2000 by Nancy S. Greif and Erin J. Johnson
The Good Neighbor Guidebook™ is a registered trademark of the authors.

All rights reserved. No part of this publication may be reproduced or transmitted in any form or by any means, electronic or mechanical, including photocopy, recording, or any information storage and retrieval system, without permission in writing from the publisher.

Published by Johnson Books, a division of Johnson Publishing Company, 1880 South 57th Court, Boulder, Colorado 80301.
E-mail: books@jpcolorado.com.

9 8 7 6 5 4 3 2 1

Cover design by Debra B. Topping
Cover and interior photographs by Kathleen Norris Cook. Visit her website at kathleennorriscook.com.

Library of Congress Cataloging-in-Publication Data
The good neighbor guidebook for Colorado: necessary information and good advice for living in and enjoying today's Colorado / edited by Nancy S. Greif, Erin J. Johnson; foreword by Charles Wilkinson.
        p.   cm.
    Includes bibliographical references.
    ISBN 1-55566-262-5 (alk. paper)
    1. Land use, Rural—Colorado. 2. Land use, Rural—Colorado—Planning. 3. Land use—Government policy—Colorado. 4. Conservation of natural resources—Colorado. 5. Environmental protection—Colorado. I. Greif, Nancy S. II. Johnson, Erin J.
HD211.C6 G66 2000
333.76′09788—dc21   00-044368

Printed in the United States by
Johnson Printing
1880 South 57th Court
Boulder, Colorado 80301

⊕ Printed on recycled paper with soy ink

This book is dedicated to
all our wonderful friends and good neighbors in Colorado

CONTENTS

Section IV: Recreation, Public Lands, and Tribal Lands

Section V: Protecting Our Western Heritage

Section VI: Avoiding and Resolving Problems

By Charles Wilkinson

For centuries, human beings touched the lands of the interior West only lightly. Until well into the twentieth century, this was true for the Indian tribes and Hispanic communities and, later, the Mormon settlements, the mountain mining towns, and the farm and ranch communities in the valleys. To be sure, the pell-mell race for gold and silver rearranged the ground and left waste piles in the mining districts. The running of cattle and sheep made the western range less hospitable to wildlife. Irrigation drew down some rivers and inundated some canyons. And the westward expansion brought profound society dislocations. The Indian tribes were now confined to reservations. The Hispanic communities along the Rio Grande now included significant Anglo populations. But by and large the land itself—with its magnificent variety of startling landforms, abundant wildlife, and wide open space—absorbed each new round of arrivals.

Traditionally, the sheer physical distance between human communities isolated and insulated them, let them be independent. There was no need for a ranching town to work with the neighboring Hispanic village, to discuss mutual problems and aspirations. The two communities probably would have had similar concerns (inadequate water, schools, and health care) and similar dreams (a good living from a harsh and beautiful land, a way of life dictated by the land and refined over the generations, and a promise of passing the way of life and the land on to the next generations). But neither saw any need to engage the other, much less the city people.

The aftermath of World War II brought nothing less than a revolution to both the land and communities. The cities ringing the interior, from Los Angeles to Denver, and from Salt Lake City to El Paso, began to grow explosively. A new wave of settlers poured in, attracted by the sunshine, informality, burgeoning industries, and inexpensive housing. The ambitious urban areas had plenty of room to grow, but they needed water and power. They turned to the desert lands and rivers of the intermountain region. They built dams and power plants, pipelines and transmission lines. They mined the coal—under Indian land, under ranch land, under federal land. The post-war boom also sent the timber harvest on the national forests skyrocketing. Still, for a generation the people carried on in their traditional ways—ignoring the outside world, still isolated, still insulated.

But it would not last. Federal funds improved and connected up the highways, the airlines added flights and launched larger planes, and Americans had more wealth and leisure. Tourism surged. At first these visitors only skied, or hiked, or camped, or fished, and after two or three weeks, went home. They left their money and did little to harm the land or disturb the local ways of life. By the 1980s, however, it had become clear that the population explosion—the West grew from 17 million in 1945 to 60 million in 2000—was taking an enormous toll. Listings of endangered and threatened species stood as testaments to the impact of development on the mountains, plains, and rivers. Tourists and residents of the new metropolises swarmed over the backcountry.

In the 1990s, the new pressures intensified even more in the rural West. Previously, virtually all of the residential population increase had been in the cities. More recently, however, increasing numbers of people, particularly from the coasts, began to buy land and move to the country. They put pressure on real estate prices. Gradually, ranches were subdivided, towns grew into small cities, and recreational demands on the land began to affect its more traditional uses. Old timers felt threatened; newcomers felt unwelcome.

The Good Neighbor Guidebook for Colorado attempts to address the stresses inevitable in the changing West in a way that is both creative and objectively sound. The editors believe, rightly, that an understanding of the law is central to the development of lasting, neighborly relations among people of diverse economic, social, and cultural backgrounds. They see the federal, state, tribal, and local laws as creating a set of societal sideboards. These sideboards give everyone—newcomers and established residents—a common set of understandings and expectations within which to work. Properly understood, this can serve to structure public relationships and ease tensions among people of good will.

This volume contains a remarkable collection of essays. The individual authors are expert in their fields, and their essays are clear, non-technical, interesting, and often humorous. The book begins with a series of articles on stewardship—choosing a building site, protecting water quality, and respecting wetlands, wildlife, and natural vegetation. It then moves on to deal with such topics as water law, land use planning, the law of nuisance, real estate transfers, eminent domain, and mineral rights. Federal public land law and tribal law are examined in some detail, for they are critical topics in a region where public and Indian lands are often adjacent to, or interspersed with, private land. The book concludes with an excellent discussion of the alternatives to subdivision: conservation easements, sustainable ranching, and tax and estate planning. Throughout, the essayists stress the need to understand and reach out to communicate with neighbors new and old, city and country, ranch and subdivision.

We all love this land—some of us because we have always loved it, some of us because we have recently fallen in love with it. Our ability to understand each other, to respect each other's rights, and to live up to our own obligations is a necessary foundation for the development of mature, enlightened communities that can, in the not-so-distant future, craft a relationship with this storied and sacred landscape that will do us and those who follow proud.

By Nancy S. Greif and Erin J. Johnson

Whether we like it or not, "The times, they are a changin'!" and the West, especially Colorado, is changing too. These days it's not so simple to build or live on rural land and to be a good neighbor in the rural West. You need a lot of basic information if you hope to achieve personal happiness and neighborhood harmony in Colorado.

The primary genesis of this book was a one-day seminar that Nancy organized in Durango, Colorado, covering a broad range of rural living and "good neighbor" issues. The seminar was sponsored by the Southwest Colorado Women's Bar Association, the Foundation of the Colorado Women's Bar Association, and Norwest Bank of Durango. After we both participated as speakers in the Good Neighbor seminar, we found a high level of demand for practical information about living in Colorado. This discovery led us to embark on a two-year effort to gather additional information and pull it together in a "presentable" manner.

Another motivating factor for this publication was former Colorado governor Roy Romer's Smart Growth Initiative. This effort encouraged everyone to help build a better Colorado—from the ground up. Although many Smart Growth directives were concentrated at community and local-government levels, we made a sincere effort in developing this book to truly start at the "ground level." We felt that providing people with the appropriate tools to encourage better communication and cooperation between neighbors of all kinds in Colorado would result in the best kind of Smart Growth.

The concept of being a good neighbor in Colorado encompasses responsibilities of stewardship of the natural elements of the state as well as respecting human interactions. To best illustrate this concept, we chose the photography of Kathleen Norris Cook, world renowned nature photographer, for the cover and section dividers. The cover photo, *Twilight at the Cimmaron Range of the San Juans in Ouray County*, displays the breathtaking beauty of the Colorado landscape and also reminds us of the inseparable human influence on the state's broad and majestic panoramas. Several other examples of Kathleen's work are used within the book.

Although the editors are both previously published authors and editors, our best qualification for putting this book together is that we both practice law and mediation in rural southwest Colorado, and we both have strong backgrounds in natural resource and land use issues. We have done our best to select appropriate experts in carefully chosen areas and to have the chapters reviewed by other experts in order to keep inaccuracy to an absolute minimum.

After begging, pleading, arm-twisting, and promising whatever we could, we ended up with thirty-seven authors contributing the forty-four chapters that make up this book. These authors, who represent a broad spectrum of specialized fields of expertise, graciously agreed not only to share their knowledge but to write "understandable" nonlegalese articles about specific topics. The contributing authors of this book possess a wealth of specialized knowledge and wisdom that we believe can make anyone's Colorado experience smoother and happier.

One of our primary goals was to present often technical and complex legal information in a format that most readers would be able to understand and use frequently. For this reason we have tried to keep notes to a minimum. However, there are necessary references in some of the chapters. Please keep in mind that if you have a specific problem, this book is just the starting point. Many authors have provided references at the end of the chapter so that the reader can obtain more detailed information and a deeper understanding of the issues and the jargon. If those resources do not answer your questions or resolve your disputes, then you should go to a professional such as a lawyer or a legally trained mediator for additional assistance.

Because we value the expertise of the contributing authors and feel that we have already asked enough of them, we as editors have not tried to "homogenize" the information for the sake of uniformity. Please be aware that authors from different professional backgrounds have different methods of citing information. We also value each author's individual style of expressing him- or herself and have tried to protect the expression of the contributors' passions for certain issues so that their importance is fully communicated. Sometimes similar feelings were expressed in two or more articles. After editing to eliminate pure repetition, we came to the conclusion that some things are stated more than once from different perspectives because they are very important, so we left some of that repetition alone.

All in all, the collection of information submitted by the contributing authors in this book constitutes an invaluable resource and reference document for the citizens of Colorado. We sincerely thank the contributing authors for the time, energy, and expertise they contributed to this book. On behalf of all of the contributing authors, we hope that Colorado will be a better place to live with the help of the information in this book.

"No man should have proprietary rights over land who does not use that land wisely and lovingly."
—Marjorie Kinnan Rawlings
Cross Creek, 1942

Land Stewardship

The Best Way to Be a Good Neighbor in Colorado

When people ask questions about living in Colorado, they often start with questions about their rights. Many landowners have strong feelings about their "right" to do whatever they wish with their property. However, everybody who owns land in the rural West is somebody's neighbor, and being a good neighbor begins with understanding your responsibilities to others as well as your rights as a landowner. People who have lived in rural areas for a long time know that the best and easiest way to be a good neighbor is to care for your own property in a responsible manner.

Good land stewardship implies building in a responsible manner and caring for your land to establish and maintain an attractive and safe environment that will not infringe on the rights of your neighbors. If you are a good steward you will probably never be confronted by angry neighbors reminding you that they too have rights. Therefore, this book about being a good neighbor starts with some tips about how you can build your home and care for your property as a good steward of the land.

Building on rural property, a popular thing to do these days, brings its own list of questions for people who are trying to be good neighbors. Some of the major concerns that you will have to deal with before you buy property and begin to construct your home in rural Colorado are summarized by **Dusty Pierce**. Have you thought about the roads and driveway access? Electric power service? Telephone lines? Fire protection? Many public utilities and services that we often take for granted in more urban areas may not be routinely available in rural Colorado. Have you thought about snowload requirements, the depth of the frostline, extra insulation, and solar energy? Being a good neighbor means building in conformance with applicable building codes and in such a way that your home can be well maintained and will not quickly take on a derelict and uncared-for appearance.

In addition to the basics of building in rural Colorado, another important concern is likely to be the source and purity of your drinking-water supply. Where will your water supply come from? Will there be enough water, and will it be pure enough to drink? When building on rural property where individual drinking-water and waste-disposal systems are needed, good land stewards try to be considerate of their neighbors by choosing building locations and installing facilities that accommodate, as much as is feasible, their neighbors' concerns and sensitivities. **Jerry Biberstine**, who has been in charge of the drinking-water program for the state of Colorado since 1987, outlines the main sources of drinking water, possible contaminants, testing programs, and treatment systems. Understanding these fundamentals is necessary so that your actions don't lead to the presence of contaminants in your neighbor's drinking-water supply.

A closely related concern for rural construction is whether a particular piece of property is well suited to the installation and maintenance of a safe and unobtrusive wastewater–septic disposal system. **David Akers** explains several alternatives for the disposal and treatment of wastewater in rural Colorado.

Another part of responsible land stewardship is taking natural hazards into account prior to construction. **Daniel Balsinger** outlines some of the dangerous natural hazards that can threaten your home. In Colorado, avalanches, floods, landslides, and other natural hazards may affect the safety of your building site, and many such hazards are not covered by standard insurance policies. Proper early detection of natural hazard risks can prevent expensive repairs and catastrophic disasters.

Good stewardship also involves taking care of fragile environments that may be located on your property. **Lauranne Rink** explains the importance of wetlands and wetland environments and discusses what good neighbors can do to preserve and protect these important natural features and habitat support systems.

Reducing fire hazard in rural areas is an essential element of good land stewardship. Natural fires of all magnitudes not only are unavoidable but have important ecological functions. If we want to limit the incidence of fires that might destroy rural residences, we must take the responsibility of doing some of Mother Nature's "housekeeping" ourselves. Additionally, we must be prepared to protect our homes and families in the event of a fire. **Frank Dennis's** chapter gives tips about how to maintain your property and neighborhood to reduce the chances of a catastrophic fire.

The "suburbanization" of rural Colorado, including agricultural land splits and significant increases in large-lot subdivisions, has had a cumulative effect on natural ecosystems. Large country homesites are a desirable alternative to urban living, but property taken out of agricultural management, for the sake of space and privacy, may result in unintended ecological disasters. When land is not carefully managed to control noxious weeds, hardy weed seeds spread to neighboring farm and ranches. Then farmers and ranchers are forced to use more herbicides and mechanical eradication techniques. Consequently, more labor and higher expenses for farmers and ranchers are the unintended result of the suburbanization of the rural West. Additionally, weed infestation on rangeland used by stock and wildlife decreases the amount of available nutritious forage. The lesson for good neighbors is to become well informed about which plants are problem weed species and to do your best to control or eradicate them on your property before they become a problem for your neighbors. **Rod Cook's** chapter describes how alien noxious weeds have invaded our pristine pastureland and cropland and what species you need to control.

One of the easiest ways to aggravate your neighbor is to have improperly controlled pets and other domestic or farm animals. Dogs can be a menace to livestock and wildlife, and cats are natural predators. What happens if your dog likes to run after the neighbor's sheep? If you don't have your tomcat neutered, are you really to blame if the neighborhood is overrun with feral pussycats? And what about other wandering animals—horses; pigs; chickens; and even exotics such as llamas, ostriches, and camels? Can you legally keep vicious animals? To be a good neighbor you need to begin with understanding responsibilities to others as well as your rights. **Peter Holton** and **Nancy Greif** outline your responsibilities as a pet owner in rural neighborhoods.

Colorado has significant wildlife populations whose territories are constantly invaded by rural population growth. Wildlife is generally considered an amenity to property when selling real estate, even if you do have to surrender your tulips to the deer. However, rural development and wildlife are not necessarily compatible. What if your development interferes with a deer or elk calving ground? Will your pets become a nice snack for mountain lions? Are your children safe from attack by bears or other dangerous animals? In order to be good stewards of our abundance of wildlife and live peacefully with our wild neighbors, we all need **Pat Tucker's** tips to enjoy wildlife experiences and to remain safe in the process.

Subdivision of land in Colorado is often viewed as a God-given right that should not be interfered with by your neighbors and that especially should not be constrained by local governments. A lot of land in Colorado is marginally suitable for development; a high level of population growth results in a lot of pressure to develop regardless of how it is accomplished. If you are considering developing or subdividing your land, a little thought and foresight about your future neighbors can result in the creation of better homesites and increased land values. **Erin Johnson's** "recipe" for low-impact rural development offers some food for thought.

The chapters in this section help us all to shift our focus from the attitude of "What is best for me and my own family?" to "What is best for my family and our neighbors?" In rural environments where people like to seek solitude and escape from rules and regulations, it is easy to forget that we have neighbors and that we continue to have responsibilities to others even if we do not have urban-level day-to-day interactions with them. If we practice good land stewardship and follow the helpful suggestions given in this section, we are likely to have far more harmonious relationships with all of our neighbors.

Be Informed Before You Build in Rural Colorado

Dusty Pierce, *General Contractor, Master Carpenter*

I. Dreams Are Important

Once there was a family who dreamed of living in Colorado. After many years of hard work and saving, they were finally on their way to realize their dream. It took them a couple of days of hard driving to reach the state line. "Welcome to Colorful Colorado," the sign beckoned. They stopped to have their picture taken in front of the sign. But as they approached it, Dad noticed what looked like fine print at the bottom—and sure enough, the sign also said, "Buyer, Beware!"

Although this is an old joke told about many places, the point is well taken. Most people moving to Colorado take for granted basic governmental services such as electricity, water, sewer, telephone, and roads. They often assume that these services will be present at the new home or homesite because such services tend to exist where people have lived most of their lives, but this is not necessarily true in rural Colorado. This chapter provides a checklist of important items to consider *before* you spend your hard-earned savings building on rural Colorado property.

II. Reality Is Essential

Access

Access generally refers to whether you can get into your property from a passable section of road in all kinds of weather. What is the access to your property? Many roads in rural Colorado, whether they are maintained by the county or not, are not plowed in the winter. If you live on a road that is maintained by the U.S. Forest Service, you may need a permit to plow snow. The same may be true of roads maintained by the Bureau of Land Management (BLM) and other public agencies. An established school-bus route may be important if you have children; in a bad snowstorm, primary roads and school-bus routes will usually be plowed first. Be prepared to be snowed in. You must keep your driveway plowed in case an emergency vehicle needs to get through. You need to own and maintain the proper equipment or arrange for a plowing service to keep your driveway clear. Who will grade the road in the summer? To find the answers to these questions, ask your county road department, homeowners' association, or neighbors.

Water

Many areas in rural Colorado have readily available drinking water from public or private water systems, but some areas do not. Even if the property has an existing well, the water quantity or quality may not be adequate for your needs. Ask the water department, county health department, or water provider about availability, hook-up and tap fees, size of water lines, and usage fees. Regardless of the source, you need to determine whether there is enough water pressure for domestic as well as fire-protection purposes. If there is no nearby water system, you may need to drill a well or haul your water. Local well-drilling companies can provide information about probable well-drilling costs in your area. Neighbors can also provide useful information on their own wells.

Electric Service

As amazing as it may seem to urban refugees, you cannot take for granted the idea that a public power supply reaches the property you are considering purchasing. Talk to the local electric company early in your investigation because it can be very expensive to bring power to your property, even if power lines are located nearby. Look for power poles or pedestals indicating underground lines. Some rural electric associations may offer photovoltaic systems. Be prepared for frequent power outages in rural areas.

Telephone

Again, don't take anything for granted. Check with the local phone company. Some areas may be served only by cellular phone service, which is usually more expensive than traditional phone service. Remember that mountains and canyons affect your cellular range.

Sewer or Septic Systems

A few rural areas in Colorado have public sanitary sewer systems, but this is generally not the case. If your property has a septic system, have an engineer or other professional check it to see if it is operating properly and is adequate for your needs. Check with the local health department to see if the required permits are in place. The county building department and planning offices are good places to start with your questions. Remember that a septic system requires special care, and "normal" conveniences, such as garbage disposals, can be very hard on a septic system.

Although most septic systems release domestic wastewater into an underground leach field, poor soil conditions may require a lagoon or evaporation pond or an "engineered" leach field. These systems are effective only if properly designed, installed, and maintained. The local health department will have specific information about requirements and alternatives, but you may need to hire a private engineer to design the proper system.

Fire Protection

The possibility of fire on your property is a serious consideration. Most of rural Colorado is served by volunteer fire departments that typically operate on very limited budgets aided by a lot of goodwill and prayers. Depending on the population and available services, expected response times may be very long compared to those of municipal services. In some remote areas there may be no fire protection service available at all. You will probably pay more for fire insurance than you would in an urban setting and may have trouble even obtaining fire insurance for your home.

You also need to give some thought to wildland fires, which can sweep large areas. Most fire districts, the U.S. Forest Service, the BLM, and county governments have information on what you can do to help protect your home from wild fires. Be conscientious about clearing a "defensible space" around your home. Most authorities recommend at least fifty feet of clear area between your home and trees or brush. You may need to consider building a separate holding tank that has an independent source of power to pump water for fire protection purposes.

Building Codes

Believe it or not, many rural areas in Colorado have not adopted the Uniform Building Code (UBC) or other uniform national building standards. If there are no building code requirements, request that construction bids be based on uniform code requirements and pay special attention to areas prone to flooding, potential snowloads, and other special needs in your particular area.

Your county government should have maps that indicate flood potential and define "hundred-year flood" areas. A hundred-year flood is usually caused by a storm that drops so much rain in a short period of time that it raises rivers and streams to a level that only happens on an average of every one hundred years.

Snowload calculations are also often based on the possibility of a hundred-year event. It is important to understand the significance of snowload requirements. Because snow in your area may remain on your roof for several months, the weight of the snow and ice may easily build up over the winter and reach or exceed the snowload capacity of the structure. The altitude of your home is directly related to snowload calculations. For example, a home built at 7,000 to 7,500 feet in elevation requires a structure that can support the weight of the roof plus an additional 65 pounds per square foot for the snowload. A 1,500-square-foot roof needs to be designed to hold 97,500 pounds of "live" snowload plus the weight of the roof itself, or the "dead" load, usually about 10 to 15 pounds per square foot. The total load for this small roof area is 120,000 pounds, or the approximate weight of 30 cars!

This is just one example of why it is necessary to build to national building standards in most areas of Colorado. Also keep in mind decks, porches, and sun exposure. You may have serious safety problems depending on where your roof "sheds" the snow, and decks may need to be built to be even stronger than your roof!

The other components of your home, such as the walls, floors, windows, and doors, also need to be strong enough to support snowloads as well as the pressure from the force of the wind.

Frostline

You probably viewed or picked out your property in the summer months, and the frostline was probably far from your thoughts at that time. In Colorado, winter temperatures of 20°F below zero are not uncommon. In some areas temperatures can be as low as 65 below zero. The depth of the frostline is essential information so water lines can be buried deeply enough so that they don't freeze. The frostline also dictates how deep to dig your foundation footings so that the house won't be affected by the ground frost in the winter.

If you are unfamiliar with ground frost, think about how water expands when it freezes. When water in the ground freezes, it also expands and can exert tremendous pressures on foundation walls. Expansive soils, found in many areas of Colorado, can also affect foundations in similar ways. Your foundation needs to be designed to withstand the negative effects of all potential site conditions. If you are buying an existing home, check carefully for cracks and other structural defects. If you find any obvious or questionable problems, get a professional opinion regarding their severity.

Insulation

Proper insulation is very important in the Colorado environment. A common temperature setting in Colorado homes is 70 degrees. If it is 90 to 100 degrees outside you will need to cool your house by 20 to 30 degrees, and if it is 20 degrees below zero outside, you will need to heat your house 90 degrees! Because of these factors, installing good insulation is important whether you are building a new home or remodeling.

Good ceiling insulation is the first consideration—in Colorado you need at least R-30 to R-40 protection. It is recommended that you use at least 6 inches of insulation in the walls as well as insulation under floors. Stopping air infiltration is a very important part of a good overall insulation job.

Most window manufacturers offer several grades of insulated glass—if you install big windows to take advantage of Colorado views, it is important to get a good grade. Some types of glass also protect carpets and furniture from fading in the sunlight. Insulated doors and airlocks (two doors—an outer door and then a second door into the home) are also a good idea. Take the time to talk to the county building department or a reputable contractor about necessary protection for your area.

HUD Versus UBC Standards for Manufactured Homes

Manufactured housing may be built to Department of Housing and Urban Development (HUD) standards rather than UBC standards. The differences between the codes may be important. In a mobile or manufactured home, for example, HUD accepts a 30-pound snowload rating for all of Colorado, so if you have a HUD house in an area that has a 65-pound snowload rating, you may have problems. Take the time to learn exactly what you are buying if you are looking at mobile or manufactured homes.

Taking Advantage of the Sun

Although most people are aware of the advantages of passive and active solar-heat systems, these systems have even more importance in Colorado. Think about the orientation of your home. Think about the areas where the roof will shed snow and ice. Proper orientation of your home and attention to eaves and roof lines can take advantage of sunlight in the winter and provide shade in the summer.

Land Use Regulations

It is important for you to be aware of and have copies of *all* applicable land use regulations for your area. These may include county planning documents, subdivision covenants, plat or deed restrictions, zoning regulations, and special district and utility regulations particular to your lot or development. Spending a little on copying charges will save you money in the long run. Put the copies you collect into a three-ring binder for a handy reference. If you sell your home, leave the notebook with the house for the next owner. Also document and keep copies of any special land use approvals or negotiations that you may conduct with a local government entity or your neighbors, such as a conditional use permit or an access easement.

Geologic Hazards in Rural Building

Most of Colorado is rated under UBC standards as Seismic Zone 1. By contrast, most of California is rated as Zone 3 or Zone 4. This rating means that Colorado has only a minor potential for earthquakes. However, there are many other types of natural hazards that occur in Colorado. Common geohazard events include avalanches, landslides, rockfalls, mudflows, and ground subsidence. Another significant problem in Colorado is the potential for expansive or swelling soils, characteristics often associated with clay soils. Certain types of soils in Colorado can expand to up to fifteen times their normal volume when they get saturated with rain, snow, lawn watering, runoff, or other forms of moisture. When these soils dry out, they shrink and create ground movement that can crack and lift foundations or cause settling. Some counties have geologic hazard maps that identify some major types of natural hazards. If you think there may be a problem, hire a geologist.

Electronic Communications

The beautiful mountains and canyons of Colorado can cause problems with your reception of electronic communications signals. Living in a remote area may cause interference with television, radio, cellular phone, CB radio, and even satellite signals. Be prepared to cuddle up with a good book instead of watching your favorite TV program during bad weather. You may have to spend considerable money to get adequate reception in some areas. Also remember that you may be "out of communication" just when you need it the most.

Other Considerations

1. Is there mail delivery to your home? You may have to get a post office box in a nearby town.
2. If you are buying a home along a state highway, check with the Colorado Department of Highways to see if your access complies with the state access code.
3. If you are going to operate a business, check to see if there are any special licensing requirements or other restrictions in your area.
4. When you buy property, you may own rights only to the surface—someone else may own the right to extract oil, gas, and minerals from your property, and they may disturb the surface to do so. Be sure to discuss this possibility with your real estate professional or the title company, or do some research at the county clerk's office yourself.
5. Home-building materials may not be as readily available in rural areas as they are in urban areas. Many items need to be specially ordered and may cost you extra time and money. Don't be upset if local businesses can't offer the same prices as Builder's Square. Remember, the "laid-back" atmosphere of a small town is one of the features of Colorado that attracted you here in the first place, so try to be patient and go with the flow instead of trying to make the local atmosphere more like the area you are trying to escape.
6. Part of being a good neighbor is being happy and enjoying Colorado. When someone tells you that you can't do something you'd like to do, it's human nature to feel your temper rise. Calm down and act responsibly. Never assume anything. Do your own homework. Ask questions when you are not sure of something. Don't be afraid to talk to neighbors and "old-timers"—they can be a big help, and you may become good friends.

III. Build Your Rural Colorado Dream

As you evaluate your plans for building in rural Colorado, don't become overwhelmed with potential problems! Approach your project one step at a time, and don't get in too much of a rush. You will be welcomed and treated like a native (well, almost) if you try to appreciate Colorado's rural lifestyle instead of trying to import your values from another area to your new home. If you have a particular expertise, special knowledge, unique perspective, or a good solution to a problem, help the rest of us learn about it instead of just demanding that everyone do things your way. You might be surprised at what new tricks you can teach some old dogs in Colorado if you use a gentle approach.

Once you settle in, don't forget to enjoy all the wonderful resources that Colorado has to offer, and do your part to protect them for future generations. Enjoy the wildlife, the majesty of the mountains, the beauty of a fresh snowfall, fantastic sunsets, and the bluest of skies. Once you have built your home in rural Colorado, you will truly know the meaning of "Home Sweet Home." So "Buyer, Beware," yes—but "Buyer, Rejoice" as well!

2

Providing Rural Drinking Water

Jerry C. Biberstine, *Drinking Water Specialist*
Department of Health and Environment, Drinking Water Program

I. Where Will You Get Your Drinking Water?

Most people in Colorado get their drinking water from a public water system. A public water system is any water supply that serves at least twenty-five people for at least sixty days per year. Such water systems are regulated by the state under the federal Safe Drinking Water Act to ensure that the water is safe to drink. The water from a public water supply is treated to remove any hazardous chemicals and to kill or remove any pathogenic organisms that may be present. It is regularly tested for seventy-five or more contaminants to verify that no health hazard exists. If you are in an area that is served by a public water supply, you can get a copy of the chemical analysis from the water system. A requirement for water systems is to provide the results of sampling analysis, a compliance history of the system, and a brief discussion of the water source and treatment to every customer of the system. This requirement is met by a publication called the "Consumer Confidence Report."

If you are not in an area currently served by a public water system, you can either put in your own water supply or have water hauled to you.

Official state policy (DWT-8) requires that commercial water haulers obtain the water from a public water system; it must be disinfected before it is put into your cistern. This type of water service is expensive, may result in periods without water, and generally is used only in areas where other types of water supply are unavailable.

If you intend to put in your own water supply, you may use a well, a spring, or a surface water supply. However, before you drill a well, tap a spring, or divert a surface water source, you must be sure that you have the legal right to use the water. To find out how much water you can use and what type of rights are available to you, you must contact the State Engineer's Office, Water Resources Division, of the Colorado Department of Natural Resources. In many areas there is a local contact for the division. Look in the state government listings in your phone book or call your county planning department.

If the water supply you would like to use will not serve twenty-five or more people, the water quality of that source will not be regulated by the state. In other words, there is no required testing to determine whether the water is unsafe, and there is no requirement to treat the water to make it safe.

II. Water Sources

Water that may be available on your land is either surface water or groundwater. This distinction is important because the type of water source will determine the types of contaminants you are likely to have in your water as well as the amount and type of treatment you may need to make the water safe to drink. Your water rights decree (for surface or spring water) or your drilling permit (for groundwater) will explain your rights to use water from a particular source.

A surface water source is one that comes into contact with the surface of the ground or contains contaminants that are usually not found below ground level. This source could be a pond or lake, a river or stream, a spring or shallow well that is open to the air and could be contaminated by exposure to the air. Surface water, even if it runs only a few feet across the ground, is subject to contamination by animal fecal material. Fecal material contains pathogens (disease-causing microorganisms) that are a significant threat to public health. Major disease outbreaks have been caused by such microorganisms as *Giardia* and *Cryptosporidium*. These microorganisms are present in the fecal material of wild animals all over the state. Public water systems are required to filter out surface water contaminants such as dirt and pathogens.

A groundwater supply comes from underground and never "daylights" until it comes out of the tap. Because there is little chance of contamination of such sources from fecal material, treatment requirements to control microorganisms are minimal. However, there may be other contaminants present in the subsurface soil and rocks that may affect the quality of the water for drinking. Also, because the groundwater must move through the pore spaces in the soil to reach the well, there is a limit to the amount of water that can be withdrawn within a given time period. If all the water is pumped out of a well, it must be given time to "recharge" before any more can be pumped. In some areas of Colorado, the recharge rate is insufficient to provide all of the water that is needed for a single-family home.

So groundwater sources may have two problems: quality and quantity. If the water is good but there is not enough of it, you have a problem. If there is plenty of water but it cannot be used for drinking, you also have a problem. You need both quantity and quality to have a safe and reliable water supply.

Groundwater in Colorado is generally "hard." This means that it is high in mineral content, primarily calcium, magnesium, iron, and "salts." Although these minerals may be considered contaminants, they are not identified as health hazards and are not regulated. They tend to form unsightly deposits on sinks and tubs and may be an aesthetic problem, so the homeowner must decide whether to remove them through treatment. No matter what type of quality problem you have with the water, it can be treated. Whether the cost of treatment is excessive or not is a decision of the homeowner.

III. Contaminants

Colorado, because most of its water comes from the mountains, has experienced very few problems with health-related contaminants. However, it is always possible that some kind of illegal disposal or spill of chemical contaminants could result in a problem in your water supply. There are also a number of naturally occurring contaminants in water supplies in the state. Public water systems are required to test for and treat these regulated contaminants, but residential wells are not. The most common contaminants found in water supplies in the state are microorganisms, nitrate, arsenic, radium, uranium, and radon.

Microorganisms can cause immediate health problems. *Giardia* and *Cryptosporidium* are two pathogens found in surface water that can cause sickness or death. Other organisms, including bacteria and viruses, can be found in both surface water and groundwater and may include pathogens that cause typhoid fever (caused by the bacillus *Salmonella typhosa*), typhus (caused by several species of the genus *Rickettsia*), and cholera. Bacteria and viruses are present almost anywhere, including the air, and can contaminate your well and the plumbing in the house.

The most common source of nitrate contamination is fertilizers, but it may also be caused by animal waste and septic-tank discharges. High levels of nitrate can be fatal to fetuses and to children up to six months of age. High nitrate levels are also an indicator of possible fecal and pesticide contamination.

Many areas of the state have elevated levels of naturally occurring arsenic. At low levels arsenic can cause cancer, and at high levels it can cause death. It is still used as rat poison.

A number of radioactive elements are found throughout the state. The most common are radium, uranium, and radon. These three are regulated contaminants and are also naturally occurring. Radium is a known cause of bone cancer. Many areas in the state have levels that exceed the established health level, or maximum contaminant level (MCL). Uranium is also suspected to cause bone cancer. It occurs throughout the state, with many areas having levels that exceed the MCL. Radon is a radioactive gas found in groundwater supplies all over the state. Many areas exceed the MCL established by the Environmental Protection Agency (EPA) for the protection of health. Radon may cause lung cancer if the gas is inhaled. The gas comes out of the water when you use it, and since it is not detectable, you inhale it without even knowing it. Drinking water is only a minor source of the radon gas that you may have inside your home.

IV. Testing

Public water suppliers are required to test for all of the regulated contaminants, but this testing may cost thousands of dollars. Most homeowners cannot afford such extensive testing. Whether you get your water from a public system or you have your own water supply, you may wish to do some sampling to determine whether the water meets your expectations. The big question is: "Just what should I be sampling for?" Even though some tests cost less than $20, there is little to be gained in sampling for contaminants that are not in your area. You should check with sources familiar with drinking water issues where you live. These could include the county health department or sanitarian, a local well-drilling contractor, a nearby water supplier that uses the same type of source, government agencies, or even other residents of the area. The Colorado Department of Public Health and Environment (CDPHE) recommends that if you have your own water supply, you should check for bacteria and nitrate at a minimum. Other contaminants, such as arsenic and the radionuclides, can be added if you are in an area where these elements occur.

In order to obtain valid results, you should use a certified drinking water laboratory. A list of these labs can be obtained from the county or from the CDPHE. Once you have selected a laboratory, the experts there can help you determine your testing needs, send you the proper bottles for sampling, explain sampling procedures, tell you the cost of testing, and help you understand the results.

V. Treatment

Testing can tell you if you have a problem with your water, but continuous treatment is the only way you can be assured that the water is always safe to drink. Treatment is required for all public water supplies. At the very least, a system must disinfect its water to protect against bacterial contamination. In some cases, chemical removal, filtration, and disinfection have all been required to make the water safe to drink. Testing is done to show what treatment is needed and also to show that the treatment is working. If you are served by a public water supply, officials there can tell you what their treatment requirements are and whether the treatment is working properly to the point of delivery to your home.

If you have your own source of water, you must decide how much treatment you need, or want, to assure safe drinking water. You should make sure that whatever treatment option you choose, you get your equipment from a well-known and reputable dealer. If the company has its reputation riding on its product, you will get better service from the dealer. There are a number of treatment options that are available to you for in-house use, whether you are on a public water system or not.

Residential treatment units come in either point-of-entry (POE) or point-of-use (POU) configurations. If you are treating for removal of contaminants to make the water safe to drink, it is best to use a POE unit. This type of unit treats the water for the entire house. Although this means that even the water in the toilet is treated, it also means that every tap used for drinking, including the shower and bath, has water that has been treated. This is especially important if there are children in the house because they are apt to drink from whatever tap is handy. If you are treating only for aesthetic reasons such as the taste and odor of the drinking water, you may wish to use POU since this system treats the water only at the particular tap where the treatment unit is installed. POU systems are smaller, less expensive, and easier to maintain, but they do not provide the protection to the whole house that POE systems do, and POU has a limited treatment capacity. The type of contaminant that is being removed will usually determine which type of treatment you use. Several types of treatment use are explained in the following paragraphs, with the type of contaminant that they control.

Activated carbon units are used for the removal of organic compounds. These units can be used to remove most of the regulated organic compounds, including most pesticides, solvents, and disinfection by-products. They will also remove chlorine. Since chlorine and organic compounds are the most common causes of taste and odor problems in drinking water, these filters are excellent for taste and odor control. This type of filter is also effective for radon control. However, radon removal leads to a buildup of radioactive lead in the filter, which can be controlled by frequent changing of the filter. Another problem with these filters is the buildup of bacteria. Organic material removed by the filter acts as a food source for certain bacteria. With prolonged use, it is common to have more bacteria coming out of a filter than going in. This problem can also be controlled by frequent changes (every three months) of the filter.

Cartridge filters are used to remove particulate matter from the water by screening it out. Iron and sediment removal filters are common and have a pore size of 5 microns. For removal of microorganisms such as *Giardia* and *Cryptosporidium*, the filter needs to be rated as "nominal 1 micron" pore size, which means that no pore is larger than one micron. These filters are very effective but must be changed regularly, as pressure buildup can force the microorganisms through the filter. Use of these filters for microorganism control should be accompanied with some form of disinfection to control bacteria and viruses.

Chlorinators are the most common form of disinfection

owing to their ease of operation and low operating cost. They are generally wired into the well pump so that the chlorine feed pump operates only when the well is pumping. The pump is fed with liquid chlorine bleach diluted with water. This type of disinfection is used by most small public water systems in the state. The use of chlorine requires storing finished (chlorinated) water for at least thirty minutes to allow the chlorine to kill the microorganisms. There may be chlorine taste and odor problems, but the chlorine stays in the water and helps to prevent bacteriological growth in the storage tank, distribution lines, and in-house plumbing. Other forms of chlorination such as the use of gaseous chlorine are available but are usually feasible only for large public water facilities.

Ion exchange units, commonly called water softeners, can treat a number of inorganic chemical contaminants. These units remove a given contaminant or contaminants by exchanging them with another chemical. A common water softener exchanges the calcium (hardness) in the water with sodium. The sodium remains in the water. The calcium is removed from the material in the ion exchange unit by backwashing it with table salt (sodium chloride). The same kind of process can be used to remove uranium, radium, iron, arsenic, and other inorganic contaminants. Depending on the type of media used, the backwash wastewater may be hazardous. Some units cannot be backwashed once the medium has been used up. These units are not commonly used for health protection but are frequently found in areas with groundwater that has high hardness or iron.

Reverse osmosis is a form of treatment that will remove most contaminants from a water supply. The process involves forcing water through a membrane at high pressure. The openings in the membrane are in the molecular range; thus, contaminants with molecular sizes larger than water are held on one side of the membrane while the water is forced through. Removals of most chemicals are in the 60 percent to 90 percent range. Such a system not only will remove harmful chemicals but will also reject minerals in the water, thus acting as a water softener as well. The rejected chemicals are continually washed off the membrane, so there is a continuous waste stream that may range from 15 to 40 percent of the water pumped. Power costs can be high owing to the need for pressurizing the water in the membrane vessel. Quite often pretreatment is needed to protect the membrane from damage. Filtration and activated carbon are used to eliminate large particulates and chlorine. This type of treatment is very effective but can be costly and can produce water only at a low rate. Water is treated constantly and collected in a storage tank of a few gallons. Water for use is then pumped from the storage unit. Due to the low rate of treatment, this is usually a POU-type unit used only for drinking water purposes. Larger units, from POE size to systems large enough to handle a town, are available.

Aeration is used for the removal of many volatile organic contaminants, tastes, odors, radon, and methane and can aid in the removal of iron and sulfur as well. Volatile contaminants are those that are gases at normal air pressures. Aeration is the process of pumping fine bubbles of air into a storage tank and letting the air carry certain contaminants out of the water. Therefore, volatile chemicals and other gases such as radon and sulfur dioxide will escape with the air exhaust. Care must be taken regarding where the air from an aeration system is discharged; airborne contaminants could be carried into nearby windows or doors. The air will also oxidize chemicals such as iron and sulfur. Once oxidized, these chemicals become solids and can be settled or filtered out of the water.

Ultraviolet (UV) disinfection can be very effective for residential water supplies, or for other supplies that do not have distribution systems. UV systems provide high energy at a given wavelength that kills bacteria and viruses. The water must be of good quality with high clarity so that the light has no problem shining through the water. Maintenance usually involves cleaning and replacing the UV bulbs. Power costs can be high, depending on the use. UV disinfects only at the point of application, and because it has no residual effects, it is ineffective in controlling bacterial regrowth in storage tanks, distribution lines, or plumbing systems.

VI. Summary

Colorado is blessed with some of the best drinking water in the world. Even so, there may be quality problems that you need to check for and possibly treat. Public water supplies are continually checked to ensure that you, your family, and guests are not put at risk from the water. If you have an individual drinking water supply, you also need to be confident that your water is safe to drink. Remember that you can have your water tested, and if there are any contaminants that may be a health problem you may be able to treat the water to remove or decrease contaminants to acceptable levels. It is also important, for the sake of your own water supply and that of your neighbors, to dispose of any wastewater from your water treatment units in a proper manner.

For Additional Information

Contact your local health department or, if your county has one, the county sanitation department. Look in the government listings (blue pages) in your phone book.

Call the CDPHE Water Quality Control Division, (303) 692-3500.

Discuss treatment options with reputable water treatment equipment manufacturers.

Call the EPA hotline, (800) 426-4791.

Call the American Water Works Association (AWWA) small system hotline, (800) 366-0107.

3

Rural Wastewater and Sanitary Systems

David Akers, *Manager, Water Pollution Protection Section*
Colorado Water Quality Control Division

The traditional method of treating wastewater in rural Colorado has been by piping it into septic tanks. These systems settle the solids and then drain into leach fields that allow the remaining wastewater to be filtered by the soil surrounding the buried perforated pipes of the leach field. The septic tank and leach field are located on the homeowner's property, and the homeowner is solely responsible for maintaining and replacing the system when necessary. With very few exceptions, these systems discharge to groundwater and, if not properly designed, could impact the quality of nearby streams, irrigation ditches, or your downstream neighbors' wells. The septic tank–leach field disposal system is the most often used type of individual sewage disposal system (ISDS).

More sophisticated types of ISDS include mound systems, constructed wetlands, wastewater ponds, aerobic systems, gray-water systems, and composting toilets. ISDS's are very different from the typical urban wastewater treatment system in which wastewater is collected from homes and businesses and transported, via sewer mains, to a central facility for treatment and discharge to a body of surface water. The use of central wastewater collection and treatment systems is becoming much more widespread in rural areas, particularly where development densities are greater than one unit per acre or where site-specific problems preclude the use of an ISDS. The homeowner who is connected to a central collection and treatment system has no responsibility for the proper operation and maintenance (O&M) of the system other than maintaining the collection line that runs from the home to the sewer in the street. They can generally stop worrying about their wastewater once it goes down the drain as long as they are not disposing of large volumes of wastes that may be toxic to the wastewater treatment process. Since the individual homeowner's responsibilities are minimal for these types of systems, this chapter will concentrate on situations in which an ISDS is to be used for wastewater treatment and disposal.

Owners, or prospective owners, of properties that use ISDS's should familiarize themselves, as far as possible, with the state and county ISDS regulations or guidelines. This chapter provides information that the prospective property or home buyer needs to consider prior to purchase as well as suggested steps to assure that the ISDS is properly operated and maintained.

I. ISDS Considerations When Building a New Home

When a new home is being planned, the owner should first determine whether central wastewater treatment is available or whether an on-site ISDS will be necessary. The county building or planning department or the regional Colorado Water Quality Control Division (WQCD) office can be consulted to determine whether there is an entity that you may be required to connect to, such as a sanitation district, city or town, or regional treatment facility.

If there is no such entity and the use of an ISDS will be necessary, the owner has a responsibility to ensure that the system is properly designed and constructed. Generally this responsibility is met through retaining a qualified professional to design the system and oversee its construction. The owner should be careful to select a consultant who has experience in designing a wide variety of types of systems, especially those types that are suited for the site where the home is to be located. Ideally the consultant should be brought in to do an initial feasibility evaluation before a property is purchased or as soon thereafter as possible.

In certain areas, the county or local health department may be able to provide information on the types of systems that are successful in certain areas. Although their experience with the area may prove to be invaluable, these local government professionals will not always be familiar with your specific situation and may not be able to conduct a site-specific assessment. Therefore, unless the county representative positively indicates that the site (soil types and suitability, depth to groundwater, lot size, etc.) is suitable for installation of a simple ISDS, you may need to hire a consultant.

If a consultant is retained to prepare a report, review it carefully, especially if it indicates that the site may be marginal for an ISDS or that an "engineered" system will be required, and make sure that the consultant provides you with a detailed analysis, including any underlying assumptions. Since the design of an ISDS is largely predicated on the ability of the native soils to infiltrate the wastewater, you may want to become familiar with the basics of soils science as well as the nature of the soils at the chosen site. There are many references for on-site wastewater disposal that can be consulted for basic design information, and engineering texts can also be consulted where a deeper understanding is desired. The county or the regional WQCD office can provide information on references used in reviewing ISDS designs. The United States Geological Survey (USGS), the Colorado Geological Survey, or the local soil conservation district can be contacted for information on the types of soils in the vicinity of the property that is being considered.

The consultant's analysis will include representative soils analyses and associated percolation rates and should also identify the depth to groundwater and bedrock. The consultant will identify the location of water bodies (streams, lakes, ditches, etc.), water lines, wells and springs, and occupied buildings to determine the minimum distance requirements between the leach field and these features. These requirements may result in an unfavorable location of the home on the chosen piece of property unless appropriate mitigation measures are taken. Review this information carefully and make sure that the consultant identifies and explains whether a simple septic tank–leach

field system will work at your location. If a more sophisticated type of system will be necessary owing to unfavorable site conditions, you will need information on the types of systems that may work under the indicated conditions, the associated costs, and any risks of system failure so that you can take these factors into account in your decision to purchase the desired property. Since the county will be reviewing the design of any new system, county officials may be willing to review and provide their perspective on any predesign advice that you obtain from the consultant.

II. ISDS Considerations When Purchasing an Existing Home

Where an existing home with an ISDS is being purchased, the prospective buyer should become aware of the system's design and its condition and be willing to make any modifications that are necessary to ensure that the system will remain viable into the future. The county should be contacted to see if the system has had problems or whether it may have failed in the past. The local ISDS maintenance company that has been servicing the system should also be contacted to determine whether the system has had problems or has required maintenance (pumping, chemical or enzyme treatment, etc.) at a higher than normal frequency. If the system does have a history of problems or has failed in the past, you may want to make your purchase of the home conditional on the receipt of a report, prepared by a qualified professional, that indicates that the ISDS will remain viable for a reasonable period. This report should indicate the date and cause of any problems or failures and contain a description, with the date of completion, of any modifications made in response to the problems or failures. It should also include an opinion on whether the modifications permanently remedied the problems or failures. Where the consultant can't provide assurance for long-term system viability, the report should provide a description of system improvements that are necessary to provide such assurance, along with an estimate of their cost. This information can then be used to negotiate a change in the price of the home or as a the basis of an agreement for presale improvements.

III. Proper Operation and Maintenance of an ISDS

A significant number of ISDS's experience some type of failure that, aside from design-related failures, could be prevented by following proper use and maintenance protocols. The proper use and maintenance of any ISDS requires understanding of the function of each of the units that make up the system and the conditions under which each unit will perform as designed.

If a consultant has been retained to design a new ISDS or modifications to an existing ISDS, the owner may want to include a provision in the contract for preparation of an operations and maintenance manual. The manual would include a description of the system, its underlying design, and maintenance schedules for each piece of equipment.

If a consultant has not been retained, then the owner of an ISDS can obtain a working understanding of the function of each of the processes in the system through review of texts on ISDS design or from summary information that the county, the WQCD, or the EPA may be able to provide. In either case, the owner should also be familiar with information on the proper use of the ISDS and the maintenance that will be required.

An ISDS will function well as long as one remembers that it is a biological process that is subject to upset from disposal of incompatible materials. Small amounts of standard household cleansers, drain cleaners, detergents, and so forth will be diluted in the septic tank and will not damage the system. Pesticides, paint thinners, disinfectants, some dyes, and other strong chemicals will cause a major upset in the septic tank. Specific items that should not be flushed into the tank include: coffee grounds, sanitary napkins, cooking fats, bones, wet-strength paper towels, disposable diapers, and cigarette filters. Other relatively indigestible material such as plastic, rubber, or nylon also should not be flushed into the tank. These materials will simply occupy space in the tank that would otherwise be used for treatment. Brine solution from water softeners can be slowly flushed into the system without harming the biota in the tank or the leach field. However, it may cause pollution of the groundwater, and this factor should be considered before purchasing a softener.

There are many products on the market that claim to be beneficial to septic tanks or to prevent problems. Many of these products will not provide any measurable benefit, and some may actually do harm to the process. Be sure to check the contents of the product before use to ensure that you are not adding a toxic chemical that will end up in the groundwater.

For most simple ISDS's, the only required maintenance is to periodically pump out the accumulated solids from the septic tank. The nominal period for solids removal for most households is every three years. Until the sludge accumulation rate for your tank has been established, the solids level in the tank should be checked every year. You can do this yourself or have the local septic tank pumper check it, but you may be charged for this service, especially if the tank does not require pumping. When the tank is pumped, make sure that the scum layer and all accumulated solids are removed and that some of the liquid is left to "seed" the regrowth of the bacteria. The amount of liquid left in the tank should be increased as much as possible if the tank was installed below the water table in order to ensure that it doesn't "float" and dislodge the inlet and outlet piping.

References and Additional Information

Perkins, Richard J. *Onsite Wastewater Disposal.* Chelsea, MI: Lewis Publishers Incorporated, 1989.

Burks, Bennette D., and Mary Margaret McInnis. *Onsite Wastewater Treatment Systems.* Madison, WI: Hogarth House, Limited, 1994.

Colorado Department of Public Health and Environment Water Quality Control Division Office Locations

Denver Office
4300 Cherry Creek Drive South
Denver, CO 80246-1530
Phone: (303) 692-3500
Fax: (303) 782-0390

Durango District Office
P.O. Box 140
Durango, CO 81302-0140
Phone: (970) 247-5702, ext. 273
Fax: (970) 247-9126

Grand Junction District Office
222 S. 6th Street, Room 232
Grand Junction, CO 81501
Phone: (970) 248-7152
Fax: (970) 248-7198

Pueblo District Office
720 N. Main Street, Suite 300
Pueblo, CO 81003-3027
Phone: (719) 545-4650
Fax: (719) 543-8441

Steamboat Springs District Office
410 S. Lincoln Street
Steamboat Springs, CO 80487
Phone: (970) 879-7479
Fax: (970) 879-7479

4

Natural Hazards in Rural Building Areas

Daniel F. Balsinger, *Professional Geologist*

Colorado Statute §34-1-103 charges the Colorado Geological Survey with addressing issues involving geologic and other natural hazards within the state. The law defines a geologic hazard as "a geological phenomenon which is so adverse to past, current, or foreseeable construction or land use as to constitute a significant hazard to public health and safety or to property."

Geologic hazards are naturally occurring dangers that pertain to rocks, soils, and landscapes and that could cause bodily harm or danger to buildings. Typical Colorado geologic hazards include snow avalanches, landslides, rockfalls, mudflows, debris flows, ground subsidence, and swelling soil and rock. Basically the hazards are things that could fall on you or a building, slide down a mountain onto you or a building, or give way under you or a building.

I. Common Hazards

Snow Avalanches

Snow avalanches are common in the mountains, and they can incorporate ice and debris such as rocks and vegetation. Generally avalanches occur in the Colorado mountains above 8,000 feet from November through April. Steepness, weather, and wind contribute to dangerous conditions. Mountain slopes greater than 45 degrees normally accumulate enough snow to produce very large avalanches in Colorado. Avalanches usually start on slopes greater than 30 degrees but less than 45 degrees. However, avalanches may occur on slopes of less than 30 degrees if climatic conditions are just right. A long period of warm weather followed by a heavy snowfall can cause the snow pack to become highly unstable. Unusual wind conditions can also trigger an avalanche.

During the summer, evidence of past avalanches can be seen, such as avalanche "chutes" that appear as cleared strips straight down the mountains. Different types of vegetation often grow along the paths of old avalanches in forested areas; trees are mowed down and replaced by grasses. Piles of broken trees and other debris at the foot of a swath of cleared forest and patches of downed trees all aligned in the same direction are also good indicators of old avalanche events.

Landslides

Landslides are a type of mass wasting in which the rock sequence has a distinct zone of weakness that separates the slide material from the more stable underlying material. Typically these slides are the downward and outward movement of a relatively dry body of rock and earth in response to gravitational stresses.

Large landslides move huge masses of material many miles down a mountainside and may even deposit material up the opposite slope of a valley. The movement can be almost imperceptibly slow or very rapid. Activities by humans can cause the movement of landslide materials if the "toe," or lower end, of the potentially unstable material is removed. For example, the excavation of hillside materials so that a building can be placed on a flat area could cause a local landslide. Even a small slide could seriously damage a building.

There are many natural circumstances that may trigger

landslides. Erosion of critically supporting materials is a common trigger. Erosion can undermine the base of a mass of potentially unstable material and cause the slope material to move downhill into the newly vacated area. The lubrication of clay or other fine-grained materials by wetting may also cause the overlying materials to slide downhill. When rock and other debris glide downslope on top of wet shales or clays, the resulting mass is not usually a jumbled mixture of these materials. This type of landslide often preserves the general stratification of the material because it is merely sliding off a slippery inclined surface onto a flatter surface where the slide stops. Earthquake vibrations can trigger a slide, but fortunately earthquakes are not frequent visitors to the Colorado Rockies and do not constitute a major threat to rural building.

Landslides are common in the Colorado mountains and can do much damage to structures. They constitute a major geological hazard. If you suspect any potential for landslides in an area where you are considering construction, you should retain a geologist or geological engineer. These professionals can identify potential risks and assist you in determining an appropriate course of action, which may include avoidance or mitigation measures. Some of the many possible mitigating efforts for building in potential landslide areas include retaining structures, improved subsurface drainage, and material removal.

Rockfalls

A rockfall is a gravity-driven fall of large loose rocks and is a common occurrence in Colorado. Rockfalls typically involve individual or a few rocks rather than the movement of a cohesive mass of earth and rock. Most of us are familiar with road signs that alert the public to the danger from rocks that may tumble into the roadway. Usually these are areas where relatively small rocks are often dislodged from steep hills or cliffs. However, rockfalls involving large boulders do occur and have devastating consequences when they fall on vehicles or structures. Rockfall boulders may weigh many tons.

Many rockfalls areas are associated with interbedded soft shale and harder, more cohesive sandstones and limestones. When the shale is eroded, the overlying rock layers slough off the face of the cliff. Falling individual rocks or blocks of rock can occur as big, rounded boulders in a mixture of glacial till or as blocks of massive and broken bedrock high on a steep slope or overhanging a ledge.

As with landslides, the wetting of an underlying slippery shale or clay by heavy rain or melting snow may lead to a rockfall. When rocks or blocks of rocks drop onto this glide plane, they move downslope more easily by rolling or sliding. Undercutting of rock slopes by streams or construction excavations can remove support for overlying or overhanging rocks and cause the rocks to move. Another geologic agent that causes rockfalls is the freezing and thawing of water in the cracks of the rocks coupled with the pull of gravity. When water freezes, the pressure created by the expansion exceeds 3,000 pounds per square inch. With each freeze the cracks widen, pushing the rocks closer to the point where they are loose enough to fall.

Mudflows

A mudflow is a process that transports a wet mass of fine-to-coarse-grained sediment turbulently downhill. Often the mudflow process is triggered by flooding. When the Big Thompson Canyon flooded in the 1970s numerous mudflows occurred. Coastal mudflows in California during the rainy season are another familiar example. In the Colorado mountains, melting snow can saturate the soils and cause them to begin their downhill movement. Water content may be up to 60 percent of the mass. The movement of a mudflow is not necessarily rapid. Some mudflows ooze or creep their way downhill, depending on the steepness of the slope and the amount of water contained in the mass.

Most mudflows in Colorado start in drainage basins whose streams originate in high, barren mountains. Such basins may be subject to rapid runoff from extensive rains or rapidly melting snows in the spring. It is possible for the activities of humans to reactivate old mudflows by excavating the toe of the deposits. Lawn irrigation could upset the equilibrium of an old mudflow and start it moving downhill again.

Debris Flows

A debris flow is different from a mudflow in that mudflows are characterized by very fine-grained clays or soils, whereas debris flows contain a high percentage of boulders and cobbles in a poorly sorted mixture. Debris flows usually occur along steep mountain ridges and valley sides. Generally they have irregular upper surfaces because of the rapid deposition of the jumbled mass. Often debris flows are recognizable by the fan or triangular shape of land forms at the mouth of mountain valleys; the debris fans can measure up to several square miles in area. Slow debris flows may move less than 3 feet a year, while rapid ones can reach 100 miles per hour. It is very difficult to mitigate either mudflows or debris flows, and they can easily ruin a building beyond repair.

Ground Subsidence

Ground subsidence can be a significant problem in some areas of the state. The two causes of subsidence that are important are hydrocompaction and underground mining.

Hydrocompaction involves two types of soils in Colorado—wind-deposited silts (loess) and certain fine-grained soils that can be any loose, poorly sorted material deposited as a dry mass of large and small rocks in a mixture of fine materials such as clays or soils. By its very nature, loess contains a large amount of air that is displaced by an excessive amount of water. The second type of deposit is usually found at the foot of a slope or cliff and brought there by gravity. When these unstable materials get wet from rain or snowmelt, the deposits undergo compaction as the air is forced out, and the surface can then collapse.

Removal of support by underground mining is a common cause of surface subsidence in many mountainous areas of Colorado. Once material is removed in the mining process, the rocks remaining are under a natural stress that can cause shifting and collapse into the mined-out areas. This collapse can affect the overlying rocks, even up to the surface. About the only defense against this problem is to avoid building over mined-out areas. It is often difficult or impossible to locate old mining maps, and many of the old maps are less than accurate. It is better to avoid building in underground mining districts if possible.

Expansive Soils

Expansive soils may also threaten buildings in Colorado. Clay materials are common in sedimentary sequences, and some types of clay can expand to as much as fifteen times their dry volume when wet from rain or snowmelt. When these clays occur at the ground surface, the pressure may be great enough to damage houses and other buildings, roads, and pipelines. The most common type of expanding clay is called montmorillonite, a soft, plastic clay formed by the chemical alteration of beds of volcanic ash. Bentonite is a rock consisting largely of hardened montmorillonite. In the past, Colorado had many active volcanoes. Therefore, there is a lot of this type of clay in many areas of the state. Either the swelling of wetted clays or the shrinking of drying clays can damage buildings, although most damage is caused by the swelling process. Most buildings built on expanding clays will have only minor damage during the life of the building, but a few will be damaged beyond repair. A geological professional can identify these soils prior to construction.

Earthquakes

Compared to many other states, Colorado has only a minor potential for earthquakes. Earthquakes are caused by the movement of very large blocks of rock. The area along which the movement occurs is the fault. Geological evidence allows scientists to map faults that could generate future damaging earthquakes. Cumulative fault displacement can be measured in inches or miles. When movement along a fault occurs, shock waves radiate out from the epicenter, the area where the movement first occurs.

Basically, two broad types of damage to structures can result from earthquakes. First, if a structure is built close to a fault, the shifting rock or ground can collapse structures by tearing them apart. Second, the surface shock waves that are generated can shake buildings and other structures to the point that they break apart and collapse.

In terms of frequency of movement along faults, Colorado is an area of low to only moderate ranking. Based on the frequency and magnitude of earthquakes as evidence of fault movement, there are several areas of Colorado where landowners and builders should exercise a higher degree of caution in the design and location of structures.

The most seismically active area in the state is northeast of Denver near the Rocky Mountain Arsenal, where the injection of fluids into the ground has triggered earthquakes. Although this area has been subjected to human influence, technical studies have concluded that the potential for earthquake activity existed before any such influences and that the injection of fluids into the rocks has not relieved all of the stress in the rock system. It must be viewed as an area of future earthquake potential. The second-most active area in Colorado is in southern Archuleta County along the New Mexico border. The area is well known for numerous small earthquakes and rockslides.

Major potentially active faults in Colorado also lie in a trend along the east side of the San Luis Valley from east of the town of Alamosa northwesterly to about Steamboat Springs. There are numerous other potentially active faults in Colorado, particularly west of the Front Range in eastern Fremont County and in Teller, Douglas, and Jefferson Counties. The counties of San Juan, Hinsdale, Ouray, and eastern San Miguel to the southeast of Montrose have experienced numerous earthquakes. Also, there is a very broad area of frequent earthquakes encompassing Gunnison, Delta, Pitkin, and western Chaffee Counties.

II. Conclusion

When selecting a building site or designing a structure, it is a good idea to visit the county engineer's office and ask about potential geologic hazards. For a comprehensive evaluation, landowners, developers, and builders should consult a qualified geological engineer when planning construction. A detailed geological study could save much time and expense if geologic hazards are present in the area you plan to build.

For Additional Information

A good place to start learning more about geologic hazards is *Geologic Hazards Avoidance or Mitigation: A Compre-* *hensive Guide to State Statutes, Land-Use Issues, and Professional Practice in Colorado,* Information Series No. 47 by the Colorado Geological Survey. The Colorado Geological Survey also has many other useful publications and will send a catalog on request.

Colorado Geological Survey
1313 Sherman St., Room 715
Denver, CO 80203
Phone: (303) 866-2611
Fax: (303) 866-2461
E-mail: katie.kellerlyn@state.co.us

5

Wetlands: Nature's Oasis

Lauranne P. Rink, *Wetlands Scientist*

Colorado has a surprisingly large inventory of natural wetlands, despite the fact that the entire state is west of the 100th meridian. The 100th meridian is the line that John Wesley Powell used to divide the eastern lands, those that receive enough natural precipitation to grow crops without irrigation, from the arid west. Some of these are pocket wetlands supported by springs in the drylands of the Four Corners region, some are bosque areas along perennial streams and rivers, and some are broad areas where the land surface intersects the water table. In any case, if you purchase property that contains land that is naturally saturated for all or even part of the year, there is a lot you need to know before you decide to make changes that affect the unique biohydrologic system that is now under your care.

Most importantly you need to know that wetlands perform a number of services that you'll probably value once you are aware of them. High on the list of the reasons people enjoy living in Colorado is the opportunity to observe wildlife of many kinds; wetlands provide water and shelter for many kinds of wild animals from muskrats to elk. They also filter the water entering streams and keep them clearer and contaminant free. Wetlands decrease erosion along stream courses and moderate flooding by providing backwater areas for floods to enter without undercutting the main banks.

There are many reasons that wetlands are protected, and if you live on property with wetland areas, you will grow to value the beauty of these wild areas as well as their utilitarian purposes. This chapter will outline the background knowledge you need to be a good steward of these beautiful areas.

I. What Are Wetlands?

Colorado wetlands occur in many shapes and sizes. They can be as extensive as hundreds of acres along the flood-plain of a major river or as small as an isolated depression 10 square feet in size. They can occur at all elevations and in the most inhospitable places, from the high alpine tundra to the roadside ditch along a highway. They can be saturated with water all year long or wet for just a week during the spring. Some contain cattails, others support trees or shrubs, and many are dominated by grasses and forbs. Most have been around for hundreds or thousands of years, while others may have popped up over the past few years owing to a change in drainage patterns or land uses.

Simply stated, wetlands are ecosystems that occupy transitional areas between deepwater habitats (lakes, reservoirs, and streams) and dry upland habitat areas. They occur when water is present at or just below the ground surface for a long enough period to support water-loving plants. They can be found along shorelines adjacent to streams, ponds, lakes, and reservoirs; along intermittent drainage-ways; in isolated depressions; where persistent snowpack lingers into the late spring and summer; in springs and seep areas in both flat and sloped conditions; or in any other wet to moist site. The characteristics of the area in terms of hydrology, vegetation, and soil are used to describe and delineate the boundaries of the wetland.

Many people say they can recognize a wetland when they see one. Yet what these people do not recognize is the fact that wetlands can be defined in a number of different ways to accommodate a number of different perspectives. The way a wetland is defined depends on the reason you find it necessary to define the wetland. For example, a wetland can be defined (1) as an ecological unit, (2) as a specific type of habitat, (3) as a type of water treatment system, or (4) as a geographic unit for legal regulatory purposes. To recognize a wetland when you see one necessarily means knowing the context of the need to define the wetland.

As a landowner in Colorado, the most important definitions that you need to understand are those that are used for local and federal regulatory programs. These definitions will be used to determine whether you own a wetland that is subject to the rules and regulations of a particular jurisdiction.

II. Why Are Wetlands Important?

Wetlands serve a multitude of functions crucial to environmental balance and human well-being (State of Washington Department of Ecology 1991). Healthy wetlands provide ecological values as well as recreational, economic, cultural, and educational benefits to society.

One of the most important functions of healthy wetlands is their ability to support local wildlife populations. Although wetlands occupy a relatively small portion of the total landscape, their contribution to biodiversity and several other key ecological functions is tremendous. Wetlands provide habitat for approximately one-third of the wild plant and animal species classified as threatened or endangered in the United States. More than 50 percent of the nation's migratory bird species use them for nesting, migratory, and wintering habitat (U.S. Fish and Wildlife Service 1990). In Colorado, twenty-nine species of birds and eleven species of amphibians that are dependent upon wetland environments are considered to be "rare and imperiled" (Colorado Natural Heritage Program 1997).

Wetlands are highly productive environments that provide critical habitat for a wide variety of organisms, including waterfowl, fish, reptiles, invertebrates, and mammals. Many species use these environments at special times during their life cycle, while others use them exclusively.

III. Other Wetland Functions

Improving Water Quality

Wetlands retain and filter surface runoff and groundwater flows and trap suspended sediments, filter out excess nutrients such as nitrogen and phosphorus, and retain and assimilate heavy metals. Runoff from urban areas, agricultural lands, mined land, and highways often carries these pollutants. Filtration and assimilation by wetlands helps to keep these pollutants from entering our streams and lakes, thereby reducing the cost for drinking water and wastewater treatment.

Decreasing Erosion

Wetlands can reduce erosion of stream banks in at least two ways. First, old stream channels and oxbow depressions can divert flood waters, lower the overall level of the flood, and reduce pressure and erosive forces on the banks of the main channel. Second, wetland vegetation with its network roots stabilizes stream banks and shorelines. Excessive erosion can result in loss of land that may be economically viable for development.

Flood Control

Wetlands act as large sponges to absorb and store excess runoff during flood events. In this capacity, they help to alleviate large-surge flood flows that can be damaging. For example, the U.S. Army Corps of Engineers (Corps) determined that it was more cost effective to acquire and preserve wetlands along the Charles River in Massachusetts than to construct flood control facilities. If these wetlands had been destroyed, there would have been an estimated $17 million in annual flood damage (Williams et al. 1996).

Contributing to Base Flows

Wetlands store excess water resulting from flood flows, snowmelt, and precipitation events. During drier periods, the wetlands slowly release the stored water to streams and rivers, adding to base flows.

Groundwater Recharge

Stored and filtered water can be transferred from wetlands to groundwater aquifers that may be tapped for domestic water supplies.

Recreational Opportunities

Activities such as bird-watching, picnicking, fishing, hunting, and boating occur in wetland environments. More than half of all U.S. adults (98 million people) hunt, fish, birdwatch, or photograph wildlife. These activities, which rely on healthy wetlands, added an estimated $59.5 million to the national economy in 1991 (Environmental Protection Agency 1995).

IV. Why Do Wetlands Require Protection?

The U.S. Fish and Wildlife Service (USFWS) has undertaken a nationwide inventory of wetlands in order to classify and quantitatively describe these little-understood wildlands. Analysis of these results indicates that less than 50 percent of the wetlands that were present in Colorado prior to European settlement are still in existence today (Mitch and Gosselink 1994). Cooper and Jones (1993) have suggested that less than 2 percent of the total land area of the state is occupied by wetland or riparian habitats.

Human actions that have contributed to wetland losses and degradation nationwide include:

- drainage, dredging, and stream channelization
- filling of wetlands with material excavated elsewhere
- diking, damming, and levee building
- tilling for crop production
- logging and mining
- construction
- surface runoff
- air and water pollutants
- changing nutrient levels
- release of toxic chemicals
- introductions of non-native species
- grazing by domestic animals

Thanks to research efforts by government agencies and universities, many citizens now realize the importance of wetland resources to the social and economic well-being of our country. Increased awareness of the importance of wetlands has been furthered by our knowledge of how much of the resource has been lost over time because of our farming and development activities. The U.S. Environmental Protection Agency (EPA) has reported that out of the 100 million acres of wetlands left in the lower forty-eight states, approximately 75 percent are located on private property (Environmental Protection Agency 1995). This realization emphasizes the need to educate landowners about wetland functions and values so that they are equipped with the information required to make appropriate land use decisions.

V. Who Regulates Wetlands?

There are international, national, state, and local laws and regulations pertaining to wetland areas. As stated by Williams et al. 1996, there is no single, overriding wetlands protection law, and the protections that do exist often are not the primary functions of the laws in which they can be found. In Colorado, no statewide wetlands laws were in existence as of the time of this publication. Therefore, a landowner should be conscious of federal and local regulations.

Section 404 of the federal Clean Water Act is the primary regulatory control governing the use and protection of all wetlands as defined in the statute. Section 404 regulations are enforced by the Corps in coordination with the EPA. Among other things, Section 404 regulates the discharge of dredged or fill material into waters of the United States, including wetlands. More simply stated, any time you want to fill or excavate in wetland areas, you need to find out if you need a 404 permit to do so.

The definition of wetlands used by the Corps for regulatory purposes reads as follows: "Those areas that are inundated or saturated by surface or groundwater at a frequency and duration sufficient to support, and under normal circumstances do support, a prevalence of vegetation typically adapted for life in saturated soil conditions. Wetlands generally include swamps, marshes, bogs, and similar areas."

This definition is quite broad and encompasses a wide variety of circumstances. To make this definition clearer, the Corps published a manual that describes how to identify and delineate wetland boundaries according to this definition. A number of professional wetlands scientists (including this author) are trained to interpret this definition for those in need of delineating wetland boundaries on their land.

Several local jurisdictions in Colorado have passed wetland regulatory programs of their own. The city of Boulder has its own permit program in addition to the federal Section 404 program. San Miguel County has a wetland protection program tied to its county land use code; it prohibits certain activities in and around wetland areas. Both the city of Boulder and San Miguel County regulate activities adjacent to or in the "buffer zone" around wetlands. Other counties and cities have elements within their land use codes that deal with protection of wetlands, and more are being added all the time. It is best to check with your local municipality or county to see if a wetland regulation or land use-related code exists. Two things to note: (1) Sometimes the local jurisdiction's definition of *wetlands* is different than that used at the federal level (as is the case with the city of Boulder), and (2) you may need to comply with the requirements of both the local and the federal regulatory programs.

VI. How Do I Know If I Have Wetlands on My Property?

If you suspect that certain areas of your property could be defined as wetlands and you have any plans for disturbing them for any reason, it is best to get the opinion of a specialist. You can call your local Corps office to request that a specialist visit your property to provide an opinion. Alternatively, the Corps office maintains a list of professional wetlands scientists and other related professionals that it will send you free of charge—no questions asked. If you own agricultural ground, the local Natural Resource Conservation Service (NRCS) office can send someone out to evaluate your property. The definitions and laws surrounding wetlands are complex enough that it is worth taking the time to get some free advice from these noted sources to keep you out of trouble.

Some communities and counties have conducted what is called an advanced identification of wetlands, or ADID. The EPA provides grant assistance to communities that want to undertake this work for planning and management purposes. If an ADID covers your area, this study can give you a pretty good idea of the extent of wetlands on your property. (Note that small wetlands [i.e., less than 0.5 acres] may not be included in these studies.) Your local city or county planning office can tell you if an ADID study has been completed in your area of concern.

VII. What May I Do to My Wetlands?

As described above, the federal Section 404 program seeks to regulate the filling and excavating of wetland areas. This covers filling for development, dams, roadways, house foundations, septic systems, tilling for crops, and similar activities. Fill material can include earth, aggregate, concrete, wood, or garbage. Excavating for the purposes of draining, pond and lake creation, and the harvesting of materials (e.g., gravel, peat) is also subject to the regulations.

Routine work or activities that have minimal effects on the environment, even though they are regulated, may be authorized by the Corps in a short time by letter. Other activities that may have a greater impact on the environment require more thorough review, more time, and more paperwork. In these cases the Corps will want to ensure that the proposed impacts are avoided or minimized to the extent practicable before authorizing the work. Compensatory mitigation, such as creating or restoring other wetlands to provide for "no net loss" of wetland resources, may be required in order to authorize a proposed impact. A detailed description of the Corps's permit program is beyond the scope of this chapter, but the best recommendation is "ask first"—to be sure your plans comply with the law.

Local wetland regulatory programs and land use codes may prohibit activities that are allowed under the federal program. Check with your local land use planning office about these matters.

Local programs may also prohibit or regulate activities that fall outside wetlands but within their "buffer zones." Buffer zones are areas that surround or are adjacent to wetlands that delineate a zone of influence between the upland area and the wetland. Buffer zones act as protective areas between developed or developable property and ecolog-

ically sensitive areas. Depending on the jurisdiction, buffer zones may vary in size and width. Usually particular activities are prohibited in buffer zones. Again, it is best to check these specifics with the local planning office.

Activities that fall outside the Section 404 purview include mowing, grazing, tree and shrub pruning or removal, and addition of plantings for landscaping. Although these activities are not regulated, they may not be advisable in all cases from an ecological standpoint in wetland areas.

VIII. Homeowner Restrictions

You may have purchased a property that is subject to certain protective covenants or restrictions that are typically enforced by homeowners' associations. As development pressures increase, particularly in the mountainous areas, developers are agreeing to restrict and control future land uses through mechanisms such as homeowner covenants. The city, county, Corps, or other governing jurisdiction may have required the developer to use homeowner covenants to avoid piecemeal environmental impacts.

For example, a landowner plans to convert a 600-acre ranch to a mixed-use residential community. Assume that 30 acres of wetlands exist within the 600-acre site prior to its subdivision. The developer must obtain a Section 404 permit from the Corps to affect 2 acres of wetlands in order to install roads, bridges, and utilities. This impact will be mitigated on site by creating 2 new acres of wetlands. The developer agrees to set aside another 13 acres of wetlands as permanent open space. This leaves 15 acres of wetlands scattered throughout twenty-five new home lots. If each landowner ends up filling or draining wetlands on his or her individual lot, then all 15 acres of original wetlands, or half of the original acreage, could easily be lost. In this particular example, homeowner covenants that restrict filling or draining of wetlands on individual parcels can be an effective mechanism for minimizing environmental impacts.

Such covenants, if any are applicable, are usually referenced in the deed to your property and may be obtained from your real estate agent or the homeowners' association.

IX. How Can I Make Wetlands Better?

Here is a short list of things that can be done to improve existing wetlands:

- avoid and minimize impacts

- install temporary "fencing" to limit sediment erosion and runoff during construction projects
- use the smallest equipment you can for the job in and around wetlands
- control noxious and invasive non-native plants
- use demonstrated good land management practices such as burning, rotational grazing, no-till and contour plowing, and limited mowing
- control discharges of any pollutants or contaminants
- plan construction to avoid conflict with sensitive species
- reduce water-quality degradation
- minimize impacts to hydrology that support the wetlands
- consider restoration or enhancement

Landowners may choose to improve the quality of their wetlands in order to increase their economic or aesthetic value. Improvements may be intended to either restore or enhance the area. Restoration refers to actions taken to correct previous alterations that have either destroyed or seriously impaired the values and functions of an aquatic area. Enhancement means increasing or improving on functions or values of an existing aquatic or wetland area.

A few voluntary government programs exist for restoring wetland resources on private property. Partners for Wildlife is a federal program administered by the USFWS aimed at restoring wetland habitats in partnership with private landowners. Both financial and technical assistance are provided through voluntary cooperative agreements. Two other federal programs exist through the U.S. Department of Agriculture. The Conservation Reserve Program and Wetlands Reserve Program are administered through the NRCS. These are also voluntary programs that encourage landowners to take environmentally sensitive lands, including wetlands, out of crop production in exchange for payment.

Contact names for these various programs:
U.S. Army Corps of Engineers Offices—Colorado
Albuquerque District (Rio Grande River Basin)
P. O. Box 294
Pueblo, CO 81002
(719) 543-9459

Omaha District (Platte River Basin)
Tri Lakes Offices
9307 State Highway 121
Littleton, CO 80123-6901
(303) 979-4120

Sacramento District (Colorado River Basin)
402 Rood Avenue, #142
Grand Junction, CO 81501
(970) 243-1199

Environmental Protection Agency
Ecosystems Protection and Remediation/Ecosystems Protection
U.S. EPA Region VIII
999 18th Street
Denver, CO 80202
(303) 312-6218

U.S. Fish and Wildlife Service
Region 6
134 Union Boulevard, P.O. Box 25486
Denver Federal Center
Denver, CO 80225
(303) 236-7904

Partners for Wildlife
Colorado Division of Wildlife
6060 Broadway
Denver, CO 80216
Contact: Bill Noonan
(303) 291-7464

Colorado Natural Heritage Program
1313 Sherman Street, Room 618
Denver, CO 80203
(303) 866-3437

Natural Resource Conservation Service (formerly Soil Conservation Service)
655 Parfet Street
Room E, 200 C
Lakewood, CO 80215
(303) 236-2886

References and Additional Information

Colorado Natural Heritage Program. 1997. *Colorado's Natural Heritage—Rare and Imperiled Animals, Plants and Plant Communities.* Oct. 1997, vol. B, no. 1.

Cooper, D. and R. Jones. 1993. *Wetlands of Colorado.* Denver, CO: Colorado Department of Natural Resources.

Dahl, T., C. Johnson, and W. E. Frayer. 1991. "Wetlands—Status and Trends in the Conterminous United States Mid-70's to Mid-80's." Arlington, VA: U.S. Fish and Wildlife Service, National Education and Training Center. Call (703) 358-1711 for a free copy.

Environmental Protection Agency. 1995. "Wetland Fact Sheets." EPA843-F-95-001, Washington, DC: Office of Wetlands,

Oceans and Watersheds. Call Wetlands Information Outline, (800) 832-7828.

Mitch, W. J., and J. G. Gosselink. 1994. *Wetlands.* New York: Van Nostrand Reinhold.

Neiring, W. 1985. *Wetlands: A National Audubon Society Nature Guide.* New York: Alfred A. Knopf Publishers.

State of Washington Department of Ecology. 1991. *Wetlands Preservation: An Information and Action Guide.* Publication No. 90-5. Call (360) 407-7472.

Steinburg, R. E. 1991. *Wetlands and Real Estate Development Handbook.* Rockville, MD: Government Institutes. Call (301) 921-2355.

U.S. Fish and Wildlife Service. 1990. *Wetlands Losses in the United States—1780's to 1980's.* Arlington, VA: U.S. Fish and Wildlife Service, National Education and Training Center. Call (703) 358-1711 for a free copy.

———1990. *Wetlands Action Plan.* Washington, DC: USFWS.

Wetlands Information Hotline, (800) 832-7828. Free telephone service provided by EPA. Also see Internet website at http://www.epa.gov/owow/ogwow/wetline.html.

Williams, C., J. Vincent, and K. Firehock. 1996. *Save Our Streams Handbook for Wetlands Conservation and Sustainability.* Izaak Walton League of America. Gaithersburg, MD. Call (800) BUG-IWLA.

6

Rural Reality: Wildfire Dangers

Frank C. Dennis, *Wildfire Hazard Mitigation Coordinator*
Colorado State Forest Service

Colorado's population is one of the fastest growing in the nation. However, many of the things that make Colorado attractive to people also present the homeowner with potentially hazardous everyday rural conditions. Colorado's extensive areas of forest and brush, relatively dry climate, frequent periods of high winds, hilly and mountainous topography, and the popularity of these areas for home and cabin sites combine to make the typical forested development highly susceptible to wildfires.

This chapter outlines the kinds of forest/human interfaces and the major types of forests that we have in Colorado. The importance of the natural fire cycle and the costs associated with humankind's suppression of the natural fire cycle are discussed. General mitigation strategies are described, and there is a list of practical actions that you and your neighbors can take to be "firewise."

I. Common Forest/Development Interfaces

Forestry experts often talk about "the interface." This term indicates what kind of boundary there is in a given area between the forest or brushland and adjacent human-made structures or communities. A "classic interface" is one in which the boundary between developed lands and undeveloped lands is very distinct. For example, the edge of a town or subdivision that abuts U.S. Forest Service land is such an interface. These interfaces tend to be easily accessible to fire control crews and equipment, and with the help of various fire control techniques discussed in a later section of this chapter, these interfaces may be fairly defensible.

An "intermix interface" is one in which the homes and

buildings are scattered through a forest or brushland area. These developments can be found throughout Colorado and are very popular, in part because of their sense of privacy and spaciousness. The developments of Evergreen, west of Denver, and Black Forest, near Colorado Springs, are prime examples. This kind of interface tends to be the most difficult to protect from fire and the most difficult to defend once fires begin.

An "occluded interface" describes an area in which pockets of wildland are completely surrounded by developed lands. Greenbelts and open-space parks in cities and towns are examples. In rural areas, undeveloped lands may be completely surrounded by developed land. These areas are often sites where wildfires begin within developed communities, either through natural causes such as lightning or human causes such as carelessly dropped cigarettes or abandoned campfires.

II. Common Forest Types in Colorado

Colorado, because of its great variability in elevation, slope, orientation to the sun, microclimate, and other features, has many different forest types. These range from low-elevation piñon, sagebrush, and juniper stands to ponderosa and Douglas fir forests at moderate elevations and lodgepole pine, mixed conifer, and spruce and fir forests at higher elevations.

In many areas of the state at lower elevations, the forest may be interspersed with dense stands of brush such as Gambel's oak, which is often referred to simply as "oakbrush." Under certain conditions Colorado's oakbrush can be as flammable and dangerous as California's manzanita. In 1994 the South Canyon fire in Garfield County that killed fourteen firefighters was ignited in a piñon/juniper/oakbrush type of forest.

III. The Natural Fire Cycle

Fire is a natural part of the ecology in most Colorado forest ecosystems. When humans choose to live within these ecosystems, naturally they attempt to suppress and control fire close to their homes and businesses. However, by so doing they inevitably change the way the ecosystem functions and can, over time, actually increase the threat of wildfire.

The natural cycle of recurring fire in lodgepole pine and other high-elevation forests is typically moderate to long intervals of 140 to 300 years or more. Fire frequency can be expected to increase where humans live and recreate. In the absence of fuel mitigation efforts, such as forest thinning, these are often large, high-intensity, destructive fires that completely burn stands of trees. These are called "stand replacement" fires. Fewer residential developments occur in high-elevation forests than in lower-elevation forests, but it is a good idea to be aware of the danger. If you are contemplating purchasing land in these forests, understand that wildfire hazards are more difficult to mitigate and that you're living on borrowed time, so to speak.

The natural cycle for the lower-elevation ponderosa stands is shorter. In the natural world, fire would typically burn given areas in a ponderosa forest every 2 to 25 years. These forests are naturally adapted to these frequent light-intensity, "cool" fires that do little harm to mature trees. This natural cycle historically led to widely spaced stands of large, mature ponderosa pines with a parklike grassy understory. The frequent fires took out the smaller trees, brush, and leaf litter.

However, starting with the advent of logging, overgrazing, and development in ponderosa forests during the late 1800s, the ecology has changed dramatically. Now the fires no longer sweep through, "cleaning house" on a frequent basis. A thick carpet of needle and leaf litter smothers the native grasses and forbs that are necessary for wildlife forage. Other species of trees that cannot tolerate fire, such as Douglas fir or white fir, begin to colonize the area. In dry years these provide a dangerous source of fuel to wildfires. These trees allow fire to climb up their branches to the crowns of older trees and are thus called "ladderfuels." Areas that were previously able to survive fire may now be burned completely. These unnaturally dense stands of trees are also more susceptible to attack by insects and disease.

IV. The Costs Associated with an Unnatural Fire Cycle

When fire is suppressed to protect people or human-made structures, the danger of catastrophic fire increases dramatically over time. It is not a question of *whether* but rather *when* fire will revisit any particular site. This certainty raises serious concerns for both civilian and firefighter safety. Any wildfire has direct costs associated with loss of life and property and the cost to control and extinguish the fire. Two examples illustrate some of the direct costs of wildfire.

In 1996 the Buffalo Creek fire in Jefferson County burned approximately 10,000 acres in five hours. The fire was in a relatively unpopulated area of the county, but even so it narrowly missed the town of Buffalo Creek and the Spring Creek subdivision. Twelve structures were destroyed. The county conducted a study that indicated that if the fire had occurred a few miles farther north, approximately 840 homes would have been endangered. Narrow rural roads in such a catastrophe could have become clogged and prevented escape. Similar potential for a disaster of major proportions is present in many areas of the state.

In 1994 the South Canyon fire in Garfield County resulted in the death of fourteen highly trained, experienced professional wildland firefighters. The interface areas discussed above are usually protected by crews of dedicated but less experienced and sometimes ill-equipped volunteer firefighters. The potential for catastrophic loss of life by men and women trying to protect homes is clear.

Another direct cost of wildfire is the cost of suppressing the fires. Recently the average cost of controlling wildfire in the Rocky Mountain region has been estimated at $350 to $400 per acre. However, the cost of controlling fires in the interfaces described in the first part of this chapter can easily run many times that average figure. It is not unusual for the suppression of fires in interface areas to cost more than $1,500 per acre.

The loss of life and property are a horrible and very direct cost of wildfire. However, we are only now beginning to understand the secondary or indirect impacts and costs of these fires. Floods following the Buffalo Creek fire took the lives of two people, and the fire's other secondary or indirect impacts were severe. The fire removed the protective cover of vegetation, and the heat was so great that the underlying soils were baked to such a degree that they could no longer effectively absorb water. The large blackened area absorbed the heat from the sunlight and created conditions that led to a series of severe local thunderstorms. The water was not absorbed by the soil but ran off in flash floods. The private water system of Buffalo Creek was completely destroyed. Public money had to be used to restructure the company and repair the damage. A large portion of a state highway was destroyed as well as numerous county and U.S. Forest Service roads. Small bridges and culverts washed out. Heavy water flows, erosion, and siltation occurred in the Platte River, damaging fish habitat, stream-bank vegetation, and stream-bank stability. Debris and silt flowed into Strontia Springs Reservoir, plugging filters and requiring flushing the system through massive releases of water from the dam. This action damaged downstream habitat and caused the loss of large quantities of valuable water. The total cost for the fire and floods is expected to top $25 million. The Buffalo Creek area has experienced more than a dozen "hundred-year flood events" since the Buffalo Creek fire was extinguished in 1996.

Areas like Buffalo Creek exist all over the state of Colorado; they are not unusual or rare. The potential for major fire with loss of life and millions of dollars in property and natural resource damage is absolutely real. Long-term secondary costs may be expected to far exceed the costs of suppressing the inevitable fires.

V. What Can You and Your Neighbors Do to Reduce Fire Risks?

Develop a Community Fire Protection Plan that includes plans for the following:

1. *Fuel breaks.* These are easily accessible strips of land of varying width (depending on fuel and terrain) in which fuel density is reduced, thus improving fire control opportunities and safety. The forest stand is thinned, and remaining trees are pruned to remove lower branches that can become ladderfuels. Brush, heavy ground fuels, snags, and dead trees are disposed of, and a more open, parklike appearance is created. These should not be confused with *firebreaks*, which are large areas in which the vegetation is completely removed.

2. *Defensible space* around each building—an area in which firefighters have room to safely and effectively do their jobs. Essentially this means thinning trees and eliminating brush close to structures. Pruning of lower branches is also useful. Stacks of firewood should not be adjacent to structures.

3. *Straightening and widening development roads and driveways*, if necessary, to accommodate the turning radius of fire trucks. Bridges should be adequate to support the weight of fire vehicles. Make sure that all roads, house numbers, and owners' names are visible.

4. *General forest thinning between structures* to reduce the possibility of crown fires in the tops of trees. Crown fires tend to spread rapidly and are so intense that suppression actions are often futile until the terrain or the weather force the fire back to the ground. General thinning occurs in areas outside fuel breaks and defensible space.

5. *Removal of dead trees* (leaving a few for bird habitat). An abundance of dead or diseased, dying trees is potential fuel for wildfires.

6. *Assessment of wildfire hazard.* Work with your local fire-protection district to assess each homesite's wildfire hazard. Develop plans that can be implemented in the event of a wildfire.

7. *Banding together with your neighbors*, both private and public, to keep the forests healthy and reduce wildfire risk. These efforts should help to establish a more fire-resistant ecosystem that will reduce the danger to the residents and the houses it contains.

Some of the groups that have already formed to protect large boundaryless areas are the Pikes Peak Prevention Partners in Douglas, El Paso, and Teller Counties; the Jefferson County Wildfire Committee; the Boulder County Wildfire Mitigation Group; the Larimer County Wildfire Council; the Upper Arkansas Valley Wildfire Council in Lake and Chaffee Counties; the Lookout Mountain Wildfire Committee; and the West Ranch and Homestead Homeowners Associations. In partnership with public entities, the community could consider large-scale activities such as ecosystem restoration, prescribed burns or localized tree thinning, and support of timber sales on public lands designed to protect residential areas. Prescribed burns are planned, human-ignited fires that are controlled in order to reduce fuel on the forest floor. Tree thinning and timber sales can produce difficult-to-dispose-of "slash," the limbs and branches remaining after the thinning harvest. This material can be piled and burned in a safe manner, chipped, hauled to the landfill, taken to the city mulch pile, or "lopped and scattered" around the forest floor to rot.

Although such activities can be expensive, the costs may be offset in part by the sale of forest products. At any rate, the remaining costs will prove to be many times less than fighting a fire at the interface between human developments and the forest.

VI. The Bottom Line

Well-managed forests that mimic the conditions brought about by natural fire cycles are healthy, wildfire-resistant forests. The open, parklike atmosphere is aesthetically pleasing. Insects and disease are less likely to cause damage to trees that would lead to an abundance of dead wildfire fuel. When fires do occur, they will be less expensive to fight and the forests will recover faster afterward. Wildlife will prosper as it utilizes the healthy grass under the high tree crowns. Stream banks will not erode, and soil will retain moisture and release it gradually into the watercourses.

Good neighbors, both public and private, contribute to the health and fire resistance of the forests.

For Additional Information

Contact your local fire department, your local U.S. Forest Service office, or your local Colorado State Forest Service office. A forester from the state Forest Service can visit your property to provide help specifically designed to the needs and conditions of your property or neighborhood.

Request the following documents or download them from the following website: http://www.colostate.edu/ Depts/CoopExt/PUBS/NATRES/pubnatr.html

Fact Sheet 6.302, "Creating Wildfire Defensible Zones"
Fact Sheet 6.303, "Fire Resistant Landscaping"
Fact Sheet 6.304, "Forest Home Fire Safety"
Fact Sheet 6.305, "Firewise Plant Materials"
Fact Sheet 6.306, "Grass Seed Mixtures to Reduce Wildfire Hazard"

Other websites include:

http://www.firewise.org
http://www.firesafe.com
http://lamar.colostate.edu/~pbarth/csfs/links.html
http://www.colostate.edu/Depts/csfs/home.html

7

The Battle Against Noxious Weeds

Rod Cook, *Weed Management and Control Specialist*

Noxious weeds are defined by federal law as "plants of foreign origin that can directly or indirectly injure agriculture, navigation, fish, wildlife or public health." Another definition is: any plant that reduces people's ability to make a living off the land or that decreases their enjoyment of the land. The simplest definition is "a plant out of place." However, "not all exotic or alien plants are considered weeds. Most crops and lawn grasses in North America are exotic plants" (Bedunah 1993).

Historically this country has always been concerned with weeds, but over the years the concern has shifted from the agrarian focus. During the seventeenth, eighteenth, and nineteenth centuries, the United States was largely a nation of farmers and ranchers. Because their very livelihood depends on the land, farmers and ranchers have always been concerned about weeds and weed control. At the turn of the twentieth century about 75 percent of the nation's population made a living from the land; today less than 2 percent of the population are agricultural producers.

As the nation expanded, the population grew and became more mobile. Concerns about alien weed populations also expanded beyond the agricultural community to include highway maintenance managers; recreational gardeners; the horticultural, lawn-care, and landscape industries; and individual homeowners. Over time a sizable segment of the population has become aware that the control of weeds is an economic as well as an aesthetic problem, and now state legislators, natural resource managers, and wildlife managers have gotten into the act. Today many different entities are involved in trying to prevent the assault on our ecosystems by exotic weeds.

This chapter will explain the origins of the weed problem in the West, the reasons that you and your neighbors should be concerned and involved, and what Colorado residents and visitors can do to prevent the spread of noxious weeds.

I. The Development of Stable Communities of Native Plants

Colorado is a rugged land shaped by time and the elements. If you can visualize a storm-tossed sea of solid rock with huge folds and faults, volcanoes and glaciers, you'll have a pretty good idea of the active geology that produced our topography and soil. Overall, the phrase "high mountain desert" best describes the middle to lower elevations of the state, where most of the people in Colorado reside.

However, the level of precipitation, which so dramatically influences the kind of vegetation that can grow, is quite variable in Colorado. Almost two hundred years ago, when the early Anglo explorers Zebulon Pike and Stephen H. Long first sighted the rugged, snow-capped peaks of the Rocky Mountains, they were standing in an endless sea of prairie grass in the area now known as eastern Colorado. They described the high prairies as "extremely arid and forbidding country," and this type of description led to the depiction of the high desert west of the 100th meridian as "the Great American Desert." However, much of Colorado isn't a true desert. The high plains receive, on average, 12 to 16 inches of precipitation each year. And the peaks the explorers could see have far more precipitation. Pikes Peak receives 25 to 30 inches per year, and Longs Peak gets 30 to 40 inches of precipitation annually. Some mountains in Colorado receive as much as 50 to 70 inches per year. The most arid areas of the state receive as little as 8 inches per year. In short, the amount of precipitation that any given patch of soil receives depends a lot on elevation.

In addition to the amount of precipitation that an area receives, the soil type is the other major control on the distribution of native plant species. Again, past geologic forces played a major role. Approximately ten thousand years ago, much of Colorado was covered with ice. Huge glaciers carved out cirque basins near the mountaintops and inched downslope like giant freight trains, gouging out valleys and grinding up the earth and rock in their paths. As the glaciers melted they left the ground-up rock behind, and the warmer temperatures at the end of the Ice Age allowed the grasses, forbs, flowers, shrubs, and trees to colonize the soils left by the receding ice. These native species spread across the land, and the ecosystems adapted to the temperatures and levels of precipitation that were largely controlled by elevation.

The land rush was on, and the flowering plants were the homesteaders. Some plants used advanced strategies to grab more land at a faster pace. Some attached parachutes to their offspring and let the wind carry them away. Some simply produced more seeds than others. Some used their extensive root systems to go deeper for water and food. Some literally choked their neighbors out. A few produced chemicals that poisoned neighboring vegetation, and then the poison-producing plants colonized the vacated land. Birds and animals spread seeds during foraging and migration. It was a massive battle in slow motion as different plant species competed with others.

While the plants were evolving reproductive strategies that would allow them to dominate the plant world, the insect and animal communities were also evolving. Insect predators and plant diseases helped to hold aggressive plants in check, to prevent domination by a single species, and to limit "monoculture stands." Fires swept the hills, and the native plant communities adapted to the recurrence of fire in the different ecosystems.

After thousands of years of natural processes and struggle, the native plants finally found the climatic conditions, precipitation, elevation, and soil where they could flourish and be in balance with the rest of the plants, insects, and animals.

II. The Invasion of the Aliens

Almost any weed expert will tell you that many of our exotic or non-native species are Eurasian in origin. At first blush, that seems to be a real mystery. How in the world could seeds be transported all the way across the ocean? Once again, history helps to explain the origins of many of our Colorado weeds.

Several thousand years before Christ, in the "fertile crescent," now Iraq, between the Tigris and the Euphrates Rivers, humankind began irrigated agriculture and developed several domesticated strains of small grains such as wheat. Many ancient people recognized the value of these crops, and over time these seeds were transported all over the world, including to North America.

However, when people transport crop seeds they almost invariably transport a few weed seeds as well, whereas insects and plant diseases that keep the weeds in check in their native locations are usually not transported with the seeds. When the grains are planted, if the overall growing conditions are congenial for the grains, they are almost certainly congenial for the development and spread of the non-native weeds as well. The climate of Eurasia is not unlike the climate of the American West, so as the grains grew, the weeds spread. Without the natural insect predators that evolved with the Eurasian weed species in their native habitat, the potential for aggressive, unchecked spread was all but certain. Historically in North America, most new weed species spread for about thirty years and infest approximately 10,000 acres before anybody notices that they are a problem. At that point eradication is all but impossible. Management is usually the best that we can do.

III. The Spread of the Non-native Aliens

After the introduction of non-native crop and weed species along the seacoasts of America, the non-native species spread along the transportation routes with the Western settlers. When the soil was disturbed by a wagon road or a pack trail, by a railroad or a mine, or by a plowed field, the disturbed land was fertile ground for the growth of weeds. Aggressive non-native perennial "stress tolerators" such as leafy spurge; yellow and dalmatian toadflax; and Russian, spotted, and diffuse knapweed initially invade disturbed areas and then have the ability to move into healthy areas of native vegetation.

Much has been said about "overgrazing of the West" contributing to the spread of weeds. Historically, herd animals traveled through an area over a short period of time, eating most of the forbs and grasses. Such short, intense periods of grazing stimulate and challenge forage plants, which increases productivity. "No grazing" policies can leave vegetation unchallenged and cause plants to become stressed and unable to fend off weed invasion. Modern improved grazing management techniques play an important role in weed management.

IV. You Don't Have to Be Pretty to Be Successful

Several exotic perennials have successfully invaded Colorado. Many of these, such as leafy spurge and the knapweeds, don't even necessarily need disturbed ground to take root. Their success lies in several factors.

Very often, these plants have deep root systems (Russian knapweed, 20 feet; leafy spurge, 15 to 40 feet) that give them a competitive advantage. It has been speculated that 1 acre of Canada thistle roots connected end to end could reach from Denver to Chicago. These extensive root systems allow the plants to seek out water and nutrients more successfully than the native species.

Additionally, many of the perennial weed species are prolific seed producers and have a very high germination rate, meaning that almost all of the seeds sprout. Spotted knapweed produces 400 to 2,500 seeds per plant with over a 90 percent germination rate.

Another adaptation that allows weed species to be successful is that many produce seeds that remain viable and alive in the soil for three to sixty years, waiting for favorable germination conditions. Houndstongue seeds can lie in the soil for twenty years before sprouting. Field bindweed may be viable for sixty years and spotted knapweed for eight years.

With these kinds of adaptive characteristics, it is easy to see why weeds are so successful in spreading into healthy stands of native vegetation. The idea of weed eradication isn't the real world. Weed management and control are about the best we can do. This means maintenance as often as it takes to prevent the weeds from spreading by roots or producing seeds.

Prevention and early detection are the least expensive forms of weed control. If it is necessary to disturb a patch of land, revegetate the disturbed area with desirable species, or nature will do it for you with aggressive, less desirable species. Nature abhors a vacuum, so if you create a vacancy, revegetate in a timely manner, or you will find that the area will eventually be covered with the most aggressive weed species in the area.

V. Pretty Weeds We've Planted on Purpose

Recreational gardening has brought a whole new group of plants to our shores. Some have characteristics that make them perfect for our gardens, such as beauty, drought tolerance, prolific seed production, and aggressive growth. Unfortunately, the same characteristics allow these plants to escape from our gardens and invade healthy stands of native plants, where they aggressively compete for nutrients and moisture and may squeeze the natives right out of existence. In time they tend to form monoculture stands with just one species; that's not a sign of a healthy ecosystem.

These plants pose some of the most difficult challenges for resource managers. After all, who would want to kill a pretty field of flowers? Some horticultural publications refer to these escapee infestations as "naturalized" populations, but they are far from "natural." These plants have not evolved naturally with the native ecosystem, and some are toxic or unpalatable to native wildlife. If they crowd the native species out, the wildlife has to go elsewhere to find forage or starve.

Widespread monocultures of exotic weeds have already altered elk migration routes in Montana. Left unmanaged, oxeye daisy, yellow toadflax, dalmatian toadflax, sulphur cinquefoil, dame's rocket, and others could eventually have the same impact on elk grazing and migration in Colorado. Of the 1,300 species of native plants in Colorado, 130, or 10 percent, have already been displaced by non-native plants. Recently the Colorado legislature passed a law prohibiting the sale of certain aggressive ornamental seeds. Colorado was one of the last states to do so, and consequently several international and national seed distributors used Colorado as a dumping ground for seeds that were prohibited for sale in other states.

Colorado already has a number of escaped-ornamental "hot spots." Yellow toadflax has infested 125,000 acres in the White River National Forest in Rio Blanco County in western Colorado. Mayweed chamomile has escaped around the Crested Butte area. Oxeye daisy and dalmatian toadflax are spreading in many areas. Dame's rocket is starting to spread along the Poudre River and Interstate 25 between Fort Collins and the Wyoming state line. Purple loosestrife has already escaped to several waterways around the state.

Escaped ornamentals will undoubtedly pose problems for the future of agriculture, grazing, wildlife habitat, and native plants in the state. It is too late to eradicate some of these plants, and their ultimate impacts are unknown.

VI. Colorado Noxious-Weed Law

On May 7, 1990, the Colorado Weed Management Act (Colorado Revised Statutes §35-5.5-101 *et seq.*) was signed into law. It requires each county to design and implement a noxious-weed management plan. Four weed species—leafy spurge, Russian knapweed, spotted knapweed, and diffuse knapweed—were declared noxious for the entire state. Individual counties could also add (through public hearing and resolution) any other weed species deemed undesirable in those counties.

Under the law, private landowners and public land managers can be notified that they need to control areas of noxious species. Control is defined as any method that "stops seed production and root spread." If the weed owner refuses or ignores the notice to control, then with due process, the county may enter the infested lands and take the necessary action to control the named weed or weeds and bill the cost plus a 15 percent administrative fee to the landowner or manager. Unpaid bills are levied in the form of a property-tax lien for private land or collected through the court system for public lands.

Section 15 of the federal Noxious Weed Law mandates that federal land managers comply with state and local weed ordinances. Counties are prohibited from exercising more stringent weed policies upon other lands than they do upon land under their own jurisdiction.

In 1997 the state law was revised to expand the noxious-weed list to ten species. The revised state law still allows counties to add other weeds as necessary and provides for some state grant funding and a full-time state weed coordinator. The 15 percent administrative fee was increased to 20 percent.

The new law requires all counties to survey and report on all federal lands within each county to determine the appropriate level of weed management activity and compliance with state law. Most counties have an active program with a weed supervisor and weed advisory boards comprised of local landowners. If the county in which you reside does not have an active weed program and weed board, encourage your county commissioners to get one started. There are noxious weeds in every county in Colorado.

VII. Tips for Prospective Landowners in Colorado

How many times have we all seen folks buy small lots in new subdivisions that once were productive farms or ranches? It looks pretty good when they buy the land, so they decide to leave it "natural." The problem is that a farm or a ranch is usually not undisturbed or natural. Grasses once used for hay production require continued management. If you are considering purchasing land in Colorado, here are a few tips:

1. Check with your local weed supervisor (a county employee) or the local extension agent to see if the prospective parcel (and neighboring parcels) has any current or historical noxious-weed problems. You can find the phone numbers in the government (blue) pages of your phone book.

Some weed problems reduce the value of the land significantly. Severely infested lands may be open to price negotiation. It may cost thousands of dollars and years of management effort to reduce weed density enough so that you can enjoy or make a living off the land. And you certainly don't want to buy land with poisonous weeds and then pasture valuable animals that could die after eating plants you didn't even know were there. Even if the ground is covered with snow, the weed professionals should be able to tell you the kinds of problems that might exist in that area. Once you have this information, you can make an informed decision to purchase or to keep looking.

2. If you plan to move to Colorado and have horses, check with the local Natural Resource Conservation Service (NRCS) office (in the blue pages) and find out the "carrying capacity" of the land. That's the number of grazing animals the land will support. Irrigated land will normally produce two to three times the forage of nonirrigated land. In any case, you need to plan on supplemental feeding on small acreages and during the winter.

The best way to invite weeds in is to put too many animals on too small a range. Horses tend to browse even when they are not hungry and will graze a pasture down to the ground if there are too many of them in a small space. You'll need cross fencing to move the animals from one space to the next to give the grass a chance to recover. Supplemental feeding, regular exercise, and weed management will be part of your future if you own horses on small lots in Colorado.

3. Be careful when you purchase hay. Personal inspection of the fields from which your hay will be cut will help to ensure that you won't end up with unwanted weed seeds or poisonous plants sprouting on your land from hay contamination. It is much easier to see foxtail, a problem native grass, in the field before baling. And remember that some weeds are still poisonous in baled hay. Animals are more likely to consume them in the winter, when they are hungry and have limited forage choices, so you need to inspect their food sources to protect them.

Colorado has a "weed-free hay" program in which the fields are certified weed-seed free before cutting. This program does not guarantee the overall quality of the hay but only its weed-free nature. Certified bales are marked with orange-and-blue twine or galvanized wire on one side and have records tracing the hay to the producer. Only certified weed-free hay may be used on Western public lands.

Contact your local Cooperative Extension office or the Colorado Department of Agriculture to obtain a list of producers or for more information.

4. If you see a field of pretty flowers, find out what they are before you transplant them or collect seeds. They may not be native wildflowers. If it turns out to be an exotic species or an escaped ornamental, notify the local weed supervisor for the county.

5. When landscaping, choose native plants or nonaggressive varieties. If you see ornamentals spreading from their settings, don't ignore them. Native wildflowers can't compete with aggressive exotic ornamentals for nutrients, water, and sunlight. Take action before your garden plants become a widespread problem. If you see aggressive ornamentals for sale, do not purchase them, and discreetly ask the management of that nursery or store to please discontinue the sale of such plants. Some packets of so-called wildflower mixes contain non-native aggressive-ornamental seeds. Before purchasing mail-order seeds, examine the list of the contents to ensure that you are not really purchasing undesirable ornamental weeds.

6. Talk to your friends and neighbors about weeds. Teach your children about noxious weeds because it will be their problem in the future.

VIII. Developing a Weed Management Program

Weed invasion isn't a condition that just happened overnight. It was allowed to happen over a long period of time. It won't go away overnight, and it takes a sustained multipronged effort to take control. Weed scientists stress that successful long-term management of noxious weeds relies on a combination of biological, chemical, cultural, and physical methods as well as improved land management practices. If you have a serious infestation, you may not be able to run down to the local hardware store to solve your problem.

The first step is to find out exactly what type of weeds you have. You need to know how each weed grows and spreads. This is a war, and everything you know about the enemy will help you plan your attack. You need to understand the plant's characteristics and where it is most likely to grow so that you can identify it during different growth stages throughout the year.

Second comes the mapping stage, where you gather information on the plant's location, density, the soil type it is growing on, the plant community around the weed invasion, and its proximity to water and your neighbors. This information will help you devise an effective treatment plan.

Third, you need to think about what you've learned from steps one and two and examine at least five alternatives, listed below, for combating the enemy.

Fourth, keep records of where the weeds were and what you did to control them. This step is frequently overlooked, and if you don't know what worked and why, then it will be more difficult to control your weeds in the future.

Fifth, follow up your weed control efforts to make sure your program is effective. You may need to repeat the control techniques several times for many years before you are able to control an infestation.

Weed Management and Control Techniques

- *Prevention and early detection.* Knowing what weed species are on neighboring lands and using sound land management practices will help you prevent weeds from spreading to your land. Visitors to public lands can assist land managers on BLM and Forest Service lands by reporting noxious-weed infestations. Some counties offer a reward if people find and report noxious-weed species.

- *Cultural.* This means planting desirable grasses for weed competition as well as fertilization and grazing management.

- *Mechanical.* This technique involves mowing, digging, or chopping up the plants. However, it is a myth that mowing alone will control noxious weeds. Close mowing every seventeen to twenty-one days during the growing season may achieve about 90 percent control of Canada thistle after four years. Research has shown that mowing is ineffective for musk thistle, Russian knapweed, or spotted knapweed and only about 25 percent effective for leafy spurge.

- *Chemical.* The judicious use of herbicides can disrupt plant growth, but it's not the whole answer. Most herbicides are toxic at a low or moderate level. Two chemical characteristics may help you to select the right herbicide for your job. All chemicals degrade in time through photochemical reactions in sunlight or microbial action. The half life of a chemical is the amount of time it takes for half of the chemical to degrade into harmless substances. In addition, chemicals are assigned a lethal dose (LD) number; the lower the LD, the more toxic a chemical is. For example, the LD for the common herbicide Roundup is 5,600, as contrasted with 3,320 for table salt or 19 for gasoline. Check the labels before you buy. And check with your county weed control department to find out if it has a program that you may qualify for that would make it less expensive for you to purchase the weed control chemicals you need.

- *Biological.* This method involves the use of an organism to prevent the plant's reproduction and spread. Biological introductions may take several years, even decades, to become established. Even then, they may not eradicate a weed problem.

An effective management plan always incorporates at least two of the above methods of controlling weeds. Never rely on just one management method. Weed management is different than weed control. Weed control happens after you've already got an infestation. Weed management is a proactive plan to prevent weed encroachment and to prevent their spread to other areas.

For Additional Information

Contact your county weed supervisor (county government listings), your local Colorado State University Cooperative Extension office (county government listings), or your local Natural Resource Conservation Service office (federal government listings).

The Colorado Weed Management Association
P.O. Box 1910
Granby, CO 80446-1910
(970) 887-1228

Colorado Department of Agriculture
Eric Lane, State Weed Coordinator
700 Kipling Street, Suite 4000
Lakewood, CO 80215
(303) 239-4182

There are also links to several Internet sites that you can find on state university home pages.

References and Weed Identification

Colorado Climate Center
Department of Atmospheric Sciences
Colorado State University
Fort Collins, CO 80523

Bedunah, Don. 1993. "The Complex Ecology of Weeds, Grazing and Wildlife." Techline, Dow Agrisciences.

Colorado Weed Management Association. 1997. *Troublesome Weeds of the Rocky Mountain West.* Granby, CO: AgWest Communications.

8

Good Neighbors Are Responsible Pet Owners

Peter A. Holton, *Planning Consultant*
Nancy S. Greif, *Attorney at Law*

Owning pets is a great joy but also a great responsibility. In many cases, proper care and control aren't just left to the common sense of pet owners but are governed by state statutes and by county and municipal regulations and ordinances. Although you should always check with the county and city governments where you live to get a copy of the local rules, the following tips apply statewide.

I. What Kind of Pets May I Have?

In general, federal and state laws regulate the kinds of animals that a person may possess. Threatened or endangered species are generally out. However, the law leaves a loophole for such species that have been bred in captivity. Unfortunately, there doesn't seem to be any easy way to check whether a particular pet that you'd like to buy is legal. If you have a question about the legality of a pet, it's probably better to be on the safe side; if you're wrong, fines can be steep.

Never try to capture and domesticate a wild animal; it's against state law. It is unlawful in Colorado to have wildlife in your possession, and "wildlife" is defined very broadly. However, there are certain commonsense exceptions: If you're properly licensed and fishing and possess fish, or if you're hunting and possess game, it's legal. However, in general, if you're thinking of making a pet of the cute squirrel, raccoon, or deer in your backyard, don't. Remember that even possession of wildlife is illegal.

There are commonsense reasons behind these strict laws against making pets of wild animals. Many wild animals carry diseases and parasites that can be communicated to humans and to domestic animals. Furthermore, if your wild animal gets too wild, you can't assume that all you have to do is turn it loose; it will probably starve and die. Before such former pets die, they could seriously frighten your neighbors who may encounter a raccoon or other animal in their kitchen or on their porch looking for a handout.

State law also discourages the ownership of another group of animals: hybrids. A hybrid in this context is an animal that was born from the mating of a domestic animal and a wild animal of the same species—for example, a domestic dog and a wolf or a domestic cat and a wildcat of some kind, such as a bobcat. The problem with hybrids is that they are cute and cuddly and quite domestic for the first few years of their lives, and then most of them remember their wild natures and become unmanageable. In fact, hybrids are often more vicious and less predictable than their 100 percent wild cousins.

In 1997 the Colorado legislature recognized that hybrid dogs and felines "may pose a significant threat to other animals and humans," that wolf hybrids have been declared responsible for killing two children each year in the United States, and that ten states prohibit the breeding and maintenance of wolf hybrids. In response to these concerns, the general assembly authorized a study of hybrid animals in order to provide the information necessary to decide whether to prohibit the breeding and ownership of hybrids in Colorado. It's not illegal yet, but owning hybrid animals is a bad idea.

In addition to federal and state laws, the protective and

restrictive covenants that govern homeowners' associations may provide additional rules and regulations regarding the keeping of animals either as household pets or as outdoor livestock. Always read carefully any covenants that apply to the property you contemplate purchasing; try to anticipate any animals you may wish to own and try to understand how the covenants would apply to keeping those animals. For example, the covenants may not specifically prohibit horses, but they may prohibit barns and barnlike outbuildings. If you are unsure how to interpret the covenants, consult the association or a lawyer for advice and clarification before you buy. Once you own a parcel governed by covenants and you plan to add pets or other animals to your household, read the covenants again and get any ambiguity cleared up or get the covenants changed before you go ahead. You could save yourself a great deal of neighborhood conflict, not to mention years of litigation and expense.

So what kind of pets can you have? A few simple guidelines might help.

- Almost any pet offered for sale by a reputable pet store or breeder is fine.
- Don't buy pets in foreign countries thinking you'll be able to bring them home.
- In general, the old standbys, dogs, cats, horses, gerbils, etc., are the best.

II. Do I Really Have to "Control" My Dog or Other Pets?

Yes. The state legislature has given boards of county commissioners the authority to adopt resolutions requiring that all pets be under "control" at all times. The county may define the degree of "control" required, for example, with a leash law, and may specify different degrees of control required at different times of the day, for different places, and for different animals.

Among other things, the law also authorizes local governments to require licensing of dogs, including the requirement of a valid rabies shot.

If county resolutions passed under this state law are violated and there is no bodily injury as a result, the statute says that the violation is punishable by up to a $300 fine and not more than ninety days in jail. If the violation involves bodily injury, it is punishable by up to a $1,000 fine and twelve months in jail.

Even though the imposition of maximum penalties is rare, the mere possibility of these penalties should help you

to realize just how seriously the legislature and other levels of government take being a responsible pet owner.

Two important state laws that every dog owner needs to understand are Colorado Statutes §35-43-126 and §33-3-106. "Any dog found running, worrying, or injuring sheep, cattle, or other livestock may be killed, and the owner or harborer of such dog shall be liable for all damages done by it." And, generally, it is lawful to kill dogs when necessary to prevent them from killing or injuring either big game or small game, birds, and mammals. This is serious business. Never let your dog harass livestock or any kind of game; it could cost your dog his or her life and could result in some stiff fines for you, the owner.

Municipalities may also pass ordinances governing the control of animals. In particular, the Colorado Supreme Court has held that a city ordinance that made it unlawful for owners to allow their dogs to run at large was a valid exercise of the city's police powers.

And don't forget to check your covenants. Frequently, homeowners' associations have leash laws even if the city and the county do not. These laws are designed to provide peace of mind for parents of children who may be playing outside in unfenced yards and for people walking or jogging in the neighborhood. Some covenants specify that a dog be within voice control; if that's true, let your dog take you to obedience school to learn how to work together as a team.

It's just good manners to respect your neighbors' rights, and it's also the law in most places.

III. Vicious and Dangerous Dogs

State law makes it unlawful to own a "dangerous dog." That means any dog that has been trained for animal fighting, has inflicted bodily injury, has caused the death of a person or domestic animal, or has demonstrated tendencies that would cause a reasonable person to believe that the dog may inflict injury or death on a person or domestic animal. There are serious penalties for owning such a dog, and the penalties in addition to fines and jail time include paying restitution to the victim or the victims' owner and paying medical expenses.

Many counties and municipalities have their own regulations governing vicious dogs. Unfortunately, the simple fact that some people choose to own vicious or badly behaved or untrained dogs often ruins the enjoyment of the owners of well-trained and well-behaved dogs. The "bad apples" are the reason for many of the restrictive ordinances.

IV. Spaying, Neutering, Vaccinations, and Veterinary Care

Good neighbors take care of their pets and don't abandon them. Many people can tell you horror stories of moving to the country and feeding a stray cat because they felt sorry for it. Pretty soon that cat had kittens, and those kittens had kittens, and so on. Before long there were cats everywhere. You may think that some governmental entity is responsible for rounding up all these cats and getting them out of your area. Wrong!

The animal control officers of most counties and municipalities are so overworked just attending to vicious animals and cruelty to animals that they barely have time for lunch, much less time to round up the stray cats that have collected around a well-meaning but ill-advised food source. Call the local Humane Society and ask to borrow a live trap to catch one animal at a time; then take each animal to the Humane Society to be adopted or put to sleep. It's much more humane to put one or a few cats to sleep than to wind up with a hundred starving cats on your property.

If that cute stray is tame enough to pick up safely, you can make the decision to keep the animal as a pet, you can try to find a responsible person who would agree to take the animal as a pet, or you can take it to the local Humane Society to be adopted or euthanized.

If you decide to keep the animal, take it to the veterinarian and get the females spayed and the males neutered so that the neighborhood isn't littered, so to speak, with unwanted kittens. Many veterinarians prefer to spay or neuter either kittens or puppies at about six months old. In addition, get the full recommended spectrum of vaccinations. This can cost you some money, but it's nothing compared to what you'll face if that cute little cat has kittens or gets sick.

Of course, the same advice applies to stray dogs, but thank goodness, there seem to be fewer abandoned and stray dogs than cats in most neighborhoods.

V. Summary

Good neighbors realize that their pets are neighbors too. Remember that you have a clear responsibility to control your pets. That can mean a leash or a dog run or even voice control depending on the jurisdiction, the kind of animal, and the circumstances. Know your local laws and try to be as considerate of your neighbors as possible. Don't let your dog run loose or bark frequently or at night.

Under no circumstances allow your dog to chase livestock. Your pet's legal death could be the result.

And remember that you may not legally own a vicious or dangerous dog.

Be sure to stay current on shots for your pets. Many pet diseases such as feline leukemia and bordatella are infectious and can be spread from one animal to another in the neighborhood.

Finally, unless you are a breeder and make a business of selling carefully bred animals, please spay or neuter your dogs and cats. The world already has enough animals that end up at the animal shelters for adoption and euthanasia; don't contribute to a neighborhood surplus of kittens and puppies.

For Additional Information

Call your local county or city animal control person (government blue pages of your phone book) to get a copy of the local regulations regarding pets.

If your subdivision has a set of covenants, check the part about animals or pets before you buy.

Call your local Humane Society, the Society for the Prevention of Cruelty to Animals (SPCA), or your local veterinarian or vet school (universities) to find out if there are special shot clinics or spay-and-neuter days that are lower cost.

9

Living With Wildlife

Pat Tucker, *District Wildlife Manager*
Colorado Division of Wildlife

Colorado is known not only for its great natural beauty but for the abundance and diversity of its wildlife. Many old-timers and newcomers alike will tell you that the presence of wildlife is one of the things they like best about living in Colorado. Living among the wild things adds to that intangible "quality of life" that causes us to live and play here.

If you'll take the time to sit quietly and observe the birds in a tree, a coyote hunting in a snow-covered field, or a herd of elk moving through a meadow, you'll find that your investment of time is richly repaid. The more we watch wild animals, the more we appreciate their beauty and resourcefulness; they bring out the sense of wonder in us all. So dust off your camera and take some photographs. Even if your snapshots are not museum quality, they will serve to remind you of a particular animal and why you stopped to look and listen.

However, some types of wildlife encounters can bring out frustration and anger. The animals don't always allow us to admire them from a distance. Sometimes they run in front of our cars, eat our newly planted landscaping, push down our fences, cause our favorite hiking trails to be closed, or break into our cabins searching for food. "Why can't they stay where they belong?" we ask.

The fact is, that's what they're trying to do. Long before humans spread out across the continent, the wild things were here. And as human populations continue to expand at accelerating rates, we displace and disrupt the wild animals as we look for our own little corner of paradise. Some of the animals leave, looking for a less congested place. Some die when they can't find a suitable home anymore. A few adapt and learn to live among the alien humans by taking advantage of human habits that provide new sources of food and shelter.

Just like humans, all animals need a suitable place to live, or a habitat. Every animal needs accessible food, water, shelter, and space. If wild animals find one or more of these necessities on your property, they are likely to move in and stay unless and until you remove these attractions. It's as simple as that. Most wildlife conflicts can be prevented if you remember that your wild neighbors are just looking for a home. Provide that home and they stay; remove the elements that signal "home" and they'll leave.

Be well informed. Few people would buy a piece of property without checking on the roads, how many gallons of water the well could pump, the schools, or some other aspect of how we judge a potential new home. Rarely is wildlife a consideration—but it should be. Before you purchase property or a home, be sure to ask your real estate agent about resident and migratory wildlife. Contact the local Colorado Division of Wildlife (DOW) office and ask about deer, elk, skunks, raccoons, bears, and mountain lions. Chances are that many of those wild animals will be present in the area where you are considering setting up housekeeping. But don't let that stop you. Humans can coexist very peacefully with most wild species if they plan ahead.

This chapter will summarize what you need to think about when wild animals are your neighbors.

I. Plan Ahead to Protect Your Landscaping

1. Choose your landscaping plants with the local wildlife

in mind and you won't have Bambi eating your tulips or elk munching on your new aspens or blackbirds chowing down on your cherries. If you're planning to do some ornamental landscaping, be sure to contact the DOW, the local Natural Resource Conservation Service (NRCS) office, and the local Cooperative Extension Service and ask for help *before* you do the design work, and certainly before you buy any plants. These agencies have lists of trees, shrubs, and plants that are more preferred and less preferred by big game for grazing. You have two choices: Pick those plants the big game doesn't care for and watch grow, or pick those plants they love and watch them disappear as deer and elk browse on them. The lists are only as good as human understanding of animal behavior, so remember, as with most things, there is no guarantee. Just because the list says deer don't like daffodils, that doesn't necessarily mean that if you plant three daffodils the deer won't decide to eat two anyway. But it certainly improves the odds of having a successful garden if you use the information available about browsing preferences. The animals are just looking for food, one of the elements of their home. The great outdoors is their home, and as far as they can tell, your shrubs, trees, and plants are part of their home.

2. Fencing can remove *your* plants from *their* home. If you don't want the wild animals to browse on your landscaping investment, protect your investment. Effectively remove the food source from the wild animals' home by erecting fencing around your plants for about four to six years after planting. That should be enough time for them to get a good start and form tougher bark and less tasty leaves. To save on fencing costs, you can plan to group plants and fence the groups rather than your whole property.

II. Livestock Fences Can Accommodate Wild Neighbors

It seems to be part of the Anglo-American heritage to want to fence things. It's a way of saying, in this complicated world, "This is mine." But the wild things need space too, and unless you are raising domestic animals that wild animals might want as a food source, there is no reason that you can't share your world with the animals.

First, ask yourself if you really need a fence. If the answer is no, you may still want to mark your property boundaries. In this situation, consider posts, signs, stone pillars, or some other method.

If you do need to fence, for example, to keep your horses from straying or to keep your neighbors' livestock out, build a fence that will not only confine your stock but also allow the resident wildlife to pass through or over it. Cows,

pigs, and even horses can't jump as elk and deer can. You can fence out unwanted domestic livestock and still be able to enjoy the beauty of an elk herd on your property if you choose to build the right kind of fence. It will also help your fence stay intact if you build one that will allow that bull elk to get to the river for water. If you aren't considerate of these big, powerful animals, they may not be considerate of your fence.

The Colorado DOW (in the blue pages of your phone book) is an excellent source of information regarding the construction of livestock-proof and wildlife-friendly fences. Electric and wire-strand fences are best suited for these dual purposes. Generally, a three- or four-strand wire fence will keep stock out (or in) and still allow the passage of wildlife if these guidelines are followed:

- Barbed wire should never be used for the top or bottom strands. This precaution will help your stock as well as the wildlife.
- These fences should not be higher than 42 inches, and there should be at least 12 inches between the two top wires. Deer and elk may get their legs caught in the fence if the top wires are closer together than 12 inches, and that wouldn't do your fence or the deer any good.
- The lower wire should be a minimum of 16 inches above the ground so that elk calves, deer fawns, and antelopes can get under the fence. Additional wires can be evenly spaced.
- Whenever a new fence is constructed, it should be flagged immediately so that wildlife and stock will quickly become aware of the new barrier.
- And of course, all fences should be maintained properly, which includes keeping the wires taut so that neither stock nor wildlife is tempted to lean them down.

If you need a taller or stronger fence, for example, to separate cows and bulls, you may need to build at least part of your fencing to specifications that will not accommodate wildlife. If that's true, consider flagging the top strand of your fence so wildlife will not be tempted to try to jump across. Wire-mesh fencing is recommended only for sheep. The purpose is to exclude predators, but it tends to keep out all wildlife and effectively seals off part of the range from the area available for wild animals' homes.

Another type of fencing that may prove useful is seasonal "lay-down" fencing that may be taken off its posts and laid on the ground. This type of fencing is most useful for pastures that are not used in the winter and are subject to heavy snowfall. You won't need to fence livestock in or out, and the wildlife won't get caught in your fence. In the spring, simply stand the fence up and rewire it to the existing posts.

Even after all these years, the technology of fencing is changing every day. High-tensile fencing, electric fencing, white vinyl-top wire fencing, and others all have a place and may someday become the norm.

Proper fence maintenance is essential. The most deadly threat to wildlife trying to jump a fence is two loose top wires. As an animal jumps, its hind feet often get caught between the two wires. Then the wires twist as the animal continues over the fence, and the animal is left hanging; often it dies in great pain. Plan for periodic maintenance, and make sure you do it.

As with being good neighbors to the humans who live close to you, the key to preventing problems is to try to understand why the wild animals do what they do and to think ahead. Animals, like humans, are likely to use the easiest available food sources. Unfortunately, all too often an animal that has become accustomed to the easy life of human handouts literally cannot be retrained to go back to wild food; too often the result is the death of the animal. The following sections will help you to anticipate and avoid this kind of accidental cruelty.

III. Living in Bear Country

Much of western and central Colorado is excellent bear habitat. The grizzly is gone, but the black bear population is estimated to be between ten thousand and fifteen thousand strong. Black bears are true omnivores; they are opportunistic feeders and eat a wide variety of both plants and animals. They have good eyesight and an even better sense of smell.

Every year many calls are received about bears causing problems. As with most wildlife conflicts, if people had given a little thought to what bears need to live and how that relates to things around the home, the problems could have been avoided with very little effort.

There are four main attractions that will draw a bear into your yard or even onto your porch:

- Bears love trash because most trash contains leftover food. Be sure that your outdoor trash bins will hold all your trash and that the tops lock securely. If possible, put trash containers in a closed garage or shed.
- Bears love pet food; what an easy meal! Always remove pet foods from outdoor locations at night, when bears usually forage.
- Bears love sweets. A hummingbird feeder full of sugar

water beats looking for a log full of nasty bees any day. Bring your hummingbird feeder in at night if you don't want a midnight visitor.
- Bears also love meat. What do you suppose your barbecue grill smells like? Keep the grill stored in the garage, shed, or barn when not in use.

When you see the world through a bear's eyes, it's a wonder there aren't more human-bear encounters. Although not all problems are preventable, most are if you follow the simple rules above.

When a bear problem occurs, a closer examination of the site will usually point out why the bear was there. In most cases, the bear will not be trapped and removed. To do so might solve the immediate short-term problem, but another bear will be quick to take over the vacancy if the problem isn't rectified. Research shows that a trapped bear must be released more than 100 air miles from where it was trapped or it may return. In addition, the Colorado DOW has found that bears are sufficiently territorial that if a new bear is removed to an area with an existing bear population, the newcomer will probably be killed by the bears who were there first.

So it's up to us to prevent bear-human conflicts by not unintentionally inviting our neighbors over for a snack.

IV. Living in Lion Country

Almost three thousand mountain lions inhabit Colorado. Although rarely seen, they are a true picture of power and grace. They are also known as pumas or cougars.

If you live in an area with a large amount of available prey, such as mule deer, or if you live near large rock walls, rock outcroppings, or canyons, you could find yourself with a lion for a neighbor. These areas are often used as travel corridors and home ranges for large predators. But don't panic; lions are known for being elusive and shy. Again, try to understand the animals' needs and follow a few simple rules based on mountain lion habits:

- If you suspect that a mountain lion is in the area, use caution. Although attacks are rare, they do happen. Small children seem to be especially vulnerable, perhaps because of their size and unpredictable movements.
- Stay aware of your surroundings. Lions and other predators frequently depend on surprise and will generally run if they realize you've spotted them.
- Most predators are opportunistic about their food. Don't chain your dogs without the protection of

a kennel or dog run, and don't allow them to run loose. Keep your cats in, or at least try to get them in before dusk.

- Tell your children that if a mountain lion has been sighted in the area, they shouldn't play in areas where it could find cover. They should watch out for areas near tall grass, thick brush, or big rocks.
- If you're walking your dog, keep the dog on a leash.
- If hiking in mountain lion country, always try to stay in a group and make plenty of noise. If confronted by a lion, stop, make yourself appear as large as you can by raising your arms, and slowly back up and leave the area. If an attack does occur, fight back. Lions have been driven away by prey that fights back.

V. Be a Good Neighbor to Wildlife: Control Your Dogs

It is illegal in Colorado to let your dog harass wildlife. Citizens and law enforcement officers can kill a dog caught in the act, and the owners can be fined.

Dogs can be a twofold problem for wildlife. If you don't take care of your family pet and it reverts back to the wild, it may form a pack with other wild dogs and harass and kill wildlife. In many instances, dogs don't kill wildlife but rather wound them, tearing at the flesh and then leaving an animal to die a slow death.

In addition, during the winter, dogs that chase deer and elk can be particularly troublesome. In deep snow, deer and elk cannot outrun dogs, especially if there is a crust on the snow. The large animals expend considerable energy that they need just to survive trying to get away from the dogs. During the winter, careful energy consumption is vital if the animal is to make it to springtime.

In short, be a responsible pet owner.

VI. Remember That Cats Are Natural-Born Killers

Cats, whether your dear pets or feral animals, are very efficient predators. A recent study in Wisconsin showed that one cat killed over three hundred songbirds in a year. Imagine that number multiplied by all the outdoor cats. Put your bird feeders or your hummingbird feeders on wires so that cats can't wait in ambush. Think about putting a collar on your cat that has several small built-in bells to warn its prey. Above all, have your animals spayed or neutered so that there are fewer unwanted feral cats roaming the countryside preying on small birds and other small animals.

Keep your cats in at night so they won't fall prey to larger predators.

VII. Please Don't Feed the Animals

This message should be a constant reminder of one of the cardinal rules for living with wildlife. It is illegal to feed big game in Colorado and strongly discouraged for other wildlife. Bird feeding is OK, but be aware that it may attract other animals and that diseases can be caused by bird food gone bad.

Feeding may attract many animals into a small area and could cause enough stress that a disease outbreak might occur. Larger predators may follow the smaller animals into the area and create more problems. Again, once an animal has become used to human handouts, getting it to accept wild food again is difficult, if not impossible—why eat something covered in fur or feathers if you can get leftover steak or a hamburger?

Remember to be considerate of your human neighbors as well. You may enjoy seeing wild animals up close, but your neighbor may not be so tolerant.

If animals have moved into a neighborhood, it often takes the cooperation of the whole neighborhood to get them out. Wild animals can move around freely, and if you evict an animal it may simply move next door. Everyone has to know what needs to be done and do it at the same time.

VIII. Don't Try to Domesticate the Wildlife

In Colorado, private possession of most native wildlife is illegal. Wildlife is just that—wild—and deserves to remain so. Although they are intriguing and hopelessly cute, wild animals do not make good pets. They are difficult to keep in captivity. Additionally, they cannot fend for themselves if they are confined for any length of time and then released. You may enjoy the animal for a time, but if you then release the animal to the wild again, the animal will suffer and probably die. Leave it alone and resist the urge to try to make it a pet. There are a few exceptions to this law—please check with the DOW about them.

If you happen to find an injured or orphaned animal, please leave it alone. Don't pick it up. Deer, elk, and other mammals often leave their young while feeding, relying on the young animals' natural camouflage to protect them. Don't assume just because you can't see their parent that the young have been abandoned.

In cases where newly hatched birds have fallen from their nests, return them to the nest if you can or place them on a high branch out of the reach of pets. Keep in mind that as young birds learn to fly, they aren't always successful the first time and often spend time on the ground before they perfect their flying skills.

IX. Thoughtful, Peaceful Coexistence Is the Key

It is literally impossible to remove all bothersome wildlife from your area. At one time or another, you almost inevitably will find yourself sharing some of your space with your wild neighbors. Remember that when they see you, they're trying to figure you out, so why don't you do the same? Mutual understanding and consideration are the keys to a happy relationship with your wild neighbors, just as they are for your human neighbors.

Although most human-wildlife conflicts can be avoided by following the commonsense rules in this chapter, try to remember if a conflict does occur that humans are sometimes part of the problem and sometimes part of the solution.

We can coexist with wildlife. Give it a chance.

For Additional Information

Free publications available at all Division of Wildlife offices:
  "Too Close for Comfort—How to Avoid Conflicts with Wildlife in the City"
  "Living with Wildlife in Lion Country"
  "Living with Wildlife in Bear Country"
  "Living with Wildlife in Coyote Country"
  "Living with Deer and Elk"

10

Low-Impact Rural Development Planning

Erin J. Johnson, *Attorney at Law, Planning Consultant*

For many Colorado landowners, their property represents not only their livelihood but their savings and retirement "accounts" as well. Frequently ranchers and farmers say they are cash poor but land rich. Often there comes a time when they need to transform some of their land into cash to pay expenses. When that happens, they need to be able to split off portions of land for various purposes. Anything that threatens that option makes them nervous for understandable reasons. "Minor" land splits, those that may create one, two, or three residential parcels from one piece of land, are common in Colorado counties, and in many areas such minor subdivisions are handled through variances or minimized land use review procedures.

However, as more and more people move to rural areas in Colorado, the cumulative effect of these types of abbreviated subdivision approvals creates burdens and impacts on local governments and citizens that are not foreseen in the approval of individual proposals. Local governments need to step back and take a good look at the overall growth trends in their region so that they can change their review procedures, if necessary, to take into account the cumulative impacts of minor land-split approvals. Landowners who plan to seek approval for minor land splits can also help achieve responsible growth in their areas.

The following "recipe" is a checklist for responsible minor land divisions:

Rural Residential Soufflé

Start with:
1 piece raw land.

Gather ingredients:
Look at area around site—existing and probable future land uses.
Project future traffic and use patterns.
Identify "attractors" for site—distance to shopping, schools, recreation.
Identify safety problems around site.
Identify views, amenities, and other special features.

Slice and dice:
Look at 1-mile-radius area as if there were no boundaries—what should it be like.
Identify limiting factors—natural hazards, slopes, geographic features.
Identify best homesites—avoid blocking others' views and consider wind, etc.
Look for economies in providing utilities.
Explore feasibility of access to best homesites.
Plan for emergency service vehicle access.
Utilize natural features but prevent fire hazards.
Fix problems—drainage, erosion, etc.

Blend and bake:
Develop several alternative lot plans.
Establish an entry feature for aesthetic and functional purposes: signs, landscaping, mailboxes, screened dumpster and recycle area, school bus pullout, community picnic table.
Swap recreational access easements between property owners.
Identify areas that need special protection.

Be creative—consider common barn for horses or storage units.

Provide parking area for boats, recreational vehicles (RVs), etc.—screen and protect with fence.

Consider covenants if necessary or desired—design theme, quality control, other purposes.

Design for attractive "street presentation"—avoid "stuff" at front of lot.

Avoid cuts and fills for roads as much as possible; restore and replant disturbed areas.

Improve all roads and driveways to county standards.

Protect from further subdivision through covenants or deed restrictions.

Clean up:

Revegetate disturbed areas.

Install landscaping or require landscaping at time of building.

Serve and enjoy better neighbors and higher property values!

Basics of
Colorado Law

The Law You Need to Know to Be a Better Neighbor

Many disputes between neighbors result from one or both neighbors not being well informed about some aspect of Colorado law. This situation is completely understandable—not many of us have the time or the inclination to study law just for the fun of it. We all develop a general sense of law related to subjects that we experience in our lives. However, our understanding may be limited, and our experiences from different areas of the country may be completely different from Colorado laws. This section does not pretend to cover every aspect of Colorado law that you may need to know, but it does provide an introduction to and overview of many important topics about living in Colorado. A good understanding of some of the fundamentals will help citizens govern their actions in accordance with a more accurate set of rules. Consequently, people will tend to get "crosswise" with their neighbors less often over basic and important issues.

No single issue in Colorado causes so many serious neighborhood conflicts as rural rights and responsibilities related to water law. **Nancy Greif** outlines the aspects of Colorado water law that frequently cause problems in the rural environment and in rural subdivisions. Although it is a complex topic, the information is presented in a readable and understandable manner.

Another mystifying source of conflict in Colorado relates to disagreements over access to and the development of various types of mineral rights. Many new Coloradans come from areas where the landowner owns any minerals that may occur beneath the land. In most of the West, it has been a common practice for decades to retain the mineral "estate" when property is sold. Some of these retained rights have value, and some don't. The important thing for surface owners to understand is that the mineral rights are in many respects "superior" to the surface rights. **John Wel-**

born explains the critical issues related to the severance of the surface and mineral rights as well as common easement and right-of-way issues.

When buying property in Colorado, the importance of "doing it right the first time" cannot be overstated. Real estate contract and title problems are easy to come by and hard to get rid of. The insights of **Gail Lyons** should be enough to convince both sellers and buyers to pay more attention in the process of buying and selling real estate. **Susan Hatter** contributes a portion of the real estate chapter dealing with "tax-deferred" or IRS §1031 real estate exchanges. Susan provides a good basic outline of the exchange parameters and process so that you can decide whether it applies to your purchase or sale situation. All owners and potential owners of land have responsibilities that cannot be transferred to the various professions involved in the transaction process, and anyone can make a mistake. Read this chapter carefully so that you can try to prevent serious problems in your property transfers.

Even if you successfully navigate the real estate purchase process, you may not be out of the swamp of boundary and access problems. Modern survey technology is more accurate than methods used in previous centuries and decades, and old fence lines are rarely in their technically correct locations. Pride of ownership in Colorado frequently results in really big disputes over incorrect boundaries, even if the actual effect is minimal. **Victor Grimm**'s summary of this important area of law will help you decide what is important and what you should learn to live with, and how to remedy either type of situation. This chapter also addresses the gnarly topic of adverse possession—law related to what happens if a nonowner uses property for a long time and the rightful owner does not evict the nonowner. This type of incremental property acquisition is surprisingly common in Colorado.

If you own property in Colorado, you have to have a road that "runs through it." Most rural properties are accessed by private roads, which may bring up a lot of problems. This is a serious issue because even if you can get to your property, you can't get title insurance unless you have "legal" access. Read the "Rural Road Law" chapter, edited by **Erin Johnson** based on materials provided by **Leslie Fields** and **John Sperber,** for more information.

William Paddock outlines the laws related to trespass, landowner liability, and agricultural leases in Colorado. Will you have a right to build a driveway that does not front on a county road in order to get to your land? Are you allowed to put on your waders and walk down the middle of a trout stream on private land?

If you are keeping up with all this information so far, what happens if you are a renter or tenant and you don't even own the land you are using or on which you reside? What are your responsibilities, and what are the landlord's? **Victor Grimm** explains basic Colorado landlord and tenant law and outlines ways that both landlords and tenants can avoid legal conflict.

Another area of potential conflict involves things your neighbors do that might be considered a downright nuisance. **Nancy Greif** and **Peter Holton** and identify the kinds of activities that might be considered impermissible neighborhood nuisances under Colorado law.

Many people build their own new homes in Colorado or contract with builders or developers to build for them. Because the work and materials of people "improve" real property, Colorado law protects the construction industry, from architects and engineers to general contractors, subcontractors, and laborers, regarding payment for their services and materials. If a dispute arises, the first thing the owner wants to do is withhold payment. The first thing a service or material provider will do in response is file a lien against the property. Daniel Gregory outlines the legal parameters of this area of law.

The information in this section is an invaluable resource for Colorado landowners and citizens, but it is by nature rather complex. Try to understand the basic concepts of the areas that affect your interests, and keep the other chapters in mind for future reference. Keep the book in a place where it will be handy to do a little reading if you have a question or need more information.

11

The Basics of Colorado Water Law and Custom

Nancy S. Greif, *Attorney at Law*

Mark Twain is reputed to have said, "Whisky's for drinkin', water's for fightin'," and on the high plains of eastern Colorado and throughout the Rocky Mountain West, truer words were never spoken. Water, or rather the lack of it, is probably responsible for more, and more serious, conflicts between neighbors than any other single source of disagreement. But it doesn't have to be that way.

Many problems arise because landowners and tenants make incorrect assumptions about their "right" to use water from rivers, streams, and ditches that cross their property or because they do not understand their responsibilities as water users. Many faulty assumptions are the result of not understanding Colorado water laws or the basic reasons behind those laws. The objective of this brief summary of Colorado water law is to provide practical information about the regulation of water resources in Colorado. An understanding of the basics, with regard to rights and responsibilities, should enable you to have rational, well-informed conversations with your neighbors about the management and use of water in your neighborhood and region.

As with most areas of the law, "the devil is in the details." If you have a specific problem, you may be able to use this general overview to help you discuss the situation with your neighbor, but it would also be a good idea to consult with a water attorney so you know how Colorado water law applies to your specific set of facts. This chapter is not intended to be a comprehensive scholarly discussion of Colorado water law; it is intended to be a practical overview that covers many of the common terms and topics that rural residents frequently encounter.

In becoming familiar with water law, half the battle is becoming familiar with the terms that are customarily used to describe water rights; therefore, much of this chapter will explain the basic classification of water rights in Colorado and discuss the terminology important to the classifications.

In order to make sense of water law in Colorado, the most important point to grasp is that there is more than one kind of water. Water that flows in rivers, streams, springs, and humanmade ditches is usually referred to as surface water, and water that comes out of a water well is groundwater. Groundwater can be either tributary to a natural surface stream or nontributary. The rules are different for these different categories of water and will be discussed in separate sections of this chapter. A third major category of water, that stored in natural lakes and reservoirs, will not be addressed in this chapter.

To complicate the picture still further, surface water is divided into at least three categories. Part of the water in a stream may have been decreed by a Colorado Water Court for the use of particular individuals or their successors in interest; that water is called "adjudicated water" because it was adjudicated to individuals and their successors by the court. In addition, some of the water that you see flowing in a river or ditch may have been retained behind a dam or impounded for use on specific parcels of land that have been classified as "irrigable" by the federal government; that water is called "project water" because the term refers to the project, or dam, that impounded the water for agricultural use. Project water is also "decreed" by the Water Court when the project water is "allocated" to particular irrigable acreage. And in a few streams, some of the water may not have been adjudicated to individuals or allocated to irrigable land; that water is considered "unappropriated."

In the first section of this chapter, the basics of Colorado law that define the "right" to use the surface waters of the state are outlined as the laws relate to adjudicated water, project water, and unappropriated water. Perhaps more importantly, the last part of this section deals with water users' responsibilities with respect to the surface distribution systems that bring adjudicated and project water to specific properties.

The second section of this chapter summarizes the basics of Colorado law related to groundwater.

The third section of this chapter addresses issues related to the value of water rights when a government or a private individual wants to buy those rights.

The last section outlines what you need to do to be a better "water neighbor."

I. Do I Have a Right to Use Surface Water in Colorado?

Adjudicated Water: The Doctrine of Prior Appropriation

As settlers pushed into the arid Western frontier, they found that most of the precipitation, in the form of summer thundershowers and winter snowfall, fell at higher elevations, where the topography forced warmer moisture-laden currents of air upward until condensation brought the moisture down as rain or snow. Unfortunately, the mountains had little level, fertile land, and they were colder and thus had a very short growing season. The only land worth tilling was at lower elevations, where there was relatively little precipitation. Though the streams and rivers conducted the water to the general vicinity of the arable land, the settlers had to find ways to conduct the water out of the streams and rivers to irrigate their fields.

Likewise the miners, who needed large quantities of water to run their placer and ore milling operations, found that they needed to conduct the water out of the streams to the locations of their claims. Water in a distant stream did them little good, but water diverted in a ditch to their mining claims could wash the gravels or transport crushed ore.

In the West, it wouldn't have made sense to say, as was the case in the East, that only those settlers who actually owned land along a watercourse could use the flow of the rivers. Diversion, often for long distances, was the most efficient way to use this scarce resource.

Historically, diverting the water meant backbreaking labor and often a significant investment of capital as well. So a system was devised to protect those investments of sweat equity and cash. The first people who diverted the waters of a stream and used the water for a beneficial purpose wanted to be sure that even when other settlers came after them and diverted water upstream from the earlier diversion point, they would be protected by the law and assured that they would always have the amount of water required to fulfill the beneficial use that was the source of their need for water in the first place. By law, beneficial uses include, but are not limited to, domestic, agricultural, mining, and manufacturing.

Thus was born the doctrine of "prior appropriation," meaning "first to take." This concept is often expressed as "first in time, first in right" or "first come, first served." In practice, what this means is that anyone who takes, or appropriates, water has the right to divert as much as he or she needs for a beneficial use as long as all earlier downstream diverters are getting the full amount that they have historically needed for their crops or mines or other beneficial uses.

So the settlers and the miners built the headgates and the ditches. The legal protection they received in return became known as a "water right." Although the Constitution of the State of Colorado, Article XVI, Section 6 states, "The right to divert the unappropriated waters of any natural stream to beneficial use shall never be denied," it was not until 1969 that Colorado enacted the Water Right Determination and Administration Act, which systematized the procedures for granting and administering water rights in the state of Colorado. That act set up a system for implementing Section 6 of the constitution. One way to understand adjudicated water rights is to examine the various parts of the wording of Section 6.

What exactly is a "water right," and how is it expressed?

The legislature has declared that the water in the streams and rivers of Colorado belongs to the people of Colorado. Therefore, the only thing a water right gives an appropriator the right to do is to use the water for a beneficial purpose for as long as it is needed for that purpose.

Water rights, for diversions in Colorado, are expressed as a certain amount of flow, with a particular priority, that may be diverted at a particular place for a particular use.

The first element of a water right is the quantity that the user may divert. The amount of water flow in a water right is the amount necessary for a particular beneficial use. Water lawyers say that the quantity is limited by the "duty" of the water, that is, the amount of water it takes to grow a particular crop at a particular elevation.

The amount is also limited by the carrying capacity of the ditch. In Colorado, the quantity of flow is measured in cubic feet per second (cfs) because it is relatively easy to construct a flume or a V-notched weir to measure flow. If there were later enlargements of the ditch or if the ditch was extended to irrigate additional fields, then additional water rights may have been added to the original right. In contrast, storage rights and project water in a reservoir are measured in acre-feet.

The second element of a water right is a priority date and number. The priority date is either the date that the water was first put to a beneficial use or the date that a potential user first began construction on the diversion and ditch system so long as the user has worked diligently to finally put the water to a beneficial use. The priority dates on a stream are arranged chronologically and assigned numbers, with Priority Number 1 (for a given year) being the oldest water right on that stream for that year. Older rights are called "senior" and newer appropriations are called "junior." The Water Court (part of the District Courts of the state) must determine what the correct priority is and assign that priority in a decree.

The location of the point of diversion and the category of beneficial use must be specified and cannot be changed without application to the Water Court.

Any irrigator has the right to take as much flow as he or she is entitled to out of the river as long as everyone with a lower priority number is also getting his or her full adjudicated flow. But if any user is unable to get his or her full flow because junior irrigators upstream are taking water out of the river, then that irrigator can put a "call" on the river. That means that all irrigators upstream with a higher priority number than that of the irrigator who called the river must cease diverting any water until the call is lifted.

If a "diversion" isn't what I do in my spare time, what is it?

Historically, in order to satisfy the requirement for a diversion, it was necessary to actually take water out, that is, divert water from a natural watercourse and conduct it to some other location. However, Colorado courts have found that as long as the water is put to a beneficial use it is not absolutely necessary to physically remove water from a natural watercourse. For example, if a farmer constructs check dams along arroyos that carry intermittent streams in order to water his or her orchards, that would be con-

sidered enough of a diversion to qualify for a water right. Physically, diversions are usually headgates that are constructed between the flowing stream and the ditch. A headgate is a metal plate or a wooden board that can be raised or lowered to let water into the ditch. Often there is a measuring flume at the headgate to quantify the flow being released into the ditch.

Generally, physical diversion from the stream is absolutely necessary, but there are a few instances in which it is not required, including fish culture, minimum instream flow, and power generation.

Does "unappropriated" mean "unattached," as in "Hello, Miss, are you unappropriated?"

Sort of. It refers to any water that has not been adjudicated to individuals or allocated to irrigable land. It is water that is still available for use by others.

In Colorado, the amount of unappropriated water in a stream depends on when you ask the question. The courts have held that when the needs of all appropriators are met at any given time, then any water remaining in the stream is unappropriated and available to be put to beneficial use. Thus, courts continue to grant water rights even though it might be reasonable to think that the amount of the total flow would not be enough to satisfy all of the rights. The rationale for continuing to "overappropriate" streams is that in a very wet year there might be some unappropriated water left for later appropriators. Of course, the end result of the application of this system would be a dry streambed. In traditional Western water law, water is only fulfilling its purpose when it's "working." That view has been modified in recent years by legislative guidance that the definition of beneficial use should be broadly construed.

Most rivers in Colorado are currently overappropriated, meaning that the most recent, or junior, appropriators have only "paper water"; in most years there is no way they'll get "wet water" because in normal or dry years there is not enough water flowing in the stream to satisfy all of the water rights that have been granted. Because senior adjudicated rights have to be satisfied in full before holders of junior rights get any water, often the holders of junior rights get nothing. The system referred to as prior decreed rights expresses this concept as "No sharing of shortages."

If a new prospective appropriator wants to take water from a stream at a time when unappropriated water is not available, it may still be possible to be granted a very junior right if the applicant files an acceptable augmentation plan. The user has to show that the plan will increase the supply of water available for beneficial use without injuring vested water interests. Although it is not intuitively obvious that humankind can produce "new" water, a classic example illustrates the concept: A stream may be "augmented" by building a dam to retain water and release it as needed for appropriators senior to the applicant.

A more common use of augmentation plans is to come up with well water for a new development. In these cases, a developer purchases an adjudicated water right (or water rights) with senior priority and sufficient flow to take care of the development. Then the developer applies to change the use of the water from irrigation to domestic use and to change the point of diversion from the old headgate to the site of a new well or wells. If the changes are approved by the Water Court, the developer may dry up the old irrigation right and drill a well or wells to supply the new development.

There are many unresolved problems regarding what constitutes acceptable augmentation, but with most of Colorado's rivers overappropriated, augmentation plans will no doubt be increasingly common adjuncts to applications for water rights determinations of all kinds.

Aren't all streams "natural"?

Just as common sense tells you, a "natural stream" is a flowing body of water that is not humanmade. Any watercourse that is tributary to a natural stream, whether that watercourse runs year-round or only occasionally, is considered a natural stream. Likewise, all groundwater that by flowage, seepage, or infiltration will eventually reach a natural stream is considered water tributary to natural streams and is governed by the same rules as surface water. Nontributary groundwater is governed by a different set of rules (see section II of this chapter).

Does "beneficial use" mean beneficial just to me?

Not anymore. Current Colorado law has begun to recognize some uses that are of general benefit to the people of Colorado. In the 1969 Water Right Determination and Administration Act, the legislature made it clear that beneficial use was to be construed broadly. The act also specified that recreation, fisheries, wildlife, and instream flow were to be considered beneficial uses. In general, whether a specific use justifies an appropriation is largely a matter of determining whether the use is more or less "wasteful" than other competing uses. Another important criterion is whether the purpose for which the water is needed could as efficiently be accomplished by another means, for example, hydropower versus a coal-fired power-generation plant.

The purpose of requiring a beneficial use is to keep the water "working." Water rights cannot be held for speculative purposes; the water must actually be used for a beneficial purpose. The Colorado constitution recognizes domestic, agricultural, manufacturing, and mining uses. Until 1969 whether a particular use was considered beneficial was left to the courts on a case-by-case basis. Some of the uses that were recognized were power generation, aquaculture, and general municipal use. Now, as noted earlier, this list is growing in response to a balancing of uses that are important to the people of Colorado.

If I want to secure a water right in Colorado, what do I do?

In order to be granted a water right in Colorado there are three basic steps: diversion, putting the water to a beneficial use, and adjudication of the right. In Colorado it is still possible to create a legal water right by simply diverting unappropriated water and putting it to a beneficial use. Then, at some later time, the appropriator may apply to the Water Court to confirm the right and establish a priority. It is a good idea to apply to the Water Court to adjudicate a right as soon as possible because the priority will depend on the year the court adjudicates the right. Even though water rights can be secured for water produced from wells, a de facto water right, by diversion and use, cannot be used for wells; to legally extract groundwater it is necessary to get a well permit from the Office of the State Engineer before a well is drilled (see section II of this chapter).

Almost invariably these days, a person who wishes to establish a water right will find out if there is unappropriated water in a stream, begin building the ditch and diversion system (to tie down the priority date), and apply to the Water Court for a conditional right that will be perfected and made final when the water is put to beneficial use. There are seven Colorado Water Court divisions that roughly coincide with the seven major watersheds in the state. The kinds of determinations these courts make regarding water rights include:

- the amount and priority of conditional and final water rights
- findings of reasonable diligence with respect to perfecting conditional rights
- change in use, point of diversion, or storage
- the abandonment of conditional or absolute rights

In order to secure a ruling, the potential user must first submit an application for the determination of a water right and pay a filing fee to the clerk of the Water Court in her or his district. This application sets forth specific facts supporting the ruling sought. Forms are available from the water clerk. Either the applicant or the water clerk prepares a summary of the application, known as a résumé, for publication in newspapers of general circulation and distribution to the division engineer of the state engineer's office and other parties who may be affected by the requested action or who are on the clerk's mailing list. The purpose of this distribution and publication is to allow anyone who believes that their water rights could be adversely affected by the proposed action to object to the application. It is a cardinal tenet of Colorado water law that any action proposed to the Water Court will not be allowed if any existing water rights would be harmed. Like the Hippocratic oath, this concept might be expressed as, "First, do no harm."

If you believe you may be adversely affected by a proposed determination, the best course of action is to file a statement of opposition with the water clerk. Be sure to check with the water clerk about the appropriate deadlines.

The application is reviewed by either the water judge, a District Court judge appointed by the Colorado Supreme Court, or by a water referee appointed by the district water judge. Generally, if no statements of opposition to a proposed action are filed, the case is referred to the water referee. Either the judge or the referee consults with the water resources division engineer of the state engineer's office, who submits a report that is sent to all parties. The referee or judge may make other investigations regarding the truth of allegations in the application or the statements of opposition. A hearing may be held. Once all of the information has been analyzed, a ruling on the application is issued. If the ruling was made by a referee, the ruling may be protested and a trial *de novo* (meaning it includes all the issues and facts examined by the referee) is held by the water judge. Orders of the water judge may be appealed in the same manner as other District Court rulings except that these decisions are appealed directly to the Colorado Supreme Court rather than to the Colorado Court of Appeals.

Once this process is complete, the applicant has a binding ruling on the particular action sought. For example, if the applicant sought a determination of a final water right, then that applicant may now divert and use the quantity of water decreed or ordered by the court in accordance with the use, point of diversion, and priority date and number in the decree.

The complexity and formality of the process protect holders of existing water rights from "injury" by new potential users or users who wish to change their existing uses. While it is possible to get through the process without a lawyer, particularly if there are no statements of opposition, many people choose to consult an attorney to draft and file the required paperwork and to make the most persuasive arguments in hearings.

Once I have a water right, can I sell it, and can I lose it?

Remember, a water right is only a right to use a certain amount of water for a particular beneficial use. However, because the use, place of use, and point of diversion may be changed by application to and ruling of the appropriate Water Court, a water right may be valuable to someone other than the original applicant. Although the case law on the precise nature of a water right is a bit confusing, in general it has been held by the courts that a water right, or the right to divert and use a particular flow of water with a particular priority, is a real property interest and, with certain limitations, may be sold independent of the land.

It is important to remember that down-gradient users may have rights to your return flow. Return flow is the water that you apply for your beneficial purpose but that is not consumed; it runs off and may be captured by other users. Down-flow users may have water rights to your return flow. This situation limits sale rights. For example, if a person holds a water right for 3 cfs, and if 1 cfs of that amount runs off and has historically been used by down-gradient return-flow users, the only amount that may be sold is the amount "consumed," not the return-flow amount. Keep in mind that others have vested rights to the historical return flow.

Remember also that the actual water in the natural watercourses belongs to the people of the state of Colorado. The courts have held that once the water is diverted into a ditch or other water-delivery system, then the water becomes the personal property of the appropriators on that ditch. If a neighbor who does not have any adjudicated water right on that ditch takes water out of the ditch, then that neighbor is guilty of the theft (sometimes called "conversion") of personal property. Obviously, theft is a very serious offense and understandably creates a lot of conflict between neighbors even if the use of the water was due to a correctable ignorance of water law.

Likewise, if one neighbor has an adjudicated right to a particular flow rate to irrigate his or her crops and that neighbor takes more than the correct amount of adjudicated flow out of the ditch, then that neighbor is taking someone else's property. All of the water in the ditch belongs to someone and is not for the use of others who do not hold vested water rights. Unless you are sure that you hold an adjudicated water right, do not take water out of a distribution ditch.

It is also possible to lose a vested water right. State law intends that rights be granted in order to put the water to beneficial use. If you stop doing that, policy dictates that the unused portion of the flow be made available to someone else who will put it to beneficial use. However, in practice the loss of a water right is rare, in part because the state of Colorado does not have an automatic forfeiture statute. In some states, if a water right is not put to beneficial use for a certain number of years, then it is automatically forfeited and may be adjudicated to another user. In Colorado, the state periodically publishes a list of unused water rights. The holders of these apparently unused rights must show that it was not their intent to abandon the right, which may be difficult to prove. The most reasonable course of action in Colorado if you no longer intend to use your water right is to sell it to someone who will use it.

Who enforces the prior appropriation system, and how does that work?

Each of the seven Water Resources Divisions of the Office of the State Engineer is divided into Water Districts. Each Water District has a water commissioner who is responsible, among other things, for making sure that the correct amount of adjudicated flow is released into each of the diversions in that district. As the irrigation season progresses, if an irrigator is not getting all the flow to which she or he is entitled, that person contacts her or his commissioner and puts a "call" on the river. That means that junior appropriators upstream from the diversion of the person calling the river will be completely shut off, starting with the most junior appropriators until the senior appropriation is completely satisfied. In dry years, only the most senior appropriators with the lowest priority numbers will get their adjudicated water.

In order to mitigate the severity of this rule, the U.S. Bureau of Reclamation, in partnership with farmers and ranchers, built dams and impoundments to store spring and late summer runoff for release to water land that the bureau classified as irrigable. This water, project water, is also carried by the distribution ditches, so when you look at the water in a ditch you may be looking at both adjudicated and project water.

Project Water

Project water is measured in acre-feet, which is the volume of water necessary to cover one acre of land to a depth of one foot. To connect the two "kinds" of water in terms of amount, 1 cfs of flow in a year is equal to 724 acre-feet in a year. As a point of reference, the rule of thumb for residential usage of water is that each person generally uses between 75 and 100 gallons of water per day. This means that a family of four normally uses between 0.336 and 0.448 acre-feet per year.

Of course, agricultural uses require a great deal more water than do homes. *Ninety percent of all the water in Colorado is used for agricultural purposes.* The dams were built primarily for the benefit of agricultural irrigators, and water is allocated to particular acreage that has been classified as irrigable by the Bureau of Reclamation. The purpose of this system is to conserve water by allowing its use only in areas that are likely to produce crops or livestock forage.

When the impoundments were built, judgments were made about how much water it would take to irrigate particular acreage. A certain number of acre-feet is allocated to certain acreage. In some areas the conservancy districts have had to reallocate project water since the original allocation. This reallocation is done in response to a petition to the board of directors of the district that controls the reservoir.

Project water is not a separate property right like an adjudicated water right. Project water is attached to particular acreage and may not be sold to irrigate any other acreage. The right to use project water stays with those particular parcels of land that are set forth in the allocation by the conservancy district. The owners of the individual lots that carry an allocation pay (as part of their tax bill) for their allocations of water. If people whose lots do not carry an allocation use project water, it is a very serious offense and is tantamount to stealing the property of another.

If you are not sure whether your land carries the right to use project water, you can consult a water attorney or check with the dam superintendent to get a list of project-water parcels that may irrigate from that impoundment. If you do have the right to use project water and you need it to irrigate, you should call the dam superintendent or your ditchwalker, if there is one on your ditch, to request release of your project water from the dam and the diversion of it into your ditch.

Unappropriated Water

For a few of the natural watercourses in Colorado, the Water Court has not completely parceled out the flow. Unappropriated flow is any water that, at that particular time, has not been decreed to individual water rights holders. Thus, in a wet year there may be unappropriated flow in a river, whereas in a dry year there may be no unappropriated flow. The practical test is that if all of the holders of water rights are getting the full flow to which they are entitled and there is still water in the river, then there is unappropriated water that may be diverted for beneficial use. If that's true, you don't have to go to the Water Court to use the water; you may simply divert the water and use it unless and until the holder of a vested downstream right no longer gets a full appropriation; if that happens, by definition, there is no longer any unappropriated water in the river and use by any upstream junior and unvested users of unappropriated water must cease.

If you use unappropriated water, it is a good idea to measure or meter the quantity of water you use and keep track of the first day you put it to use. Then, if you want to establish a water right, you may go through the application procedure discussed in section I of this chapter to establish a water right.

What are my responsibilities with regard to the surface distribution ditches?

Historically, when the number of users was smaller, citizens would often band together to build and maintain a ditch as a voluntary association. Today a more common practice is for the users to form a not-for-profit corporation called a mutual ditch association or ditch company. These organizations will have articles of incorporation, usually a set of bylaws, minutes summarizing past actions taken, and sometimes a set of policies and procedures. These documents govern the transfer of equity stock to the shareholders, election of officers, number and timing of meetings, dues for insurance and maintenance, regular maintenance duties, and the like. If you have a right to use some of the water flowing in a particular ditch, you should get in touch with the ditch company to ask what your responsibilities are and when the next general meeting will be held.

If the dues (sometimes known as assessments or ditch fees) cover all of the required maintenance, your main duty may be to pay your dues on time and possibly to assist in the management of the ditch by serving as an officer or as a volunteer ditchwalker. Ditchwalkers, either paid or volunteer, are responsible for making sure that the proper amount of flow is entering the ditch at the headgate and for organizing volunteer work crews to maintain the ditch walls and remove vegetation that clogs the water flow (or for contracting for maintenance chores). Usually they walk the length of the ditch on a regular basis to spot potential problems and respond to complaints from users.

Most of the smaller ditch companies do much of the ditch maintenance themselves, either by asking individual shareholders to clean the sections that run through their property or by forming volunteer work crews. If you are a user of water carried by that ditch, you have a responsibility to help keep it well maintained.

If you live in a subdivision that has a ditch through it, it would be a good idea to contact the general counsel of the subdivision in order to find out more about your rights and responsibilities regarding the ditch.

And please, please, please be aware that just because a ditch runs through your property, that does not automatically mean that you have any right to use the water in that ditch. Any water right you may have must be obtained via the procedures above, not simply from owning property by a river, stream, or ditch. You must hold a valid water right to use any of the water flowing through a ditch.

In addition, if you have a ditch on your property, even if you are not a user, the ditch company and people with water rights in the ditch have the right to enter your property along the ditch for the purpose of maintaining the ditch, the flow, and the headgate. Owners of water rights have the constitutional right to condemn a right-of-way from the headgate off the source stream to the place of use, and they have the right to use the right-of-way for ingress, egress, and maintenance. The obligations of ditch owners and the statutory rights are found in the Colorado Revised Statutes (C.R.S.) from §37-84-101 through §37-84-125 and from §37-86-101 through §37-86-113. It's the law, so be graceful about providing access when necessary.

II. Do I Have a Right to Use Groundwater in Colorado?

Groundwater is any water that is contained in the pore spaces of the soil or rock below the surface of the earth. Some of these pore spaces are connected, which may allow the water to flow in response to a pressure differential. The degree of connectedness is called the permeability of the soil or rock. The general stratum where water exists in the pore spaces is referred to as an aquifer; an aquifer is essentially an underground reservoir that stores water. If the aquifer is permeable in such a way that the water, if not blocked by an impermeable barrier, will eventually reach a natural watercourse, then the water in that aquifer is said to be "tributary" to a natural stream. If the water in an aquifer will never naturally reach a surface watercourse, then it is "nontributary." This distinction is important to the regulation of groundwater.

In 1965 the Ground Water Management Act established the twelve-member Ground Water Commission, which was authorized to determine the groundwater basins within Colorado. To date, the designated basins are on the

Eastern Slope. The Office of the State Engineer regulates designated basins under rules passed by the commission and administers undesignated areas under a separate set of rules and regulations.

Tributary Groundwater

In 1969 the Colorado General Assembly passed the Water Right Determination and Administration Act with the goals of integrating the administration of surface water and groundwater and allowing for the maximum utilization of groundwater while at the same time protecting vested rights. Tributary groundwater is governed by the same system of prior appropriation as is surface water. Tributary groundwater wells are either "exempt" or "nonexempt." Exempt wells are statutorily exempt from administration as part of the priority system of water rights. Domestic use, household use, and, rarely, very limited-use commercial wells are considered exempt.

Under the statute, the yield of existing wells may not be increased, nor may new wells be drilled without the express approval of the Office of the State Engineer. In order to receive a permit to drill any water well, an application must be submitted to the local Water Resources Division office of the Colorado Office of the State Engineer. These offices have the authority to issue permits for exempt, nonexempt, and geothermal wells.

Exempt wells are usually low-yield wells for household use, the watering of domestic animals, the irrigation of not more than 1 acre of lawn or garden, the limited watering of livestock on a ranch, or drinking and sanitary facilities at a small business. The latter is known as an exempt commercial well.

The applicant for a nonexempt water well permit must show by hydrologic, geographic, and geologic evidence that the intended well will not materially injure existing water rights and that there is unappropriated water available. This high standard is used to evaluate all applications for nonexempt water-well permits in Colorado. Nonexempt wells are used for irrigation, commercial, industrial, and municipal uses. Applicants must show that any injury to existing water rights can and will be prevented and that there is unappropriated water available. Nonexempt wells must be located at least 600 feet from any existing well.

Nontributary Groundwater

Nontributary groundwater can be thought of as an underground "reservoir" in the pore spaces of an aquifer that is surrounded by impermeable strata; the water is static and does not flow toward a natural watercourse. Even if the

groundwater below a desired well location is not tributary to natural watercourses, a well permit must nonetheless be obtained from the Office of the State Engineer. That office calculates the available nontributary groundwater by multiplying the amount of land owned by the applicant times the saturated thickness of the aquifer and the specific yield of the aquifer. Then, in order to make the confined aquifer last at least one hundred years as it is "mined out," the division issues a permit to withdraw only 1 percent of the amount available in any given year. Some local governments have more stringent requirements. Based on these limitations, there is a presumption that such a well will not injure other users of that nontributary groundwater reservoir. The underground water statute also states that nontributary groundwater will be allocated on the "basis of ownership of the overlying land."

III. If I Own Water Rights and the Government or a Private Individual Wants to Buy My Rights, What Are the Ground Rules?

Generally, the initial negotiations are the same. Either a private individual or a representative from a governmental entity will approach the owner of the water right and try to negotiate a price both parties can accept. However, assuming the government can establish that it needs the water for a public purpose (such as a school, an airport, or a municipal water supply), the government has powers to "take" the water right that a private individual does not have. In both processes, "just compensation" must be determined to establish the value or the price for the water right.

The framework under which a governmental entity may "take" a water right and the ground rules that both the government and private individuals use to value water rights are described below.

Governmental Condemnation of Water Rights

Several sections of the Constitution of the State of Colorado prohibit governmental entities from taking your property for public purposes without just compensation. However, so long as just compensation under the law is paid, governments may take private property for public purposes. This right derives from the old sovereign right of the king to exercise the right of eminent domain for the public good. In Colorado the power of eminent domain, with certain restrictions, has been held to apply to water rights as well as to other forms of real and personal property.

Another relevant section of the Colorado constitution says that "those using water for domestic purposes shall have the preference over those claiming for any other purpose, and those using the water for agricultural purposes shall have preference over those using the same for manufacturing purposes." Case law makes it clear that this order of preference in no way abrogates the requirement to pay just compensation.

Thus, the state and municipalities that identify a need for water may first attempt to negotiate an acceptable price for the water rights they wish to acquire, but, failing that, they may acquire the desired rights by using statutory eminent-domain procedures.

Three separate sections of the statutes now exist that establish procedures by which governmental entities may conduct this process: C.R.S. §§38-1-101 *et seq.* establish general procedures for conducting eminent domain actions; C.R.S. §§36-6-101 *et seq.* identify particular procedures to be used by cities and towns; and the third procedural section is C.R.S. §§38-6-201 *et seq.*

When, under the existing articles of the statutes, the city of Thornton attempted to condemn water rights in the Farmers Reservoir and Irrigation (mutual ditch) Company in 1975, the legislature passed the Water Rights Condemnation Act (C.R.S. §§38-6-201 *et seq.*), which purported to establish different procedures for the condemnation of water rights by municipalities. In 1978 the Colorado Supreme Court found, among other things, that because Article XX, Section 1 of the Colorado constitution specifically provides that a home-rule municipality "shall have the power, within or without its territorial limits, to construct, condemn and purchase, acquire, lease, add to, maintain, conduct and operate water works, … as in taking land for public use by right of eminent domain," the General Assembly had no power to enact a law that denied a right specifically granted by the constitution. The court also approved an earlier holding that a home-rule municipality could elect to utilize the procedures in C.R.S. §§38-1-101 *et seq.* or the procedures in C.R.S. §§38-6-101 *et seq.*, depending on the procedural statutes best suited to its circumstances.

These kinds of considerations mean that if a governmental entity wishes to condemn your property, a careful analysis of the appropriate procedural statutes that must be followed is important at the outset. You will need to consult with a water lawyer.

In additional to procedural statutory limitations on the condemnation of water rights, the courts have held that water and sanitation districts do not have the power to acquire water rights by eminent domain and that while conservancy districts may condemn "any property necessary" to exercise their enumerated powers, they may not do so in order to acquire "title to or beneficial use of vested water rights for transmountain diversion."

What are the ground rules for determining what just compensation should be paid by either the government or a private individual?

First, the person who conducts the valuation of water rights need not be a licensed real estate appraiser.

Second, water rights should be valued as an integral component of the overall value of the property rather than as a discrete value. This area of the law is still developing, and the distinction between presenting evidence as to the separate value of the water rights and the need to integrate the value of the water into the value of the overall unit is not completely clear. In any case, when property is condemned the value of any appurtenant water rights needs to be considered.

Third, the valuation of water rights may not be "speculative" but should stick as closely as possible to a comparison with the value of comparable rights. If a value is found to be too speculative, it may not be accepted by the court. Table 11.1 outlines some of the more important factors that a court may analyze in determining if a value, based on "comparable" sales, is too speculative.

IV. Summary of Good Water-Use Practices for Good Neighbors

Before you use any water source, be sure you have a right to do so.

Carefully research your rights to any adjudicated, project, unappropriated, or groundwater. Be skeptical. Because normal title insurance does not examine the status of title to any water rights or valid but unexercised rights to drill wells, it is important to be an informed consumer and to critically analyze all the information you can obtain about any and all water rights that are said to be transferred in a real estate deal or deed. For example, a developer will frequently subdivide a big farm that has project water allocated to it. It is not unheard of for that developer to put in the individual tract deeds that she or he is transferring a percentage of the project water that was originally appurtenant to the farm to individual owners within the subdivision. However, unless project water was allocated to specific acreage, it would be an invalid transfer of project water to include such wording in a deed. Unfortunately, it happens occasionally, so be skeptical and analytical about all purported transfers of project water. The problem is that if you believe that you have adjudicated or project water and you do not, and if your water use injures the vested rights of a neighbor who really does have such rights, you may be unintentionally harming your neighbor, and you may be liable for damages.

If in doubt, don't use the water in a ditch.

This simple rule will prevent most water conflicts.

Once you truly understand your rights, get to know your neighbors, your ditchwalker, and your water commissioner.

Let them know that your have carefully looked into your water interests and that you will do everything in your power to conform to water law and ditch customs in your use of the water that you have a right to use.

Find out when the next meeting of your local ditch association will be held; go and participate.

After water is turned into a ditch from the river, it passes beyond the administrative purview of the state. In general, the ditch association for each ditch is responsible for the administration of the water after it leaves the river. Ditch companies almost always need volunteers' help to plan ditch maintenance, organize spring ditch cleanup, and keep the minutes and records of the association. Along with your water rights come responsibilities to help maintain the ditch, to keep it clean, and to pay dues to the association for insurance and maintenance. Be sure you fulfill your responsibilities and you will be a good neighbor. Volunteer to hold the meetings at your house or to provide the refreshments.

TABLE 11.1 Valuing Tributary Water Rights: The Spectrum of Certainty

Certainty	*Uncertainty*
Previous sales of identical water right for identical purpose	No previous sales of "comparable" water right
No further governmental approvals required for proposed use	Numerous approvals required; outcome doubtful
Previous court decree(s) for the change of a "comparable" right	No previous change decrees for a "comparable" right
In previous sales, buyer lacked power of condemnation	Sale is being forced under threat of condemnation
In other sales used for comparison, the buyer was not facing an emergency need	Buyer is desperate for water
Unassailable evidence of nonabandonment	Chronic nonuse may create a presumption of abandonment
Strong current market for identical purposes	No market for identical or any other purpose
Marketable title to water right established	Title disputes exist
Historical use of water is tied to specific land under the water right holder's control	A "paper" right may exist, but there is no established historical usage
No approvals are required by a ditch company or a similar entity	Ditch company may prohibit or oppose
A surface water right is absolute, or a groundwater permit in a designated basin is final	Conditional right or a permit
The water supply is historically both legally and physically reliable	Water is frequently either legally or physically unavailable

Source: Derived from a chart presented by James S. Witwer, Esq., of Trout and Raley, P.C., Denver, Colorado, in his presentation "Valuing Water Rights: Mission Impossible?" given at the Western Agricultural and Rural Law Roundup in 1999. I thank Mr. Witwer for graciously consenting to its publication in slightly modified form.

Never violate the law.

If you don't have any project water and you are able to determine that owing to a call on the river there is only project water in the ditch, then don't use any of the water in the ditch. Period. If your domestic-use well permit allows you to irrigate 1 acre, don't irrigate 2. If your adjudicated right is for 0.4 cfs, don't use 0.5 unless you work out a sharing arrangement with other holders of adjudicated rights on your ditch. If you have a question about what you can and cannot do, don't just do it and see if somebody complains; consult a water lawyer or your water commissioner.

In short, be well informed and take your responsibilities as seriously as your rights.

For Additional Information

See "A Summary of Colorado Water Law," 21 *Colorado Lawyer* 63 (1992) and other more specialized articles you may find in the annual *Colorado Lawyer* index (December issue).

Read the *Colorado Citizens Water Handbook* by George Vranesh, P.E., E.M. L.L.B., published by Colorado State University in Information Series No. 67. This may be ordered from Colorado State University, Bulletin Room, Aylesworth Hall, Fort Collins, Colorado 80523.

Read *The Rural Homeowner's Water Guide* published by the New Mexico State Engineer Office and the New Mexico Environment Department in June 1991. Copies may be ordered from the New Mexico State Engineer Office, P.O. Box 25102, Santa Fe, NM 87504-5102. Even though this guide was published in New Mexico there is a lot of useful information, such as typical well construction, that applies in both states.

Look in the blue pages (government) of your phone book and go to the local office of the Water Resources Division of the Colorado Office of the State Engineer. Get to know your water commissioner, and pick up a booklet called *Synopsis of Colorado Water Law*, by Joseph Grantham, revised edition, May 1991. That office may also have other interesting brochures and pamphlets that will help you learn more about the complex world of Colorado water law. If you're interested in dams, ask for the *Guide to Construction and Administration of Dams in Colorado*, June 1994.

Call the League of Women Voters and ask for the most recent edition of their excellent publication, *Colorado Water*.

Call the National Wildlife Federation and ask for a copy of an article written by Christopher H. Meyer, "Western Water and Wildlife: the New Frontier."

If you have a specific question, ask around and check your attorney listings in the phone book to find a water lawyer who can help you to understand the way in which Colorado water law applies to your specific situation.

12

Split Estates and Mineral Development

John F. Welborn, *Attorney at Law*

I. What Is a Mineral Estate?

Severing the Mineral and the Surface Estates

The term "estate" refers to "the degree, quantity, nature, and extent of interest which a person has in real and personal property."[1] At its most basic, ownership of land means ownership from the heavens above one's land straight down to the center of earth. This is understood to be ownership in *fee simple,* that is, ownership of the largest estate recognized by law. However, humankind's increased dependence on natural resources dictated that property interests in land be divided into the *surface estate* and the *mineral estate.* In effect, ownership of the minerals located beneath the surface can be *split,* or *severed,* from ownership of the surface itself.

When the mineral estate and surface estate are severed, the minerals are commonly referred to as having been *reserved.* A landowner who initially holds title to both the surface and mineral estate but then sells only the surface estate retains title to the minerals; she or he has reserved, or *split,* the mineral estate and therefore has a right to come onto the surface estate at some time in the future and develop the minerals. In short, one estate can be bought, sold, conveyed, exploited, and developed apart from the other estate. However, it is because the mineral estate can be reserved and because ownership of either estate can rest in any number of entities, each with differing visions for present and future uses of their estate, that the potential for conflict between mineral and surface owner should be impressed upon every Colorado landowner.

Historical Foundation for the Mineral Estate

In nineteenth-century England, the response to the conflicts between uses of the surface and the subsurface was guided by the economic importance placed upon the development of natural resources. Developed within the context of an industrializing England that was dependant on the coal located beneath moors, farmlands, villages, and cities, public policy required recognition by the courts that the mineral estate be *dominant* over the surface estate and that the surface estate be *servient* to the mineral estate. Put simply, owners of the mineral estate (1) could employ any and all methods required to get at the minerals, (2) were granted an automatic *easement* over the surface to employ these methods (known as the right of *egress* and *ingress*), and (3) could use as much surface land as was reasonably necessary for all aspects of mineral development. Years of land development and changing economic priorities have tempered the starkness of this rule, and certainly its modern version in this country better addresses the competing uses and interests of each estate. However, in no way is the mineral estate diminished in importance, a fact that every Colorado landowner needs to appreciate. Recent events in one Colorado county only emphasize the need for all Coloradans to be familiar with the issues.

Modern Conflicts Between the Surface and the Mineral Estate

Colorado is host to a variety of natural resources. Predominant among these resources is natural gas, and in the early 1990s, natural gas production intensified in Colorado. Natural gas operations became especially active in the Denver Basin, a rich natural gas reservoir located in part beneath the surface of Weld County, a large county due north of Denver that stretches to the Wyoming border. Development of the San Juan Basin in southwest Colorado and northern New Mexico also intensified at that time.

Because of its proximity to Denver and favorable land prices, Weld County has fast become home to an increasing number of people, many of whom were unaware of the intensified gas production operations. What was business as usual for gas producers was an unpleasant surprise to new homeowners ignorant of the fact that their property rights covered the surface estate but excluded title to the minerals. Their surprise was not so much because they had no right to the mineral wealth (although this was an issue as well); it was owing in large part to the many nonresidential types of activities that ensued as gas producers explored, drilled, and operated production facilities on the surface.

The affected Weld County inhabitants soon learned that not only did gas producers have a right to the gas but they could do all that was reasonably necessary to exploit this right, including setting up exploration, drilling, and pumping activities on the surface. The ensuing battle between surface and mineral owners, though nothing new to Colorado (or any other mineral-rich state), was nonetheless a battle that could have been mitigated had all parties been cognizant of what was contained in their respective deeds and been aware of their respective rights and duties pursuant to these property interests. There have been modifications to Colorado law regulating oil and gas production, but no statute or rule has been enacted that eliminates conflict or the potential for conflict altogether.

With every new Colorado landowner, the potential for conflict between owners of the surface estate and owners of the mineral estate increases. This chapter attempts to present the basics of Colorado law regulating that tenuous relationship as well as suggesting a common contractual solution to those issues not regulated by law. The chapter then ends with brief mention of one federal law (out of many federal laws) that addresses the split estate in the context of federally owned minerals and privately owned surface.

II. Dominance of the Mineral Estate

Have the Minerals Been Severed?

The deed.
Whether one has a split-estate problem is a question answered by determining who exactly owns the minerals be-

neath one's land. Has there been a previous reservation? Examining the deed to one's property is the first step. The language can take any number of forms, but be aware that looking at one's deed is often only the first step. Performing a title search on the property in question at your county clerk and recorder's office or hiring a title company to run a check for you is always a good idea. One should also consider a visit to federal offices to research whether any federal reservations exist. In fact, title searches should be part of buying any real estate when one has decided not to take a chance on what one is purchasing (such as in the case of quitclaim deeds, which carry no guarantees). If title insurance is part of the transaction, one must look closely at the title exceptions (Schedule B) to determine outstanding mineral ownership.

Another thing to keep in mind is that no Colorado law requires that the mineral estate owner announce to every new surface owner the existence of a mineral severance. Nor should mineral owners have to do so. By having their interests recorded with the county clerk and recorders' offices, the mineral owner has done all that is legally required to preserve her or his title to the subsurface estate. *It is the responsibility of every landowner to be aware of what they are taking title to and what is specifically excluded from their property interests.*

After the research is complete and a purchaser reasonably believes[2] they are legally taking title to both the surface and the mineral estate, any subsequent questions regarding title will probably be an issue for the courts to decide (in the absence of successful negotiations between the parties), especially if mineral wealth is already proven and the money involved is significant.

The absence of a state subdivision mineral recording statute.
Something to be aware of is that mineral severance questions become especially heated in the context of subdivision plats. A statewide statute requiring that all mineral interests be divulged by a subdivider prior to filing a plat would significantly reduce later conflicts. Although this issue has come up from time to time in the state legislature, no legislation has ensued. This is unfortunate, especially in light of the successes enjoyed by other states that have enacted such statutes. For example, Texas has long had the Mineral Use of Subdivided Land Act,[3] legislation that was passed and based upon a legislative finding that full and efficient utilization of land resources and full development of all minerals are equivalent state goals. The statute gives the Texas Railroad Commission (TRC), the same agency that regulates oil and gas operations in the state, the au-

thority to establish as "qualified subdivisions" those that contain mineral development sites, that is, a site where 2 or more acres may be dedicated to use by the owner of the mineral estate interest for exploration and production of minerals. The TRC then regulates that surface use so that there is no conflict between the surface and mineral owners. The statute is a helpful step in avoiding the problems created when local governments approve plats without the participation of the severed mineral owner.[4] Although some Colorado county zoning regulations do require that anyone filing plats for subdivision approval note on the plats where mineral severance has taken place, these regulations are difficult to enforce in the absence of meaningful enforcement mechanisms, and developers do not always comply.

Private Mineral Estate and Private Surface Estate

What constitutes a "mineral" in Colorado?

Assuming a mineral severance has occurred, the next question to be answered is what part of the mineral estate has been severed. Some conveyance instruments (deeds, for example) specify that "all minerals" are held by another entity. Sometimes only the phrase "oil and gas" is used. Coal, another abundant natural resource found in Colorado, may also be severed. Generally, the rule in Colorado is that unless specifically defined, the term "mineral" applies to oil, gas, coal, and minerals as minerals are commonly understood to mean precious and semiprecious metals or stones. The term "mineral" does not mean water, although it may or may not mean sand or gravel. If the wording of a conveyance is such that the mineral owner has rights to all minerals exclusive of gas, oil, and coal (these being reserved to the owner of the surface estate), then any attempt by the mineral owner to develop natural gas is expressly outside his or her property rights. The importance placed upon defining the exact nature of the mineral estate is reflected in the countless court battles that have raged over just this question.

The legal setting for mineral exploitation in Colorado.

Generally. So, how does the mineral estate come into being, and what exactly does the "dominant mineral estate" mean within Colorado law? The legal relationship between severed surface and mineral estates has been developed in Colorado by its Supreme Court in a

traditional manner. The following outlines the concept of mineral dominance as it has evolved in more specific state rules:

- Until severance of the surface and mineral estates, ownership of the surface includes ownership of the mineral estate.[5]
- The mineral estate may be severed from the surface, thereby creating a separate estate in real property that is an estate in fee simple, not limited by term or event, unless the severance document provides otherwise.[6]
- The mineral estate is the dominant estate, that is, the owner of the mineral estate, without paying additional consideration or compensation, owns the right of ingress and egress as well as the right to use so much of the surface as may be reasonably necessary to explore for, develop, and produce the severed minerals. An easement for such purposes is implied without express language.[7]
- Colorado common law (nonstatutory law) does not clearly define what is unreasonable and therefore compensable surface use by the mineral owner. However, the mineral owner does not own the right to destroy the surface (e.g., strip mining) unless there is an express agreement to the contrary or circumstances at the time of the grant an intent to allow destruction of the surface.[8]
- If a surface owner unreasonably interferes with the mineral owner's right of entry, the surface owner may be liable in damages to the mineral owner.[9]

The Colorado Oil and Gas Conservation Commission. With respect to oil and gas operations in the state, a seven-member state agency exists to regulate oil and gas questions statewide: the Colorado Oil and Gas Conservation Commission (COGCC), created by the Colorado Oil and Gas Conservation Act.[10] The COGCC's authority was predicated on Colorado's interest in conserving and maximizing production of oil and gas, a nonrenewable resource. In the realm of oil and gas, the word "conserve" means to minimize waste through the enforcement of certain drilling procedures, spacing of wells, etc. However, the commission also has some general authority to regulate adverse environmental, surface, and safety impacts from oil and gas operations.

The COGCC and Senate Bill 177. In 1994 the Colorado legislature passed an amendment known as Senate Bill 177 (SB 177) to the Colorado Oil and Gas Conservation Act. The bill did not deal directly with surface damage compensation, but it did address surface owner issues in the following ways:

- SB 177 included in the legislative declaration the requirement that the production of oil and gas be fostered and encouraged in a manner consistent with protection of public health, safety, and welfare.
- SB 177 increased the membership of the COGCC to seven (it was originally six) and required that at least two of the commissioners have formal training or substantial experience in agriculture, land reclamation, environmental protection, or soil reclamation.
- SB 177 required the COGCC, in consultation with the State Agricultural Commission and the commissioner of agriculture, to promulgate statewide rules to insure proper reclamation of the land and soil affected by oil and gas operations and to ensure protection of top soil.
- Finally, SB 177 required that the COGCC provide a means for giving reasonable advanced notice of the commencement of oil and gas operations to local government entities and to surface owners who will be affected by the operations.

The COGCC and local government control. What SB 177 did not clarify was the boundary between the COGCC's jurisdiction and local government jurisdiction. This has been an especially complex issue, especially in light of what many municipalities and counties have wished to do as their local populations grow and oil and gas interests become less politically important. However, the boundary remains defined by the courts: Traditional land use authority, such as zoning, is reserved to local government.[11] The question then becomes what exactly is traditional land use authority. The issues are by no means simple:

- The COGCC has clear authority to regulate the environmental and surface impacts of the oil and gas operations. This means that increases in well density[12] necessary to conserve and produce each mineral owner's fair share create new problems for the COGCC; that is, how can it maximize production, protect the environment, *and* accommodate surface uses all at the same time?
- Efforts by other agencies, local governments, surface owners, or environmental groups to be included in the COGCC process greatly expand the issues that the commission must consider.
- Oil and gas ordinances have been promulgated in La Plata County, Mesa County, and Larimer County in

Colorado. In addition, the towns of Greeley, Broomfield, Thornton, Westminster, Lafayette, Frederick, Erie, and Platteville have all passed comprehensive oil and gas ordinances. Whether any of these go beyond local land use authority is not always clear.

- Many Colorado towns have also written master plans, without input from mineral owners, that provide for homes, roads, and businesses but no mineral development. Simple compensation or damage procedures will not solve the resulting problems.

The role of the COGCC in surface damage issues. By statute since 1977, the COGCC has had the authority to require the furnishing of reasonable security "by lessees of land for the drilling of oil and gas wells, in instances in which the owner of the surface of lands so leased was not a party to such lease, to protect such owner from unreasonable crop losses or land damages from the use of the premises by said lessee."[13] The theory is that the surface owner who created the severance by deed or lease can write his or her own surface protection into that document and that only *unreasonable damage* is bondable. This is consistent with Colorado common law, which now provides that only unreasonable damage is compensable.

The few hearings that have been held under this section of the act have usually devolved into a public confrontation between the mineral owner or lessee and the surface owner over basic questions of what is meant by "unreasonable damage." The COGCC has been given no guidance by the legislature as to what standard should be used when trying to define this phrase.

Finally, this section of the act is not a comprehensive surface damage act, and it was left untouched by SB 177. There have been some efforts to enact an overall surface damage act that could be enforced throughout Colorado, but mineral owners are leery of the impact that changes in the dominant/servient relationship might have on the economic viability of their oil and gas operations.

Surface owners, on the other hand, typically feel that they should be entitled to full compensation for all damages occurring as a result of mineral exploration and development, reasonable or unreasonable. As was mentioned previously, the concept that the mineral owner owns the right to use any portion of the surface without compensation is not one that surface owners accept. Furthermore, the issues vary from region to region in Colorado, and what might work in one area is not always acceptable in another. This means that, absent an agreement between the parties, the following questions remain:

1. What is "unreasonable damage"?
2. What is, or should be, legally compensable?
   • Crop loss—present, future?
   • General soil damage?
   • Decreases in land values—present use, future use?

Reclamation costs, or those costs required to return the surface to a condition close to its original state, should govern any requirements. The absence of a surface-damage law intensifies the issues because areas of intense surface development seem to be juxtaposed with areas of intense mineral development and are also areas where there has been a great deal of mineral severance (i.e., Weld County).

Surface damage agreements. In most cases, the oil and gas mineral owners and the surface owners should be able to solve all the uncertainties and conflict by agreement. This is probably the most important means by which conflict may be avoided. For example, some damages may be covered by additional payments to cover defined damages. Some agreements may contemplate payment for other rights, such as the contractual and property rights that the mineral estate operator acquires under the agreement. This latter option may do no more than repeat those rights already owned by the operator, such as the right of egress and ingress. However, clarifying the respective parties' positions never hurts, especially when money is changing hands. One of the most important provisions that could be contained in a surface damage agreement is a clause that deals with well spacing and well location.

The extent to which agreements address all of the potential issues is dependent on the uses that the surface owner has for the surface and the needs of the mineral estate operator. Well-written surface-damage agreements are very useful tools, and all responsible operators will provide surface owners with the option of entering into such an agreement. However, it is the surface owner's responsibility to find someone to help define the issues. Defining the potential damages before they become a problem will always save everybody a lot of time and money in the long run.

Summary.
Recently the Colorado Supreme Court handed down an opinion that addressed in part the conflict between surface owners and mineral owners. In it, the court wrote the following:

> The fact that neither the surface owner nor the severed mineral rights holder has any absolute right to exclude the other from the surface may create tension between competing surface uses. "The broad principle by which these tensions are to be resolved is that each owner must have due regard for the rights of the other in making use of the estate in question." This "due regard" concept requires mineral rights holders to accommodate surface owners to the fullest extent possible consistent with their right to develop the mineral estate. How much accommodation is necessary will, of course, vary depending on surface uses and on the alternatives available to the mineral rights holder for exploitation of the underlying mineral estate. However, when the operations of a lessee or other holder of mineral rights would preclude or impair uses by the surface owner, and when reasonable alternatives are available to the lessee, the doctrine of reasonable surface use requires the lessee to adopt an alternative means.[14]

The opinion provides a bit more clarification as to the rights and duties of all involved, but there is debate as to what the court was attempting to do when it chose to employ certain terms. For example, what exactly did the court mean when it chose the term "accommodate," which is a term of art in this particular area of the law? And do we have any better idea as to what could constitute unreasonable damages? There is no clear answer, though plenty of opinion. Of course, this court decision was handed down after several years of expensive litigation. If nothing else, the opinion and underlying case should only underscore the importance of executing a surface-damage agreement in which the parties' expectations, rights, and duties are clearly defined.

Federal Mineral Estate and Private Surface Estate

Historical background.
Property interests are typically thought of as being private. However, as is evidenced by the extensive system of national forests, national parks, federal wilderness areas, etc., federal lands actually extend throughout the western United States. What is not as easily discernable is the fact that the federal government also holds title to minerals beneath a good deal of privately held surface-land estates. The history behind this federal severance of the mineral and surface estate is part of the history of this country's westward expansion. The ramifications of the federal mineral estate are part of the present and future of many private surface owners.

Title to most[15] of the land now recognized as being part of the United States was originally held by the federal government. As each territory was acquired from foreign governments and Native Americans, the U.S. government began turning around and disposing of this land through *disposition* statutes so as to ensure a happy, land-rich populace as well as a protected and secured territory. Indeed, several hundred federal statutes provided the authority by which thousands of settlers obtained lands upon which to homestead.

About the turn of the nineteenth century, the then administration's approach to federally sponsored settlement of federal lands changed drastically. With the administration of Teddy Roosevelt, the emphasis became one of conservation and preservation. There was also concern that the government was being too generous with respect to its mineral wealth, which could one day be an important source of revenue. Due in large part to the efforts of the then secretary of the interior, great expanses of federal land were withdrawn from settlement in order to preserve and ensure a rich public domain. The result is this nation's public land system that we all enjoy today.

With respect to the remaining disposition statutes, the government specifically reserved for itself various mineral interests while it disposed of the surface. Unfortunately, the mineral reservation language was somewhat inconsistent from statute to statute, a fact that has spawned very serious litigation today as individuals and companies fight over rich mineral wealth.[16] However, some statutes were quite explicit in what was reserved to the federal government, and the only issue today is the extent to which the privately held surface estate is servient to the federally owned mineral estate.

The common practice by the government toward its mineral wealth is to lease out its mineral rights, typically to companies wanting to locate the minerals and subject them to subsequent production. Cognizant of the potential for conflict between surface and subsurface uses, the government has tried to address and minimize conflicts through subsequent amendments to some of the original disposition acts as well as enacting new legislation to help define the respective roles of the mineral and surface owners. One federal act in particular exemplifies the response by the government to uses that may be made of the surface estate: the 1993 amendment to the Stock Raising Homestead Act.[17]

Under the Stock Raising Homestead Act of 1916, the mineral locator or lessee owns the right of entry and may occupy only so much of the surface as may be required for all purposes reasonably incident to mining and removal of minerals. No damages are payable if there is no negligence. However, this traditional relationship between the federal mineral owner and the private surface owner is changing. In 1993 Congress amended the act to better define the

rights and duties of the surface and subsurface owners. The effect is to require the following:

- No person (other than the surface owner) may enter lands subject to the act to explore or locate a mining claim without filing notice of intention with the secretary of the interior and providing notice to the surface owner.
- During the ninety-day period following filing of such notice, no other person may file such a notice, explore or locate a mining claim on the lands, or file applications for or acquire any interest in such lands. If the person who files the notice also files a plan of operation, the ninety-day period shall be extended until the plan of operation is acted upon by the secretary.
- Notice to the surface owner must be made at least thirty days prior to entry, and if the mineral operator is unable to secure permission from the surface owner, the secretary may grant permission.
- A bond is required to ensure the completion of reclamation and to ensure (1) payment to the surface owner, after the completion of such mineral activities and reclamation, to compensate for any permanent damage to crops and tangible improvements of the surface owner that resulted from mineral activities; and (2) payment to the surface owner of compensation for any permanent loss of income of the surface owner.

If mineral severance has occurred, and the minerals are federally owned, the question then becomes through what legislative vehicle the minerals were severed and which federal laws apply. Only then can one determine the extent to which the surface uses should be considered by the mineral locator or lessee.

III. Conclusion

This chapter is not meant to be a comprehensive examination of all the potential factors that could affect the surface estate, but it should give some guidance to those new to the topic. Colorado is a beautiful state, but the same natural forces that created such beauty also provided for a wealth of natural resources upon which this state was built, which continue to play a part in the state's economy. Ignorance of the property issues attendant upon the presence of natural resources can lead to grief. As a final note, if readers who have a split-estate problem remember nothing else from this chapter, they should remember the importance of the surface-damage agreement. Such an agreement, properly drafted, will save a lot of time, a lot of money, and a lot of aggravation for all involved.

Notes

The information contained in this chapter is meant to offer Colorado landowners some background on mineral and surface issues within the state. It is in no way meant to be comprehensive, nor should it suffice as a substitute for obtaining counsel in the event that readers find themselves confronted with mineral-severance questions.

The author gratefully acknowledges the assistance of his daughter, Rebecca Welborn, in the preparation of this article.

1. BLACK'S LAW DICTIONARY 379 (6th ed. 1990).

2. The question of whether one has legal title to property is a question that must be considered in light of one's state's recording statutes. The issue should not be neglected, but it is beyond the scope of this chapter.

3. TEX. NAT. RES. CODE ANN. §§92.001–92.007 (West 1997).

4. During my tenure on the Colorado Oil and Gas Conservation Commission, we commissioners routinely heard complaints from homeowners in subdivisions along the lines of, "How can you permit a gas/oil well there? We were told by the realtor that once the land is platted and subdivided, mineral owners cannot come on." The answer was rarely what the homeowners wanted to hear, and the Texas statute would have provided a welcome mechanism for avoiding the problem.

5. *Radke v. Union Pacific,* 334 P.2d 1077 (Colo. 1958).

6. *Mitchell v. Espinosa,* 243 P.2d 412 (Colo. 1952).

7. *Rocky Mt. Fuel Co. v. Heflin,* 366 P.2d 577, 580 (Colo. 1961); *Frankfort Oil Co. v. Abrams,* 413 P.2d 190, 194 (Colo. 1966). *See also Beebe Draw Farms, et al. v. Gerrity Oil and Gas Corporation,* Case No. 91CV611 (Weld Co. Dist. Ct. 1993).

8. *Smith v. Moore,* 474 P.2d 794 (Colo. 1970); *Barker v. Mintz,* 215 P.534 (Colo. 1923).

9. *Davis v. Cramer,* 793 P.2d 605, 608 (Colo. Ct. App. 1990), *rev'd on other grounds,* 808 P.2d 358 (Colo. 1991).

10. COLO. REV. STAT. §§34-60-101–34-60-126 (1999).

11. *See Bowen/Edwards Associates, Inc. v. Board of County Commissioners, La Plata County, Colorado,* 812 P.2d 656 (Colo. Ct. App. 1990) *rev'd in part, aff'd in part,* 831 P.2d 1045 (Colo. 1992); *Lundvall Bros., Inc. v. Voss,* 812 P.2d 693 (Colo. Ct. App. 1990), *aff'd; Voss v. Lundvall Bros.,* 831 P.2d 1061 (Colo. 1992); *Osborne v. County Commissioners,* 764 P.2d 397 (Colo. Ct. App. 1988).

12. "Well density" refers to the number of wells that the COGCC allows to be drilled per unit area. Drilling density affects the production of oil and gas and is thereby a factor in monitoring waste of these nonrenewable resources.

13. COLO. REV. STAT. §34-60-106(3.5) (1999).

14. *Gerrity Oil and Gas Corp. v. Magness,* 946 P.2d 913 (Colo. 1997) (citations omitted).

15. With the exception of the original thirteen colonies, Texas, and Hawaii, title to all U.S. land is vested in the U.S. government and was acquired through trade, purchase, and disposition.

16. Most notable is the recent litigation over ownership of certain coalbed methane gas deposits in Colorado. As successor in interest to a statutory reservation of coal to the United States, the Southern Ute Tribe is arguing that coalbed methane gas is part of its coal estate and not part of the oil and gas estate held by Amoco and others. *See Southern Ute Indian Tribe v. Amoco. Prod. Co.,* 874 F.Supp. 1142 (D.Colo. 1995), *rev'd,* 119 F.3d 816 (10th Cir. 1997), *aff'd en banc,* 151 F.3d 1251 (10th Cir. 1998), *cert. granted,* No. 98-830, 67 U.S.L.W. 3465 (Jan. 26, 1999), *rev'd,* 526 U.S. 865 (1999).

17. Stock Raising Homestead Act 43. U.S.C. §§291-299 (1994) (§§291-298 repealed 1976) (§299 amended 1993).

13

Real Estate Transfers

PART A: BUYING AND SELLING BASICS
Gail G. Lyons
Real Estate Broker

Whether you are a first-time property purchaser or a seasoned real estate trader, you need to have a good understanding of Colorado contract and real estate law. Remember that the best time to prevent legal battles or financial losses is *before* you sign any documents. Also keep in mind that real estate professionals are there for a purpose: to facilitate the transfer of real property. They have a wealth of information about the market and about transferring property, but they are no substitute for the advice of your own professional advisers, such as your attorney and accountant, and others directly involved in the industry, such as home inspectors, engineers, and architects.

All real estate transfers in Colorado require a written contract in which the buyer and seller "mutually assent" to the terms of the transaction. There must be some "consideration," usually money, the parties must be "competent" and the transaction must have a "legal purpose." Let's briefly look at each of these essential elements of a contract before discussing the typical items and common contingencies of a contract to buy and sell real estate.

I. Essential Contract Elements

Mutual assent occurs when an offer to purchase is made by the buyer and the seller accepts the terms of that offer. The parties' signatures are evidence of the offer and acceptance. When both parties have signed, the offer becomes a contract. To be effective, acceptance must be given knowingly and voluntarily and according to the terms specified in the offer. Should the seller want to change the terms of the buyer's offer, the seller makes a counteroffer, which the buyer then either accepts or counters. This process con-

tinues until either the parties reach agreement or the offer or counteroffer is rejected.

Consideration is usually the exchange of the buyer's money for the seller's deed. However, legally, consideration may be defined simply as a promise bargained for and received in return for a promise. Although the buyer's promise to pay at some future date (closing) is good consideration, most buyers also make a partial payment at the time of their offer to indicate the seriousness of their intent. This is called earnest money or good-faith money.

In Colorado all adults (eighteen years of age or older) are legally considered to be able to enter into a real estate transaction unless determined by the court to be incompetent, meaning that they are found to be incapable of understanding the nature of the transaction. Minors may contract but also have the right to cancel their contracts with no liability; the burden to ascertain that a person is of legal age is upon the adult.

Finally, to be valid and enforceable, a contract must have a legal purpose. Its object must not violate the laws of either the United States or the state of Colorado. Examples of illegal purpose include an agreement to defraud someone, to slander a person, or to operate a house of ill repute or dual contracting to induce a lender to make a loan on real estate without knowing the true terms of the sale.

II. Who May Prepare Contracts?

Contracts may be prepared by members of the public, by attorneys, and by real estate licensees. By law, real estate licensees may prepare contracts only on standard forms approved by the Colorado Real Estate Commission. Even if you are not using a real estate professional, the Colorado Real Estate Commission forms are an excellent outline of the necessary contract elements and functions. You can buy blank contract forms at most office supply stores, but make sure that the forms are not obsolete. Attorneys may draft their own contracts, although many choose to use the standard forms for basic types of transactions. Regardless of who prepares the contract, the four essential elements described above still apply.

III. The Contract Procedure

In order for a real estate agent to have the right to sell a property on behalf of an owner, they need to have a valid listing contract for the property, which may be obtained through an arrangement such as belonging to a multiple listing service in the local market area. This contract sets forth the terms of the agreement between the listing broker and the property owner. Some properties are sold without the assistance of real estate professionals, and in these situations you must take extra precautions in order to be aware of the risks involved.

Real estate contracts approved by the Colorado Real Estate Commission have recently been updated. Generally the changes made some obligations more date specific, and there is now a summary of the contract dates on the first page of the contract. This makes it easier to understand and use by all involved but also more vulnerable to breach of contract if the dates are not met. Remember that the dates can be extended, but the contract has to be modified in writing. There is a specific form for modifying the terms of a contract, and all parties must agree to the changes or the original contract controls the situation.

When someone wants to buy a property, a written contract is prepared. This contract establishes a series of obligations by both parties, each of which has a set date for completion. If any item cannot be completed by the set date, the contract may be invalid. Under certain circumstances, either the buyer or the seller may terminate a contract. Sometimes a buyer or seller wants a contract to terminate, but most of the time both parties want the transaction to be completed. If the contract is terminated by the buyer for a legitimate reason, their deposit or earnest money is usually returned to them.

The signed contract becomes the road map for the actions of the parties from the date of the acceptance of the offer to the date of closing. It is very important that all information is correct on the contract because the title company and other professionals involved in the transaction rely on the contract information to do their jobs. Pay particular attention to the spelling of names, the correctness of the legal description, and whether all of the negotiated terms of the contract can be clearly understood and accurately reflect the intentions of the parties. Even small mistakes can lead to big problems, so review every word

carefully and verify all information through outside sources. Paying an attorney to conduct the review and research is money well spent. All agreements between the parties related to the transaction should be included in the contract; otherwise, what you thought you agreed to may not happen.

Once all the contract obligations are met, that is, inspections and repairs, surveys, title research and acceptance, and financing, the transaction is ready to "close." At the closing, all obligations of the contract itself are fulfilled or waived unless separate arrangements are made for any agreement to "survive" the closing. In Colorado, taxes are generally prorated to the date of closing, and the buyer assumes the responsibility to pay any actual increase in tax responsibility after closing. The result is a "clean" transaction, with no ongoing association between the buyer and the seller unless the seller finances the purchase.

Once the transaction is complete, the deed to the property is in the buyer's name, even if a third party has provided financing. If the purchase is financed, there will be a written promissory note between the buyer and the financer that states the amount of indebtedness and how it is to be repaid. The financer typically also has a deed of trust granted by the buyer, which, in the event of default of the note, gives the financer the right to foreclose on the property. In a foreclosure action, the buyer has a right to "cure" before the forced sale of the property, and a certain amount of time after the sale to "redeem" the property by paying the indebtedness and all costs.

The person conducting the closing generally has the responsibility to record the appropriate documents, get the original documents to the correct parties, and get copies of the other recorded documents to all parties. The final title insurance policy will be sent to the buyer within a few weeks after the closing. Title insurance is not required in Colorado, but a buyer would be very foolish to purchase a property without it, even if there are significant exceptions to the policy. Typically, title insurance is an expense of the seller.

The most important thing to remember is that if you are buying a property, it is your responsibility to be aware of all the conditions and circumstances associated with the property. Significant information, such as whether the property is zoned for the buyer's intended use or whether there are natural hazards on the property, may not be included in any of the normal transaction processes. After the transaction is closed, it is generally too late to hold anyone else accountable. Don't be shy about asking questions, doing your own research, or hiring appropriate professionals for inspections, analyses, or opinions. Do your research early in the contract process or, with permission, before you make an offer on a particular parcel.

IV. Typical Contract Items

The following points should be used as a checklist to make sure that each item is properly understood and addressed in a real estate contract.

1. *Names and signatures of the parties.* Both buyer and seller must be named and identified as either buyer or seller. When there is more than one buyer or more than one seller, all must be named and appropriately identified. Likewise, all must sign the contract. Make sure that the contract reflects the correct manner in which the buyers wish to hold title, either with their correct individual names and as joint tenants or tenants in common or as the correct entity that is to hold title (i.e., partnership, corporation, trust, etc.).

2. *Sale price and payment provisions.* To be enforceable, the contract must contain the price. If there is no provision for method of payment, the law presumes a cash transaction. If it is not a cash sale, the contract should also state the amount of earnest-money deposit, the amount to be paid at closing, and the balance either by assumption of an existing mortgage (very rare in today's marketplace) or a new mortgage. When a mortgage is used, the terms (interest rate, term, and monthly payment) should be described.

3. *Description of the property.* The property must be described with reasonable certainty. This description may be a street address, but it is preferable to use the legal description contained in either the seller's deed or the title insurance policy. If any personal property is being transferred, this property should be listed as well.

4. *Type of deed.* Property is legally conveyed by a deed, and the type of deed to be used should be identified in the contract. The most common deeds are general warranty and quitclaim. The general warranty deed is used to transfer title in most purchase and sale contracts; in it the seller guarantees the title against defects existing before the seller acquired title or arising during the seller's ownership. A quitclaim deed is one in which the grantor warrants nothing and that conveys only the grantor's present interest in the property, if any. Such deeds are frequently used to change the name of the owner, to clear up a technical defect in the chain of title, or to release lien claims against the property.

5. *Condition of title.* Title is generally supposed to be "merchantable." This means that it is free from defects other than those a reasonably prudent buyer would be willing to accept, for example, property taxes that are paid in arrears. To prove that title is merchantable, the seller, as a condition of the contract, usually provides the buyer with a title insurance commitment. After closing, this is converted to a title policy. If the commitment indicates title defects that the buyer finds unacceptable, the contract should provide for the buyer to so notify the seller; the seller must then correct such unsatisfactory title conditions or the contract terminates.

6. *Default provisions.* These provisions should describe the remedies should either buyer or seller default. If the buyer is in default, the contract should define the disposition of the buyer's earnest-money deposit. Many contract disputes arise over earnest-money deposits. Typically, the buyer finds a reason that they do not want to complete the transaction and believes that they are entitled to the return of their earnest money. The seller's typical reaction is to allow the buyer to back out of the contract at the cost of the earnest money. Make sure that you specifically address the status of the earnest money in all negotiated contract provisions, and make sure that you can perform all obligations within the allotted time. You can usually close earlier than the contract states if all obligations have been met, so be sure to give yourself plenty of time when you are setting up a contract. A period of forty-five to sixty days from the date of the contract is not unusual for a projected closing date.

7. *Contingency provisions.* Usually the buyer includes a number of contingencies that must be met before the buyer is willing or capable of buying. If a contingency is not met, the contract can be canceled by the appropriate party. Contingency provisions should carefully describe the method and time period to accomplish the contingent requirement or terminate the contract. All contingent provisions should directly address the disposition of the earnest money in the event that the provision is not met or otherwise resolved. Some of the more common contingency provisions are described in the next section of this chapter.

8. *Possession.* Since the time of closing the transaction and the time of possession of the property may not be the same, the contract should clearly state the date and time of possession.

9. *Apportionment or adjustment.* There are a number of charges against the property that are not determined by who owns the property, for example, property taxes, assessments, interest on assumed encumbrances, and rents. The contract should state how these will be apportioned; usually this is done based on the closing date relative to the end of the year.

10. *Risk of loss.* Since it is possible that the property could be damaged by fire, flood, storm, earthquake, etc., the contract should clarify who suffers the loss, buyer or seller, and

how the loss may affect the transaction. Usually the risk of loss remains with the seller, but the buyer retains the right to terminate the contract if the loss is more extensive than the buyer is willing to accept.

11. *Dispute resolution.* The standard forms contain a provision requiring the parties to address disputes through some form of alternative dispute resolution (ADR), typically mediation, prior to filing lawsuits over the disputed matter. This can be an effective manner of resolving unforeseen problems that arise during the contract process.

V. Common Contract Contingencies

The following is a checklist of other important contract elements that require specific decisions to be made by the buyer and seller:

1. *Mortgage loans.* In Colorado, the security for a real estate loan is the property itself. Instead of a true "mortgage," as is used in many states, Colorado statutes provide that the debt is secured by a deed of trust. The primary difference between "mortgage" states and "public trustee" states is that in Colorado the remedy of foreclosure following default of the loan is conducted through the office of the County Public Trustee rather than through the courts, as would happen in a mortgage state. Otherwise the two instruments are nearly identical. As a contingency, the contract should clearly describe the terms the buyer is willing to accept relative to interest rate, term, fixed or adjustable rate, and dates for loan application and loan approval.

2. *Appraisal.* Most lenders require an appraisal indicating a property value equal to the sales price. If the appraisal is lower than the sales price, the loan amount is usually reduced proportionally. Even if the buyer is paying cash, it is a good idea to have an appraisal.

3. *Survey or Improvement Location Certificate (ILC).* This too is usually a lender requirement. Effectively, these are maps that show the location of any improvements, encroachments, and easements within the property boundaries. Even if the buyer is paying cash, it is a good idea to obtain a survey (boundaries are clearly staked or flagged) or an ILC (no staking or flagging).

It is important to understand the different functions of an ILC and a survey. An ILC is intended to establish that all of the improvements are actually located on the parcel and that their value is not negatively affected by the location of any easements, lot lines, rights-of-way, or other restrictions. An ILC cannot establish a legal description or a new parcel.

A survey plat defines and illustrates the legal description of the parcel. Other than the boundary, other features or improvements may be shown on the plat if it is arranged with the surveyor that the plat is to meet certain standards. The surveyor places pins in the ground at each corner of the property boundary.

In most real estate transactions, a title insurance policy is obtained to protect the buyer from defects in the title. A title company verifies the legal description on the survey plat and researches the public record for recorded documents that may affect the title of that parcel. The title policy may include exceptions, or references to certain situations or documents that are not covered under the policy.

If the parcel is in a subdivision, the land has been surveyed as a part of establishing the lot. The subdivision plat, a survey plat that may include many parcels, is kept on file in the county clerk's office, and these plats provide the legal description for each individual parcel, as approved by the local government. In these situations, the ILC is an inventory of improvements, usually requested by the lender, and a survey is not necessary to transfer the property unless a specific need or concern exists.

If the parcel is not in a subdivision, the legal description of a parcel may be established by a metes and bounds description or described as a part of a section in a particular township and range. If there is no survey, it is a good idea to have the property surveyed to identify encroachments and boundary disputes that may need to be resolved.

4. *Inspections.* This contingency gives the buyer the right to have the property thoroughly inspected. Such inspections are usually done by a professional and include structural, electrical, plumbing, heating, and other characteristics of the improvements. The inspection may also include soil tests, water rights, condition of plants or crops, etc. The contingency usually gives the buyer the right to object and request repair and the buyer and seller a time period to reach resolution on the buyer's objections.

5. *Title.* As discussed earlier, most contracts require that the title be merchantable and that the seller provide the buyer with a title commitment acceptable to the buyer. Occasionally when there is no commercial loan, abstracts are used instead of title commitments; however, this has become increasingly uncommon. Many title companies will no longer update an abstract. If an abstracts is used, make sure that it includes all current recorded documents and have it reviewed by an attorney who is willing to issue a written opinion of title.

6. *Closing.* The contract should state a specific date on which the buyer will provide cash and, if necessary, loan proceeds equivalent to the sales price and the seller will provide a deed, usually a general warranty deed, in exchange. At the same time, most of the costs for completion

of the contingencies are divided appropriately between buyer and seller. The majority of closings in Colorado are handled by a title insurance company. The remainder are done by real estate brokers, attorneys, or escrow companies. The settlement documents should be available within twenty-four hours prior to closing so that you can review the closing information.

VI. It's Up to You ...

Many items in a real estate contract are unique to your property and transaction, and there is a multitude of information that you need to gather or understand. This type of information may or may not be addressed elsewhere in the closing process or documents. The following checklist includes some of these types of issues:

1. *Remedies.* Make sure that the real estate agent or your attorney discusses the contract remedies with you so that you fully understand them as they apply to the buyer and the seller.

2. *Allowances.* The seller may have escrowed funds for repairs based on an estimate or allowance. Verify actual costs of replaced items and get written estimates or proposals on items to be replaced after the closing. Make sure the proposal will be valid after the closing, with enough time for you to complete the repair. Discuss any discrepancies or shortfalls prior to closing.

3. *Access prior to closing.* In the rare situations when you have access or possession prior to closing, make sure that you have a valid lease or other written agreement. Make sure you have insurance in place adequate for the nature of your use.

4. *Soils report disclosure.* For certain residential sales in Colorado, the seller is obligated to provide a copy of a soils report to the buyer fourteen days prior to closing. Make sure that you get a copy, verify that it applies to your property, and read carefully any concerns regarding soil conditions.

5. *Engineering and other reports.* If any studies have been conducted to prepare the property for sale or at the buyer's request in the negotiation process, make sure that they are certified to the buyer, even if paid for by the seller.

6. *Construction.* Sometimes sellers contract to improve the property to the buyer's specifications prior to closing. Make sure the proper insurance is in place and that the earnest money or other deposit is held in a safe escrow account until improvements are complete.

7. *Real estate professionals.* Make sure that you understand the specific responsibilities of any real estate professionals involved in the transaction. By law, they can act as seller's agents, seller's subagents, buyer's agents, or transaction brokers. Any agent owes a fiduciary duty to their client and acts as their client's adviser and advocate. Transaction brokers have very specific duties, and they cannot act as an advocate for either side of the transaction. Be sure you understand whether you are being represented by an agent or whether you are working with a transaction broker. Ask lots of questions.

8. *Zoning and subdivision.* Do your own research with the local government entity to verify the existing regulations and to discuss how you intend to use the property. Ask the government if any regulatory changes have been made recently, if any changes are anticipated in the near future, and if they have experienced any problems with the existing zoning and subdivision regulations. Identify and understand neighboring zoning districts and the uses allowed in those areas.

9. *Building permits.* If you plan to build or remodel, talk to the building inspector prior to closing to identify any problems regarding obtaining a building permit.

10. *Water, sewer, septic, ditches, wells, drainage easements, etc.* Independently verify the source and amount of all water rights and taps. Get historical use figures from the seller—you will not be able to get them later without their permission. Have septic systems and wells inspected by a qualified person, and discuss them with the county health department. Make sure you are aware of any ditch easement on the property and know whom the water belongs to. For irrigation water, talk to the water company and meet the ditchrider. Understand the rules and the system and ask about any problems.

If water or water rights are being transferred, make certain that original certificates are presented or accounted for and that all transfer documents are signed.

11. *Legal access.* It is very important to understand your legal access and your physical access prior to closing. Many deeds lack a specification of width for easements, and many modern zoning and subdivision codes require specific widths that are wider than historical use. Check with the local government to identify the requirements, particularly if you want to subdivide, and correct any problems prior to closing. Check your title commitment for any exceptions addressing "lack of access."

12. *Roads.* Find out whether the roads to your property are public or private, and understand your obligations with regard to each. Check for special improvement taxes that may be due. If any portion of the access to your property is through public lands, be sure you understand any limitations and how and when they are maintained.

13. *Fences.* Examine your survey to determine whether

any existing fences are on the actual property boundaries. You may want to make a boundary agreement with your neighbors prior to closing if there are any boundary issues. If so, such an agreement should be recorded along with your deed.

14. *Title insurance.* Review the preliminary commitment carefully, and discuss with the title company the exceptions, endorsements, and exclusions. Make sure you understand them. Get copies of and review all documents that affect your title. If you are using a real estate professional, they should review all aspects of the title commitment and closing with you.

15. *Legal description.* Make sure the deed includes the complete legal description and that all easements and other items transferred in the deed are accurate and correct. Read through the legal descriptions with another person to check for typographical errors.

16. *Liens.* Make sure that there are no liens on the property that are not your responsibility. These can be from a variety of sources, including mechanics, attorneys, the Internal Revenue Service (IRS), other tax liens, child support, and homeowner associations. Any existing liens will remain with the property even though the title transfers unless they are paid and appropriately released.

17. *Home warranty.* If you are buying a new home with a warranty, or a warranty on an existing home, understand what the policy covers and make sure it is in your name.

18. *Construction and remodeling.* Get a set of the construction plans and the contractor's name and address. Make certain that all debts incurred by contractors for materials or work are paid and evidenced by signed lien waivers.

19. *Homeowners' associations, covenants, and deed restrictions.* Make sure you are aware of any covenants or deed restrictions and your financial or other obligations regarding a homeowners' association.

20. *Utilities.* If utilities are not installed to the property, get cost estimates for their installation. Get separate estimates for extending the utilities from the property line to the building site. Get inspections to identify any geologic conditions that may prohibit installation.

21. *Grazing or agricultural leases and hunting and fishing rights.* Find out if there are any previous or existing rights, who holds them, and who granted them.

22. *Personal property and fixtures.* If you are buying property with associated equipment or personal property, get an inventory, make sure titled items are properly transferred, and inspect all items to verify their working condition.

23. *Plats.* Review the subdivision plats for your parcel, and check carefully for any restrictions in the form of plat notes.

24. *Condominiums, townhouses, duplexes, etc.* Make sure you fully understand the type of ownership and your rights and obligations in regard to both your unit and any commonly owned areas.

VII. Conclusion

The fundamentals of transferring real estate in Colorado are well established and have endured the test of time. State statutes and legal principles establish specific obligations and protections for buyers, sellers, and professionals associated in real estate transactions, and most transactions are completed without legal problems. However, the fundamental elements are only the background that applies to the terms and conditions of your purchase or sale. Problems do occur for many reasons—it is a complex process, and there are many things that can go wrong.

If you have a contract problem, it would be a unique situation if you were the first to have that particular experience. If you do have a problem or sense that one might arise, hire experienced legal counsel as soon as possible to assess the situation. They can help you plan an appropriate course of action based on the applicable statutes and how courts have interpreted the statutes and principles. Also, many professionals involved in the real estate industry are licensed by the state or their professional organizations and are bound by established ethical codes of conduct. If you feel that someone you are working with in a transaction is acting unethically, seek help immediately. Remember, the best cure is prevention; any legal challenge that you have to bring at a later date will be an expense to you, and you may not recover the expense.

Many real estate transfers occur without problems in Colorado every day, and most real estate professionals want to make sure that your transaction is successfully completed. Almost all transfers are accomplished under a formal purchase and sale contract. Of the residential transactions, about 85 percent are handled by real estate licensees. Whether buying or selling, real estate transfers are important moments in everyone's life—they mark financial stability, meeting the needs of a growing family, liquidating capital for retirement or other purposes, investments, and business purchases and sales. They should not be conducted in haste or without proper analysis or assistance from professional advisers. Conducted properly, a real estate transfer should be a rewarding and fulfilling event, but its success is dependent on the buyers, sellers, and others involved conducting themselves in an honest and responsible manner.

PART B: 1031 DEFERRED EXCHANGES OF REAL ESTATE INTERESTS
Susan W. Hatter
Escrow and 1031 Exchange Specialist

When selling investment property and replacing it with other investment property, one might wish to consider using a Tax Deferred Exchange as defined under Section 1031 of the Internal Revenue Code. In normal real estate transactions, the property owner is required to pay taxes on any gain realized in the sale of property. Under these regulations, the owner can sell one property and purchase another to replace it, and the tax is transferred, or "deferred," to a replacement investment property. They are sometimes called "tax-free exchanges" because the tax is not paid at the time of the transaction. The owner can buy and sell many times under these regulations. However, if a property is sold and not replaced with another qualified property, or if the regulations are not carefully followed, the owner will be responsible for the tax on the gain, which relates back to the original investment.

Qualified exchanges can be simultaneous (both transactions take place at the same time), or they may be deferred (sell first, then buy, or buy first and then sell). The properties being exchanged must be considered to be of "like kind." In the case of real estate, this merely means real property held for investment. As a result of this definition, equity in vacant land can be exchanged for a rental house, or equity in a farm or ranch can be exchanged for an apartment building.

A qualifying exchange occurs when two owners desire to trade properties of equal value. However, it is a rare experience to find a buyer for your property who owns a property you wish to purchase, which must be of the same value if both owners want to take advantage of the exchange. The 1031 exchange allows you to sell your relinquished property and have a third party (intermediary) hold your proceeds until you can find and purchase the property with which you wish to replace it.

Under the rules, a 1031 exchange can occur when the taxpayer sells (relinquishes) one investment property and reinvests the funds (equity) from that transaction in the purchase of another investment property (replacement property). If this transaction is completed successfully, the taxes on this equity are deferred until the new property is sold, unless it is also sold through another exchange. A 1031 exchange must be completed with six months of the date of the sale of the relinquished property. Because the seller cannot control the equity funds between the sale and the reinvestment, a third party, usually called an "intermediary" or "facilitator," is used to hold the funds from the sale of the relinquished property until those funds are used to acquire the replacement property.

In order to qualify as a 1031 exchange, the following basic parameters must be met:

1. The taxpayer who is exchanging must never have receipt (real or constructive) of the proceeds of the sale of the relinquished property. The intermediary or facilitator receives the funds and holds them in a separate account that is in the intermediary's name until such time as the replacement property is identified and acquired. This may be an interest-bearing account, and according to the terms of the agreement with the intermediary, the exchangor may or may not be entitled to any portion of the interest accrued during the exchange period. If the funds are held in "trust" for the exchangor, then the IRS holds that the exchangor has control of the funds and the exchange can be defeated. Since the exchangor cannot receive the sale proceeds directly, an intermediary would need to be employed under a written contract prior to the close of the sale of the relinquished property.

2. The property that is being sold (relinquished) must have been held by the exchangor for two years prior to the exchange (the sale of the property).

3. The properties must be owned (sold and bought) by the same taxing entity. In this case, if the property is owned by Joe Jones, the replacement property must be purchased by Joe Jones, not Joseph J. Jones or Jones Incorporated.

4. As the exchangor, you have forty-five days from the closing or recording date of the sale of the relinquished property to identify the property that will replace the relinquished property.

5. You must then close on the purchase of the replacement property that you have identified within six months of the date of the sale (not the identification date) of the relinquished property.

6. Any funds received directly by the exchangor before taking title to the replacement property, called "boot," are considered a "taxable event." Any "boot" or exchange funds not reinvested in the replacement property are considered taxable and not sheltered by the exchange.

These are the basic rules. There are some specific rules for special circumstances regarding properties involved in the exchange. These circumstances includes situations where the replacement property is being built; when the exchange involves family or related parties; when the replacement property is acquired before the relinquished property is sold; and other such cases. The exchange can be structured in many ways depending upon the circumstances. Consult your tax professional and your intermediary to determine if there are any special requirements or documentation applicable to your transaction.

The IRS does not identify the specific documentation with which to accomplish this series of events. So you will find that each exchange company or intermediary has their own documentation to validate the exchange. These documents normally include:

- An exchange agreement that is the agreement between the exchangor and the intermediary.
- The assignment of the contract that the exchangor has negotiated for the relinquished property and for the replacement property.
- A notification to the buyer of the relinquished property and the seller of the replacement property that the exchangor is participating in an exchange.
- An identification form for the replacement property that is the exchangor's notification to the intermediary that a replacement property has been identified, which property it is, and as of what date. This is the exchangor's evidence that the property was identified during the proper time frame.

It is the taxpayer's responsibility to determine whether they might benefit from the use of a 1031 exchange (and if so, to what extent) when selling and buying investment property. Many things are taken into consideration when determining the exchange funds (amount of equity that might be taxed) on any transaction. Such things as the amount of the loans against the property and the costs required to sell are considered in determining the amount of exchange funds, against which taxes would be deferred by the use of an exchange. A review of the proposed transactions with your accountant may help you decide if you could benefit from this type of exchange.

If you are using a 1031 exchange to complete the sale of your current income property and purchase of a replacement income property, here are some things to consider:

1. If you intend or are considering using a 1031 exchange to accommodate the sale of your investment property, your real estate contract should reflect this intent. Most realtors have a standard wording that they use when they are working with a client using a 1031 exchange. The inclusion of this intent in the contract helps establish your intent to use a 1031 exchange in the case of IRS audit of the exchange, and you still have the option of deleting this wording from your contract prior to closing should you choose not to use the exchange.

2. Intermediaries can be individuals who are not your accountant, real estate broker, or lawyer. These types of people are considered by the IRS to be in your employ and therefore under your control. Funds they hold on your behalf might be considered by the IRS to be under your control or direction while they are held. Intermediaries can also be companies established for the purpose of handling 1031 exchanges (there are quite a few such companies nationwide that are as close as their toll-free numbers). In any case, each intermediary will have their own policies and documentation that they have developed to meet the IRS criteria and provide you with a valid exchange under the IRS code definition. The fees charged by intermediaries will also vary greatly. As with anything else, it pays to shop around and carefully check the knowledge and qualifications of people you are considering to handle your transaction.

3. Your closing agent will need to know who your intermediary is prior to preparing the documents for your closing on your relinquished property and again on your replacement property. Your intermediary will have specific instructions for your closing agent as to the manner in which the documents for your closing should be prepared. You will need to advise your closing agent (or have your realtor notify the closing agent) that you wish to use an intermediary, and who that intermediary is, well before the closing of the transaction.

4. When you find the replacement property, make sure any earnest money required comes from the funds held by the intermediary so that you maximize the dollars that are sheltered by the exchange.

5. Once you have exchanged into ownership of a property, you can exchange out of the ownership of that property as well. As long as the property still qualifies under the tax code for this type of exchange, the taxes on the sale of the property will continue to be deferred until such time as an exchange is not used to sell the replacement property. Remember that the code is constantly being revised, and new revisions can affect how this exchange is used by the taxpayer to accomplish his or her goals. The exchange can be as complex or as simple as you wish or need to make it.

This outline is a simplified overview of the 1031 exchange process. Always consult with your tax professional (accountant or tax preparer) to determine what the benefits of the exchange might be before participating in the exchange.

14

Boundary, Possession, and Access Issues Between Neighbors

Victor M. Grimm, *Attorney at Law*

If there is a dispute between neighbors in Colorado and it is not about water, it is more than likely a problem related to boundary, adverse possession, or access issues. These issues are distinct but have related legal principles, and any such disputes can be complex and expensive to resolve. The best approach to a boundary or access problem is to work it out directly with your neighbor. Because tempers tend to get fired up over these types of problems, using a mediator or neutral third party is a good idea to effectuate a lasting resolution. If you do reach a solution to a problem, document it or have it surveyed and recorded so that the next generation or the next owner does not have to repeat the same exercise.

The most common problems in this area concern boundary disputes and adverse possession. Modern survey technology produces much more accurate data than technology used in previous years; a new survey may indicate a boundary problem that has gone unnoticed for decades. Many people in Colorado have questions such as, Where does my property end and my neighbor's begin? What happens if a neighbor uses a portion of my property for an extended period of time without my permission? What happens if a fence line is not on "the actual lot line" and encroaches on my property or on my neighbor's property? What if my neighbor's barn was built on part of my driveway more than twenty years ago?

Another set of issues concerns access to property and using the property of another for a purpose such as access. This kind of use is called an "easement." People frequently ask, If my driveway goes over a neighbor's property, can the neighbor block my access? What if I have a "landlocked" piece of property; can I force my neighbor to give me access over their property to get to the road? What if the public uses a pathway on my property to access public space for an extended period of time; could this pathway become a public highway? It could!

This chapter outlines some of the basic legal principles applied to resolve these types of questions in Colorado. If you have a boundary or access problem, use this chapter as a basic introduction to the issues and then get appropriate professional assistance.

I. Public Records

Most interests in real property are obtained through a conveyance or grant from one owner to another. These conveyances are memorialized in written legal documents, such as deeds and easements. Each county in Colorado maintains an office of clerk and recorder. Deeds and other legal documents affecting property must be recorded with the clerk and recorder. If they are not, with a few exceptions, they are not valid as to third parties who do not have actual knowledge of the existence of these documents (*see* C.R.S. §38-35-104).

Therefore, one of the most important things to do before commencing litigation is to review the county records to determine what documents exist that affect your and your neighbor's property. Although it is possible to do the research yourself, it is much more expeditious to hire a local title company to obtain such information. The research might reveal that your neighbor has some type of recorded interest in your property. For example, perhaps your predecessor-in-title (the person who sold or conveyed your land to you) had earlier granted to your neighbor a right to place their driveway over a portion of your property by a recorded easement. This situation frequently happens in the mountains, where access is a valuable commodity. If this is the case, depending upon the language of the document, you might be stuck with the situation. This is why careful review prior to purchasing land is essential, as is hiring a good attorney. It could save you in the long run.

II. Boundary Issues: Survey Plats

An accurate and detailed survey plat is generally required to substantiate a boundary dispute. A survey plat is simply a map that depicts the location and boundaries of individual parcels of land. The survey plat will also generally depict improvements that exist upon the properties, including fences, outbuildings, and ditches, but surveys are made for many different purposes and are drawn under different standards. Colorado law sets forth certain minimum standards for land survey plats (*see* C.R.S. §38-51-101 *et seq.*). Additionally, private associations, including the American Land Title Association (ALTA) and the American Congress on Surveying and Mapping (ACSM), promulgate more standards concerning survey plats.

The more detailed a survey plat is, the more expensive it will be. For most boundary dispute issues, a landowner should obtain at the very minimum a land survey plat as defined in C.R.S. §38-51-101 *et seq.* Many people believe that they have a survey plat when they actually have an Improvement Location Certificate (ILC). An ILC is a specialized document utilized for real estate transfers and is not really a survey. The statutory language requires that ILCs contain disclaimers on the ILC certificate itself. For example, an ILC must state, "This is not a land survey plat, and is not to be relied upon for establishment of fence, building or other further improvements." An ILC is simply a "representation of the boundaries of a parcel of land and the improvements thereon." Therefore, though a review of an ILC might give a landowner the first indication that there are some problems with the boundaries of the property, it is imperative that a more detailed survey plat be obtained before taking any legal action concerning the property.

When obtaining a survey plat, it is important to hire a surveyor who is familiar with the particular area where your property is located. Many registered surveyors who focus on city and suburban settings are not particularly well versed in surveying mountain or agricultural properties. A surveyor who is familiar with your area can usually do a more expeditious and economical job and usually will have specific knowledge about monuments and potential surveying problems that may exist. Local banks, title companies, or real estate agents are good referral sources to locate competent, efficient, reasonably priced surveyors.

As soon as a survey plat is obtained, it should be carefully reviewed to see if it depicts boundary issues that you believe might exist. For example, does the survey plat show that your neighbor's fence is actually located on your property? Does it show that your fence is located on your neighbor's property? Does the plat show that your neighbor's improvements encroach on your property, or vice versa?

If you detect a potential problem, you should at least try to communicate with your neighbor concerning this issue. Meet with your neighbor and discuss the plat and see if you can remedy the situation through removal of the offending improvement or by working out some sort of an agreement concerning this improvement. If an agreement is worked out, it is important to consult an attorney to assist you in drafting an appropriate document memorializing this agreement. It may be in the form of a boundary agreement (*see* C.R.S. §38-44-112), an easement (essentially a grant to use another's property for a specific purpose), or a lease or conveyance of a portion of the property. It is important that legal counsel be consulted before any type of conveyance of the property is made so that the conveyance complies with applicable state or county rules. In some cases subdivision or other review procedures or additional steps may be required, such as a county lot-line adjustment procedure (*see* generally C.R.S. §38-20-101 *et seq.*).

In trying to find a reasonable and legal solution, it is important that you try to understand the basic legal principles; if you do, it can save you a lot of money and hard feelings as you and your neighbor work together to find a solution that works for both of you. If you are unable to work out some sort of acceptable solution through direct negotiations with your neighbor, your attorney can help you assess the strengths and expenses of other available options, including mediation or litigation. It is also important to remember that a solution agreeable to all parties is important because you will continue to be neighbors, and even if your neighbors move away, the problem will remain.

III. Adverse Possession

What if your title research reveals that your neighbor has no recorded interest in, over, under, or upon any portion of your property? You may be surprised to learn that a person may also obtain a legal property interest in another's property if he or she illegally trespasses or otherwise uses the property for an extended period of time. This is known as adverse possession. This concept of rewarding a long-term trespasser with legal ownership may at first appear absurd. However, the legal concept of adverse possession has its roots in our country's philosophy of manifest destiny and encouraging the populace not to let any land go "wasting." Once again, adverse possession is quite popular in the mountains, where squatters may establish claims to the land simply by staking out a tent and fulfilling the requirements described below.

In order to establish a claim of adverse possession, one must prove possession of the disputed parcel was hostile, adverse, actual, under a claim of right, exclusive, and uninterrupted for the statutory period of eighteen years (*Smith v. Hayden*, 772 P.2d 47 (Colo. 1989); *see also* C.R.S. §38-41-101(1)).

Open and Notorious

The first element that must be established is that the possession is "open and notorious." What this means is that the use must be apparent or visible so that others are put on notice that the claimant is occupying or otherwise using the property. This element can be satisfied in numerous ways, including erection of buildings, fences, or tipis or other visible uses of the property (*Smith v. Hayden*, 772 P.2d 47 (Colo. 1989)). A burro staked out next to one's tent would be hard to miss.

Actual

Somewhat tied into the first element, this element requires that the claimant use the property as an owner would use it (*Anderson v. Cold Spring Tungsten*, 458 P.2d 756 (Colo. 1969)). For example, planting and harvesting crops on farm land or living upon residential land while building improvements may be part of the use; however, actual evidence of the use is more important. It should also be noted that actual possession "does not require constant, visible occupancy or physical improvements on every square foot of the parcel claimed" (*Smith v. Hayden, supra*). This would cover the situation of one's burro occasionally taking shade in the woodlands outside the claimed area.

Hostile, Adverse, and Under Claim of Right

Hostility does not mean that there need be any violence connected with the entry or that there exists a deliberate attempt to steal a neighbor's property. (One need not stand guard with a rifle at the claimed property in order to be "hostile.") This element is established from the intention of the claimant to claim exclusive ownership of the property that is occupied (*Moss v. O'Brien*, 437 P.2d 348 (Colo. 1968); *Anderson v. Cold Spring Tungsten, supra*). These intentions may be determined by reasonable deductions from the acts and statements of the involved persons, such as building a fence or making the statement, "That's my property" (*Vade v. Sickler*, 195 P.2d 390 (Colo. 1948)). (If it sounds similar to "That's my sandbox," you are on track.) Finally, a claim of right may be established by the claimant owing to the "acquiescence or silence of a property owner" (*Auslaender v. MacMillan*, 696 P.2d 836 (Colo.App. 1984)). Take, for example, the fact that the landowner attended your cookouts at your tent or fed your burro carrots and said nothing about your tent.

Exclusive

The claimant cannot be successful in an adverse possession claim if the property claimed is used or shared by the claimant and other individuals or the public at large (*Raftopoulous v. Monger*, 656 P.2d 1308 (Colo. 1983)). If you share the claimed land with others, exclusive use cannot be established.

Continuous and Uninterrupted

The use of the property by the claimant must be continuous and uninterrupted for the statutory period. If the claimant stops the use or it is interrupted prior to the expiration of the statutory period, adverse possession will not be completed, and the period must begin all over again. (If you moved your tent, packed up the burro, and sought higher ground, you couldn't return later and resume squatting.) However, it should be noted that a claimant may pass on their claim to a new claimant, and the new claimant may use the previous claimant's years in computing the time of possession. This is known as "tacking" or, informally, "tag-team settling."

Statutory Period

The statutory period for adverse possession in Colorado is eighteen years (*see* C.R.S. §38-41-101). All of the discussed elements must be in existence for the entire period. Note that there is also a shortened seven-year statutory period that applies to special circumstances, such as the claimant having "color of title" (*see* C.R.S. §38-41-106, 108, and 109). In a nutshell, color of title means that the claimant has some document that purportedly conveyed record title but in fact did not.

Effect of Adverse Possession

If a claimant has satisfied all of the elements of adverse possession, the claimant is legally deemed to be the owner of the property. In a majority of adverse possession and boundary dispute cases, the main issue is, however, whether all of these elements do in fact exist. Case law makes clear that the determination of these elements is very fact sensitive. Therefore, testimony of longtime residents and neighbors will be some of the most important evidence presented at trial. And quite often, this testimony can be among the more interesting and entertaining.

IV. Boundary by Acquiescence

Another method whereby boundaries may be modified or altered through the use or claim of land by one party and inaction by the adjacent owner is under the principal of boundary by acquiescence. As codified in C.R.S. §38-44-109, if it is found that certain boundaries and corners "have been recognized and acquiesced in for twenty years … such recognized boundaries and corners shall be permanently established." Building a fence for one's wandering buffalo on claimed land may be good evidence of a boundary. Note that in a boundary by acquiescence situation, it is not necessary to satisfy all of the adverse possession criteria. This is a separate approach in which the aspects of acquiescence and recognition alone are the issues to be determined by the court. Cases applying this rule include *Forristall v. Ansley*, 462 P.2d 116 (Colo. 1969), and *Brehm v. Johnson*, 531 P.2d 991 (Colo.App. 1974) (this case deals with both the concept of adverse possession and boundary by acquiescence).

V. Boundary by Estoppel

Another legal concept that is important to boundary disputes is the common-law concept of boundary by estoppel. If a property owner makes a representation regarding a boundary line that an adjacent property owner reasonably relies upon to their detriment, the boundary as represented may become the boundary line. The representing property owner is said to be "estopped" from asserting the true boundary line. Although commentators are unanimous that this principle is alive and well in Colorado, no on-point cases have been discovered. However, an example of a court applying similar equitable principles to a boundary dispute case can be found in *Pull v. Barnes*, 350 P.2d 828 (Colo. 1960).

VI. Parol Agreements

Although it is certainly advisable to have all agreements concerning boundaries in writing, Colorado courts have in the past upheld unwritten, oral ("parol") agreements concerning boundaries. This concept was articulated by the Colorado Supreme Court in a 1933 case, *Sobel v. Gulinson*, 28 P.2d 810 (Colo. 1933), and thereafter quoted in more recent cases: "When there is a doubt or uncertainty, or a dispute has arisen, as to the true location of a boundary line, the adjoining owners may by parol agreement establish a division line; and, where the agreement is executed and actual possession is taken under such agreement, it is conclusive against the owners and those claiming under them" (*Schleining v. White*, 431 P.2d 458, 459 (Colo. 1967), quoting *Sobol v. Gulinson, supra*).

VII. Remedies

Once a boundary dispute has been identified, one of the first issues that should be explored is, *What is it worth?* The question of worth should be explored in economic terms as well as time, "brain damage," and neighbor relations. Many feuding neighbors have wasted a lot of time, money, and sleep over a 5-foot-wide swath of dirt that has absolutely no economic impact upon their respective properties—and not just during the days of the Hatfields and the McCoys but well into the 1990s. If you have determined that the dispute is important enough to pursue, several different legal avenues are available.

Boundary Line Adjustment (C.R.S. §38-44-112)

The most straightforward way to resolve a dispute is to determine the boundary by written agreement. This agreement will probably be preceded by some type of negotiations between the parties: perhaps some type of nonbinding mediation, and maybe one party paying the other some type of monetary consideration for resolution of the issue. A $500 check can sometimes go quite far in preserving neighborhood peace, allowing parties to "save face," or perhaps, covering the other parties' attorneys' fees so that they can be assured that this agreement is not "signing away the farm." Colorado law provides, in C.R.S. §38-44-112, "Any line or disputed corner or boundary may be determined and permanently established by written agreement of all parties thereby affected, signed and acknowledged by each as required for conveyances of real estate, clearly designating the same, and accompanied by a map or plat thereof which shall be recorded as an instrument affecting real estate, and shall be binding upon their heirs, successors, and assigns."

Therefore, what you will need to resolve a boundary issue by agreement is the following:

- Written agreement of *all* of the parties affected
- Signature and acknowledgment of each party (just as required on a deed)
- Clear legal descriptions of affected property (this usually will include "before" and "after" descriptions prepared by a licensed surveyor)
- A map or plat of the affected property (once again, this will usually be "before" and "after" land survey plats prepared by a licensed surveyor)
- recording of the document with the clerk and recorder of the appropriate county

The document should be prepared by an attorney and accompanied by plats and legal descriptions prepared by a licensed surveyor. Thereafter, the boundary line adjustment application will be submitted to the county in which the land is located.

Statutory Action to Establish Disputed Boundaries (C.R.S. §38-44-101)

In the event that an agreement is not possible, litigation may become necessary. Colorado has a special legal procedure for resolving boundary disputes (*see* C.R.S. §38-44-101 *et seq.*). Essentially, the case is commenced by a complaining party filing a complaint in District Court (called a "petition" in the statute) naming all interested parties (i.e., adjacent land owners, lienholders, etc.). If a public road is affected, the county must also be named as a defendant (C.R.S. §38-44-101, 103). Consulting an attorney is essential in this situation.

The court may then appoint the county surveyor (if one exists) or a commission of one or more disinterested surveyors "to locate the lost, destroyed or disputed corners and boundaries" (C.R.S. §38-44-103). Additionally, the surveyor(s) may hold hearings and take testimony as to the boundary issues. The surveyor(s) then file a report with the court as to the boundary issues (C.R.S. §§38-44-106-107). Thereafter the court may hold an additional hearing and will issue an order establishing the boundaries or corners previously in dispute (C.R.S. §38-44-108, 109). The court is empowered to tax costs (which will probably be substantial if they involve surveyors' fees) against the parties to the action "as the court thinks just" (C.R.S. §38-44-111).

If embarking upon a statutory boundary action, it is probably prudent to budget a minimum of $10,000 for attorneys' and surveyors' fees, and perhaps much more.

Quiet Title Actions (CRCP Rule 105)

A quiet title action is a court proceeding to establish a party's title to land by bringing into court one or more adverse claimants and thereby compelling the claimants either to establish their claims or be forever barred from asserting them. What this means is that through the court system, one can seek to establish ownership of a piece of land or use of an easement. It is similar to "Daddy" having the final say: *"That's Joe's sandbox, not Emily's."*

A quiet title action is brought pursuant to Colorado Rules of Civil Procedure (CRCP) Rule 105(a), which provides: "(A) Complete Adjudication of Rights. An action may be brought for the purpose of obtaining a complete adjudication of the rights of all parties thereto, with respect to any real property and for damages, if any, for the withholding of possession. The court in its decree shall grant full and adequate relief so as to completely determine the controversy and enforce the rights of the parties. The court may at any time after the entry of the decree make such additional orders as may be required in aid of such decree."

Although at one time there was some question as to whether a quiet title action may be used to resolve boundary disputes, it is now well settled that this type of action is available (*see Durbin v. Bonanza Corporation*, 716 P.2d 1124 (Colo.App. 1986)).

The person or persons seeking the decree quieting title will be the plaintiff. The defendants will be all parties who have an outstanding *recorded* interest in the subject property, all parties in *actual possession* of the property (remember, these may not be recorded, e.g., tenant or adverse possessor), and every party who could *possibly* claim an interest in the property. Further, if there is a deed of trust on property (money is owed to someone for the property), the public trustee must be named. Finally, included is the statement, "All unknown persons who claim any interest in the subject matter of this action" (*see* CRCP Rule 10(a), C.R.S. §38-35-114, and CRCP Rule 105(b)). The legal description of property involved must be provided. The more detailed, the better (*see* CRCP Rule 105(g)). Once again, legal counsel is imperative as there are numerous court rules one must follow, and failure to do so may result in redoing the entire case.

A complaint is filed with the court informing the court and defendants of the specified relief that the plaintiff is requesting. All of the elements of the specific claim should be pled. For example, if a plaintiff was seeking a quiet title decree by virtue of his adverse possession of property, he would allege in a claim for relief that his claim is valid because he has "openly, notoriously, hostilely, adversely, continuously and uninterruptedly occupied the property for the statutory period."

If any defendants file answers or counterclaims disputing the complaint, it is a *contested* matter. If the time for filing an answer expires (twenty days after in-state personal service; thirty days after last publication date for those parties served by publication), it will be an *uncontested* matter.

If the plaintiff is successful, the court will enter a Decree Quieting Title at the conclusion of trial (known as the "final say"). The decree should set forth all parties and decree their relative interests in the subject property. It is also important that the legal description of the subject property be precisely contained in the decree. After one receives the decree, one should obtain a certified copy and record the decree with the clerk and recorder as soon as possible. Typically, title companies will require that six months pass before they will insure after the decree. This is to allow time for appeals or motions pursuant to CRCP Rule 60 (Relief from Judgment).

VIII. Access and Other Easements

Nature of Easements

An easement is a right of one party to use the property of another for a specific purpose. Most of the time when a property owner speaks of an easement they are referring to an access easement or easement for right-of-way, specifically, a right to pass over another's property for the purpose of entering and exiting ("ingress and egress") your own property. In the mountains, this is referred to as the right to four-wheel over that gravel swatch you call a road. However, easements also exist for many other purposes, including, without limitation, easements for utility lines and pipes, easements for drainage, easements for water ditches, and even easements for views and solar exposure.

An easement can be held by a private person (for example, a driveway easement), a corporation (for example, an easement for power lines held by Public Service Company), or governmental entities (for example, easements for water and sewer services).

An easement may be attached to an adjacent piece of property (an "appurtenant easement"), such as a driveway easement. Appurtenant easements will "run with the land" and follow the conveyance of the respective parcels from one owner to the next.

An easement may be granted to a specific entity unrelated to any other piece of property (an "easement in gross"), for example, a utility easement granted to a cable television company.

The property that has the easement over, upon, or through it is called the servient estate. The property that is benefited by the easement is called the dominant estate.

How an Easement Interest Is Created

Legally valid easements can be created in a number of different ways.

Express grant.

The most obvious way to create an easement is through a document expressly granting or reserving an easement. For example, if a property owner wanted to obtain an access easement over his neighbor's property, the parties could enter into an express easement agreement whereby the neighbor expressly granted a right of ingress and egress to the other property owner. Typically, the express grant will specify the servient and dominant estate, the use for which the easement is granted, terms and conditions for the use of the easement (e.g., who is responsible for maintenance, any payment required for the easement), specific legal description of the location of the easement on the servient estate, and signatures and acknowledgments of the parties' signatures. The easement agreement will then be recorded with the clerk and recorder of the county where the properties are located in order to put all third parties and successive owners of the respective parcels on notice of the existence of the easement. An attorney can prepare this document quite inexpensively.

When you purchased your property, you in all likelihood received a title commitment followed by a title insurance policy. These documents will list the express easements that benefit or burden your property.

An easement can also be reserved in a deed. For example, a property owner may own two tracts of land: one that is immediately adjacent to a public road (let's call this parcel Blackacre) and another parcel that lies immediately adjacent to Blackacre that must obtain access through Blackacre (let's call this parcel Whiteacre). If the property owner sells Blackacre but retains Whiteacre, in his deed to the new owner, he may reserve a right of access over Blackacre between the public road and Whiteacre. This deed will then be recorded and will provide notice to all successive owners of Blackacre and Whiteacre of said easement.

It should be noted that some express easements will not state a specific, legally described course for the easement to follow. If this is the case, Colorado common law has provided that a "reasonable and convenient way" will be implied (*see Isenberg v. Woitchek*, 356 P.2d 904 (Colo. 1960)). If it is easier to drive through the creek rather than at an angle to the mountain, the creek may be the way to go.

Prescriptive easements.

A second way to create an easement is through prescription, which is very similar to the concept of adverse possession discussed earlier (*see* Section IC2, *supra*). The same elements that must be proven in order to create adverse possession must also be proven to create a prescriptive easement (*see Wright v. Horse Creek Ranches*, 697 P.2d 384 (Colo. 1985)). Prescriptive easements can be acquired by private persons, other entities, or by the public. Probably the biggest issue litigated concerning prescriptive easements is the element of hostility, because if the use by a claimant of an easement is deemed to be with the permission of the owner, then the element of hostility is lacking and a prescriptive easement will not be created. (*See*, e.g., *Lang v. Jones*, 522 P.2d 497 (Colo. 1976) and *Allan v. First National Bank of Arvada*, 208 P.2d 935 (Colo. 1949). Both of these cases discuss situations where a use of an easement was considered to be permissive, and thus a claim for a prescriptive easement was defeated.)

Although most prescriptive easements arise relative to access, prescriptive easements can also arise as to drainage, utilities, and other uses for which an express easement can be granted. If a prescriptive easement arises, it should be noted that the prescriptive easement is not a right of ownership upon the affected property but rather simply a right of *use*. Thus, the servient estate property owner can continue to use their property for any other purpose that does not interfere with the use of the prescriptive easement.

As with adverse possession, it is usually necessary to proceed with a quiet title action and obtain a court order recognizing the prescriptive right, which may then be recorded with the clerk and recorder of the county where the land is located. However, sometimes neighbors, after realizing that a prescriptive right has arisen, may arise, or is alleged to have arisen, will enter into an express easement agreement that will memorialize an agreement between the parties, thereby eliminating any possible confusion that could be raised by a prescriptive easement claim and keeping the peace.

Implied easements.

A third way easements can be created is through implication. This arises in one very special circumstance: If a property owner owns a large tract of land and subsequently divides the ownership into two or more parcels, and different entities own the divided parcels, and by this division a landlocked and inaccessible parcel is created (or cannot receive utilities, water, or drainage, etc. without necessarily burdening one or more of the other parcels). In such circumstances, the owner of the landlocked parcel is deemed to have an "implied easement" over the other parcels (*see Wagner v. Fairlamb*, 379 P.2d 165 (Colo. 1963)).

Easement by necessity.

Another way that a party may obtain an easement is by necessity. An easement by necessity applies to landlocked parcels, whether or not they were at one time a portion of a larger tract of land (unlike implied easements). Easements by necessity can also be taken for certain uses other than access, including ditches for agricultural and mining purposes. The right to obtain an easement by necessity is even specified and guaranteed by the Colorado constitution (Art. II, Sect. 14): "Private property shall not be taken for public use unless by consent of the owner, except for private ways of necessity, and except for reservoirs, drains, flumes or ditches on or across the lands of others, for agricultural, mining, milling, domestic or sanitary purposes."

The procedure for obtaining these easements by necessity is specified in C.R.S. §38-1-102 *et seq*. Essentially, this procedure is a condemnation proceeding whereby the claiming party, in a role similar to a condemning governmental entity, must commence a legal proceeding whereby the court, a jury, or a group of "commissioners" will ascertain the fair market value to be paid to the servient estate property owner. Upon the determination of the amount to be paid, the claiming party must pay said amount to the servient estate property owner.

In an easement by necessity situation, the court will provide a route that is the least intrusive or damaging to the servient estate (*see West v. Hinksmon*, 857 P.2d 843 (Colo. App. 1992)).

Easement for public highway.

Although there are several other common-law and statutory methods for creating easements, the scope of this text does not permit discussion of all of these. However, one last type of easement merits a brief discussion. Colorado law provides (C.R.S. §43-2-201) that "The following are declared to be public highways ... All roads over private lands that have been used adversely without interruption or objection on the part of the owners of such lands for twenty consecutive years."

The impact of this statute is essentially to codify the

common-law method by which the public can obtain title to a right-of-way by adverse use (*see Mahnkee v. Coughner,* 458 P.2d 747 (Colo. 1969)).

Remedies Concerning Access and Other Easements

The remedies concerning disputes over access and other easements are very similar to those discussed earlier concerning boundary disputes. By far the most important method of resolving issues relative to access and other easements is to reach some type of agreement between the parties and memorialize the agreement in the form of an easement agreement, which may then be recorded with the clerk and recorder. In the past such agreements may have been memorialized on tree bark or bar coasters. Nowadays an attorney can draft these quite easily.

If an agreement is not possible, in all likelihood resort to a quiet title action will be necessary. The procedures are identical to those discussed previously concerning boundary disputes. The specific legal language of CRCP Rule 105 provides that the court may determine "the rights of all parties thereto with respect to any real property." This would include easement rights, whatever their nature or origin.

IX. Conclusion

Boundary and access disputes can be some of the most emotionally charged litigation in the courts. At first blush, one might wonder why issues concerning strips of dirt and chunks of air can trigger such sentiment. However, one need only recall grade school history or basic psychology for the answers. First, the history. Most wartime and peacetime history can be traced to issues concerning use of lands, be it through conquest, war, or immigration by the peaceful masses. All living humans (and dead ones for a time as well) require a bit of valuable and finite real estate known as the earth for their survival. People will inevitably bump up against each other, and disputes and confrontation may follow.

As to the psychology, we are all familiar with the sayings about a man's home being his castle as well as the need for everyone to have their own "personal space." In the present day, this is becoming even more of an acute issue. When these ideals become less than ideal, once again disputes and conflicts may arise.

The key to amicably resolving these disputes comes down to obtaining a sense of perspective regarding the issues involved. Is it so important to have all 5 feet of disputed strip? Or is it more important to compromise with your neighbor and gain the peace of mind that comes with cooperation, tolerance, and a sense of community among neighbors? The answer is up to you, and I hope that you will be as reasonable as you desire your neighbor to be.

Bibliography

The following materials contain more in-depth discussions of the topics discussed in this chapter.

Carpenter, Willis. *Adverse Possession in Colorado* (materials provided at 12th Annual Real Estate Symposium, Continuing Legal Education, 1994).

Dahl, Gerald E., David C. Difulvio, and Frederick B. Skillern. *Boundary Law in Colorado* (National Business Institute, Inc., 1994).

Dahl, Gerald E., James L. Kurtz-Phelan, and James L. Wheat. *Boundary Law in Colorado* (National Business Institute, Inc., 1992).

Madson, T. S., II. *Madson, on Colorado Real Property Boundary Law* (LSS Publishing, 1983).

15

Rural Road Law

Erin J. Johnson, *Editor*

Private property rights are near and dear to all Colorado landowners, and proper access is an essential element of enjoying private property. If you are considering buying property or think you might have a "legal" access problem, whether or not you have "physical" access, read on. This chapter outlines some of the common issues associated with the establishment, use, and extinguishment of roads and highways, with a particular emphasis on the issues facing landowners in rural and mountain areas of the state.

The chapter begins with a discussion of statutory and common-law methods for establishing the existence and right to use public and private rights-of-way. It then examines issues regarding the use of roads, including utility installations and relocations, the ownership of underlying mineral rights, the ability to expand the width and scope of uses of the road, and the taking and regulating of access rights. The chapter concludes with a discussion of methods of extinguishing roads, including abandonment, merger, and vacation.

This chapter is intended to provide general guidelines only, and the reader should review and analyze the cited authorities and conduct independent research before reaching any legal conclusions regarding the applicability of this chapter's provisions to any particular circumstance.

I. Establishment of Roads

R.S. §2477 Claims

An 1866 federal act, R.S. §2477 (Act of July 26, 1866, 14 Stat. 251, R.S. §2477 [a.k.a. 43 U.S.C. §932]), provided the authority for the establishment of many roads in Colorado. This act was repealed in 1976 by §706(a) of the Federal Land Policy and Management Act (FLPMA) but is still cre-

ating controversy because roadways in existence before the act's repeal can still be adjudicated under the act today.

The language of the act is deceptively simple: "The right of way for construction of highways over public lands, not reserved for public uses, is hereby granted." It is commonly understood that R.S. §2477 constitutes an offer from the federal government to individual states and territories to legitimize existing miner and homesteader access routes across public lands. It can be utilized to establish access across both present or former public lands. However, there are no real guidelines to define the acceptance of the offer.

Applying the act today is not simple. There are controversies in the case law, among politicians, and among users regarding the meaning of the terms "construction," "highway," and "public lands, not reserved for public use." There is also some debate over whether federal or state law should be used to interpret R.S. §2477.

In Colorado, *Brown v. Jolley*, 387 P.2d 278 (Colo. 1963), is probably the most often cited case interpreting these terms. This case established the following principles:

- The statute created an *express* dedication of the right-of-way for roads over unappropriated government lands, and acceptance resulted from use by members of the public for whom it was necessary or convenient.
- It is not necessary that work be done upon the road or that public authorities take any action with respect to it. The mere fact of its being used was sufficient.
- Moreover, that use could be by "any who have occasion to travel over public lands, and if the use be by only one, still it suffices."

A recent case, *Barker v. Board of County Com'rs*, 49 F.Supp.2d 1203 (D. Colo. 1999),[1] reaffirmed *Brown* by:

- confirming that state law resolves when an offer is accepted
- adopting the *Brown v. Jolley* standard
- defining public lands as any land to which any claims or rights of others have not been attached
- making the entry date of the mining claim, not the date title passes, the relevant date when a claim attaches

Several other cases help to interpret the federal statute,[2] and a similar Colorado statute addresses access across state lands.[3]

For access across federal lands in Colorado, FLPMA provides that access rights across public lands now require permit approval.[4] For information regarding BLM lands, see www.blm.gov/nhp/landfacts/row.html.

Another federal statute, 28 U.S.C. §2409(a), provides a procedure and method to name the United States as a party defendant in a civil action to adjudicate disputed title in real property.[5] U.S. District Courts have exclusive jurisdiction over such actions pursuant to 28 U.S.C. §1346(f).[6]

Private Prescription and Use

C.R.S. §38-41-101 generally controls the establishment of private roads and easements by prescription and use. The statute requires eighteen years of adverse use and limits causes of action against the state and its political subdivisions. Essentially the statute applies the law of adverse possession in the context of easements. To establish a claim of adverse possession, the necessary elements must be proven. These include actual, adverse, hostile, exclusive, and uninterrupted possession of the prescriptive use area (*Lovejoy v. School District*, 269 P.2d 1067 (Colo. 1954); *Anderson v. Cold Spring Tungsten, Inc.*, 458 P.2d 756 (Colo. 1969)).

First, you must be able to prove actual occupation or a visible and open use of property. The route chosen has to be relatively well defined (*Starr v. People*, 30 P. 64 (Colo. 1892)). Next, you must show that the actual occupation was adverse and hostile. Establishing an adverse and hostile use does not mean resorting to violence or deliberate attempt to steal. Rather, the use must be under a claim of right, that is, against the rights of the owner (*Smith v. Hayden*, 772 P.2d 47 (Colo. 1989)). On the other hand, if the use is permissive, or consensual, it is not adverse. If it is conducted in a neighborly or friendly fashion, it is not adverse. If the road goes across vacant and unenclosed land, there is a presumption that it is not adverse, but like all presumptions, it can be defeated. If there is a recognition of the landowner's title, it is not adverse.

The next element that must be proved is exclusive pos-

session. If an individual is claiming private adverse possession rights, he cannot rely upon use by others. His claim must rest upon his own exclusive use, and sometimes use by predecessors in title. The use of an easement doesn't have to be exclusive of the owner or others but only the type of use that an easement holder would make of the property.

The final element is uninterrupted possession. To prove this element, the use must be continuous for the statutory length of time. It cannot be intermittent or sporadic. If it is interrupted for even a short time period, the right can be defeated. However, don't confuse this with having to use the road or route every day. The law requires the use of the land only when necessary in order to carry out the objectives of the possession. In the case of *Gleason v. Phillips*, 470 P.2d 46 (Colo. 1970), the court established a presumption of adverse possession where eighteen years of use were adequately proven. Additional cases illustrate various aspects of adverse possession.[7]

Public Highways Through Prescription

A public highway may be established through prescription under C.R.S. §43-2-201(1)(c). This statute requires a showing that:

- members of the public used the road under a claim of right and in an adverse manner
- the road was used without interruption for statutory period of twenty years
- the landowner had actual or implied knowledge of the public's use and made no objection

The statute and common law interpreting it lay out essentially the same requirements as a private prescription claim, except the use period is extended an additional two years and the use must be by the public rather than a single user.

To establish a public highway, the burden of proof is upon the party claiming the public use, by a preponderance of evidence (*Board of County Com'rs v. Masden*, 385 P.2d 601, 603 (Colo. 1963); *Gerner v. Sullivan*, 768 P.2d 701, 706 (Colo. 1989)). The 1984 case of *Board of County Com'rs v. Flickinger*, 687 P.2d 975 (Colo. 1984), provides a good example of evidence courts find probative. In this case, it was found that:

- the road was used by the general public for the twenty-year period
- the county maintained the road (removed snow, graded)

- the road was put on the highway users' tax list in order to get state aid
- official maps showed the location of the road
- the road went to public recreational areas, so there was a reason for the public to use it

Several cases have dealt with the issue of what happens when the course of the road wavers. In *Sprague v. Stead*, 139 P. 544 (Colo. 1914), the court determined that the road "must be confined to reasonably definite and certain line." In *Board of County Com'r v. WHI*, 992 F.2d 1091 (10th Cir. 1993) the court stated, "It has long been the law that the course of a right-of-way may be altered without destruction of the right-of-way. This may be by mutual consent, evidenced by acquiescence, or it may be the result of changes resultant from natural causes."

One predominant legal question is what constitutes a "highway."[8] In Simon v. Petit, 651 P.2d 418, the Colorado Court of Appeals said an 18-inch footpath across a vacant lot in Boulder could be a public highway but found that the use was permissive because the lot was vacant and unoccupied. The Supreme Court affirmed the decision on other grounds by holding that the footpath was not a road under the facts of the case.

Generally, there is a presumption of permissive use if the land crossed is vacant, unenclosed, and unoccupied.[9] The placement of gates across the roadway typically defeats adverse use claims, but it depends on the circumstances.[10] County maintenance is important evidence of a public road, but it is not dispositive.[11] Inclusion on county maps or other public documents is again not dispositive, but it is strong evidence of a public road. It may be notice of hostile intent, and if maps are in existence for twenty years, there is a presumption of public use.[12]

The amount of Colorado case law provides an indication of how often these types of issues arise:

- *Starr v. People*, 30 P. 64 (Colo. 1892). Owner's intent to set apart land for road purposes and use by public for prescribed period of time can constitute public dedication of road.
- *Martino v. Board of County Commissioners*, 360 P.2d 804 (Colo. 1961). Sale of land by state was subject to road that had previously been created over public lands.
- *Board of County Commissioners v. Ogburn*, 554 P.2d 700 (Colo. App. 1976). Trial court should specify in decree location, width, and extent of public passageway acquired by prescription. See also *Lovvorn v. Salisbury*, 701 P.2d 142 (Colo. App. 1985).

- *Collins v. Ketter*, 719 P.2d 731 (Colo. App. 1986). Road was not a public road upon evidence that county never accepted its dedication, county never maintained road, and use of road had been limited to occupants of particular tract, other owners of adjacent property, and their invitees and guests.
- *Board of County Com'rs. of Saguache County v. Flickinger*, 687 P.2d 975 (Colo. 1984). C.R.S. §43-2-201(1)(c) states that public highways include all roads over private lands that have been used adversely without interruption on the part of the owners of such lands for twenty consecutive years. This provision does not implicate equal protection safeguards or constitute an unlawful taking of property without compensation.
- *Board of County Commissioners v. Masden*, 385 P.2d 601 (Colo. 1963). Evidence held insufficient to sustain county commissioners' determination that road extending across private property was a public road under statute.
- *Williams v. Town of Estes Park*, 608 P.2d 810 (Colo. App. 1979). Use of road by public that was casual, intermittent, and generally with permission of landowners could not be found adverse.
- *Walter v. Hall*, 940 P.2d 991 (Colo. App. 1996). Public highway was not established across landowner's property where use of road had been permissive and landowners erected fences with chains and locked gates.
- *Allen v. First Nat. Bank of Arvada*, 208 P.2d 935 (Colo. 1949). When one constructs passageway over one's own land, at one's own expense, and thereafter it is used by others, their use is presumed permissive unless subsequently changed to an adverse use.
- *People ex rel Mayer v. San Luis Valley Land and Cattle Co.*, 5 P.2d 873 (Colo. 1931). Road that was generally used by people living along it, and had a gate erected that was maintained by owner, was not a public road by prescription.
- *Simon v. Pettit*, 651 P.2d 418 (Colo. App. 1982) and *Simon v. Pettit*, 687 P.2d 1299 (Colo. 1984). Highways and roads may include footpaths depending upon context in which terms appear.
- *Lovvorn v. Salisbury*, 701 P.2d 142 (Colo. App. 1985). Once a road has been declared to be "public," all uses that are proper for a public road are permissible uses. Decision criticizes *Board of County Commr's v. Ogburn*, 554 P.2d 700 (Colo. App. 1976).
- *Goluba v. Griffith*, 830 P.2d 1090 (Colo. App. 1991). The width of a public highway acquired by prescrip-

tion must be limited in the decree to that established by public use; however, it is not limited to actual beaten path but extends to such width as is reasonably necessary to accommodate established public use.

- *Sprague v. Stead*, 139 P. 544 (Colo. 1914).

Common-Law Ways of Necessity

Another way to establish legal access is through a common-law way of necessity. The elements necessary to establish a common-law way of necessity include (1) original ownership of the entire tract by a single grantor prior to division; (2) necessity existing at the time of the severance; and (3) a great necessity for the particular right-of-way.

Typically this type of easement is an implied *grant* (i.e., conveyance of a severed parcel carries with it access easement across the grantor's remaining land), but it can also be an implied reservation of an easement across conveyed lands if the grantor landlocks himself (*see Wagner v. Fairlamb*, 151 Colo. 481, 379 P.2d 165 (1963)). Many times it is an oversight that occurs when subdividing small parcels from a larger tract.

Normally the location of an implied easement established by a common-law way of necessity will be the same as the traditional means of access to property, or if no route has previously been established, then over a reasonable way of necessity to be delineated by the owner of the servient estate. Even if not absolutely necessary, an easement by necessity may be implied if no other practical way to access the property exists.[13] However, a way of necessity is extinguished when another means of access becomes available.

Despite the fact that common-law easement is fixed by intent of the grantor at time of conveyance, it nonetheless can accommodate reasonable new uses, that is, uses the parties reasonably might have expected based on normal development of the property (*see, e.g., Thompson v. Whinnery*, 895 P.2d 537 (Colo. 1995)). Additional case law:[14]

- *Crystal Park Co. v. Morton*, 146 P. 566 (Colo. App. 1915). Way of necessity at common law is an easement implied when one grants land separate from the public highway by land that one retains, and is grounded upon the maxim that every grant includes that without which the grant will be without effect.
- *Martino v. Fleenor*, 365 P.2d 247 (Colo. 1961). Where owner of land in question conveyed to others a portion of land to which there was access only over a particular road, a way of necessity over the road was created.
- *Collins v. Ketter*, 719 P.2d 731 (Colo. App. 1986). Easements of necessity are not implied where necessity did not exist at severance and necessity was not great.

- *Lee v. School District No. R.1 in Jefferson County*, 435 P.2d 232 (Colo. 1967).
- *Wagner v. Fairlamb*, 379 P.2d 165 (Colo. 1963). Way of necessity exists when there is a practical inability to have access any other way than by the way of necessity.

Easements Implied from Prior Existing Use

Where a grantor conveys a portion of the grantor's land, and the grantor's retained land has historically been used for the benefit of the land conveyed for a road to access the granted land, the right to continue this prior existing use will be implied.[15] In these situations, the prior use must have been apparent, continuous, and necessary to the normal use and enjoyment of the dominant estate.

An easement implied from prior existing use is similar to a common-law way of necessity except that it requires actual use of the road *prior* to severance. It also does not have to be the only access to conveyed property.[16]

Condemning Private Ways of Necessity

Article II, Section 14 of Colorado's Constitution allows private individuals to condemn rights of access across other private lands under certain circumstances. The constitutional provision states that "private property shall not be taken for private use unless by consent of the owner, except for *private ways of necessity*" (emphasis added). The state statutory provision, C.R.S. §38-1-102(3), includes virtually the same language.

Condemning a private way of necessity is distinct from a common-law way of necessity in proof and procedure.[17] A condemning landowner must adhere to all condemnation prerequisites, including:

- obtaining a competent appraisal to value the property to be taken and any damages to the remainder
- good-faith negotiations with the condemnee
- a survey and accurate legal description of the area to be taken
- the payment of court costs and expert fees of the condemnee

It is constitutionally permissible to condemn for private uses in this context. In *Bear Creek Development v. Genessee Foundation*, 919 P.2d 948 (Colo. App. 1996), the court determined that establishing a private way of necessity serves the public purpose of unlocking land and promoting sensible utilization. In *Childers v. Quartz Creek Land Co.*, 946 P.2d 534 (Colo. App. 1997) (*cert. granted and then dismissed as improvidently granted*, 964 P.2d 509 (Colo. 1998)), the court upheld the right to condemn against public policy and statutory construction arguments.[18]

Two Colorado cases discuss the issue of who has standing to condemn. In *Coquina Oil Corp. v. Harry Kourlis Ranch*, 643 P.2d 519 (Colo. 1982), a federal oil and gas lessee (as a nonowner) was precluded from instituting a private way of necessity case. In 1990 the court in *State Dept. of Highways v. Denver and Rio Grande Western R. Co.*, 789 P.2d 1088 (Colo. 1990), determined that the private condemnation statute and constitutional provision did not give the highway department authority to condemn a private way of necessity to furnish access to a property owner landlocked by a state highway project.

In order to prove a "necessity," the plaintiff must show that there is no other reasonable alternative route available. Cases dealing with this issue have an interesting twist: Because the condemnor has discretion to select the location of the road, the burden of proof is on the *condemnee* to establish no legally permissible and presently available feasible alternative route.[19] However, under C.R.S. §38-1-122, if the condemnee proves alternatives do exist, then the condemnor has no authority to condemn and must pay the condemnee's attorney fees (*Billington v. Yust*, 789 P.2d 196 (Colo. App. 1989)). Other relevant cases:

- *Freeman v. Rost Family Trust*, No. 97CA2123 (February 4, 1999). Private party had legal authority to condemn way of necessity where original easement was extinguished by merger of dominant and servient estate.
- *Bear Creek Development Corp. v. Dyer*, 790 P.2d 897 (Colo. App. 1990). Leasehold interest in condemned property does not preclude condemnation of private way of necessity.
- *Mikolitis v. Spruce Valley Land Co.*, 96 CA0359 (Sept. 11, 1997) (n.s.o.p.). Court reversed trial court's granting of motion for dismissal on plaintiff's claim that he was entitled to condemn a private way of necessity. Indicated that under proper circumstances a landowner may condemn to widen an existing roadway across other lands if justified by past, present, or future use of property.

Another related legal difficulty is the valuation of an easement condemned over an existing roadway. Because the expanded use of an existing road may cause little additional impact on the road and on surrounding property, little compensation may be necessary. Just compensation is measured by what is lost by the landowner, not what is gained by the condemnor (*see Colorado Mountain Properties, Inc. v. Heineman*, 860 P.2d 1388 (Colo. App. 1993); *Bear Creek Development Corp. v. Genessee Foundation*, 919 P.2d 948 (Colo. App. 1996)).[20]

The scope of uses and width of right-of-way that may be condemned are different than those of a common-law way of necessity. A condemned way of necessity is not based on historical use at the time of severance. Instead, the right-of-way is determined from the historical, existing, and reasonably expected future uses considering the property's current zoning.[21] Additionally, the easement will be eliminated if and when the necessity is eliminated.

Another potential defense by a condemnee is estoppel or laches. Colorado has not directly decided, but virtually all jurisdictions have found, that if a landowner subdivides his own property in a way that leaves no access to the remaining portion, he is precluded from condemning way of necessity.[22] This rule is contrary to the general principle that eminent-domain powers can never be waived or abrogated. A 1993 Colorado case, *Minto v. Lambert*, 870 P.2d 572 (Colo. App. 1993), suggests laches may also be a defense against a private condemnation. The court in *Childers, supra*, however, rejected arguments that the condemnor was estopped from bringing an action where she knew of the landlocked status of the property when it was purchased and may have known for the statutory period for adverse possession.

Some Colorado cases suggest that a private way of necessity does not include utilities.[23] Other cases have held that utilities are implied as part of the necessity for the road.[24] Under the Colorado Constitution and statutes, a person may be allowed to condemn for utilities, even without a showing of necessity, under the Constitution and statutes, as a private "drain, flume or ditch" for "domestic or sanitary purposes."[25]

Roadway Petitions

A series of archaic statutes first enacted in the late 1800s and ultimately repealed in 1953 provided methods to establish public roads through road petitions. One method was for a county to accept donations of a roadway upon the submission of a petition signed by the owners of all the land included within a road, which was then filed in a "road book" and recorded in the county clerk and recorder's office. A second method provided that any ten freeholders residing within 2 miles of the proposed road could petition the county to create a public road. The county then appointed viewers to mark out the road, assess damages and benefits, arrange for a survey and plat, and then recommend the appropriate action to the board of county commissioners. The board could then hear objections and determine whether the road would be established after compensation was paid. The viewers' report and plat were recorded in a road book.[26]

Two older Colorado cases and one recent one discuss roadway petitions:

- *Boothroyd v. Board of Com'rs. of Larimer County*, 97 P. 255 (Colo. 1908). Discusses procedure whereby a road can be established based upon freeholder's petition and viewers' report after compensation is paid to landowner through whose property the road crosses.
- *Board of Com'rs of Boulder County v. Brierly*, 88 P. 859 (Colo. 1907). Upon filing of road petition, appointment of viewers, and survey of road on recorded plat, road is lawfully established as a public highway.
- *City of Lakewood v. Mavromatis*, 817 P.2d 90 (Colo. 1991). Although public highways can be created under road petition procedures without compliance with Recording Act, such compliance is necessary in order to give constructive notice to bona fide purchasers.

Dedication

Roads in Colorado can be established through dedication. A dedication is defined as a landowner's designation or appropriation of land for some public use and acceptance by the public. There are two types of dedications: statutory and common law. The theoretical difference between the two is that statutory dedications are considered express grants. Common-law dedications are based upon principles of estoppel. A landowner is estopped from challenging the dedication of her property for public use based upon words or conduct that unequivocally indicate an intent to dedicate for public use.[27]

The practical difference is the presumption of title transferred. Under C.R.S. §31-2-106 and §31-23-107, statutory dedication presumes a fee-simple transfer. Common-law dedication presumes an easement.[28]

Under appropriate circumstances, however, a court may find that the parties intended either a fee transfer or easement regardless of whether it is a statutory or common-law dedication. In *City of Greenwood Village v. Boyd*, 624 P.2d 362 (Colo. App. 1981), the court stated that whether the dedication of a greenbelt was categorized as a statutory or a common-law dedication did not change the evidence that the landowner intended only to grant an easement necessary for greenbelt and drainage and utility purposes.

Colorado statutes give specific dedication authority to municipalities. Under C.R.S. §31-2-106(3), all streets, parks, and other places designated or described as for public use on the map or plat of any city or town are public property, and the fee title thereto is vested in such city or town. Additionally, C.R.S. §31-23-107 provides that all streets, parks, and other places designated or described as for public use on the map or plat of any city or town or of any addition made to such city or town are public property and the fee title thereto vested in such city or town.

There is no equivalent statutory provision for dedication to counties. C.R.S. §30-28-133 requires the preparation and presentation of a subdivision plat to counties before the land is developed but provides no specific procedures for the dedication of streets or roadways. Therefore, all dedications to county entities are dependent upon common-law dedication principles.[29]

If you fail to meet prerequisites for a statutory dedication, you may still have a common-law dedication.[30] Dedication is a question of fact, and the burden of proof is on the party claiming the dedication.[31] The content of the burden may be greater as a practical matter depending on why you're trying to prove dedication. Case law from other jurisdictions indicates that the burden may be greater where a finding of dedication is a prelude to finding liability for failure to repair a public street, or to require that the public pay condemnation costs for the closing of a street, than it is in cases where dedication merely establishes the right of free public passage, the privilege of repairing a road for public use, or the loss of exclusive rights by the former owner.[32]

Common-law dedications are never presumed. Evidence must be presented of an unequivocal intent of the owner to make the dedication and the acceptance of the dedication by the governmental authority or the general public.[33] There must be an offer and acceptance within a reasonable time. An offer requires unequivocal intent to dedicate and can be revoked prior to acceptance. This is a fact-based inquiry based on all of the surrounding circumstances. Any of the following may constitute an unequivocal offer:

- an offer to dedicate roads depicted on a plat by a statement such as "Future Road," "Reserved," "Dedicated," or even a blank area (*Sherrill, supra*)
- platting property with depiction of roads and selling lots consistent with that plat
- statement in deeds or contracts offering to dedicate for public uses

A mortgager cannot make a dedication of mortgaged

property without consent of the mortgagee. The consent of the mortgagee is based on the same strict standard as dedications in general.[34]

Acceptance can be established by public use or by public authority acceptance. Use only by surrounding neighbors and invitees and guests may *not* be sufficient to constitute public use under some circumstances.[35] Public authority acceptance can be evidenced by legislative act, possession, improvement, or use as a public road. It is possible to accept only a portion of a dedication.

"Reasonable time" for acceptance depends on the circumstances and intervening activities. In *Thornton v. City of Colorado Springs, infra*, there was an eight-year delay before building the road, and was held by the court to be sufficient acceptance, particularly where construction of portion of road began earlier than that. In *Board of County Commr's v. Warneke, infra*, there was a twenty-four-year period before acceptance was sought; in the meantime predecessors in title established adverse possession and withdrew the offer. In *Lidvak v. Sunderland, infra*, there was no acceptance in a sixty-six-year period.

There are specific guidelines for obtaining dedications and donations in highway projects with federal funding. If the project for which you are seeking dedication of right-of-way is a highway project with federal funding, be aware that, amongst other things, the government entity cannot use coercion. Landowners must also be informed of their right to receive just compensation.[36]

There is a significant amount of case law in this area of the law:

- *City and County of Denver v. Publix Cab Co.*, 308 P.2d 1016 (Colo. 1957). In Colorado a dedication of land to the public use may be made either according to the common law or pursuant to statute.
- *Town of Center v. Collier*, 144 P. 1123 (Colo. App. 1914). A common-law dedication is not a grant but operates instead from principles of estoppel.
- *Board of County Commissioners of Jefferson County v. Warneke*, 276 P. 671 (Colo. 1929). Incomplete or defective statutory dedications may be sustained as common-law dedications, and if the streets are accepted by the public, they will become public highways.
- *City of Greenwood Village v. Boyd*, 624 P.2d 362 (Colo. App. 1981). Statutory dedication operates by way of a grant and ordinarily conveys full fee title, whereas common-law dedication operates by way of "estoppel in pais" and ordinarily only conveys an easement.
- *Near v. Calkins*, 91-CV-1645 (Colo.App. 1997). Stat-

utory dedication to public results in conveyance of fee title; common-law dedication grants an easement only.

- *Buell v. Sears, Roebuck and Co.*, 205 F. Supp 865 (D.Colo. 1962), mod. 321 F.2d 468 (10th Cir. 1963).
- *Board of Commissioners of Jefferson County v. Warneke*, 276 P. 671 (Colo. 1929). Where plat contained statement that streets and alleys were granted to public, there was no dedication under then existing statutes.
- *Collins v. Ketter*, 719 P.2d 731 (Colo.App. 1986). Recording of plat dedicating public road is only offer to dedicate road, and general public or public authorities must accept dedication within reasonable time.
- *Overland Machine Co. v. Alpenfels*, 69 P. 574 (Colo. 1902). Holder of a deed that describes property as bounded on a roadway is presumed to have title up to the center of the roadway, unless language of the deed clearly states an intention to restrict the boundaries of the conveyance. *See also Near v. Calkins*, 946 P.2d 537 (Colo. App. 1997).
- *Hand v. Rhodes*, 245 P.2d 292 (Colo. 1952); *Litvak v. Sunderland*, 353 P.2d 381 (Colo. 1960); and *Thornton v. City of Colorado Springs*, 478 P.2d 665 (Colo. 1970).
- *See also Hecker v. City and County of Denver*, 252 P. 808 (Colo. 1927).

Exactions and Reservations

The law of exactions involves the relationship between new development and its impact on governmental services and facilities. The theory is that it is constitutionally permissible for government to impose certain conditions upon the granting of discretionary governmental benefits if those conditions are designed to mitigate the impacts of the proposed development. County, city, and town land use regulations now routinely require the dedication of roads and streets. It is something that developers have come to expect as the inevitable cost of doing business.

There are two primary legal principles that guide exactions. The first is the sufficiency of the legal authority to impose the dedication or exaction requirement. The second is whether the dedication or exaction is constitutionally permissible.

In order to constitutionally require dedications or other conditions to development, the authority to impose such requirements must be contained in relevant statutes and local regulations. These enactments taken together must be sufficiently detailed to provide all users and potential users of land with notice of particular standards and requirements to be imposed for development approvals. Case law illustrates the necessity for such legal authority:

- *Beaver Meadows v. Board of County Commissioners*, 709 P.2d 928 (Colo. 1985). The court rejected requirement that developer pave a 4.7-mile road as a condition to approval of Planned Unit Development (PUD) application without sufficient standards and safeguards to insure that the county acted in response to the PUD application.
- *Board of County Commissioners v. Bainbridge*, 929 P.2d 691 (Colo. 1996). County regulations imposing additional fees to benefit school district payable at time of building permit were improper where state subdivision statutes contained specific provision proscribing developer exactions for school districts.
- *Cimarron Corp. v. Board of County Commissioners of El Paso County*, 563 P.2d 946 (Colo. 1977). Subdivision regulations adopted by county allowing for collection of funds from developers in lieu of land dedication were not statutorily authorized.
- *Cherry Hills Resort Develop. Co. v. City of Cherry Hills Village*, 790 P.2d 827 (Colo. 1990).

Thus, any analysis of dedication obligations should begin with a review of the relevant statutory provisions and county or town regulations.

In analyzing the second legal principle, whether a condition is constitutionally permissible, the question essentially boils down to one of reasonableness. Are the conditions imposed reasonably related in nature and extent to the burdens the new development will place on the system? If not, they are unlawful. Colorado case law on the issue includes the following:

- *Bethlehem Evangelical Lutheran Church v. City of Lakewood*, 626 P.2d 668 (Colo. 1981). As a condition to the issuance of a building permit, city could require the dedication of street right-of-way and payment of fees for curb, gutter, sidewalk, and street improvements because requirements were reasonably necessary to offset traffic impacts of proposed development.
- *Wood Brothers Homes, Inc. v. City of Colorado Springs*, 568 P.2d 487 (Colo. 1977). City council could not condition approval of a subdivision plat on developer bearing entire cost of construction of a major drainage channel that would serve an area far greater than the subdivision.

Additionally, several federal standards apply. In *Dolan v. City of Tigard*, 512 U.S. 374 (1994), the U.S. Supreme Court laid out the following test: (1) There must be an essential nexus to a legitimate state interest, and (2) the condition must be "roughly proportional to the burdens the development will create." In *Dolan*, the Court held that the city could not condition approval of a building permit upon dedication of a portion of the landowner's property for a storm drainage system, public greenbelt, and bicycle path. The Supreme Court stated that it was not enough for the city to say that the traffic increases caused by enlarging the retail store *could* be offset by a bicycle pathway leading to the facility. Rather, the city had to demonstrate that such traffic impacts *would* or *were likely to be* mitigated by alternative forms of transportation.

Thus, the *Dolan* opinion imposes two additional requirements before a forced dedication is constitutional:

- The government must make an individualized determination regarding the expected impacts from the development and the necessity of the requested condition to accommodate those impacts.
- The government bears the burden of proof that such dedication is proper.

Colorado recently enacted a new statute regarding the "Regulatory Impairment of Property Rights," at C.R.S. §29-20-201 *et seq.* (effective July 1, 1999). The statute codifies the *Dolan* "rational nexus" and "rough proportionality" standards. It also:

- requires that the condition imposed is based upon duly adopted standards that are sufficiently specific to ensure that the condition is imposed in a rational and consistent manner
- places the burden of proof on the government
- clarifies that the statute will not apply to legislatively formulated assessments, fees, or charges imposed on a broad class of owners
- provides an expedited timeline:

  * Within thirty days after final action imposing the condition, the owner must notify government in writing of the alleged violation. This is a condition precedent to an action under the section.
  * Local government has thirty days to respond.
  * Sixty days after the government's time to respond, the landowner must file a petition in District Court for the district where the property is located. Failure to file within sixty days bars relief.

* Thirty days after the service of the petition, the government must file with the clerk all documents relating to the condition, including records of any hearings.
* The court can then decide the issue without a hearing, or, if it needs more information or there are contested issues of fact, will hold a hearing "as soon as docket permits."

If the condition is not warranted, the court shall order appropriate relief, by requiring modification or invalidating the condition if not based on appropriate standards. The court may also award the prevailing party its costs and attorney fees. The statute does not preclude separate actions for relief for inverse condemnation or Rule 106 review (subject to certain qualifications).

As development increases in Colorado, there is an increasing trend toward considering exactions in condemnation proceedings. This trend is because local government entities may require dedications for roadway improvements as a condition for development approvals not because of any particular impact from the project but in an effort to avoid subsequent eminent-domain actions. Such efforts are unconstitutional.

For example, in *Hermanson v. Board of County Commissioners*, 595 P.2d 694, 695-96 (Colo. App. 1979), the Colorado Court of Appeals recognized that governmental entities may not impose land use restrictions on the property for purposes of depressing the value of the property in anticipation of future acquisition by a condemning agency. Where a governmental entity creates zoning restrictions or other impositions on property for such purposes, courts should properly exclude evidence of those restrictions in valuing land in subsequent condemnation proceedings.[37] Beware, however, of waiver, estoppel, and acquiescence arguments if the landowner had the opportunity to challenge a condition prior to condemnation and failed to do so.[38] A landowner is often well advised to challenge the condition under Colorado Rules of Civil Procedure 106 or other appropriate actions immediately upon the imposition.

Condemnors also sometimes claim that property would need to be dedicated in the future upon rezoning or other development, which affects the value of property. Such evidence is undoubtedly relevant in valuing the property pursuant to *City of Aurora v. Webb*, 585 P.2d 288 (Colo. App. 1978), which allowed the condemnor to present evidence regarding the cost associated with rezoning and developing the property after landowner presented evidence of the property's value if rezoned. But what if that dedication would be unconstitutional under *Dolan?* Courts in other jurisdictions have held that such evidence is only admissible where a condemnor meets its initial burden of proving the likelihood of the dedication being imposed upon the property *and* the constitutionality of such a condition.[39]

Another issue that arises in this context relates to reservations or land banking. The question here is whether the government can require *reservation* (as opposed to dedications) of areas for future roads in plats or in development plans. Generally it comes down to an assessment of the following issues:

* As with other exactions, is the landowner who is being required to set aside property for future roadway purposes creating the need for this road, or is it simply a situation where the municipality is attempting to carry out some community-wide master plan or transportation plan that has nothing to do with the landowners' property?
* Is the road something that will be constructed in the foreseeable future or some speculative idea that is ten to twenty years out? If neither element is met, then you may have an unlawful taking of property.[40]

Public Condemnation

Several Colorado statutes apply to public road condemnations, depending on the circumstances. However, a condemnation case cannot be brought on behalf of the public against a private landowner unless the right is specifically granted or necessarily implied.[41] The following statutes provide explicit authority:

* Colorado Department of Transportation:
  * C.R.S. §43-3-106 (state can condemn local service roads and access rights)
  * C.R.S. §43-3-107 (counties and state can jointly condemn for highway)
  * C.R.S. §43-1-208; §43-1-210 (state can condemn excess right-of-way or a right-of-way deemed necessary for future needs within five-year highway program)
* counties: C.R.S. §43-2-112; §43-2-204; §43-3-107
* statutory municipalities: C.R.S. §38-6-101
* home-rule municipalities: Colo. Const. Art. XX, Section 1, and Home Rule Charter
* metropolitan districts: C.R.S. §32-1-1004(4).

II. Use of Roads

Utility Installations

C.R.S. §38-5-101 allows utilities to be placed in public highways. Issues frequently arise with respect to who pays for the relocation of such utility lines when the public street itself is relocated or otherwise improved. The following case law applies:

- *City and County of Denver v. Mountain States Tel. and Tel. Co.*, 754 P.2d 1172 (Colo. 1988). Abolishing governmental or proprietary distinction in context of utilities relocation, court holds utility required to pay cost of relocating its facilities from public streets when necessary pursuant to exercise of municipality's police power.
- *Board of County Commissioners v. Southwest Metropolitan Water and Sanitation District*, 895 P.2d 1073 (Colo. App. 1994); *aff'd Meadowbrook-Fairview Metro. Water and Sanitation Dist. v. Board of County Com'rs*, 910 P.2d 681 (Colo. 1996). Following the holding in *Mountain States*, court holds that county commissioners can compel special districts to assume substantial costs of relocation of district's lines necessitated by roadway improvement project in furtherance of police power, despite fact that districts are also quasi-public entities. *See also US West v. City of Longmont*, 948 P.2d 509 (Colo. 1997) (city could properly require undergrounding pursuant to police powers based on same authority discussed above for relocation).
- *City of Greeley v. Poudre Valley Rural Elec. Ass'n., Inc.*, 744 P.2d 739 (Colo. 1987). Home-rule city has exclusive power to grant public utility a franchise to use city streets and alleys; Public Utility Commission (PUC) could not grant appropriate approval.

Underlying Mineral Rights

Two statutes address the ability to condemn mineral rights when streets are acquired:

- C.R.S. §38-1-105(4). No right-of-way acquired by condemnation shall give the condemnor any right or title to any underlying "vein, ledge, lode or deposit" except to the extent of subsurface support.
- *See also* C.R.S. §43-1-209(1) (need for subsurface or lateral support).

Old Colorado case law and other sources have also considered who owns minerals under public streets:

- *City of Leadville v. Coronado Mining Co.*, 67 P. 289 (Colo. 1901); subsequent appeal at 86 P. 1034 (Colo. 1906). In the first appeal, the court suggested that the minerals under the streets belonged to city because it owned the streets in fee simple. In a subsequent appeal, the court said original statements were *dicta* and found that it was not a fee-simple acquisition because it failed to meet prerequisites for statutory dedication; accordingly, city did not own the minerals.
- *See also City of Leadville v. Bohn Mining Co.*, 86 P. 1038 (Colo. 1906) (decided on same day as second *Coronado* appeal). "Fee" as used in statutory dedications didn't mean fee in technical legal sense; meant only that interest in surface to depth necessary for utilities, etc., but no ownership interest in minerals and ores.
- Subsequent law suggested "fee" means "fee," and law from other jurisdictions suggested that if there is a statutory dedication, the government has rights to minerals (39 Am Jur.2d *Highways, Streets and Bridges* §165).
- *See also William E. Russell Coal Co. v. Board of County Com'rs*, 270 P.2d 772 (Colo. 1954). Where mineral deposit underlies proposed highway, owner of land has duty not to remove minerals to extent support for highway is jeopardized. However, that does not mean that the landowner is not otherwise entitled to damages for the loss of the right to extract minerals.
- *See also* Gregory D. Penkowsky, "Mineral Ownership Under Highways, Streets, Alleys and Ditches," 17 *Colo. Law* 43 (1988).

Width and Scope of Use

The width of an existing road and the ability to expand the width and uses depends upon the circumstances surrounding the original establishment and reasonably foreseeable uses. It is clear, however, that an easement cannot be used to service property other than dominant estate.

If there is an express grant, the width and scope is determined by interpretation of the conveyance instrument according to the law of contracts. The court can consider extrinsic evidence provisionally to determine if the instrument is unambiguous. The court will examine the circumstances surrounding the grant, including the location and character of properties involved, uses made before and after easement was granted, general plans for development, and the consideration paid.[42]

In a situation involving private prescription, the outcome may be different. In Smith v. Hayden, 772 P.2d 47 (Colo. 1989), the court determined that the adverse possessor gains control over only the area actually occupied and used by the adverse. Nonetheless, once a road has been established by prescription, the beneficiary of that right may be able to enlarge or expand the easement to accommodate future uses of the property under certain circumstances. In *Wright v. Horse Creek Ranches*, 697 P.2d 384 (Colo. 1985), the court held that the change of use of the dominant estate (i.e., the land that is benefiting from the use of the easement) from a single large agricultural enterprise to 40-acre recreational residential parcels unlawfully altered the physical characteristics of the road and placed additional nonconsensual burdens upon the servient estate (estate being encumbered by the easement), principally traffic burdens. However, contrast this case with *Westland Nursing Home v. Benson*, 517 P.2d 862 (Colo. 1974), wherein the court found that the use of an easement to serve a nursing home (as opposed to the original single-family residence) was not an overburden of the use. These cases may turn on what is established as the initial prescriptive use. In *Wright, supra*, the court found that the original easement was intended for hunting and ranching, not residential uses. A reasonable and foreseeable extension or expansion of the easement will probably be allowed unless it places undue burdens or hardships upon the servient estate.[43]

The case of *Thompson v. Whinnery*, 895 P.2d 537 (Colo. 1995) illustrates the situation of a common-law easement of necessity. The court held that despite the fact that a common-law easement is fixed by the intent of the grantor at the time of conveyance, it nonetheless can accommodate reasonable new uses, that is, uses the parties reasonably might have expected based on normal development of the property. This fact did not, however, allow broader uses such as multifamily housing on a property that was traditionally used for hunting and fishing.

The width and scope of public roads also depends on their circumstances and origin. If the land for the road was dedicated in fee simple, its uses can probably be expanded. If it is an easement, it may depend on the circumstances. In *Lewis v. Lorenz*, 354 P.2d 1008 (Colo. 1960), the court held that the definition of "highway" in state statute is broad enough to include a borrow pit as part of the highway.

If the public road was created by public prescription, the Colorado Court of Appeals held in *Lovvorn v. Salisbury*, 701 P.2d 142 (Colo. App. 1985), that the uses are not limited to historical uses but that instead the road can be used in a similar manner as any other public road. In *Goluba v. Griffith*, 830 P.2d 1090 (Colo. App. 1991), the court held that the width of such a road is based upon historical uses plus any additional width necessary to accomplish the established use.[44]

The leading case in defining the scope of the right-of-way under R.S. §2477 is *Sierra Club v. Hodel*, 848 F.2d 1068 (10th Cir. 1988). Here, the court determined the scope to be "that which is reasonably and necessary to ensure safe travel … including improving the road to two lanes so travelers could pass each other."

III. Access to Roads

New Access Code

Colorado adopted a new Access Code (effective August 31, 1998), which has modified access permit issues in several ways. First, the old code had five highway categories, with no distinction between urban and rural roads or the level of existing development on a road. The new code has eight categories, which more accurately reflect these issues, and provides particular access guidelines for each category.

Second, local jurisdictions are allowed input as to the appropriate categories. Modifications also require consideration of implications of prohibiting highway access from local streets. Local streets will be allowed to access a state highway if it is determined that there is less impact than other options. Further, representatives of local jurisdictions are invited to preapplication meetings.

Third, there is now a two-step application process. The old code required engineering and design of the driveway at time of application. The new code lets an owner process the permit first, then deal with design and construction issues.

Fourth, the new code modifies access requirements for redevelopment properties. The old code provided that if traffic increased 20 percent or more, the owner was required to make an application for a new access permit; this often resulted in access being taken away. The new code encourages redevelopment through the following standards:

- Less than one hundred vehicle trips per day requires no new application
- Less than 20 percent increase requires no new application
- Even if the situation doesn't meet either of the above criteria, the redeveloper will retain at least 50 percent of the old access (resolve odd number of driveways by rounding up)
- The state can require relocation of driveways

Fifth, there is an internal administrative review committee to consider permit denials. The committee is appointed by the Colorado Department of Transportation's (CDOT's) chief engineer. Two CDOT employees and one non-CDOT employee review the denial. The committee provides a recommendation to the chief engineer, who then decides the outcome. If the landowner is not satisfied, a legal appeal may be filed. Case law and resources include:

- *Magness v. State Dept. of Highways*, 844 P.2d 1304 (Colo. App. 1992). Provisions of Highway Access Code may be applied to treat public and private applicants differently without violating equal protection rights.
- Kathleen L. Krager, "State Highway Access Code, 1998," CLE International Eminent Domain Conference, Denver, August 19–20, 1999.
- http://www.dot.state.co.us/business/accessmgt (contains copy of 1998 code, category assignment for highways, access permit forms, historical traffic counts and twenty-year traffic projections)

Acquiring and Regulating Access Rights

Generally, C.R.S. §§43-2-147 and 43-3-107 govern access to state highways. Colorado law is clear that a property owner has an indefeasible right of access to a street upon which their property abuts.[45] The general rule is that this right of access cannot be taken away, or materially impaired or interfered with, without compensation.[46] Nonetheless, this right of access may be reasonably regulated for the public's safety or welfare under the government's police powers. If such governmental regulation goes too far, however, it is treated as a "taking" for which compensation is compelled by the court.[47]

Stated another way, an abutting landowner has a right to compensation for the limitation or loss of access if the limitation or loss substantially impairs the landowner's means of ingress or egress to the property.[48] Whether substantial impairment exists depends on the peculiar facts of the case, and per se legal rules are inappropriate. *State Dept. of Highways v. Interstate–Denver West*, 791 P.2d 1119, 1121 (Colo. 1990), is the leading case in defining the circumstances under which substantial impairment may be found.

In determining whether a landowner's access has been substantially impaired, pertinent factors would include the use of the property, its contiguity to the highway, the topography of the land, the location of the improvements, the expected flow of traffic, and all other characteristics that are relevant to the property's "access needs" (*State Dept. of Highways v. Interstate–Denver West, supra*). In *Shaklee v. Board of County Commissioners of Weld County, et al.*, 176 Colo. 559, 491 P.2d 1366, the court stated that the present and future uses of property should be considered. To prove substantial impairment of access, a landowner may be required to show that the damages to him are specific,

that is, that they are "different in kind, not merely in degree, from those suffered by the public in general."[49] Several other cases also address substantial impairment.[50]

IV. Discontinuance of Roads

Abandonment

Two elements must be proven to establish abandonment. First is the intent to abandon, and second is an overt act displaying that intent.[51] Several cases address this issue:

- *Board of County Com'rs of Mesa County v. Wilcox*, 533 P.2d 50 (Colo. App. 1975). Whether undeveloped portion of highway right-of-way has been abandoned is question of fact. Generally mere nonuse will not be sufficient to show an intent to abandon.
- *U.S. v. W.H.I*, 855 F. Supp. 1207 (D. Colo. 1994). No evidence "of a clear intent to abandon" to warrant summary judgment on that issue, despite the fact that there were maps prepared by the county's surveyor indicating the road would be abandoned, the owner put locked gates up, the road was not maintained, and county employees testified as to their understanding it had been vacated. There was a resolution refusing to vacate in 1959.
- *Koenig v. Gaines*, 440 P.2d 155 (Colo. 1968). Nonuse combined with evidence of intent to abandon, such as construction of alternate route, is sufficient evidence of abandonment.
- *Westland Nursing Home v. Benson*, 517 P.2d 862 (Colo. App. 1974). Occasional use of road even after another street has been constructed did not manifest an intent on landowner's part to abandon the easement.

Merger

If the owner of a dominant tenement acquires the servient estate, the easement merges into common ownership and is extinguished.[52]

Vacation

Vacation proceedings for roads, streets, and utilities in Colorado are governed by C.R.S. §43-2-301 *et seq*. Once the road is vacated, title to it vests immediately in accordance with C.R.S. 43-2-302(1)(c), generally but not always to the abutting landowners.[53] If the vacation is on a subdivision boundary, then the ownership reverts to adjoining land to the same extent that roadway area was part of subdivided lands. If the vacated portion is less than the entire width, only the landowner on the side abutting the vacated portion gets the land. No portion vests to any abutting roadway.

Title reverts to the present landowners, and not any prior landowners. Two cases illustrate this issue:

- *Buell v. Redding Miller*, 430 P.2d 471 (Colo. 1967). Where landowner made statutory dedication of portions of his property for public street, landowner had no right left in the dedicated premises when street later vacated by proper dedicator.
- *Buell v. Sears, Roebuck & Co.*, 205 F. Supp. 865, aff. 321 F.2d 468 (D.C. Colo. 1962). Upon vacation of dedicated street, property goes to adjoining landowner and not original dedicator.

The decision to vacate a road is a legislative act and not a quasi-judicial one. Therefore, you cannot bring a Rule 106 action to overturn that decision once made. You cannot rescind the ordinance vacating it, and the title vests immediately in the receiving parties. Case law:

- *Sutphin v. Mourning*, 642 P.2d 34 (Colo. App. 1981). Resolution of county vacating street was a legislative act that was not subject to review.
- *Fry v. Board of County Com'rs*, 7 F.3d 936 (10th Cir. 1993). County commissioners entitled to absolute legislative immunity in vacation of roadway allegedly done in retaliation for owner's exercise of protected First Amendment rights.
- *LeSatz v. Deshotels*, 757 P.2d 1090 (Colo. App. 1988). If ordinance or other document vacating road is on record for seven years, it is prima facie evidence of effective vacation.

The vacation statute also provides that a road cannot be vacated if it would leave adjacent property without access. However, what constitutes reasonable access may not be what all parties desire. In *Adelson v. Board of County Com'rs*, 875 P.2d 1387 (Colo. App. 1993), the court determined that landowners had "reasonable access" to property so as to allow vacation because alternative access did exist, even though it was over a road that was only passable during the summer months.

If you would like to pursue the vacation of a road, here is a general checklist of the procedure:

- Review the statute and local regulations.
- Meet with local planning staff.
- Survey what is to be vacated with a metes and bounds legal description.

- Contact utilities; vacate subject to reservation for utilities (or, if none exist, get letters from utilities documenting that fact).
- Notify abutting landowners.
- File application containing the above information and all other required information.
- Attend meetings and hearings as needed with the planning commission, board, and city council.
- When vacation ordinance is complete, attach the survey and legal description and record the document in the clerk and recorder's office.
- Ask your title company to update your policy.

Disposing Pursuant to Statutory Provisions

Three statutes apply to disposing of state highways and county roads. The relocation and abandonment of state highways is governed by C.R.S. §43-2-106. Relocation and abandonment of county primary roads is governed by C.R.S. §43-2-113. A detailed procedure for disposing of highway property is provided in C.R.S. §43-1-210(5). This process entails appraising the property, giving an abutting landowner a first right of refusal, or (if the abutting owner is not interested) giving right of refusal to the political subdivision wherein the property is located. The statute sets forth procedures for an exchange of property as well.

Notes

This chapter is based on Continuing Legal Education materials originally prepared and presented by Leslie A. Fields and John R. Sperber, attorneys at Faegre and Benson LLP in Denver, Colorado. The materials have been modified from an outline format to a narrative format by Erin Johnson and are presented in this format with the permission of Ms. Fields and Mr. Sperber.

1. Earlier SJ motions in same case found at 24 F.Supp.2d 1120 (D. Colo. 1998).

2. *See Sprague v. Stead*, 56 Colo. 538, 139 P.2d 544 (1914); *Leach v. Manhart*, 102 Colo. 129 177 P.2d 652 (1938); and *Nicolas v. Grassle*, 83 Colo. 536, 267 P.2d 196 (1928). *See also Central Pac. Ry. Co. v. Alameda County*, 284 U.S. 463 (1932) (the court provides a comprehensive discussion of the historical conditions that led to the enactment of RS §2477); *Sierra Club v. Hodel*, 848 F.2d 1068 (10th Cir. 1988) *overruled on other grounds*, 956 F.2d 970 (10th Cir. 1992) (the leading case in defining the scope of the right-of-way under RS §2477 to include "that which is reasonably and necessary to ensure safe travel … including improving the road to two lanes so travelers could pass each other.")

3. The Colorado statute, C.R.S. §43-2-201(1)(e), was discussed in *Martino v. Board of County Com'rs*, 146 Colo. 143, 360 P.2d 804 (1961).

4. *See* Wendy J. Thurm, AR.S. 2477: "Is This as Good as It Gets?" *Right-of-Way*, Paper No. 7, Rocky Mt. Min. L. Fdn. 1998.

5. *See* Martin Heit, *Real Property Quiet Title Actions Against United States under Quiet Title Act*, 60 ALR Fed. 645 (1982).

6. Several cases have applied 28 U.S.C. §2409(a): *Burdess v. U.S.*, 553 F. Supp. 646 (E.D. Ark. 1982) (the landowner had right pursuant to 28 U.S.C. §2409(a) to establish an easement by necessity across lands owned by the United States to reach private land that had no other means of access); *Kinscherff v. U.S.*, 586 F.2d 159 (10th Cir. 1978) (the cause of action filed by a private landowner under 28 U.S.C. §2409(a) seeking to use a road across public lands would have to be remanded to the federal trial court to determine whether landowners could establish an implied easement of necessity); *Cummings v. U.S.*, 648 F.2d 289 (5th Cir. 1981) (held that the federal court must dismiss a 28 U.S.C. §2409(a) claim that falls within its exclusive jurisdiction if case is first instituted in and then removed from state court); *Board of County Commr's v. W.H.I. Inc.*, 992 F.2d 1061 (10th Cir. 1993) (examines RS §2477 and other public road claims in quiet title action).

7. *See Board of County Comm'rs v. White and Welch*, 754 P.2d 770 (Colo. App. 1988); *Wright v. Horse Creek Ranches*, 697 P.2d 384 (Colo. 1985) (a change of use of dominant estate from single, large agricultural enterprise to recreational development that altered physical characteristics of road established by prescription constituted an unlawful change of use); *Westland Nursing Home, Inc. v. Benson*, 517 P.2d 862 (Colo. App. 1974) (a right-of-way may be used for any purpose for which the dominant estate may then, or in the future, reasonably be devoted, provided that any use different than established at time of creation of right-of-way does not impose an additional burden upon servient estate); *Gleason v. Phillips*, 470 P.2d 46 (Colo. 1970) (the use of an easement in excess of the prescribed period creates a presumption that the use is adverse.)

8. *See Simon v. Petit*, 651 P.2d 418 (Colo. App. 1982), *aff'd on other grounds* 687 P.2d 1299 (Colo. 1984).

9. *See Simon, supra; Barker v. Board of County Com'r*, 49 F.Supp.2d 1203 (D.Colo. 1989). *But see WHI, supra* (presumption not applicable because sheepherder, some fencing, irrigation, and homesteader in area).

10. *See Walter v. Hall*, 940 P.2d 991 (Colo. App. 1996) (gates established that use was permissive); *People ex rel Mayer v. San Luis Valley Land and Cattle Co.*, 5 P.2d 873 (Colo. 1931) (same); *Barker, supra* (same). *But see Flickinger, supra,* and *Board of County Com'r v. Ogburn*, 554 P.2d 700 (Colo. App. 1976) (gate not dispositive—it could be used for cattle control).

11. *See Mayer, supra* (not dispositive); *Flickinger, supra* ("important factor"); *Simon, supra* (same).

12. *See Flickinger, supra; WHI, supra.*

13. *See, e.g., Thompson v. Whinnery*, 895 P.2d 537 (Colo. 1995); *Wagner v. Fairlamb*, 151 Colo. 481, 379 P.2d 165 (1963). *See also Michael J. Uhes, Ph.D., P.C., Profit Sharing Plan and Trust v. Blake*, 892 P.2d 439 (Colo. App. 1995) (required degree of necessity not proved); *Adelson v. Board of County Comm'rs*, 875 P.2d 1387 (Colo. App. 1993) (access available only during summer months deemed adequate where owners previously accepted that limitation); *LeSatz v. Deshotels*, 757 P.2d 1090 (Colo. App. 1988).

14. *See also Michael J. Uhes, Ph.D., P.C. Profit Sharing Plan and Trust v. Blake*, 892 P.2d 439 (Colo. App. 1995) (laying out elements). *See also* Willis Carpenter, "Rural and Agricultural Easements," CLE materials presented at Rural and Western Law Roundup (June 18, 1999); David Masters, "A Survey of Colorado Easement Law," *Colo. Lawyer* (June 1993).

15. *See Wagner v. Fairlamb*, 379 P.2d 165 (Colo. 1963); *Proper v. Greager*, 827 P.2d 591 (Colo. App. 1992); *Bromley v. Lambert & Sons, Inc.*, 752 P.2d 595 (Colo. App. 1988); *Brown v. McDavid*, 676 P.2d 714 (Colo. App. 1983).

16. *Cf. Bromley v. Lambert & Sons, Inc.*, 752 P.2d 595 (Colo. App. 1988) (implied easement not extinguished even after other means of access became available).

17. *See, e.g., State Dept. of Highways v. Denver and Rio Grande Western R. Co.*, 789 P.2d 1088 (Colo. 1990) (laying out differences).

18. *See also Crystal Park v. Morton*, 146 P. 566 (Colo. App. 1915) (seminal case in Colorado).

19. *See Bear Creek v. Genessee, supra. West v. Hinksmon*, 857 P.2d 483 (Colo. App. 1992).

20. A recent Washington case provides a contrasting application. In *Shields v. Garrison*, 957 P.2d 805 (Wash. App. 1998), the court determined that the roadway was an improvement contributing substantial value to the easement area being acquired, just as a building would be if condemning across a commercial development. The court stated that this is a legitimate factor to consider when setting the fair market value of the easement.

21. *See Bear Creek v. Genessee Dev., supra.*

22. *Cf. Coquina Oil, supra.* (noting in *dicta* that landowner cannot condemn where he voluntarily landlocks himself).

23. *Cf. Gilpin Investment Co. v. Blake*, 712 P.2d 1051 (Colo. App. 1985) ("we are not aware of any case that has specifically allowed a [common law] easement of necessity for a television cable"); *cf. Wilkinson v. Gaffney*, 981 P.2d 1121 (Colo. App. 1999) (discussing award of attorney fees to condemnee for portion of private condemnation action seeking utility easement).

24. *See Jackson v. Pressnell*, 506 P.2d 261 (Ariz. App. 1973); *Morrell v. Rice*, 622 A.2d 1156 (Maine, 1993).

25. *See* C.R.S. §38-1-102(3) and Colo. Const. Art. II, Sec. 14.

26. *See* Willis V. Carpenter, "Mavromatis and Before," *Real Estate Law Newsletter, The Colorado Lawyer* (February 1992) (providing a detailed discussion of the statutory provisions and methods for road petitions).

27. *See Town of Center v. Collier*, 144 P. 1123 (Colo. App. 1914); *Hecker v. City and County of Denver*, 252 P. 808 (Colo. 1927).

28. *See Near v. Calkins*, 946 P.2d 537 (Colo. App. 1997); *City of Greenwood Village v. Boyd*, 624 P.2d 362 (Colo. App. 1981).

29. *See, e.g., Board of County Com'rs v. Sherrill*, 757 P. 1085 (Colo. App. 1987).

30. *See Board of County Com'rs v. Warneke*, 276 P.2d 671 (Colo. 1929).

31. Powell on Real Property & 926(3).

32. Ibid.

33. *See State Department of Highways v. Town of Silverthorne*, 707 P.2d 1017 (Colo. App. 1985); *Board of Com'rs v. Sherrill*, 757 P.2d 1085 (Colo. App. 1987).

34. *See Stagecoach Property Owners Ass'n v. Youngs Ranch*, 658 P.2d 1378 (Colo. App. 1982). *Compare with* 23 Am.Jur.2d *Dedications* §19. (Dedication by mortgager may transfer only equitable right, still subject to mortgagee's right of foreclosure.) *But compare with City of Westminster v. Brannan Sand and Gravel; City of Westminster v. Brannan Sand and Gravel Co., Inc.*, 940 P.2d 393 (Colo. 1997). (Subcontractor that paved roads that were subsequently dedicated to public could not avail itself of statute providing that mechanics' lien relates back to time when lienholder commenced work to obtain priority date preceding dedication; thus foreclosure prohibited under law that lien cannot be filed against public property.)

35. *See Collins v. Ketter*, 719 P.2d 731 (Colo. App. 1986).

36. *See* 23 U.S.C. §323.

37. *See, e.g., E-470 Public Highway Authority v. 455 Company*, 983 P.2d 149 (Colo. App. 1999), *cert granted; State Dept. of Highways v. Copper Mountain, Inc.*, 624 P.2d 936 (Colo. App. 1981). *See also Salton Bay Marina, Inc. v. Imperial Irrigation Dist.*, 218 Cal. Rptr. 839 (Cal. App. 1985); *Department of Transportation v. Amoco Oil Co.*, 528 N.E.2d 1018 (Ill. App. 1988); *Department of Public Works v. Exchange National Bank*, 334 N.E.2d 810 (Ill. App. 1975); *Sarasota County v. Taylor Woodrow Homes*, 652 So.2d 1247 (Fla. App. 1995).

38. *Cf. Exxon Co. v. State Highway Admin.*, 731 A.2d 948 (Md. 1999) (distinguishing *Exchange Bank, supra*, on grounds that landowner in case before it failed to challenge, and in fact acquiesce in, condition prior to condemnation).

39. *See, e.g., State v. Sturmfels Farm, Ltd.*, 795 S.W.2d 581, 587–88 (Mo. App. 1990); *State Dept. of Transportation v. Altimus*, 905 P.2d 258 (Or. App. 1995); *State Dept. of Transportation v. Lundberg*, 825 P.2d 641 (Or. App. 1992).

40. The following cases deal with this issue: *State of Delaware v. Rehoboth*, 89 C-SE-35, 1992 Del. Super. LEXIS 96 (Feb. 26, 1992) (conditioning issuance of access permit upon landowner "setting aside" property for a future roadway extension constituted a de facto taking); *Lackman v. Hall*, 364 A.2d 1244 (Del. 1976) (statute that allowed Highway Department to designate "corridor routes" through private property for purposes of future roads was unconstitutional despite the Highway Department's argument that it was merely "setting aside" such right-of-way for possible use sometime in the indefinite future); *Unlimited v. Kitsap County*, 750 P.2d 651 (Wash. App. 1988) (requirement that developers dedicate a strip of property along southern por-

tion of property for future extension of road as condition for issuance of PUD permit was invalid. Records showed that county had no immediate plans for the extension but rather intended to hold the property until some undefined future time when the road would be extended to connect with other, as yet unbuilt, roads).

41. *See, e.g., State Dept. of Highways v. Denver and Rio Grande Western R. Co.*, 789 P.2d 1088 (Colo. 1990).

42. *See Lazy Dog Ranch v. Telluray Ranch Corp.*, 965 P.2d 1229 (Colo. 1998).

43. *See also Scope of Prescriptive Easements* 79 ALR 4th 604 and Restatement of Property §479 (1944).

44. *See also Width and Boundaries of Public Highway Acquired by Prescription or Adverse User*, 76 ALR2d 535 (1961).

45. *See State Department of Highways v. Davis*, 626 P.2d 661, 663 (Colo. 1981); *Radinsky v. Denver*, 159 Colo. 134, 410 P.2d 644, 646 (1966); *Minnequa Lumber Co. v. City and County of Denver*, 67 Colo. 472, 494, 186 P. 539, 540 (1919).

46. See *Minnequa, supra*, 186 P. at 540.

47. *See Interstate-Denver West*, 791 P.2d at 1121. ("One fact for consideration in determining such limits is the extent of the diminution. When it reaches a certain magnitude, in most if not all cases there must be an exercise of eminent domain and compensation to sustain the act.") *See also Davis*, 626 P.2d at 664. ("The question of when the regulation of land under the police power becomes a 'taking' for which compensation is constitutionally required is a matter of degree.")

48. *See Davis*, 626 P.2d at 644. *See also State Dept. of Highways v. Interstate–Denver West*, 791 P.2d 1119, 1121 (Colo. 1990).

49. *See Radinsky v. City and County of Denver*, 410 P.2d 644 (1966), and *Troiano v. Department of Highways*, 170 Colo. 484, 463 P.2d 448 (1969).

50. *See Boxberger v. State Highway Commission*, 126 Colo. 526, 251 P.2d 920 (1952); *City of Boulder v. Kahn's Inc.*, 543 P.2d 711 (Colo. 1975); *Gayton v. Department of Highways*, 149 Colo. 72, 367 P.2d 899 (1962); *Majestic Heights Co. v. Board of County Commissioners of Jefferson County, et al.*, 173 Colo. 178, 476 P.2d 745 (1970); *Monen v. State Department of Highways, et al.*, 33 Colo. App. 69, 515 P.2d 1246 (1973); *Roth v. Wilkie*, 143 Colo. 519, 354 P.2d 510 (1960); and *Department of Transportation v. First Interstate Commercial Mortg. Co.*, 881 P.2d 473 (Colo. App. 1994).

51. *See Gjovig v. Spino*, 701 P.2d 1267 (Colo. App. 1985). *See also Uhl v. McEndaffer*, 225 P.2d 839 (Colo. 1950).

52. *See Freeman v. Rost Family Trust*, 973 P.2d 1281 (Colo. App. 1999).

53. *See Morrissey v. Achzinger*, 364 P.2d 187 (Colo. 1961). (Upon vacation of street, abutting owner became fee owner of that portion abutting his property to the center line of the vacated area.)

16

Trespass, Landowner Liability, and Leases

William A. Paddock, *Attorney at Law*

> I gave my heart to the mountain the minute I stood beside this river with its spray in my face and watched it thunder into foam, smooth to green glass over sunken rocks, shatter to foam again. I was fascinated by how it sped by yet was always there. Its roar shook both the earth and me.
> —Wallace Stegner, *The Sound of Mountain Water*

I. Trespass

At such moments as the one described above it is difficult to remember, or even to think it important, that by climbing the fence and walking the meadow to view this splendid river, you may have violated someone's property rights. But the rancher whose gates have been left open, whose fences have been broken, and whose land has been carelessly littered is dumbfounded by careless people's lack of respect for the land his family has ranched for more than a hundred years.

Do not be a trespasser.

Private property is protected from such unwanted invasions by the law of trespass. A person can be subject to both civil and criminal liability for trespassing. Civil trespass occurs when a person without invitation or permission intentionally goes onto another person's land. Criminal trespass occurs when a person unlawfully enters or remains in or upon another person's land or dwelling. In both civil and criminal trespass, the nature of the remedy or the severity of the punishment varies depending upon the circumstances.

The law of trespass defines a person on the property of another as either an *invitee*, a *licensee*, or a *trespasser*. An *invitee*,[1] as the name implies, is a person who is invited to enter or remain on the land of another to transact business

in which both parties are mutually interested. A *licensee*[2] is a person who enters or remains on the land of another for the licensee's own convenience or to advance his own interests, with the permission or consent of the landowner. A *trespasser*[3] is a person who enters or remains on another person's land without their consent.

The distinction between a *licensee* and an *invitee* depends upon the relationship between the landowner and the person who enters or remains on the land. A hunter who pays a fee to hunt on private lands is an *invitee*. A game warden who comes on those same lands to catch poachers is a *licensee*. The poacher is a *trespasser*.

Criminal Trespass

Criminal trespass may be in either the first, second, or third degree. First-degree criminal trespass is a Class 5 felony, punishable by one to three years of prison and two years of mandatory parole. A person commits this crime by knowingly and unlawfully entering or remaining in the *dwelling* of another or by entering any motor vehicle to commit a crime.[4] A trespasser is a person who "unlawfully enters or remains" in or upon the premises when he or she is not licensed, invited, or otherwise privileged to do so.[5] An example of a person who is otherwise privileged to be on someone else's property could be a building inspector who is on the property to check for building-code violations.

Second-degree criminal trespass occurs when a person "unlawfully enters or remains in or upon the *premises* of another which are enclosed in a manner designed to exclude intruders or are fenced."[6] Except as otherwise provided in C.R.S. §33-6-116, a person who enters or remains upon unimproved and apparently unused land that is neither fenced nor otherwise enclosed in a manner designed to exclude intruders does so with license and privilege, that is, is not trespassing. It is trespassing, however, if notice against trespass is personally communicated to the person by the owner or some other authorized person, or if notice forbidding entry is given by posting with signs at intervals of not more than 440 yards, or if there is a readily identifiable entrance to the land posted with signs forbidding entrance to part of the land.

If the land is classified as *agricultural land* pursuant to C.R.S. §39-1-102 (1.6), the offense is a Class 2 misdemeanor, punishable by from three months in prison and/or a $250 fine to twelve months in prison and/or a $1,000 fine.[7] If the person trespasses on agricultural lands with the intent to commit a felony, the offense is a Class 4 felony, punishable by two to six years in prison plus two years of mandatory parole.[8]

A person commits third-degree criminal trespass by "unlawfully entering or remaining in or upon the *premises* of another."[9] This is generally a Class 1 petty offense, punishable by a fine up to $500 and/or up to six months in prison somewhere other than at a state correctional facility. If the premises are classified as agricultural land pursuant to C.R.S. §39-1-102 (1.6), it is a Class 3 misdemeanor, punishable by from a $50 fine to six months in jail and/or a $750 fine.[10] If a person trespasses on premises classified as agricultural land to commit a felony, it is a Class 5 felony, punishable by one to three years in prison plus two years of mandatory parole.[11]

Civil Trespass

Civil trespass is any entry upon the land of another person without invitation or permission from the lawful owner or possessor of the land. To establish a trespass, it must be shown either that there was no consent to the entry or that, if there was consent, the consent was exceeded by the trespasser. The landowner has the burden of proving the trespass.[12] A simple example of such a trespass is pulling your raft out of a stream to picnic on private land. You are not trespassing so long as you are floating on the water, but you are trespassing as soon as you step onto the land.

Liability for a trespass requires only that the trespasser *intended* to do things that constitute or cause the intrusion; there is no need to demonstrate that the trespasser was negligent.[13] A slightly different standard applies when the interest in land is an *easement*. In that case, the owner of the easement becomes a trespasser when the owner, or their employees, goes onto land outside the authorized area and does damage.[14] For example, if an easement is granted for a private road, and rain makes the road impassable, a trespass occurs if the easement holder makes a new road around the wet area.

The civil remedy for the landowner injured by trespass is to recover damages both for loss of use and enjoyment of property and for annoyance and discomfort. The measure of damages for trespass to real estate is, in most cases, the difference in the market value of the land before and after the trespass, but this rule is not applied where it will not do substantial justice.[15]

Landowner's Rights and Liabilities Against Trespassers

A person who owns or is in lawful possession of any premises, or a person who is licensed or privileged to be on the premises, may use reasonable and appropriate physical force upon another person, when and to the extent that it is reasonably necessary, to prevent or terminate what he or she reasonably believes to be the commission or attempted commission of trespass.[16] A person may use deadly force only in defense of him- or herself or another as described in C.R.S. §18-1-704,[17] or when he or she reasonably believes it necessary to prevent what he or she reasonably believes to be an attempt by the trespasser to commit first-degree arson.[18]

A word of caution is needed here. Despite what is shown about the West in old and new horse operas ("Westerns"), individual vigilantes are seldom heroes in real life. The better practice in the case of trespass is to call the sheriff and then take photographs of the trespassers. The photographs provide evidence of the trespass, and the sheriff provides coercion to stop the trespass. Use of physical force is best reserved for those situations in which there is a real danger of substantial property damage or injury to a person.

This is particularly true because a trespasser can sue the landowner for use of excessive force. In any civil action brought against a landowner by a trespasser for injuries sustained while on the landowner's property, the landowner is liable only for damages willfully or deliberately caused by the landowner.[19]

II. Landowner Liability

Premises Liability in General

Ownership of land or property carries with it a duty of care to those who may come on the property. The duty of care depends upon the status of the injured person. As stated above, a trespasser may recover only for damages willfully or deliberately caused by the landowner. A licensee, on the other hand, may recover for damages caused by (1) the landowner's unreasonable failure to exercise reasonable care with respect to dangers created by the landowner of which the landowner actually knew, or (2) the landowner's unreasonable failure to warn of dangers not created by the landowner that are not ordinarily present on property of the type involved and of which the landowner actually knew.[20]

An invitee is owed the highest duty of care. An invitee may recover for damages caused by the landowner's unreasonable failure to exercise reasonable care to protect against dangers of which he or she actually knew or should have known. In the case of real property classified for property tax purposes as agricultural land or vacant land, an invitee may recover for damages caused by the landowner's unreasonable failure to exercise reasonable care to protect against dangers of which the landowner actually knew.

Each of these legal standards is amorphous, seemingly circular, and above all subjective. In the case of the trespasser, the injury must result from something deliberate or willfully done by the landowner. In the case of the licensee or the invitee, a landowner may be liable for dangers on his property he did not warn of or did not protect the licensee or invitee against. The law does not require heroic measures to protect a person from injury, but it does require reasonable effort. In practice, what is reasonable will be judged with hindsight and by community standards, not by the personal subjective standard of the landowner.

Permissive Recreational Use of Private Land

In an effort to encourage private landowners to open their lands to public recreation, the Colorado General Assembly adopted the Recreational Use Act of 1965. This act limits the liability of such landowners by classifying all recreational users as trespassers for liability purposes.[21] Under that law, a landowner who directly or indirectly invites or permits any person to use his or her property for recreational purposes, without charge, does not thereby give any assurance that the premises are safe for any purpose and does not confer upon the person the legal status of an in-

vitee or licensee or assume responsibility or incur liability for any injury to person or property or for the death of any person caused by an act or omission of such person.[22]

This protection is not without limitations. There is no protection under the act for an injury "received on land incidental to the use of the land on which a commercial or business enterprise" is being carried out, such as a recreational resort. The law does not apply to conduct constituting willful or malicious failure to guard or warn against known, dangerous conditions, uses, structures, or activities likely to cause harm, or where the landowner maintains an attractive nuisance.[23] An attractive nuisance, generally, is any condition on public or private land, which reasonably could be understood to be a danger to children and which reasonably could be expected to attract children to come there to play.

Other Property Crimes and Misdemeanors

Criminal mischief

Bashing mailboxes is an adolescent pastime in some rural areas. It is also called "criminal mischief," and the punishment can take all the fun out of it. A person who knowingly damages the real or personal property of another person in a single criminal episode in which the aggregate damage to property is less than $100 commits a Class 3 misdemeanor, punishable by from a $50 fine to six months in jail and/or a $750 fine.[24] If the adolescent mailbox smashers had a lot of fun, they may want to know that if a person knowingly damages another person's property (in a single criminal episode) and the aggregate damage to the property is more than $100 but less than $500, they have committed a Class 2 misdemeanor, which is punishable by from three months in prison and/or a $250 fine to twelve months in prison and/or a $1000 fine.[25]

As the damages mount, so does the punishment. The adolescents who really got carried away destroying the mailboxes and knowingly damaged another person's property (in a single criminal episode), and the aggregate damage to the property was more than $500 but less than $15,000, committed a Class 4 felony, which is punishable by two to six years in prison plus two years of mandatory parole.[26] If the adolescents caused property damage of $15,000 or more, they committed a Class 3 felony, which is punishable by four to twelve years in prison, plus five years of mandatory parole.[27]

Poaching

If you don't have a hunting license for the type of animal

that you shot, or if the hunting season is over, you are *poaching*. In Colorado, all game and fish not held under legally acquired private ownership are property of the state. It is unlawful for any person to hunt, take, or have in their possession any wildlife that is the property of the state, except as allowed by hunting, fishing, and trapping laws or other laws. Any person who violates this law is guilty of a misdemeanor and, depending upon the wildlife involved, can be punished by a fine or imprisonment, or both, and license suspension points or suspension or revocation of license privileges.[28]

Trespassing to hunt

It is also illegal to hunt, trap, or fish on privately owned land without first obtaining permission from the owner or person in possession of the land. Failure to get permission is a misdemeanor, punishable by a $100 fine and assessment of twenty license suspension points.[29] So, always ask before you hunt, trap, or fish on private lands.

Wrangling Hunters, a.k.a. Ranching for Wildlife

In order to provide large landowners with incentives to manage their lands for wildlife benefits, in 1985 the Colorado Wildlife Commission started its Ranching for Wildlife program. In exchange for preserving and enhancing prime wildlife habitat, landowners can operate fee hunting programs, a substantial economic benefit to landowners. To be eligible to participate, the landowner must have 12,000 contiguous acres that contain significant numbers of the species that they (their customers) wish to hunt. The landowner must enter into an agreement with the Division of Wildlife on management of the land for the benefit of wildlife. There is an annual review of the land management and consultation with the Division of Wildlife on land management practices that will affect wildlife habitat.

This program has numerous advantages for both the landowner and the general public. The benefits to the landowner include (1) the ability to sell up to 90 percent of the male animal licenses at trophy fees; (2) a ninety-day season within which to hold hunts; (3) the fact that hunting with rifles is allowed during the public archery and muzzleloader seasons; and (4) the knowledge that prime wildlife habitat is being preserved and enhanced. The advantages to the public include (1) the opportunity to hunt trophy animals for just the cost of the license; (2) the sale to the public of 100 percent of the female animal licenses issued for the ranch; (3) equal access to all parts of the land that are

hunted by paying clients; (4) quality hunting on prime habitat with lower hunter densities; and (5) the fact that the state has no liability for wildlife damage on these ranches.

There are a number of landowners throughout the state who participate in this program. More information on the program and its participants can be obtained from the Division of Wildlife.

What's Mine Is Mine and What's Yours Is Mine—Land or Easements Acquired by Trespass

What starts out as a trespass, intentionally or not, can ripen into either title to or the right to use the land of another. This can occur either through the law of adverse possession or prescriptive easements.

Easements

There are several ways to acquire an *easement*. An easement is an interest in real property and in most instances, should be established and transferred by a deed describing the location and purposes for which the easement may be used. But often such interests are established by consensual use. A landowner who consents to the use of his land for a particular purpose by someone else may be deemed to have granted an easement for a continuation of that use. For example, if an irrigation ditch is constructed across lands of another person without objection by the owner, then the owner is deemed to have given his consent to the construction of the ditch and an easement for operation and maintenance of the ditch. An easement also can be acquired without a deed and without the consent of the landowner. An easement obtained in this way is called an "easement by prescription." This is essentially adverse possession of the land for the statutory period of eighteen years.

A common problem in agricultural and other rural areas is the conversion of a limited easement into a more general easement or public road by adverse use. A landowner can protect himself against this, but it requires diligent efforts. For roadways, whether across farm lands or along irrigation ditches, it is a good practice to place gates on the roads at places where there is access from public roads. Likewise, the road should be posted with "no trespassing" signs. Both the gates and the signs should be maintained because all roads over private lands that have been used adversely without interruption or objection on the part of the owners of such lands for twenty consecutive years are declared to be public highways.[30] Failure to prevent such use may result in a formerly private road being used to serve a subdivision. So unless a landowner wants the general public to have access across his or her property, private roadways should be posted and gated.

Now, if you own an easement, you can have the same type of problem, but for a different reason. Most easements are nonexclusive. This means that the easement holder is entitled to use the land for their purposes, but the owner of the land may use it for any purpose that does not unreasonably interfere with the easement holder's use of the land. For example, if you are the owner of an irrigation ditch, it is unwise to permit houses or other structures to encroach on the easement. This is an increasingly common problem in areas where development is occurring on lands that were historically farmed. If such structures are placed on an easement or right-of-way, you should take immediate action to require their removal. Likewise, if you are a new landowner and want to build your garage by the ditch, be certain that you either get the ditch owner's consent or stay far enough away that you do not interfere with the ditch's use. Be sure to leave enough room for vehicles and heavy equipment to get in to clean and repair the ditch. Above all, never relocate a ditch without first securing the consent of the ditch owner.

Adverse possession

A landowner can lose title to his or her land through adverse possession by another. Adverse possession is a means of acquiring someone else's land by possessing it for the statutory period of eighteen years, under conditions that the law considers to be hostile, adverse, actual, under a claim of right, exclusive, and uninterrupted.[31] As with many legal terms, the common usage of these words is not the legal meaning. For possession of someone else's land to be considered hostile, the claimant must show that he or she occupied the property with a belief that the property was his or her own. This belief must be as against the true owner and as against the world.[32] To establish hostility, a showing of force or actual dispute is not necessary. Rather, hostility depends upon the intent of the claimant, which is determined from declarations of the parties and from reasonable deductions from the surrounding facts.[33]

There is a strong presumption that use of land by a nonowner is not adverse to the real owner. The claimant therefore must have lots of evidence that his claim has been adverse to the true owner before a court will conclude that the claimant established that the nonowner's possession has met the elements of adverse possession. It is possible, however, to sidestep the requirement to prove adversity. The unexplained use of land for a statutory period is presumed to be under claim of right and, therefore, is adverse.[34]

The requirement of exclusivity is not what it sounds like.

Whether possession is exclusive depends upon the claimant's actions in asserting possession, as compared with those of an average landowner taken under similar circumstances to assert exclusive nature of his or her possession. Therefore, it is a comparative standard, and it is not necessary for the claimant to prohibit any and all use of the property by others. For example, the casual entry for a limited purpose by the real owner is not always sufficient to prove that use of the property was joint and would destroy adverse possession. The claimant need only act as an "average landowner" would to assert the exclusive nature of his or her possession.[35]

The requirement of continuity is the test of time. The statutory period for adverse possession is eighteen years. Actual occupancy requires the ordinary use of which land is capable and such as an owner would make of it. The requirement of continuous possession does not mean that the claimant must physically possess it every moment of the day; rather, the nature of the right claimed is the right to passage whenever passage is desired, and it is this right that must be continuously asserted for the eighteen-year statutory period.[36] For example, seasonal grazing of livestock and construction of a fence may be sufficient continuous possession.

There are limits on the types of real property that may be acquired by adverse possession. One cannot adversely possess against the state, county, city and county, city, irrigation district, public, municipal, or quasi-municipal corporation, or any department or agency thereof. No possession, no matter how long it is continued, of any land, water, water right, easement, or other property whatsoever dedicated to or owned by the state of Colorado, or any county, city and county, city, irrigation district, public, municipal, or quasi-municipal corporation, or any department or agency thereof, shall ever ripen into any title, interest, or right against the state of Colorado, or such county, city and county, city, public, municipal, or quasi-municipal corporation, irrigation district, or any department or agency thereof.[37]

Likewise, a water right may not be acquired by adverse possession against the stream. In other words, you do not get to step to the head of the priority system simply by taking water from a stream when you are not entitled to do so. This does not mean that there is not adverse possession of water rights. In appropriate circumstances, adverse possession of a water right may be established against the owner of water that has been diverted from the stream. An example of this could be cotenants in an unincorporated ditch where one user of the ditch always took more than his or her share of the water.[38]

III. Agricultural Land Leases

Was a farming' on the share, and always I was poor
My crops I laid into the banker's store.

Although the poor chap in this Woody Guthrie song was not in a very good spot, not all agricultural land leases are the same. Agricultural leases fall into two broad categories: leasing on shares (share cropping) and farm leasing. Similar, but not identical, considerations go into both types of leases.[39] A share-cropping agreement may or may not be a lease, depending upon what the grower is being compensated for. If the grower is being compensated for his labor in growing the crop, then the grower is considered to be a "cropper" and not a tenant.

On the other hand, if the farm owner is being compensated for the use of his farm, then the grower is a tenant, and a landlord-tenant relationship is established.[40] A written agreement should be made in either case, and when "cropping" is involved, the agreement should clearly state that neither a landlord-tenant relationship nor a partnership is intended by the parties.

The key element of the landlord-tenant relationship is the transfer of exclusive possession of the land to the tenant for purposes of growing a crop. The payment for the lease may be a cash rental, a share of the crops, or a combination of both. If both cash and crops are involved, it is important to define how much money and what share of which crops are to be paid. Will there be a sharing of the costs for raising the crop, such as seed, fertilizer, pesticides, water-pumping costs, ditch assessments, and the like? If the amount of cash paid depends upon the yield or value of the crops, or the cost to raise them, then the agreement must clearly define how total compensation will be determined.

It is also important to define what land and what improvements are subject to the lease. For example, if the land is irrigated with a sprinkler system, is the sprinkler included? Will the tenant live in the farmhouse? Will the tenant be able to store his equipment in buildings on the farm, and may the tenant use the shop to repair farm equipment? The lease should carefully define all land, improvements, fixtures, and equipment that will be included in the lease.

All agricultural leases should be recorded in the county in which the lands are located when the lands are leased for a share of the crop. Recording the lease makes any purchaser of the crop accountable to the landlord for the landlord's share of the crop purchase price.[41]

The length of the lease is also an important consideration. If it is for more than one year, or the lease allows for renewals from year to year, the parties must carefully consider the termination date. The grower needs to know if the land will be available for the next growing season, while the lessor needs to know if he will have a tenant to farm the land. These considerations point to a termination date after harvest of the crops typically grown and far enough before the next planting season to allow the grower to obtain seed, supplies, and equipment for planting.

Going into the lease, it is important to know if the lessor has planted any crops that must be harvested during the lease term. If so, the lease must address who will care for these crops, who will harvest them, and who will be entitled to the proceeds from their sale. Likewise, if the lease expires or is terminated before the tenant has harvested his crop, provision must be made for the care and disposition of those crops. Absent an agreement to the contrary, Colorado law permits a former tenant to cultivate and harvest crops planted prior to the end of a lease, provided that the tenant pays in advance the reasonable cost of use of the land.[42]

When the farm ground is irrigated, the tenant must have access to legally valid water rights for irrigation. Since most water rights are conveyed in the same manner as real property, it is important for the lease to identify the water rights provided with the land. If the water rights are provided by a mutual ditch or reservoir company or by an irrigation district, water conservancy district, or water conservation district, the lease should define who is to pay the water assessments. If the water is supplied by a well, the lease should specify who pays the power bill and any augmentation or similar assessment on the use of groundwater. If the lease fails to state that water rights are included, then whether any water rights are included becomes a question of intent of the parties, principally the intent of the lessor.[43]

Farming methods and care of the land should also be addressed in the lease. If the lessor wishes to prescribe certain farming practices or prevent the use of certain agricultural chemicals or practices, these matters should be addressed in the lease. For example, if the land is to be used for organic farming, the lessor may well proscribe the use of chemical fertilizers and all herbicides, pesticides, and fungicides. Tillage practices may also be a concern for soil conservation purposes. If the last crop is harvested after the time for planting a cover crop, then the lessor may wish to require minimum tillage, wind breaks, conservation strips, or other measures to protect the soil. Finally, the lease should address crop rotation; noxious-weed control; and maintenance of fences, ditches, and similar improvements.

Consideration should also be given to any equipment to be leased with the land. If equipment is to be included, the lease should list every piece of equipment to be furnished by one party or the other. The lease of these types of personal property is covered by U.C.C. Article 2.5. The intricacies of that article are beyond the scope of this chapter. The landlord and tenant, however, should obtain competent advice on the requirements of Article 2.5 of the U.C.C.

An agricultural lease should address improvements and repairs to the property. If improvements are furnished as part of the lease, then the lease should address who is responsible for repair of the improvements, who insures the improvements, and how the risk of loss is allocated between the parties. The parties should also consider the effect of floods, droughts, fires, hail, insect plagues, or other "acts of God." For example, what are the landlord's responsibilities if a building is destroyed by fire? If lease payment is the share of a crop, what happens if inadequate water is available or hail destroys the crop? A good lease should address all of these issues.

The layman need not despair of being able to draft a satisfactory lease. The Bradford-Robinson Company publishes several form leases that are serviceable for many uses. Both forms can have additional provisions included so that the lease can address the issues unique to the parties. The lease forms are No. 262, a general farm lease, and No. 770, an irrigated farm lease. Copies may be obtained at a nominal cost. If the lease is for a substantial sum, a long term, or covers large land areas and many improvements, it is the better practice to seek competent legal advice in drafting the lease.

Notes

1. *See* C.R.S. §13-21-115(5)(b).
2. *See* C.R.S. §13-21-115(5)(c).
3. *See* C.R.S. §13-21-115(5)(a).
4. *See* C.R.S. §18-4-502.
5. *See* C.R.S. §18-4-201.
6. *See* C.R.S. §18-4-201.
7. *See* C.R.S. §18-1-106.
8. *See* C.R.S. §18-1-105.
9. *See* C.R.S. §18-4-504.
10. *See* C.R.S. §18-1-106.
11. *See* C.R.S. §18-1-105.
12. *See Plotkin v. Club Valencia Condominium Ass'n*, 717 P.2d 1027 (Colo. Ct. App. 1986).; *Direct Mail Services, Inc. v. State of Colorado*, 557 F. Supp. 851 (D. Colo. 1983), aff'd 729 F.2d 672 (10th Cir. 1984); *United States v. Doyle*, 468 F.2d 633 (10th Cir. 1972).
13. *See Gerrity Oil and Gas Corp. v. Magness*, 923 P.2d 261 (Colo. Ct. App. 1995), aff'd in part, rev'd in part 946 P.2d 913 (Colo. 1997).
14. *See Evans v. Colorado Ute. Elec. Ass'n, Inc.*, 653 P.2d 63 (Colo. Ct. App. 1982).

15. *See Miller v. Carnation Co.*, 564 P.2d 127, 39 (Colo. Ct. App. 1977); *Engler v. Hatch*, 472 P.2d 680 (Colo. Ct. App. 1970).
16. *See* C.R.S. §18-1-705.
17. *See* C.R.S. §18-1-704(2). Deadly physical force may be used only if a person reasonably believes a lesser degree of force is inadequate and: (a) the actor has reasonable ground to believe, and does believe, that he or another person is in imminent danger of being killed or of receiving great bodily injury; or (b) the other person is using or reasonably appears about to use physical force against an occupant of a dwelling or business establishment while committing or attempting to commit burglary as defined in §§18-4-202 to 18-4-204; or (c) the other person is committing or reasonably appears about to commit kidnapping as defined in §§18-3-301 or 18-3-302, robbery as defined in §§18-4-301 or 18-4-302, sexual assault as set forth in §§18-3-402 or 18-3-403, or assault as defined in §§18-3-202 and 18-3-203.
18. *See* C.R.S. §18-1-705.
19. *See* C.R.S. §13-21-115.
20. *See* C.R.S. §13-21-115
21. *See* C.R.S. §33-41-101.
22. *See* C.R.S. §33-41-103.
23. *See* C.R.S. §33-41-104(1)(a), (c) and (d).
24. *See* C.R.S. §18-1-106.
25. *See* C.R.S. §§18-1-106, 18-4-501.
26. *See* C.R.S. §§18-1-105, 18-4-501.
27. *See* C.R.S. §§18-1-106, 18-4-501.
28. *See* C.R.S. §33-6-109.
29. *See* C.R.S. §33-6-116.
30. *See* C.R.S. §43-2-201(1)(c).
31. *See Bd. of County Comm'rs of Cheyenne County v. Ritchey*, 888 P.2d 298 (Colo. Ct. App. 1994); C.R.S. §38-41-101 (1998).
32. *See Brahm v. Johnson*, 531 P.2d 991, 993 (Colo. Ct. App. 1974); *Lovejoy v. School Dist. No. 46 of Sedgwick County*, 269 P.2d 1067, 1069 (Colo. 1954).
33. *See Anderson v. Cold Sprint Tungsten, Inc.*, 458 P.2d 756, 757 (Colo. 1969).
34. *See Collier v. City and County of Denver*, 716 P.2d 1124 (Colo. Ct. App. 1986).
35. *See Smith v. Hayden*, 772 P.2d 47 (Colo. 1989); *Hanes v. Olson*, 470 P.2d 933, 935 (Colo. Ct. App. 1970).
36. *See Palmer Ranch, Ltd. v. Sonsiest*, 920 P.2d 870 (Colo. Ct. App. 1996); *Gleason v. Phillips*, 470 P.2d 46 (Colo. 1970).
37. *See* C.R.S. §38-41-101(2).
38. *See Bagwell v. V-Heart Ranch, Inc.*, 690 P.2d 1271 (Colo. 1984); *Mountain Meadows v. Park Ditch*, 130 Colo. 537 (Colo. 1954).
39. A good discussion of this topic is located in 2A Colorado Methods of Practice, 9th §§70.32–70.44.
40. *Burton v. Miller*, 86 Colo. 106, 279 P.51 (1929).
41. *See* C.R.S. §38-30-137.
42. *See* C.R.S. §13-40-104.
43. *See Kinoshita v. North Denver Bank*, 181 Colo. 183, 508 P.2d 1264 (1973).

17

Colorado Landlord and Tenant Relations

Victor M. Grimm, *Attorney at Law*

Most landlord-tenant controversies in Colorado arise either from disputes over possession of the premises and evictions or security deposits. Many of these controversies can be avoided with a clear, detailed lease agreement that sets forth the rights and obligations of all parties. If you are a landlord or a tenant, make sure you have a clear understanding of the terms and conditions of the lease agreement. If you don't understand the provisions, make sure they are explained to you, or retain an attorney to assist you. Try to negotiate or mediate a resolution to provisions that seem to be unfair, and don't agree to anything you don't understand or know can't be complied with or accomplished. Always put your agreements in writing and document any mutually agreed-upon amendments. If your relationship with your landlord or your tenant begins to be tense or strained, document your communications and seek outside assistance from a mediator or an attorney before the situation becomes out of control.

This chapter provides a general outline of the legal principles and procedures involving evictions and security-deposit issues. Technically there is no such thing as an "eviction" in Colorado, but outside the statutory language the term is widely used. Under Colorado law, the legal procedure for a landlord to regain possession of leased premises from a tenant is called an action for "unlawful detainer." Unlawful-detainer actions are civil court actions brought in either County or District Court pursuant to the Forcible Entry and Detainer (FED) statute, C.R.S. §13-40-101 *et seq*.

If you are a landlord or a tenant, try to get a basic understanding of the basic principles, and do the best you can to keep the terms sorted out. If you are a landlord, don't lock out tenants or take their possessions. If you are a ten-ant, communicate with your landlord even if you are not in compliance with the terms of the agreement.

I. Basic Steps in the Eviction Process

The eviction process can be broken down into three fundamental steps: (1) prelitigation notice, (2) litigation, and (3) postlitigation actions.

Prelitigation Notice

Except for certain clearly delineated exceptions, all eviction cases must be preceded by a notice from the landlord served upon the tenant. Depending upon the situation, this may be: (a) *demand for compliance or possession* (also known as a *three-day notice*); (b) *notice to quit* (also known as a *ten-day notice*); or (c) *notice as set forth in the lease*. Any of these forms of notice are intended to make sure that the tenant is aware that a problem exists; these documents (depending on the situation) may give the tenant options relating to the tenancy.

Litigation

After the proper notice is given, the formal court proceedings are commenced by the filing and serving of a *complaint*. The complaint is the landlord's request to the court for relief in recovering possession and possibly damages from the tenant. The filing of a complaint opens a file with the court that is assigned a *civil action number*. After being served with the complaint, the tenant is given until a specified time, the *return date*, to file an *answer*. The answer sets forth the tenant's response to the complaint, including defenses and counterclaims against the landlord. A trial date is then set. At the trial, the court hears the landlord's and the tenant's cases and renders a decision, or *judgment.*

Postlitigation Actions

If the trial results in a judgment against the tenant for possession of the leased premises, a *writ of restitution* will be issued after forty-eight hours. This writ orders the sheriff to remove the tenant and the tenant's possessions from the premises. The sheriff will then physically remove the tenant and possessions if the tenant does not cooperate by leaving voluntarily.

Approximate Time Frame

Although eviction proceedings can drag out for long periods of time, the state statutory language sets up a relatively expeditious procedure. From prelitigation notice through recovery of possession, an eviction can taken anywhere from three days to three months, depending on numerous factors. If an appeal occurs, years can be added. However, the average contested eviction takes approximately three to ten weeks.

Approximate Expenses

Eviction actions may be brought either in the County Court or the District Court. Different filing fees apply to the different courts. Cases involving amounts under $10,000, which include almost all eviction actions, are brought in the County Court. The current fees for county courts in Colorado are:

- complaint filing fee: $31
- answer (no counterclaim): $26
- answer (with counterclaim): $31
- service of process: minimum $15
- writ of restitution: $15–$35 plus actual transportation costs

Negotiation and Mediation

Negotiation or mediation of settlements between landlords and tenants is almost always preferable to court proceedings and judgments for numerous reasons, including the following:

- Many problems arise from misunderstandings or communication problems.
- Tenants fail to read their leases.

- Parties reaching resolution "on their own" tend to be more cooperative in carrying out their respective resolutions (e.g., vacation of premises, payment of rent).
- The procedure of negotiation or mediation is less costly.
- Negotiation or mediation is usually considerably faster than litigation.
- Parties reaching a negotiated or mediated settlement feel better about themselves, each other, and the resolution process than those who must go through the legal system.

II. Understanding Default and Termination Issues

There are two basic situations that give rise to an eviction or unlawful-detainer action. The first situation is known as a *default* and occurs when (a) the tenant fails to pay rent required under the terms of tenancy or (b) the tenant acts in a manner violating a covenant or condition under the terms of the tenancy (e.g., keeps a llama in a studio apartment when the lease stated, "No pets allowed").

The second common scenario giving rise to an eviction action occurs when (a) the tenant has done nothing wrong, (b) the terms of tenancy provide for a termination at certain time intervals or upon a certain notice, and (c) the landlord desires to *terminate the tenancy.* This is known as termination of tenancy. The distinction between these two situations is important because there are different procedures for dealing with each type of problem.

Default

Failure to pay rent

A majority of evictions are commenced because of defaults under the terms of tenancy. The most common default is the failure to pay rent (*see* C.R.S. §13-40-104(d)). The law requires that before the tenant is technically guilty of an unlawful detention and subject to eviction, the tenant must be served with a document known as a *written demand,* also known as a *demand for possession,* a *three-day notice,* or a *demand for compliance or possession.* The designation *demand for possession* is actually misleading because the landlord is more properly giving the tenant a *notice to pay or quit.* The form generally used is referred to as a *demand for compliance or possession.*

The demand for compliance or possession must give the tenant three days to either (a) pay the rent due and owing or (b) vacate the premises.

Violation of terms

The second type of default occurs when a tenant violates a condition, rule, or covenant of the tenancy other than nonpayment of rent. Conditions and rules are limitless. Some common examples are "No dogs allowed," "No waste/desecration of premises," or "No loud parties." The legal requirements regarding this type of default are identical to those regarding nonpayment of rent (*see* C.R.S. §13-40-104(e)). The tenant must be served with a demand for compliance or possession and be given three days to either comply with the condition or vacate the premises.

Procedure for Defaults

The demand for compliance or possession, also known as the three-day notice, is required to be served prior to the institution of a default eviction proceeding. The case will be dismissed from court if this requirement is not carefully complied with. The statutory requirements must be satisfied to the letter of the law. Even though strict compliance is necessary for an effective action, the demand is a simple one-page document that notifies the tenant to either (a) cure the respective default or (b) vacate the premises within three days of the receipt of the notice. A demand must be served even if the lease does not contain default provisions. The form and contents of the demand are mandated by statute, and it is best to use a preprinted form—"Demand for Compliance or Possession" (Bradford Form No. 235PA)—which you can obtain from most office supply stores.

The statutory provisions specifically set forth how service of the demand must be made. The first thing a defendant will do is try to get the case dismissed owing to a technicality, so remember that strict compliance with the statutory requirements is necessary to prevent a defective notice (C.R.S. §13-40-108).

Unlike service of process in other civil actions in Colorado courts (i.e., the summons and complaint), the statutes do not require that service of the notice in an unlawful-detainer action be made by a nonparty. Therefore, the landlord or the landlord's representative, agent, or employee may serve the notice. Remember to make photocopies of the notice before you serve it. Proper notice and proof of notice are essential to a successful case.

On the reverse side of the demand, there is a form for *proof of service*. This form should be filled out on your copy after service. There is a certain confusion regarding what days to count and which days not to count in calculating the three-day period (*see* C.R.C.P. 6(a); C.R.C.P. 306(a)).

However, conservative construction of the applicable law yields the following general rules:

- The day the notice was served does not count, and hours do not count.
- Saturdays, Sundays, and legal holidays are excluded.
- The last day of the period (i.e., the third day) is included.

It is always better to err on the side of giving more than three days rather than less. If within the three-day period the tenant cures the default, then your case is over before it begins. If the three-day period passes without a cure, you may then proceed to the litigation stage of the process.

Termination of Tenancy

A termination of tenancy is distinguished from a default by the fact that the tenant has done nothing "wrong." In this situation, the landlord may simply end the tenant's occupancy of the premises at a legally appropriate time. Depending upon the type of situation, different procedures and different time periods are applicable.

End of term

This is the simplest type of termination. It is well-settled law that no prelitigation notice (notice to vacate) is required to be given to a tenant at the end of a term certain (C.R.S. §3-40-107 (4)). The tenant is deemed a trespasser, and an eviction proceeding may be commenced immediately.

The landlord must be careful not to neglect the fact that the tenant's term has expired. If the landlord handles the situation as if a tenancy still exists, for example, by collecting further rents, a court may deem a holdover tenancy to have been created. However, the simple fact that a landlord does not immediately undertake an eviction action does not, without more, create a holdover situation.

Holdover tenancy

If a tenant remains on the leased premises after the expiration of a term certain, and the landlord continues to treat the tenant as such (i.e., continues to collect rent or undertake other affirmative conduct), a holdover tenancy has been created.

Periodic tenancy

Service of a *notice to vacate* upon the tenant is required to effect a termination of a periodic tenancy. The notice to vacate is also known as *notice to quit* and informally called a *ten-day notice* because ten days is the most common period required. This chapter will refer to this document as the notice to vacate because that is what the form is titled. It is of utmost importance that this notice to vacate be properly timed. Timing of the notice depends upon the period involved. The most typical tenancy periods and their respective notice requirements are:

- year-to-year: three months
- month-to-month: ten days
- week-to-week: three days (*see* C.R.S. §13-40-107(1)(a), (c), (d))

The law further requires that the notice must be served "not less than the respective period fixed before the end of the applicable tenancy." In other words, the notice must be served so that its deadline for termination coincides with an end of the applicable period.

Termination: Notice to Vacate

Contents of notice to vacate

The contents of a notice to vacate are specified by statute (*see* C.R.S. §13-40-107). Unlike the demand for compliance or possession, the notice to vacate does not give the tenant alternatives but simply informs the tenant that the tenancy is terminated and that the premises must be vacated upon a date certain (Bradford Form No. 219).

Service of notice to vacate

The requirements of service of a notice to vacate are identical to those of the demand for compliance or possession. The same general rules regarding timing of the demand for compliance or possession apply to the notice to vacate, with one major exception: In periods over seven days (e.g., ten-day notice), weekends and holidays do count toward the period (*see* C.R.C.P. 6(a); C.R.C.P. 306(a)). However, if the last day of the period is a weekend day or legal holiday, the period then runs until the end of the next day that is not a Saturday, Sunday, or legal holiday.

III. Responding to an Attempt to Evict

Complaint

If, after the landlord has complied with the applicable pre-litigation notice requirements, the appropriate time period has passed and the tenant has failed to comply with the request set forth in the demand or notice, a complaint may then be prepared, filed, and served upon the tenant. The filing of a complaint officially commences an eviction proceeding. The law sets forth specific requirements regarding the contents of a complaint filed in an eviction case as well as additional matters that may be included (*see* C.R.S. §13-40-110 [Form No. 94]).

Contents of Summons

A summons is a document that informs the defendant that a legal action has been commenced against them. Further, it informs the defendant of the time by which and place where they must file an answer, and when to appear in court (*return date*). The summons must be prepared at the same time as the complaint. Technically, service of the summons brings the defendant under jurisdiction of the court. Once the summons has been served, the court may enter judgment(s) against the defendant without further notice. It should be noted that a summons for forcible entry and unlawful detainer is different than that for a conventional County Court case. Care should be taken to use the appropriate form.

Where to File

The eviction action *must be filed in the county where the property is located.* As discussed previously, if the amount sought is over $10,000, the action must be filed with the District Court. If the amount is under $10,000, it should be filed with the County Court.

Service of Process

Each defendant named in the case must be served with their own individual copy of the summons and complaint. This is known as *service of process.* This is essential because if a defendant is not served, then that party is not subject to the court's orders. Improper service will hold up a case while the problem is being resolved; thus, it is better to get "good service" the first time around. The rules regarding proper service upon a party are set forth in C.R.S. Section 13-40-112 and C.R.C.P. Rules 4 and 304.

Unlike in other civil cases, process may also be served by "posting" C.R.S. §13-40-112. This act is also known as *constructive service.* This must be accomplished by a person authorized to serve process and *may be carried out only after the server has made a "diligent effort" to make personal service.* If service is by posting, the court will not consider any claim for money damages and is only empowered to consider the issue of possession of the premises.

Timing of Service

Statutes require that the return date on the summons shall not be less than five days or more than ten days from the date of issuance. Service of summons, whether by posting or personal service, must be made upon the defendant at least five days before the return date. Therefore, there is only a small window of one to five days in which to serve the defendant.

Tenant's Pretrial Procedures

A tenant facing eviction proceedings must keep in mind that the single most important thing a tenant can do is to pay attention to the situation. *Do not ignore* phone calls, pretrial notices, or process.

Early Letters and Phone Calls

At least 75 percent of the time, before a landlord even considers pursuing legal action, the landlord will attempt to contact the tenant by phone or letter regarding an actual or perceived problem. A large number of problems are resolved in this manner.

Upon receipt of a letter or phone call from the landlord, a tenant should respond promptly. There is nothing that will expedite the onset of litigation more rapidly than a stonewalling tenant. If a problem exists regarding such things as the timely payment of rent or a barking dog, the tenant should be cognizant of the interests and concerns of the landlord.

Prior to almost all eviction proceedings, the tenant is entitled to a prelitigation notice. This is typically either a demand for compliance or possession or a notice to vacate. A tenant's possible action depends on what type of notice is sent.

Demand for Compliance or Possession

Upon receipt of a demand for compliance or possession, the first thing a tenant should do is check the lease to see if any longer or additional notices are required. If a longer period than three days is required by the lease, then the tenant should inform the landlord of that provision. Document this communication.

As long as the landlord has complied with the statutory requirements of posting, there is no requirement that the tenant actually see the notice within the three-day period. In other words, a tenant can be on a two-week vacation and be legally served with a three-day notice that expires before the tenant returns.

Next, evaluate the demand contained in the notice. Is the demand correct? Is there a default? If so, you must decide whether to comply with the demand (i.e., pay past-due rent or comply with covenants or conditions) or vacate the premises. *Note that if you vacate the premises, you may still be liable for subsequent rental payments through the term of your lease!* If you decide that you will cure the default, immediately contact the landlord and inform the landlord of your intentions. Make arrangements to cure the default before the three-day period has expired. The payment or cure must be timely and for the full amount (i.e., no partial payments). A letter should accompany payment.

Notice to Vacate

Unlike a demand for compliance or possession, a notice to vacate gives no alternatives and simply states that the tenancy is terminated and requires that the premises be vacated by a specific date. Upon receipt of a notice to vacate, the time periods involved and required should be examined. If there is a defect in the timing or method of service, there may exist a defense. Otherwise, the landlord is entitled to terminate your tenancy and dispossess you of the property.

Receipt of Process

If no cure or vacation of the premises has occurred, after the requisite prelitigation notice period has passed, the sheriff or private process server will serve you with process. The summons will specify the return date that serves both as (a) the deadline for you to file your answer, and (b) the date and time that you must appear to set trial upon the case.

If you agree with everything in the complaint and do not dispute any of its facts and have no defenses and no counterclaims (claims against the landlord), there is not much more you can do except to show up at the return date, watch the judge enter a judgment against you, and be ready to get dispossessed by the sheriff within approximately two to fourteen days. However, it is rare that a tenant agrees with everything that a landlord alleges or does not have a defense. If you do have a defense or counterclaim, it is essential that a timely answer be prepared and filed.

Answer

The answer is a document that is filed with the court and served upon the plaintiff by the defendant. The answer must be filed "at or before the time specified for [defendant's] appearance" (i.e., the return date). The statute mandates the contents of the answer and gives a suggested form. A written answer must be filed by every defendant wishing to contest an eviction action. If an answer is not filed, it is conclusively presumed that the defendant admits all of the allegations contained in the complaint. Further, any answer that fails to specifically admit or deny the allegations of the complaint will be deemed to have admitted the allegations. Finally, the answer must contain each and every defense that the defendant intends to rely upon.

Defenses Against Eviction

The following is not an exhaustive list of defenses against evictions but only some of the most common and most recognized by the courts.

No default

Obviously, if no default exists under the lease, an eviction will not be successful. Typically, a defense under this category would involve alleging facts showing that:

- The rent at issue was timely and fully paid or tendered.
- The covenants claimed to have been violated were cured in a timely manner or the violation had, in fact, never occurred.

Waiver

A waiver is a situation wherein a default did in fact occur, but the landlord either by word or conduct, explicitly or implicitly, assented to it or "let it go." A waiver may be demonstrated by a written agreement, verbal statements, or conduct. If a waiver is established, this will serve as a defense against an eviction action served upon the alleged default.

Defective notice

It is not required to give notice before serving a summons and complaint if the term of the lease has ended. However, any other type of termination requires proper prelitigation notice. Notice may be defective for several other reasons:

- improper time period
- improper party or parties named or served
- improper method of service
- improper contents

One seeking to assert a defense of defective notice should review the statutory requirements for notice and allege all defects to which the facts give rise. A successful allegation of defective notice will cause the eviction action to be thrown out and will require the landlord to comply with the notice requirements and refile the action.

Return Date and Setting of Trial

On the return date, the parties must appear at the time and place designated on the summons. If a sufficient answer has been filed, the case is deemed "at issue" and the case will be set for trial. If no answer has been filed, the court will enter a default judgment against the tenant.

Possession

At the time of judgment, a court may enter an order for immediate possession by the landlord. *However, the court may not issue a writ of restitution until forty-eight hours after judgment is entered* (C.R.S. § 13-40-122).

Writ of Restitution

The *writ of restitution* is the written document issued by the court to the sheriff, directing the sheriff to physically remove the tenant and personal property from the premises.

Service of writ

Only the sheriff is authorized to serve the writ. It may be served only in the daytime, between "sunrise and sunset." The sheriff will charge an additional fee for this service of the writ. The statute does not set forth the specific procedures that the sheriff must follow in acting upon the writ. Depending upon the county, some sheriffs will call or send a postcard prior to serving the writ. Finally, in some counties the sheriff will serve the writ, wait for a period, and then return to physically dispossess the tenant if the tenant has not moved out. The sheriff of your county should be contacted to ascertain the specific procedures.

Execution of writ

The sheriff or deputy executing (carrying out) a writ is obliged to remove not only the tenant but also "to remove the tenant's personal property and effects from the premises." Notwithstanding this language, it is generally the practice that the sheriff will not physically remove the property, and the landlord should make arrangements for a moving company to be present. A landlord should be available at the time of the execution of the writ to allow access to the premises. *However, beyond letting the authorities in, the landlord should do nothing. Do not remove the property. Do not make efforts to store the property.* Let the sheriff and the moving company handle it. If the landlord follows this directive, they will not be liable for damages for the manner in which a sheriff executes the writ in the course of lawful eviction or removal of the tenant's property.

Appeals

An eviction case tried in the County Court may be appealed to the District Court. The appeal will "stay" (i.e., stop) all further proceedings, including action in the writ of restitution while the appeal is pending. If an appeal is contemplated, an attorney familiar with the appeal process should be consulted at once. There are many deadline requirements, bonds, and undertakings that must be complied with or the case will be thrown out (*see, e.g.*, C.R.S. §§13-40-117, 118, 120, 121; C.R.C.P. 411; County Court Forms 4 and 5). The first of these deadlines is fifteen days from the date of the judgment. Therefore, timing and fast action are critical if an appeal is pursued. In addition to the regular appeal bond, a defendant appealing an eviction action must also deposit with the court the amount of money that was found due and owing as rent, plus additional rental payments as they become due during the pendency of the appeal (C.R.S. §§13-40-118, 120). These payments may be distributed to the landlord upon order of the court (C.R.S. §13-40-121). If the defendant fails to pay any of these, the appeal will be dismissed (C.R.S. §§ 13-40-118, 120). Finally, an additional bond may be ordered by the court upon request of the appellee (nonappealing party) after a hearing.

IV. Security-Deposit Issues

A constant source of confusion for both landlords and tenants is the status of security deposits in relation to evictions and the other aspects of the tenancy. A typical question is: Can a tenant use the security deposit as an offset against the last month's rent? Like almost all other landlord-tenant issues, the first place to look is the provisions of the particular lease involved. One major exception to this rule relates to the refund of security deposits at the end of a tenancy.

Statute: Security Deposits— Wrongful Withholding

The statute relating to the return of residential security deposits is definitely the most (and some say the only!) protenant provision in the Colorado statutes. This statute sets forth requirements as to how a landlord must return security deposits to tenants and imposes severe penalties for failure to comply. This statute cannot be waived by oral or written agreement (e.g., in the lease) (C.R.S. §38-12-103(1)).

Return of Security Deposit

Within one month after the termination of a lease or surrender of the premises, the landlord is obliged to return the security deposit to the tenant. The lease may specify a longer period, but this period may not exceed sixty days (C.R.S. §38-12-103(1)). Note that there may exist local ordinances also requiring payment of interest upon security deposits. However, no such state law exists in Colorado.

Written Statement Regarding Retention of Security Deposit

If the landlord retains any portion of a security deposit, a written statement setting forth "the exact reasons" for the retention of said portion is required (C.R.S. §38-12-103(1)). This statement must be accompanied by a return of the balance of the deposit.

If the landlord fails to comply with the above requirements and does not deliver a written statement or refund within the required time, the landlord forfeits all of their rights to withhold any portion of the security deposit. Additionally, if the retention is "in willful violation," the landlord may be liable to the tenant for treble (three times) the amount of the security deposit wrongfully withheld plus attorneys' fees and court costs (C.R.S. §38-12-103(3)).

Tenant Action to Recover Security Deposit

If a landlord willfully retains a security deposit, a tenant has the right to institute legal proceedings for recovery. A successful tenant may recover treble (three times) the amount of that portion of the security deposit wrongfully withheld as well as costs and attorneys' fees (C.R.S. §38-12-103(3)). If a tenant contemplates an action against the landlord, it is imperative that the statutory requirements of a prelitigation notice be complied with and further that the tenant be aware of the law as it relates to "wrongful withholding."

Prelitigation Notice

The law requires that prior to the filing of a security-deposit action, a tenant give notice to the landlord of their intent to file a legal proceeding. This notice must be given at least seven days prior to the filing of the action. It is suggested that this notice be sent via certified mail, return receipt requested, so that you will have proof that the landlord received the notice and you are sure that seven days have passed before you file your action.

V. Conclusion

Participating in an eviction or trying to get a security deposit back, whether as a landlord or tenant, can be an emotional, anxious, and mystifying experience. No matter how "professional" the parties' conduct, it is human nature to be emotional about rights and responsibilities related to your home or your property. Furthermore, it is impossible to eliminate the anxiety and mystery from the process altogether simply because litigation is, by its very nature, unpredictable. However, this guide attempts to give readers a better idea of what to expect throughout the process, which should help to alleviate at least some of the mystery and anxiety.

18

Not in *My* Backyard! The Simplified Law of Nuisance

Nancy S. Greif, *Attorney at Law*
Peter A. Holton, *Planning Consultant*

Where do your rights stop and your neighbor's rights start? That question is the reason we have a concept in the law called nuisance. In general, we all have the fundamental right to use our property as we wish, *but* our individual rights stop at that invisible line where the rights of others begin. Statutes and case law related to the term "nuisance" are society's attempt to define that line. A nuisance, generally, is any activity that is conducted on privately owned property that causes sufficient annoyance, inconvenience, or discomfort to the general public or to individuals that the law will not allow that activity to continue unabated or unmitigated. In other words, your right to use your property as you wish stops cold when it interferes with your neighbors' rights to the peaceful enjoyment of their own property. For example, the adjoining suburban residential property is sold and the new neighbors move in and start raising two thousand hogs for market immediately upslope from your private well. As a consequence, your drinking water becomes polluted. Now, *that's* a nuisance!

Clearly, if you plan to try to be a good neighbor you will not engage in activities that could be considered nuisances. The concept of "nuisance" has been classified into three main categories: public, private, and mixed public/private nuisances.

I. "Public" Nuisances

In general, the law of public nuisance is controlled by Colorado statutes §16-13-301 through §16-13-306. Public nuisances are acts or circumstances that injure rights shared by the public at large. The point is to protect the general public from activities that society as a whole declares are just plain bad. Many of these public nuisances are defined in state laws and are intended to protect the public from various health hazards and from a number of categories of vice and crime. In Colorado, the General Assembly has declared that it is state policy "that every public nuisance shall be restrained, prevented, abated and perpetually enjoined."

The kinds of activities that are enumerated include prostitution, gambling, drug activities, receiving and transporting stolen goods, hit-and-run accidents, drive-by shootings, disturbance of the peace, and telephone solicitations that use prohibited recorded messages. Also included as public nuisances are buildings and businesses that are open to the public that are found to be dangerous or hazardous and unused, dilapidated buildings that may attract trespassers and transients and put them at risk. Establishments that sell or distribute food products or maintain public restrooms must conform to the health and sanitary statutes and regulations or risk being declared a public nuisance. Activities that violate the state or local noise regulations may be declared public nuisances. Pollution of the air or public water supply may be classified as a public nuisance. Obstruction of public streets is a public nuisance.

The definition of "nuisance" is very broad and may include activities that are not defined in the statutes but are found to injure the general public. If by a particular act, or by failing to perform a legal duty, a person endangers or injures the public health, safety, or welfare, then that act or omission is considered to be "maintaining a public nuisance." All the residents in a particular area are potentially affected, although not necessarily all to the same degree; the number of people affected is indefinite.

The legislature, in an attempt to deter public nuisances, has enacted some tough forfeiture laws in connection with statutory public nuisances. That means that if you own a vehicle or a building or cash or equipment or other property, and you use those things in the commission of a public nuisance, then the state could require you to forfeit those things to the state; it could legally take those things away from you.

Landlords need to be aware that if they lease premises to a business that is found to be a public nuisance, it is conceivable that their property could, at least temporarily, be forfeited because of the activities that were taking place there. In order for the forfeiture to be valid, it would have to be proved that the landlord was either involved in the public nuisance or "knew or reasonably should have known" about the public-nuisance act. In other words, as a landlord you have a responsibility to stay aware of the activities of your renters and not condone or allow public-nuisance acts to take place on your premises. If you allow others to use your property, be sure you know that it will be used for a legitimate purpose.

II. "Private" Nuisances

In general, the law of private nuisance is defined in the recorded case law of the state of Colorado. The essential question in determining whether a private nuisance exists is whether one person has unreasonably interfered with another person's right to use and enjoy his or her own property. The interference must be "substantial"; it must be such that a normal person in the community would be offended, inconvenienced, or annoyed by the act or omission.

Many private nuisances are difficult to define. They result from acts or omissions by a property owner on his or her own property that may be perfectly reasonable to that person but may be unreasonable to the neighbors.

If this statement sounds like the introduction to the "Lawyers' Full Employment Act," it is. (Just kidding.) Ambiguous words such as "reasonable" or "unreasonable" keep lawyers busy. However, if you think about the things your neighbor might do that would annoy you, you will probably find that there are many gray areas that are almost impossible to define.

Imagine that your neighbor has one dog that barks oc-

casionally. No problem—your dog barks sometimes too. But then what if your neighbor decides to open a kennel, and all of a sudden there are fifteen barking dogs? Kennels are not prohibited by the subdivision covenants or by city or county regulations governing that area, *but* ... you're not getting any sleep at all. If you talk to your neighbor about what could be done, you need to be informed about whether you have grounds for a nuisance lawsuit and very gently let them know that you've been looking into it and that even though there is no statutory violation, the activity could well be prohibited under nuisance law. Frequently people are more willing to mitigate a problem and find a solution that works for everybody if they realize they could lose in court.

Nuisances are often in the eye of the beholder: "I know one when I see one." It's often up to the courts to determine whether the person doing the complaining is being "reasonable." Two common problems with winning nuisance lawsuits are: (1) If the problem existed and was known to you before you bought your property, it is difficult to find that the activity or circumstance is a private nuisance; and (2) if the problem seems terrible to you but doesn't much bother your other neighbors, then the law may find that you are abnormally sensitive. If you buy property right next door to a coal-fired power plant, and then you complain about the soot and dust, you may have a valid air-pollution complaint under federal guidelines, but you probably don't have a nuisance claim. The plant was there before you bought the property, and you either knew or should have known that coal-fired plants produce soot and dust.

Because there is a lot of legal risk involved in most private nuisance suits, it would be a good idea to turn to the alternative-dispute-resolution section of this book to find out how to resolve problems with your neighbor without going to court.

III. Mixed Public and Private Nuisances

These nuisances affect the general public, but they also result in special injuries to private rights. Often statutory public nuisances and the conduct of abnormal and unduly dangerous activities (e.g., explosives) constitute both public nuisances and a private injuries.

IV. Lessons for Neighborhood Peace

Don't allow criminal activities to take place using any property you own.

If you have a business that caters to the general public, keep the premises clean and in good repair.

Find out what zoning or other land use restrictions govern the use of your property, and comply with them.

Keep your property cleaned up.

Don't pollute your neighbors' air, water, or view.

Don't create levels of noise that are likely to irritate your neighbors.

19

Colorado Mechanic's Lien Law for the Property Owner

Daniel A. Gregory, *Attorney at Law*

Property ownership is one of the fundamental rights and privileges enjoyed by citizens of this country. The enjoyment you derive from owning real property can be negatively affected when someone places a lien against your property. An unsatisfied lien can result in the inability to sell your property; difficulty in refinancing an existing mortgage; or, the ultimate consequence, the loss of the property through forced sale. In order to avoid any of these consequences, it is important for the individual property owner to understand how certain types of liens can attach to their property and how these liens can be defended against or removed from their property.

Property owners can have liens on their property that arise from a number of different circumstances. When someone finances the purchase of real property, a lender will secure the promissory note with a document called a deed of trust.[1] A deed of trust constitutes a lien on the property. If the obligation to the lender is not paid in a timely manner, then the lender can foreclose on the deed of trust and sell the property at a judicial or a public sale to satisfy the loan obligation.

Property in a development with a homeowners' association may also be subject to a lien from the homeowners' association for unpaid assessments imposed by the association. These liens typically arise when a homeowner fails to pay the association's billings for items such as road maintenance, common area maintenance, and snowplowing. These liens are typically governed by rules to which all homeowners in the association agree when they purchase their property.

A third type of lien, and the type that this chapter will discuss, is a lien called a mechanic's lien. Contrary to what many people assume, a mechanic's lien has nothing to do with the repair of an automobile. A mechanic's lien is a right created by the Colorado legislature that allows an unpaid contractor, subcontractor, material supplier, or design professional to place a lien against a person's property that has been improved through construction labor, materials, or other services.

A mechanic's lien can exist on property as the result of an owner failing to pay for certain construction work performed on his or her home or as a result of a developer failing to pay for certain labor or service work on homes within his or her development project that are then sold to third-party purchasers. This chapter will explore the following questions: (1) What services can give rise to a mechanic's lien? (2) When and how must that lien be recorded in order to be effective? (3) How can an individual homeowner challenge the validity of the lien? and (4) How can the individual homeowner protect himself or herself when purchasing property from a developer or a previous owner who may have failed to pay for construction work on the property?

I. Services That May Give Rise to a Mechanic's Lien

In general, a mechanic's lien can arise because of the nonpayment of any person who provides any type of service in furtherance of the construction of a building or certain types of property improvements. A lien may arise, therefore, from a material supplier such as a lumber yard that has supplied lumber that, in turn, was used by a contractor to construct a portion of a building on a person's property. If that contractor fails to pay for the lumber, the lumber yard may place a lien on the property and ultimately foreclose on that lien even though the property owner may never have met the owner of the lumber yard, picked up any materials from the lumber yard, or even known which lumber yard was supplying the materials for his or her home. Similarly, a subcontractor who has performed certain work on a project can place a lien on the owner's home if the general contractor does not pay for the services performed.[2] A typical subcontractor on most construction projects is the person who installs the drywall. Although a drywaller is normally a subcontractor, he would be a contractor if he had a contract with the owner. If the drywaller is, however, a true subcontractor because he has a contract with the general contractor rather than the owner, that drywaller may still place a lien on the owner's property if the general contractor fails to pay him for the work performed. This would be true even though the owner does not have a contract with the drywaller, may never have met the drywaller, and did not know that the drywaller was not being paid by the general contractor. If a homeowner has paid an amount sufficient to satisfy his complete contractual obligations, including change orders, however, then the owner has a potential defense that can eliminate the subcontractor's lien. This defense will be discussed later in this chapter.

In addition to a material supplier or a subcontractor, the general contractor who has a direct contract with the owner also has the ability to place a lien on the project if he is unpaid for his services. If either the owner or the general contractor has contracted with a design professional such as an architect, an engineer, or a draftsman who has furnished designs, plans, plats, maps, specifications, estimates of cost, or surveys, those persons will also have the right to place a lien on the property if they are not paid for their services. If the owner contracts with an individual to provide services commonly described as construction administration services (overseeing the project for the owner), those supervisory services can also result in a lien against the project if the person is not paid by the owner.

The lien placed on an owner's property by any of the above persons would be for the amount of their contract less payments already received. Typically, the lien of a general contractor will be for the amount of his contract less what he has been paid, and this amount should include any amounts not paid to his subcontractors.[3] Although the general contractor's lien should be for an amount that en-compasses amounts due to the subcontractors, the subcontractors may also place their individual liens on a property. This is important to realize when a homeowner is trying to determine the extent or value of the liens that may encumber his property. One cannot simply add the amount stated in the general contractor's lien to the amounts of the respective subcontractors' liens because there may be a duplication of the amounts due between the various contractors and subcontractors on the project. As an example, a general contractor might place lien on a project for $100,000. A drywaller subcontractor may place a lien on the same project for $25,000. Another subcontractor who did the framing work on the project may place a lien on the same project for $50,000. Finally, the lumber yard may place a lien on the same project for $10,000. The amount of the liens on this hypothetical project could not be determined simply by adding all of the above numbers. Both of the subcontractors' liens and the material supplier's lien are probably encompassed in the general contractor's lien. In addition, the lumber yard's lien may be part of the framer's lien amount. Where an owner faces a situation in which a number of liens have been placed on the property, a careful analysis should be done to determine the total dollar value being claimed by all of the lienors. This analysis can include a demand on the contractor for an affidavit stating the amounts he has received, the amounts that he has paid out, and the exact amount paid to each individual subcontractor on the project. This information should be readily available because Colorado law requires that every contractor and subcontractor maintain separate records of account for each project or contract.[4]

II. The Legal Requirements for a Valid Lien

When an owner encounters a situation where a lien is on property that he or she already owns or that is being considered for purchase, the fundamental question that arises is how to eliminate the lien from the property. Prior to considering the defenses against an otherwise valid lien, an owner or prospective owner would be well advised to first determine the validity of the lien itself. This analysis can generally be performed by looking at the lien document in light of certain time requirements that must be met in order to make a lien valid. In general, the failure of a lienor to comply with any one of the three key time requirements contained in the Colorado Mechanic's Lien Law will result in the lien being invalid. If a lien is determined to be invalid, the lienor can typically be convinced to remove his lien from the property. How one might attempt to convince the lienor to remove an invalid lien from the property is discussed later in this chapter.

A majority of lienors in the state of Colorado are required to record their lien within four months after the last work performed by that lienor.[5] Failure to record the lien statement within this time period will render the lien invalid.[6] Prior to a lienor recording its lien within four months of that lienor's last day of work, however, the lienor is required to have sent to the owner a document titled, "Notice of Intent to Lien." This document is a mandatory prerequisite to the filing of the lien statement. In other words, if the notice of intent to lien is not sent prior to the recording of the actual lien, then the actual lien would be deemed invalid. This notice must be sent at least ten days prior to the recording of the actual lien document.[7] One other important criterion that can affect the validity of the lien if it is not satisfied is the requirement that the lienor execute an affidavit (generally, a notarized statement) that the lienor has served the prelien notice at least ten days prior to the recording of the statement of lien. This affidavit that the prelien notice has been served is often a part of the lien statement itself. Occasionally, however, an owner will find a lien statement that complies in all other respects with the lien law but does not include an affidavit of serving the notice of intent. The failure to record this affidavit invalidates the lien.[8]

Finally, an owner should check to determine whether the lien is recorded in the county where the property is located. Occasionally a lienor will record in the wrong county if the property is located in one county and the lienor's business is located in another. The failure to record in a timely manner in the county where the property is located will invalidate the lien.

In evaluating the timeliness of a lien on a piece of property, an owner should determine when the last work of the lienor was performed on the property. The lienor generally has four months from that date to record its lien but must have sent his notice of intent to lien ten days before the actual recording of the lien. Assuming that the last month is a month that contains only thirty days, a lienor must send his prelien notice (the "Notice of Intent to Lien") within three months and nineteen days of his last day of work in order to satisfy the condition of the notice of intent to lien while still satisfying the four-month time period for actually recording the lien. The lienor need not prove that the owner received the prelien notice ten days prior to the recording of the lien. It has been held that it is the date of the mailing of the prelien notice, not of its receipt, that establishes the commencement of the ten-day waiting period prior to the recording of the actual lien doc-

ument.[9] Where a lien is encumbering certain property, the owner should determine the last day of work by that lienor and calculate whether the lien was recorded within four months of that lienor's last day of work. The owner should also determine whether a prelien notice was sent at least ten days prior to the recording of the lien. The failure to comply with either of these conditions can and will result in the lien being invalid.

The next important time period for an owner to consider in evaluating the validity of a lien is whether the lienor has commenced an action to foreclose his lien against the real property within six months of anyone's last day of work on the project. There is an important distinction between the six-month time period for filing a lien foreclosure lawsuit and the four-month time period for initially recording the lien. The four-month time period for initially recording the lien runs from the date of that lienor's last day of work. The six-month time period for actually commencing a lien foreclosure lawsuit runs from the last work by any person on the project.[10] In addition to actually filing the lien foreclosure lawsuit within this time period, the lienor must also record in the office of the county clerk and recorder of the county in which the property is located a notice that an action has been commenced to foreclose the lien. This notice is often called a "Notice of Lis Pendens." Unless the lienor has both commenced his action and recorded his notice of lis pendens within the six-month period, the lien is invalid. Owners should not overlook the requirement for the notice of lis pendens. It is not unusual to find a lienor who has sent his prelien notice in a timely manner, recorded his lien, and filed his action but forgotten to record a notice of lis pendens along with the filing of the lawsuit. The omission of this requirement will result in the lien being invalid.

In calculating either the four-month time period for the recording of the lien or the six-month time period for the commencing of the lien foreclosure lawsuit, the question that often arises is what exactly constitutes the last work by the lienor or any person on the project. This is an important question to answer in determining whether the lienor has complied with the statutory time periods required to make his lien valid. Colorado lien law provides that "no trivial imperfection in or omission from the work or in the construction of any building, improvement, or structure ... shall be deemed a lack of completion ... nor postpone the running of any time limit within which any lien statement shall be filed for record."[11] Where a contractor's lien is arguably late, the dispute that typically arises is one in which the contractor is claiming that work done at the end of the project was not work to correct a trivial imperfection but was in fact work that was essential to the completion of the home or project. The owner on the other hand typically argues that the later work performed on the project was simply punchlist or warranty work that ordinarily does not extend the time for filing the lien or the lawsuit.

A review of Colorado case law reveals the following holdings that should provide some guidance for those who are faced with the difficult analysis of when the last work was actually performed. One decision has held that the work is completed for purposes of commencing the time periods when the essential parts of the job are done. In that case, all of the roofing work was done except for the "hot-mopping" necessary to seal the seams of the roofing material. This hot-mopping was done approximately two months after the completion of the earlier work. The court held that because the hot-mopping of the seams was necessary for the roofing work to be completed, so the time periods did not begin to run until that later work had been finished.[12] In another decision, it was held that where a mantel and fireplace were not completed, then the work of constructing the entire home had not been completed.[13] In yet another case, however, labor performed by a plumber several months after he had completed the plumbing in a building, which labor had a value of $6.75, was deemed trivial. The time for the plumber to file his lien was held to have started, therefore, when he had finished his original work and not when he came back to do his miscellaneous labor, which was in the nature of warranty work.[14] In general, it has been held that punchlist work, or work where the contractor is coming back and simply touching up his work and making minor corrections to his work, does not extend the time requirements for the recording of the lien. Instead, the lienor's time requirements commence when he has completed the essential work necessary for the home or project to be utilized for its intended purpose.[15]

The four-month time limit for the recording of the lien statement itself may be extended if the lienor has within that time recorded in the public records in the county in which the property is located a particular type of document designed to extend the time for recording a lien. If a potential lienor is uncertain as to whether a lien would be necessary, therefore, he can record a notice with certain information contained in it, and this notice will extend the time for filing the lien statement to either four months after the completion of the entire structure *or* six months after the date of the filing of the notice, whichever is earlier.[16] Further, prior to the earlier of these two dates occurring, this same lienor may file a new or amended notice that will remain effective for an additional period of six months after the date of the filing or four months after the date of completion, whichever occurs first. Prior to determining that a lien is invalid because it has not been recorded within the original four-month period, therefore, an owner should search the public records to see if that particular lienor has recorded a notice extending the time for the recording of a lien. This notice extending the time must, however, be recorded within the original time for recording the lien.

Most lienors are familiar with the four-month limitation within which they must file their lien against a person's property. This familiarity with the general four-month time requirement can, however, cause certain lienors to lose their lien rights because of a different, more limited time period that governs those situations in which a bona fide purchaser is buying either a single- or double-family dwelling from a seller. In such cases, a lienor must have filed his lien statement within *two months* after the completion of the building. If a lienor waits until the expiration of the ordinary time period of four months after his last day of work before recording his lien, and that four-month period is greater than two months after the project was completed, then the lien will be invalid. The determination of when the building is complete for the purpose of calculating when the two-month period commences is not as difficult a determination as attempting to calculate the time periods for the four-month or six-month periods previously discussed. When a bona fide purchaser is buying a single- or double-family dwelling from a seller, the dwelling is deemed to have been completed at the time it is conveyed to the bona fide purchaser if it is not completed before that time. A bona fide purchaser is someone who is buying from the seller in exchange or valuable consideration and without notice that any liens or potential liens exist on the property.[17]

III. Avoiding Liens

Once it has been determined that the lien is valid because the lienor has complied with the time requirements mentioned earlier in this chapter, the owner of a single-family residence may still be able to demonstrate that the lien against his or her property is invalid. One of the risks that an owner takes in contracting to have improvements done on his or her property is that the general contractor (the person with whom the owner has a direct contract) might take the owner's money and not pay the subcontractors. The subcontractors may then turn around and place liens on the owner's property because they were not paid by the general contractor. Without the statute discussed below, an owner could therefore pay twice for the same work. The Colorado legislature has seen fit, however, to protect the owner from just these circumstances.

Colorado law provides that with respect to a single-family dwelling, an owner who can demonstrate that he has paid the full amount due to the general contractor, including any amounts due for change orders, has a complete defense against any lien placed on the property by a subcontractor or a material supplier who has not been paid for the services rendered on that project.[18] In effect, the legislature has determined that where the owner can prove he has paid the full amount of the contractual price that he agreed to pay for a home to be constructed, the owner is not liable to a subcontractor to pay twice for the same work. The effect of the law is to force the subcontractor to look to the general contractor rather than to the owner to collect the money that is alleged to be due.[19] The owner who can prove full payment of his contractual obligation can therefore avoid the lien of a subcontractor who is unpaid by the general contractor for work performed on the project.

An owner can also help himself avoid being placed in this situation by including a contractual provision that requires lien releases as a condition precedent to payment to the general contractor. The amount of a potential lien will increase as more labor, services, and materials are furnished by a particular contractor or subcontractor. It is important for an owner, therefore, to obtain from the contractor a partial release of lien equivalent to the amount being paid to the contractor with each pay request. This partial release of lien by the contractor should be a release of lien for the full amount of the money being received and expressly release the contractor's lien rights up through the date of the pending payment request. Similarly, the owner can demand of his contractor that the contractor not only provide his own partial lien release with each pay application but also partial lien releases from any subcontractors or material suppliers. The partial lien releases from the subcontractors should also be for the amount of money they have been paid and provide for a release of their lien rights through the date of the pending application for payment. Many potential lienors will resist providing these partial lien releases. It is a good idea, therefore, for the owner to provide in his contract with the contractor an express provision that requires the contractor to provide not only his own lien release but lien releases from each of his subcontractors and material suppliers as a specific condition precedent to receiving payment. The contract should go on to provide that the contractor will provide a final lien release from himself and from all subcontractors and material suppliers work-

ing on the job as a condition to receiving final payment for the job.

Once an owner has received all partial lien releases for an interim pay request or final lien releases for the final pay request, the owner can be assured that he has a good defense to a lien claimed by one who has already given his release.

A contractor, subcontractor, or material supplier can create a duty on the part of the owner or his lender to make sure that each payment made on the project is in fact disbursed to those persons entitled to payment. A potential lienor has the opportunity under the Colorado Mechanic's Lien Law to send a document titled "Notice to Disburser" to the person or entity who is disbursing the funds on a construction project. The disburser can be either the owner, the owner's lender, or an escrow agent whom the owner has chosen to administer the payments for the construction project. If the disburser receives a notice, that notice then creates a duty to that disburser to ascertain the amount due to the person sending the notice as of any disbursement date and to pay that amount directly to that person instead of paying it to the general contractor.[20] If the disburser fails to comply with this duty, then the disburser will be liable for payment to the person sending the notice if the contractor receiving the funds fails to pay that person.

IV. Removing or Defending Against the Lien Claim

An owner has a few alternatives that may provide leverage in demanding the removal of liens or providing a defense against a lien claim. Some of these alternatives are more appropriate in defending or a removing a lien where a lawsuit has already been commenced. Some alternatives may be more appropriate before a lawsuit is commenced. One cause of action arises by virtue of a particular statute previously mentioned, which provides that a general contractor holds funds received in trust for the payment of services on the particular job. Demanding records to determine compliance with this requirement may encourage a lienor to give up the fight before an action for breach of his statutory trust obligation is even commenced. Not only does a contractor who violates this provision subject himself to criminal law sanctions for theft but he also may be liable to the owner for damages in a civil lawsuit.[21]

An owner also has the opportunity to bond off a lien that is on his property, thus freeing his property for purposes of selling or refinancing. An owner may bond off a lien by filing a cash or surety bond with the clerk of the court in the county where the property is located. The amount of the bond will be 1.5 times the amount of the lien plus certain costs. Although this does not eliminate the lien claim, it removes the lien from the real property and places it on the bond. If a general contractor has allowed a lien to be placed on the property by one of his subcontractors, an owner can often successfully demand that the general contractor bond off the subcontractor's lien to keep the owner's property free from encumbrances. Indeed, it is a good idea for an owner to create a provision in his contract with the general contractor requiring the general contractor to bond off any liens from any of the general contractor's subcontractors or material suppliers.

If an owner encounters a lien that may be valid but is clearly claimed for an excessive amount, the owner has another available defense that could result in the total invalidity of the lien. If an owner can prove that a contractor, subcontractor, or material supplier has filed a lien for an amount greater than is due without a reasonable possibility that the amount is due and with knowledge that the amount claimed is greater than what is due, then the lienor suffers a penalty of forfeiting his entire lien and will additionally be liable for the owner's costs and attorney's fees in proving that the lien is excessive.[22]

Where an owner wishes to take the initiative in filing a lawsuit regarding an apparently invalid lien, at least two causes of action may be viable. First, Colorado law provides a specific procedure titled "Complaint for an Order to Show Cause." This procedure allows one to file a lawsuit that will result in an order demanding that the lienor appear and show cause as to why his or her lien should not be discharged. If the lienor fails to appear within twenty days after service, the court will enter an order automatically discharging the lien. If the lienor appears and shows sufficient cause, then the parties would proceed to argue the facts of the case in the context of the legal proceeding.[23] This particular course of action is probably most appropriate when the owner does not believe that the lienor will respond in a timely manner in an attempt to defend the legal sufficiency of his lien. If the lienor has already filed an action or is likely to do so, this procedure is not appropriate.

A second action that is available to contest a disputed lien is an action for slander of title. Colorado law provides that where a document has been recorded in the public records without justification, the owner is entitled to the actual damages suffered or damages in the amount of $1,000, whichever is greater, plus court costs and attorney's fees.[24] If an owner believes that an invalid lien has been placed against his property and the lienor refuses to remove the lien voluntarily, a slander of title action is a good tool to take the offensive against the invalid lien.

V. Summary

An owner or potential owner must certainly be wary of existing liens or potential liens that may encumber his or her property. Liens arising from construction-related services are called mechanic's liens. These liens represent a special right given by the Colorado legislature to contractors, subcontractors, material suppliers, and design professionals to enforce payment for their services. In order to take advantage of these rights, the lienor must specifically comply with certain stringent time requirements set forth in the law. The failure to comply with these time requirements will result in an otherwise valid lien being invalid.

Even where a lien is valid, however, a single-family-home owner may be able to avoid liability for a lien claim from a subcontractor or material supplier where the homeowner can demonstrate that he or she has satisfied all of the contractual obligations, including change orders, for the construction of the improvement. Certain clauses can be inserted in a construction contract between an owner and a general contractor to protect the owner. These clauses include but are certainly not limited to clauses requiring partial and final releases of lien and clauses requiring liens to be bonded off. It is highly recommended that an attorney be consulted by any homeowner prior to purchasing a property or contracting for the design or construction of a new home so that an appropriate contract can be created that anticipates and avoids many of the risks normally encountered in the construction process.

Finally, certain actions are available for a homeowner in attempting to defend or remove a lien. These actions include bonding off the lien, demanding certain accounting information from the contractor, contesting the contractor's lien as excessive, suing the lienor for slander of title, and suing the lienor for an order to show cause. These and other potential actions should be evaluated carefully by an owner working in consultation with competent legal counsel to determine the most appropriate course of action. Although one cannot protect oneself from all possible risks associated with purchasing or constructing a home, understanding the basic rules of the Colorado Mechanic's Lien Law should help homeowners and potential homeowners to identify the risk and therefore make an informed decision on the course of action most appropriate for their interests and objectives.

Notes

1. In some states, a lender would use a document called a mortgage instead of a deed of trust.

2. Many people consider a contractor or a general contractor to be the person who coordinates and supervises the construction of an entire project or entire home and a subcontractor to be a person who performs only some specific function in constructing a project or home. The true distinction between a contractor and a subcontractor in the context of the Colorado Mechanic's Lien Law, however, is that a contractor is any person who has a direct contract with the owner, and a subcontractor is any person who has a direct contract with the contractor but not with the owner.

3. C.R.S. §38-22-101(2) (1998).

4. C.R.S. §38-22-127(4) (1998).

5. C.R.S. §38-22-109(5) (1998).

6. *John F. Rice Lumber Company v. Chipeta Mining, Milling and Smelting Company*, 234 P. 1066 (Colo. 1925).

7. C.R.S. §38-22-109(3) (1998).

8. *Everitt Lumber Company v. Prudential Insurance Company of America*, 660 P.2d 925 (Colo. App. 1983).

9. *Weyerhauser Company v. Colorado Quality Research, Inc.*, 778 P.2d 290 (Colo. App. 1989).

10. C.R.S. §38-22-110 (1998).

11. C.R.S. §38-22-109(7) (1998).

12. *Western Elaterite Roofing Company v. Fisher*, 237 P. 19 (Colo. 1928).

13. *Lichty v. Houston Lumber Company*, 88 P. 846 (Colo. 1907).

14. *Boise-Payette Lumber Company v. Longwedel*, 295 P. 791 (Colo. 1930).

15. *Kaibab Lumber Company v. Osburne*, 464 P.2d 294 (Colo. 1970).

16. C.R.S. §38-22-109(10) (1998).

17. C.R.S. §38-22-125 (1998).

18. C.R.S. §38-22-102(3.5) (1998).

19. If the owner has contracted directly with someone who would typically be construed as a subcontractor in addition to the owner's contract with his or her general contractor, then the owner will have to demonstrate that he or she has satisfied all of his or her contractual obligations to all persons with whom he or she has a direct contract in order for this provision to apply.

20. C.R.S. §38-22-126(6) (1998).

21. *Alexander Company v. Packard*, 754 P.2d 780 (Colo. App. 1988).

22. C.R.S. §38-22-128 (1998).

23. C.R.S. §38-35-204 (1998).

24. C.R.S. §38-35-109 (1998).

Local Governments

Understanding Local Government Functions Makes Better Neighbors

You can't escape being affected by local government; wherever you live in Colorado you are within the jurisdiction of at least one, and often more than one, local government entity. Towns, cities, counties, and special districts have direct impacts on the ways we can use our land, what and where we build, how and when we vote, how much we are taxed, etc. These public organizations affect every one of us.

Often people seem to think of local government as something we can neither understand nor control. We do know that local governments collect taxes and provide services, but just as often you'll hear dissatisfaction with the level of taxes collected or the kinds of services provided. Perhaps a more constructive way to look at local government could be called the "local government game." Like any game, first you need to know why you'd want to play. Second, you need to know how you get into the game. Third, you need to know the rules of the game. Without this basic information, you won't know how to "win" the game. And, as the lottery slogan goes, you can't win if you don't play. Every rural citizen needs to understand the basics of how local governments function and how they go about making decisions because once you know the rules of the game you can interact intelligently and influence decisions.

Why would you want to play the local government game in the first place? There are two main reasons. First, you need to be able to defend yourself if local government wants something you don't want (for example, if government wants to take your land for a public purpose). Second, you may have an idea that would benefit you and your fellow citizens, so you need to know how to bring your idea to the attention of the right officials who make those kinds of decisions and to persuade them that your idea might make government better.

So how do you get in the game? To sit down at the table, you have to ante up your commitment to be a responsible citizen in three areas. First, take the time to become well informed about local issues, and then vote in all local elections and on the local ballot issues as well. It isn't reasonable to complain that a particular issue or person lost an election if you didn't vote.

Second, actively participate in the processes that help the elected officials make decisions that affect your area. You may not have the time or inclination to run for office yourself, but if you sit back and let others draft the local laws without your input, it's tough to complain that you weren't consulted. Essentially every public decision involves both oral and written comment prior to the elected (or appointed) official's decision. Your testimony is the information they need to make a decision that is in the overall best interest of the jurisdiction. Your input, and that of your neighbors, is the essential foundation for reasonable decisions.

Third, if you have the time and inclination, run for (or seek appointment to) some local government office. Local governments are always looking for good people to serve on commissions and committees or as employees. You can learn a lot and make a real impact by being willing to share your time for a while by representing the people of your area.

So after you've anted up your good citizenship, how do you know what the rules are? Read this section of this book. It provides basic information about how municipalities, counties, and special districts work in Colorado.

One term that is repeated throughout these chapters is the "police power" of the government. That sounds a lot worse than it is; in fact, the police power is quite benign and beneficial. Simply put, it means the power of the government to protect the health, safety, and, welfare of its citizens by preserving the public order, preventing conflicts of rights among citizens, and ensuring that citizens will be able to enjoy the rights conferred by the general laws.

Many people in Colorado live in incorporated towns or cities embedded in rural environments. Even if you don't live in town, you can bet you pay sales taxes, and possibly real property, personal property, and business taxes. Municipal governments have broad police power authority and affect rural citizens who do not even live within their boundaries. Municipalities offer many opportunities for citizens to have an influence on decisions that affect the entire community. **Barbara Green**'s chapter illustrates how a concerned citizen could interact with the basic functions of a municipal government to affect the outcomes of proposed development plans.

The other major local government entity that affects the everyday lives of rural residents is the county. All municipalities are also part of one of Colorado's sixty-three counties. These counties are the "unincorporated" areas outside our municipalities and are home to a large percentage of the population of Colorado. In recent times, many of the people who have moved to Colorado have not moved to our cities and towns but instead have sought out the unincorporated areas. Sometimes it's hard for county government to provide adequate services to its citizens because counties often have a smaller tax base than municipalities and therefore have lower operating budgets.

Land use issues may be the single most important cat-

egory of decisions that county governments have to make. Many conflicts arise as areas evolve from agricultural use into residential, commercial, and industrial uses. The governments themselves are "neighbors" in this process and must learn to objectively address conflicting issues and work toward solutions that may result in annexation or intergovernmental agreements. **Beth Whittier** provides an in-depth primer on county land use powers in Colorado.

If you live in rural Colorado, sooner or later you will probably need to know that local governments have very direct power over your land and how you use it. **Erin Johnson**'s chapter on takings, exactions and impact fees, eminent domain, and growth management tools provides an introduction to several land use regulatory tools that are used to implement government policies designed to protect the health, safety, and welfare of citizens. Actions taken in support of these kinds of policies are sometimes said to derive from the government's police power. Many laws are based on this broad and powerful legal tenet and can easily be perceived as being "against" the rights of private citizens and property owners. Exercising the police power is a fundamental function of local governments, including towns, cities, counties, and federally based agencies, precisely because they have the responsibility to protect all of their citizens.

After you've put up your commitment and learned the rules, you're ready to play. Pick an issue you care about, know a lot about, or want to learn a lot about, and get out there and contribute to your community.

20

Understanding Municipalities

Barbara J. B. Green, *Attorney at Law*

Imagine that you are a resident of Rockledge, Colorado. You have read in the local newspaper that Rockledge is considering approving a rezoning request for a new shopping center directly across the street from your house proposed by a company known as Shop 'n' Drop. The shopping center will include the Toast of the Town Tanning Salon, Curl Up and Dye Beauty Shoppe, Hardsell Hardware, and Perky Pat's, a coffee shop catering to teens. You are really worried about this proposal because it will create traffic, dust, noise, litter, and loiterers. Not only that, it will also ruin your view of the mountains. You've talked to your neighbors, and they are worried too, but they are sure that there is no way to fight city hall. So what can you do, if anything?

I. Who Is in Charge Here, Anyway?

Municipal government is probably the most responsive level of government there is in Colorado. If there is any hope of having an influence on governmental decisions, this is the place to try. Although there are several different forms of municipalities within the state, they are all run by boards or councils made up of community residents who have been elected to office without assistance from political parties. These people are in close contact with the citizens they serve and have been granted substantial authority to address a wide variety of community concerns that go far beyond street maintenance and dog control.

The elected officials are where the buck stops in local government. In statutory towns, the governing body is called a board of trustees; in cities, it is known as the city council. But regardless of the name, the governing body sets the policy direction of the community, which is carried out by the staff. Statutory towns are required to appoint or provide for the election of municipal officers, including a clerk, treasurer, and town attorney. By a majority vote of the town board, the mayor, clerk, treasurer, or any member of the town board may be removed from office after a hearing.

The election of town board and city council members, as well as their terms of office, is set by state statute and municipal charter. All municipal elected officials in Colorado are subject to constitutional recall provisions. To recall a member of the board or council, it is first necessary to circulate a petition signed by the number of voters stipulated by state statute or the municipal charter. If the clerk deems the petition to be sufficient, the clerk must file the petition with the town board or city council. If the elected official whose recall is sought does not resign, then the recall question is submitted to the voters at a municipal election.

Some Colorado towns have an appointed administrator who is charged with carrying out day-to-day municipal functions, and most cities, with the exception of Denver, have a city manager who acts as the chief executive officer of the municipal corporation with the power to hire and fire municipal employees. Where there is no manager or administrator, either the town board or the mayor is responsible for day-to-day management. But deciding how the community will be taxed and how the public's money is spent; passing laws and regulations to protect the public health, safety and welfare; setting policies regarding the enforcement of those laws and regulations; and reviewing and approving important land use matters are all functions of the governing body.

The governing body is also responsible for "legislative" functions, that is, passing laws known as ordinances. There are two ways ordinances can be developed. One way, and the most common, is for the staff and council to develop an ordinance to address a particular problem or subject. The ordinance is then considered at public hearings and adopted by the council or board. Another way that an ordinance may come about is through a process known as an initiative. This process allows citizens to petition the governing body to ask that a proposed ordinance be enacted. If the governing body declines to enact the initiated ordinance, then the voters are allowed to decide whether the ordinance should become law. Similarly, if citizens do not like an ordinance that was adopted by the governing body, they may ask that the ordinance be referred to the voters in a process known as referendum.

In most municipalities, all ordinances are organized by topic in a document known as a municipal code. Typically all of the regulations dealing with zoning and land use are in separate documents known as zoning and subdivision regulations. Sometimes these regulations are combined into a single document known as the land use code. Ordinances may cover any topic necessary to carrying out municipal duties.

State law requires a statutory municipality to determine the time and place of regular municipal meetings. The method for establishing the time and place for city council meetings in home-rule cities is governed by their charter. Municipalities prepare an agenda that is available to the public in advance of the meeting. The agenda is available from the town or city clerk. There are two types of meetings in which a governing body may take official action: regular meetings and special meetings. All meetings are required to be open to the public. Under certain circumstances, which are spelled out in a state law known as the Public Meetings Law, portions of a meeting may be closed to the public. These sessions are called executive sessions. Generally, executive sessions are allowed to discuss pending litigation and negotiations. Even where a topic is appropriate for executive session, no final policy decision, rule regulation or ordinance, or other formal action can be taken in an executive session. Decisions made in violation of this requirement are void. The public is usually given two opportunities to speak at a council or board meeting: at a portion of a meeting designated as a public hearing and during any time on the agenda specified for public comment. Usually the governing body will set a time limit on public testimony or comment at the hearing.

Here in Rockledge, the first thing you need to do is find out the names of the city council members and learn whether the members are elected at large or by districts, whether there is a manager or administrator, and when and where the city council meets. A good place to start is with a phone call to Vicki Goldman, the city clerk.

II. Finding Out Who Knows What

Every municipality has a person known as the clerk. Even in cities where there is a city manager in charge of municipal management, often the city clerk is hired and fired by and reports directly to the city council. Despite the title, this position is not a clerical one. The clerk is the official record keeper for the government. All public records, with some exceptions, must be made available for inspection by any person at reasonable times. This does not mean that the clerk has to provide a copy of all requested documents, but the clerk must allow the public to come in and look. It is perfectly appropriate to charge the public for copies. Vicki tells you that the city councilperson who has responsibility for your neighborhood is Morton Bertaux, that a city council discussion of the shopping center has been scheduled within the next month, and that no ordinances regarding the rezoning have been proposed. She also tells you that Rockledge has the council-manager form of government, and she gives you the name of the city manager, Ray "Rock" Merkel. You borrow Vicki's phone to place a call to your councilperson, Morton, and pick up a copy of the municipal charter.

Morton Bertaux is cordial but cannot provide you with a lot of information. First, he explains that he cannot discuss the pros and cons of the shopping center because he must review the rezoning request when it is brought before city council. He informs you that any comments you wish to make need to be made at the rezoning public hearing. Second, he does not really know a lot about this proposal because rezoning applications are initially reviewed by the staff before the council learns much about them. He does tell you that he believes in a policy on new development as "managed growth" and that he intends to apply the zoning-code requirements vigorously. At this point, he recommends that you stop by to visit Ray "Rock" Merkel, the city manager.

III. Municipal Management

In a city like Rockledge where the council-manager form of government is in effect, the manager is analogous to the chief executive officer of a corporation, and the city council is like the board of directors. The city council is charged with policy-making responsibility, and the manager carries out those policies; the manager is responsible for hiring, firing, and directing activities of the staff. In statutory towns, the manager is usually called a town administrator and may or may not have authority for hiring and firing employees. In small communities, the mayor is often the administrative official in charge of day-to-day municipal operations;

sometimes communities can afford no staff at all. In most municipalities, there is a department of public works that oversees the construction and maintenance of streets and other public facilities; a police department responsible for law enforcement; a utility department that may be responsible for water, sewer, and electric service; a finance department that handles accounts payable and receivable, payroll, and other accounting and bookkeeping functions; and possibly a building inspector, if not a building department, that takes care of the building-permit process.

In your meeting with the city manager, you learn that Rockledge is a full-service city providing an amazing array of services to the community. And according to Rock, the community development department is responsible for land use mapping, public information, long-range master planning, zoning and rezoning requests, subdivision review, and similar land use functions. There also is a citizen board known as the planning commission that makes policy recommendations on certain land use matters and that will hold a public hearing to consider the Shop 'n' Drop application later this month. He suggests that you make a visit to Herman Hess, the community development director.

IV. Boards and Commissions

Municipal governments frequently turn to a number of citizen boards and commissions, appointed by the governing body, to assist in recommending policy and making administrative decisions. Some boards or commissions are created by resolution or ordinance; others may be required by state statute. Common boards and commissions include planning or zoning commissions, boards of adjustment, liquor licensing authorities, architectural review boards, and similar groups. For statutory towns, the membership, qualifications, and powers of many boards or commissions are established by state statute, whereas in home-rule cities, the charter may provide the basis for these organizations. Like the meetings held by the city council, the meetings of boards and commissions must be open to the public. In Colorado, the busiest of the citizen boards and commissions is usually the planning commission.

The planning commission is responsible for adopting a master plan, sometimes called a comprehensive plan, that is submitted to the town board or city council for approval. Typically, the plan is not adopted until the municipality has held public meetings and workshops to gather input from the community. Once a master plan has been adopted, nothing can be authorized or constructed in the municipality until the location, extent, and character of the pro-posal has been approved by the planning commission. A master plan is implemented through zoning regulations and subdivision regulations. In most municipalities, the planning commission hears initial land use requests and then makes a recommendation to the city council to approve, deny, or approve with conditions the particular zoning or subdivision proposal.

V. So How Do They Make Land Use Decisions Around Here?

You learn from the Rockledge community development director, Herman Hess, that the site of the proposed Shop 'n' Drop is zoned residential and that he has received a complete application for rezoning the property to allow commercial uses. Herman tells you that the planning commission will consider whether the rezoning request is consistent with the master plan. Looking at the master-plan map, you discover that the property is designated for commercial uses, and your heart sinks. Does this mean that the Shop 'n' Drop is free to go ahead without any other requirements? Herman assures you that the master plan is an advisory document and that there are many more "hoops" for the developer to jump though before the project can begin. In fact, before the rezoning will be approved, the project must demonstrate compliance with certain standards and criteria ensuring compatibility with neighboring properties. And before actual development of the shopping center can begin, site-planning criteria are applied to minimize impacts such as noise, traffic, erosion, drainage, and parking.

Herman recommends that you participate in the planning commission hearing by describing your concerns about the shopping center's impacts on you and your neighbors. He also advises you that the final decision on the rezoning request will be made by the city council after another public hearing, where you can also participate. Herman assures you that the public hearings are fairly informal, but that you will probably be given a time limit for the presentation by you and the neighbors. He advises that it would be best to base your presentation on whether the Shop 'n' Drop rezoning satisfies the criteria in the zoning code for rezoning requests. But Hess also warns you that the Shop 'n' Drop has a lot of support because of the revenue it is likely to generate for the city. He suggests that you touch base with Sharon Davis, in the finance department, to gain a better understanding of the economic issues. He also indicates that there is an opening on the planning commission right now and hands you an application.

VI. How Do They Get My Money, and Where Does It Go?

All municipalities are empowered to levy property taxes and sales and use taxes. The Colorado Constitution, state statutes, city charters, and local ordinances all influence the nature and scope of this taxing authority. The amendment to the Colorado Constitution known as the taxpayers' bill of rights (TABOR) limits the amount of tax revenue that can be collected and spent in a year and specifies when an election will be necessary if the government desires to exceed the limitations. Under TABOR, any increase in the rate of taxes and certain spending increases must be approved by the electors. Statutory municipalities may assess only the types of taxes that are spelled out in state law. These include property taxes, sales and use taxes, occupation taxes, and special assessments. Home-rule cities have more flexibility in the types of taxes that they may levy.

In most Colorado municipalities, sales and use taxes are the primary source of municipal revenue. Sales or use taxes are collected by retailers at the time of purchase of certain goods, services, and equipment. Property taxes are actually collected by the county, along with county taxes, school district taxes, and taxes for other special districts. You may be surprised to learn that the municipal share of your property tax bill actually is very small when compared to the extent of the services such as snow removal, street maintenance, or police protection that are provided by the municipality. Large portions of property taxes go to the county, the school district, and other special governmental districts. Recently there has been a trend toward reliance on service charges and user fees to finance municipal services, the idea being that the user should be charged for the services received. Examples of these fees and charges are fees to use recreational facilities, building-permit fees, and water and sewer charges.

In your meeting with Sharon, she explains that the land use patterns in Rockledge have resulted in too much residential development. According to Sharon, the amount of revenue collected by the municipality from property taxes on single-family houses is not enough to cover a lot of the necessary services. The reason that Shop 'n' Drop is getting so much support is that it will provide Rockledge with much-needed sales tax revenue so the city can provide additional services. Sharon explains that unlike the federal government, municipal governments cannot operate under deficit conditions. The annual budget, approved by the city council, must be balanced. Sharon notes that municipal governments hold extensive budget hearings, and it is during this process that revenues are allocated to different functions and funds are appropriated. Although municipalities can borrow money, borrowing authority is limited by state and federal constitutional limitations as well as statutory restrictions. Cities and towns can issue bonds to finance long-term projects or capital investments, but day-to-day operations typically are not considered appropriate for bond financing. Sharon observes that the police department has been operating with too few officers to handle the recent increase in crime in Rockledge. You find this comment interesting, considering that Shop 'n' Drop will no doubt result in the need for additional law enforcement. You begin to wonder whether the city council and the planning commission will make an impartial decision about the rezoning request. Do they have a conflict of interest because of financial considerations? Sharon suggests that you stop by to see the city attorney to discuss the rules that apply to municipal decisions of the council and planning commission.

VII. So What Is a Conflict of Interest?

The general public often wonders why citizens run for city council or seek to be appointed to boards and commissions. Often there is an impression that members of elected or appointed boards and commissions must be receiving benefits from the position because they generally receive little or no compensation for their duties. Besides, they are usually active members of the community with ties to many different businesses and activities. But in reality, government officials are subject to a labyrinth of statutory or charter constraints designed to ensure that their decisions are made in the best interest of the community instead of being influenced by self interest.

The state law requires any member of the governing body of a city or town that has a personal or private interest in a matter proposed or pending before that body to disclose the interest and not vote on the matter. They must also refrain from influencing the decision of other members. Even where a member has a personal or financial interest in the matter, the member may vote if his participation is necessary for a quorum and he discloses the interest to the Colorado secretary of state. In addition to these disclosure requirements that apply to city councils and town boards, there are other ethical rules that apply to local governmental officials. The term "local governmental official" includes members of boards and commissions in addition to members of the governing body. Under the ethical rules, a local government official may not disclose or use confidential information acquired in the course of his official duties to further his own financial interests or accept certain gifts or economic benefits of "substantial value." Finally, members of boards and commissions who receive no compensation other than per diem or expenses may not perform an "official act" that may have a direct economic benefit on a business or other undertaking in which the member has a direct or substantial financial interest.

Geraldine Doll, the city attorney, reminds you that state laws regarding conflicts of interest are in addition to provisions of the Rockledge charter that require a member of the city council or the planning commission to refrain from voting on an issue if the member would stand to gain or lose money as a result of the decision. She adds that constitutional principles of due process further constrain the city council or planning commission while they are making land use decisions that involve a zoning application or other permit request affecting individual property rights. These decisions are known as "quasi-judicial" because the decision-makers are acting like a judge and jury, finding facts and making decisions that affect individual rights. All quasi-judicial decisions require fundamental fairness. An application may be denied only if there is competent evidence on the record that demonstrates that the application fails to satisfy the applicable regulations. Armed with this understanding of the quasi-judicial process, you purchase a copy of the Land Use Code so that you can begin a review of the rezoning regulations. You next arrange for a meeting with the chief of police to get a handle on the impacts to law enforcement that might be caused by the Shop 'n' Drop proposal.

VIII. It's a Crime

In statutory municipalities, law enforcement is carried out by a marshal or chief of police who often reports directly to the governing body. Home-rule cities typically appoint a chief of police to oversee law enforcement. Municipal police are charged with enforcing certain municipal ordinances and state criminal laws. Among other powers, police have the authority to make arrests, issue citations for violations of traffic laws and other violations, and serve summonses requiring people to appear in court.

An important element of municipal law enforcement is the Municipal Court system. By state statute, the govern-

ing body must establish a Municipal Court to hear and try only alleged violations of municipal ordinances. Other violations are handled in County Court or state District Court. The statutes also provide for the qualifications, appointment, and removal of a municipal judge. In home-rule cities, the charter may spell out the structure and functions of the court system.

The police department of Rockledge is very sophisticated, employing state-of-the-art equipment and advanced technology. The chief is glad to meet with you to show you the reams of crime data that have been generated over the last few years. Luckily, he knows exactly how many hours of law enforcement effort will be required to address a shopping center like the proposed Shop 'n' Drop. He is very concerned that there simply are not enough officers to do the job. It isn't only crime to think about, he adds. There also are issues such as weed control and other code enforcement responsibilities that will be triggered by Shop 'n' Drop. He reminds you that dogs in Rockledge must be licensed and on a leash at all times. You thank the chief for his time but decline his invitation to participate in the ride-along program. Your hands are full at this point just trying to digest everything that you have learned today. At this point you are anxious to get home and begin preparing your presentation for the Shop 'n' Drop planning commission hearing.

IX. Conclusion

Colorado municipal governments have responsibility for most of the functions that directly affect day-to-day life in an incorporated community. Because of their structure and purpose, they are able to work properly only if municipal residents and property owners take the time to participate either by voting, attending meetings of the governing body, participating in public hearings on matters of concern, or communicating directly with elected officials. With a little bit of research into the form of government under which your community operates and an understanding of where decisions are made, you will discover a wide variety of opportunities to influence local government decisions. It is amazing how responsive even the largest municipal government can be if you are a good neighbor.

21

A Primer on Colorado Counties' Land Use Powers

Beth A. Whittier, *Attorney at Law*

Colorado is committed to the local control of land use decision-making. One of the most important players in the land use process is the local government's planning department. This department is generally responsible for the processing and review of a land use proposal, pursuant to the local government's land use regulations, and the formulation of recommendations to the local decision-making bodies. A property owner interested in changing the use of his or her property or in another's proposed land use would be smart to consult with the local planning department to determine the applicable land use procedures and requirements. You need to know the rules to play the game. Continual cooperation and establishment of a professional working relationship with the local planning department can also be beneficial in proceeding through the often convoluted review and public hearing processes used by local government.

Colorado is presently divided into sixty-three counties. With the exception of the City and County of Denver, counties have general land use regulatory authority over all lands within their respective boundaries that are not located within an incorporated municipality. Colorado counties possess only those regulatory powers expressly conferred upon them by the state constitution and statutes and such incidental implied powers as are reasonably necessary to carry out their express powers. Colorado counties possess no inherent powers. Express powers granted to counties include the ability to exercise traditional land use regulatory tools, such as zoning, subdivision, and building regulations, as well as limited express and implied grants of regulatory authority in the more innovative land

use areas such as impact fees, growth management systems, and transfer of development rights.

By state law, a county is required only to enact subdivision regulations. Hence, many unincorporated areas within Colorado do not have "master plans" and are not zoned or governed by building-code regulations. It is essential to ascertain the specific county's land use restrictions and the development potentials of one's property and surrounding areas prior to proceeding with a land use proposal.

This article provides a general overview of the various statutory land use powers delegated to Colorado counties as well as some as helpful pointers in pursuing or objecting to a land use matter or development proposal.[1]

I. General Legal Principles

State Delegation of County Land Use Powers

Counties do not have the unfettered discretion to regulate and control land uses within their respective boundaries. The land use regulatory authority of a county emanates from the police power of the state through statutory and constitutional delegation. A land use regulation exceeding the authority granted by the state will be held invalid.[2] A county land use regulation may coexist with state regulation on the same land use matter so long as the county regulation is not in conflict with or preempted by state statute.[3]

A county's exercise of this police power in the enactment of land use controls or in decisions enforcing such controls must bear a rational relationship to the health, safety, and welfare of the community.[4] Additionally, any delegation and subsequent implementation must contain sufficient standards and procedural safeguards to ensure that any action taken by a county in response to a land use proposal will be rational and consistent and that judicial review of the county's action will be available and effective. At a minimum, a county's land use regulations, when coupled with the procedural protections required by state statutes, must be sufficiently detailed to provide all users and potential users of land with notice of the particular standards and requirements imposed by the county for land use approvals.[5] In other words, a county cannot haphazardly and on a case-by-case basis impose review standards and conditions on a development proposal. The requirements must be provided for by the enabling state statutes and the county's implementing land use regulations, must bear a rational relationship to the general community needs, and must bear a rational relationship to or be reasonably necessitated by the specific land use proposal.

Nature of the County's Land Use Action

Different review standards and procedures may be applied depending on the nature of the request being considered. Land use actions are generally characterized as "quasi-legislative" or "quasi-judicial." A quasi-legislative action, such as a county's enactment or amendment of land use regulations, is prospective in nature, is of general application, and requires the balancing of questions of judgment and discretion.[6] Quasi-legislative actions are presumed to be constitutional and will be upheld in the absence of evidence beyond a reasonable doubt demonstrating that they do not foster legitimate governmental purposes.[7] In the quasi-legislative context, individual public officials have greater flexibility than in the quasi-judicial context in considering evidence outside the formal public hearing process, such as local constituency concerns and desires, and in taking a prior public stance. If the final determination is supported by competent evidence in the record, the motivations actuating the public official are irrelevant.[8]

A quasi-judicial action, such as an individual development proposal, generally involves a determination of the rights, duties, or obligations of specific individuals, based on the application of presently existing legal standards or policy considerations to past or present facts, developed at a hearing conducted for the purpose of resolving the particular interests in question.[9] During the 1999 legislative session, Senate Bill 218 was enacted, which codifies certain constitutionally based standards that have been established and applied by the federal and state courts in reviewing a

local government's individual land use decisions. In imposing conditions upon the granting of land use approvals, such as the dedication of real property or the payment of money, a county must now show that there is an essential nexus between the dedication or payment and a legitimate local government interest and that the dedication or payment is roughly proportional in both nature and extent to the impact of the proposed use or development of such property.

Additionally, a county cannot impose any discretionary condition upon a land use approval unless the condition is based upon duly adopted standards that are sufficiently specific to ensure that the condition is imposed in a rational and consistent manner. Applying these standards, a land use decision of a local governmental body will be upheld unless there is no competent or substantial evidence in the record to support it. This judicial standard of review has been interpreted to mean that based on a review of the record in the light most favorable to the local government, there does not exist a sufficient amount of evidence to support its decision.[10]

A heightened standard is also imposed on local governmental officials when acting in their quasi-judicial capacity. Although local public officials are cloaked with a presumption of integrity, honesty, and impartiality in serving in a quasi-judicial capacity, they are also required to provide minimum due process in ensuring a basic fairness in the public hearing procedures and decision-making processes employed in determining the rights and obligations of an individual.[11] These due-process safeguards require advanced notice and an adequate opportunity to be heard by all parties before an impartial and unbiased public body, as well as the assurance that the action taken will be based on the evidence and facts brought forward in the public hearing process, to the exclusion of other matters of which the individual decision-makers might have outside knowledge or on which they may have taken a prior public stance.[12]

Prior to taking action on an individual land use proposal, a local decision-making official should avoid: (1) ex parte contacts with either the applicant, supporters, or objectors; (2) advocating a position; (3) attending or participating in local community forums or on-site visits; or (4) otherwise conducting an independent assessment and review of facts and evidence outside the local government's formal public hearing process. Likewise, a property owner interested in an individual land use proposal should avoid inappropriate contact with any member of the local governing bodies reposed with the responsibility to make land use decisions. Although prior contact may be considered a politically acceptable and generally recognized practice in the local community, a subsequent legal challenge, if sustained, will only unjustly delay and potentially overturn the local action and could subject the locale to otherwise unnecessary economic losses and public expense. A property owner, whether advocating or opposing a land use proposal, is best served by adequately preparing for and actively participating in the local government's public review and hearing processes in accordance with the local government's land use regulations.

Administrative Interpretation

Property owners are encouraged to seek initial advice from county land use officials in pursuing or objecting to a land use proposal, but they should be cautious in relying on such advice to the exclusion of conducting their own independent review and investigation. Administrative interpretation of a land use regulation by county officials charged with administration and enforcement is generally entitled to deferential weight and will not be overturned on judicial review unless there is no competent evidence to support the county official's decision or it is determined that the county official has misconstrued or misapplied the law.[13] However, unequivocal reliance on a county official's representation may be misplaced and unjustified. The Colorado appellate courts have been hesitant to prevent, or equitably estop, a local government such as a county from denying liability based on a property owner's asserted reliance on the local government's dissemination of incorrect information.[14]

A property owner, in seeking advice from a county planning department, should: (1) fully disclose all relevant facts necessary for the county land use official to accurately and completely assess and address the issues presented; (2) obtain all county land use regulations pertinent to the county official's interpretation; (3) inquire as to whether any other county, state, or other local governmental agencies should also be consulted; and (4) obtain written confirmation of the county official's representations based on the facts presented. The property owner should also independently verify the bases for the administrative interpretation and whether the county's land use regulations provide any further review and appeal procedures in contesting such administrative interpretation.

II. Traditional Land Use Powers

The board of county commissioners of each respective county in Colorado is directed to provide for the physical development of the unincorporated territory within its county. In fulfilling these statutory land use responsibilities, a county board is required to appoint a planning commission for at least the purpose of adopting subdivision regulations. County planning commissions also generally serve as an advisory and recommending agency to the county board in a broad range of land use matters. Counties with zoning regulations also have a board of adjustment to hear appeals and consider variances from the strict application or enforcement of the zoning regulations.[15] If a county board has enacted building-code regulations, it may provide for a board of review to hear appeals and consider variances from their application or enforcement.[16]

Master Plans

A county, through its planning commission, is authorized, but not required, to make and adopt a master plan for the physical development of the unincorporated territory of the county. The master plan may consist of one comprehensive document encompassing the entire county or several plans encompassing portions of the county or addressing one or more specific planning areas such as transportation, flood control, drainage, etc., throughout the county.[17]

A master plan is the county planning commission's recommendation of the most desirable use of land and serves as a guide to development rather than an instrument to control land use. The master plan itself is only one source of comprehensive planning. It is generally held to be advisory only and is neither the equivalent of zoning nor binding upon the zoning discretion of the board of county commissioners.[18] A landowner disenchanted with a purely advisory master plan has no legal right or standing to challenge the same in court unless and until the county applies the master plan as a restrictive limit on development.[19]

Zoning

A county planning commission may develop a zoning plan for all or portions of the unincorporated county.[20] Upon adoption by the board of county commissioners, land uses within such zoned areas will be either prohibited, permitted subject to conditions or restrictions, or permitted without conditions. A zoning plan and regulations will generally specify the allowed uses, such as residential, commercial, industrial, and agricultural, in each zone; the intensity or density of such uses, such as minimum lot sizes, number of dwelling units per acre, or floor-area ratio; and the allowed bulk of buildings on land, such as building height limitations, lot coverage requirements, building setback requirements, or yard requirements. Enactment of a comprehensive zoning plan and regulations is quasi-legislative in nature.

Land use changes that are not consistent with a county's zoning plan or regulations will, in most instances, require rezoning approval by the board of county commissioners in its quasi-judicial capacity. The general standard for granting a rezoning request is whether the proposed rezoning is in compliance with the county's master plan, in which case the rezoning need only relate to the general welfare of the community. Where the rezoning is in violation of the county's master plan, the applicant must show a change in the conditions of the neighborhood to support the rezoning request.[21] Rezoning has also been upheld owing to a mistake in the original zoning or based upon a showing by the applicant that, under present zoning, the applicant has been denied all reasonable economic or beneficial use of his property.

Conditional or Special Uses

A conditional or special use is a use that is permitted within a zoned area, but because of the possibility that the permitted use could become incompatible in certain respects with other uses within the zone, special permission is required before the land may be put to that use. The issuance of a conditional or special use permit creates no greater rights in the property owner than he would have possessed had he developed in conformance with any other use permitted within the zone; rather, such issuance only represents a determination as to the subject property that a use additional to those generally permitted will be allowed.[22] A county board, in its quasi-judicial capacity, may impose reasonable conditions on the granting of a conditional or special use permit designed to carry out the purposes for which the permit requirements were imposed.[23] Such conditions must be based on established criteria and standards and sufficiently detailed to provide affected parties with notice of the particular standards and requirements imposed by the county on its land use approval.[24]

Accessory Uses

An accessory use is a use customarily incident to the principal use and so necessary or commonly to be expected in conjunction with the principal use that it cannot be supposed the zoning regulations were intended to prevent it. An accessory use is one that is deemed to be permitted by implication where the zoning regulations are silent on the particular use. A use expressly prohibited in the zoning regulations cannot be an accessory or incidental use.[25]

Variances

A variance is an authorization for the construction or maintenance of a structure, or for the establishment or maintenance of a use of land, that is prohibited by zoning. A variance is authorized where the strict application of the zoning regulations would result in peculiar and exceptional practical difficulties to, or exceptional and undue hardship upon, the property owner, and the granting of a variance would not be a substantial detriment to the public good or substantially impair the intent and purpose of the zoning plan and regulations.

Variance requests are generally determined by the county board of adjustment in its quasi-judicial capacity.[26] An applicant has the burden of showing that the need for the variance is not self-created and is of a type peculiar to the applicant and not shared by others.[27] The grant of a variance runs with the land and is not a personal license given to the property owner.

Nonconforming Uses

The use of land or structure preexisting and lawful at the time of the adoption or amendment of a zoning regulation may be continued even though such use does not conform with the provisions of the current zoning regulations.[28] The board of county commissioners may provide for the restoration, reconstruction, extension, or substitution of nonconforming uses upon such terms and conditions as set forth in the zoning regulations, and they may legally restrict the right to extend or enlarge a nonconforming use.[29] The county board may also provide for the termination of nonconforming uses through abandonment by specifying the period in which nonconforming uses shall be required to cease or by providing a formula whereby the compulsory termination of a nonconforming use may be so fixed as to allow for the recovery or amortization of the investment in the nonconformance.[30] A prior nonconforming use runs with the land, and the mere transfer of the land neither terminates the right to continue the nonconforming use nor constitutes an unlawful extension of the use.[31]

Subdivision

For county purposes, subdivision is defined as a division of land into two or more parcels, separate interests, or interests in common and specifically applies to multiple dwelling units. The enactment of subdivision regulations has been mandatory for counties since 1972.[32]

County subdivision regulations are limited in application to developments involving the division of land and thus may not apply to large industrial developments, power plants, road construction, pipeline laying, water impoundment, ski-area development, park development, and similar activities. In addition, county subdivision statutes provide several statutory exemptions that cannot be regulated by the county, the most notable of which are divisions resulting in parcels of land in excess of 35 acres.[33] A board of county commissioners is authorized, pursuant to regulation, to additionally exempt any division of land upon a determination that such division is not within the purposes of the subdivision statutes; to establish a subdivision exemption platting process for the purpose of correcting legal descriptions of unplatted or irregular parcels or parcels platted prior to the establishment of current subdivision regulations; and to adopt a rural land use process for cluster development.[34]

Zoning and subdivision regulations are separate and distinct legislation and serve different purposes. Zoning presupposes that the needs of the community have become sufficiently crystallized to delineate permissible and impermissible uses, building location, and density of individual properties. Subdivision regulations are general and inclusive and are designed to govern the layout and platting of the subdivision. The primary role of subdivision control is to prevent ill-conceived development that is beyond the reach of essential public services and to ensure that the subdivision will not be detrimental to the community.[35]

The subdivision statutes require county quasi-judicial review in three stages: sketch plan, preliminary plan, and final plat. The subdivision review process and regulations address and control such matters as lot size and shape, site characteristics of the property, development layout, and technical standards for the construction of required public infrastructure.[36] The county's review and approval processes must be conducted pursuant to duly adopted county regulations that are available to the applicant prior to commencement of the subdivision process. Any county denial of a subdivision proposal is based on the applicant's failure to conform to the requirements of the county's regulations and is supported by written findings specifying the regulatory provisions the subdivision plat, plan, or agreement failed to address or satisfy.[37] State law also provides an administrative dispute-resolution process and expedited public hearing requirements on behalf of a subdivision applicant.[38]

A board of county commissioners may require appropriate financial guarantees from the subdivider, generally by way of a subdivision improvements agreement, to ensure that the county is protected against the failure of the subdivider to provide adequate infrastructure investments that might later become public expense.[39] Further, a county may require the dedication, or payment of a fee in lieu thereof, for the construction of public infrastructure, facilities, and improvements, such as schools, parks, open space, recreational facilities, and drainage, reasonably necessitated by the subdivision.[40]

Utility Location Approval

State law provides an exception to full compliance with a county's subdivision and zoning regulations for the location of a road, park, or other public way, ground, or space; a public building or structure; or a public utility, whether publicly or privately owned. The governing body proposing the public project location is required to submit the proposal to the county planning commission and, in certain instances, to the board of county commissioners, the disapproval of which can be overruled by the governing body of the proposal or, in the case of a utility, by the Colorado Public Utilities Commission.[41]

Building Code Regulations

A board of county commissioners may adopt building-code regulations in all or portions of the unincorporated areas of the county.[42] Building-code regulations shall apply only to new buildings or structures or substantial improvements to existing buildings or structures and shall be uniform for each class of dwelling, building, or structure. The county may exempt from such regulations buildings or structures used for the sole purpose of providing shelter for agricultural implements, farm products, livestock, or poultry.

Building codes, although they may have land use consequences, are not generally treated as land use control devices because the primary purpose of such codes is to address matters of construction and maintenance, not land or the relationship between land and buildings.[43] A county's duty to grant a building permit is mandatory if the application is in conformance with both the county's zoning and building regulations.[44]

III. Nontraditional Land Use Powers

In addition to traditional land use powers, Colorado has specific enabling legislation allowing counties to implement planned unit development (PUD) regulations, to establish vested rights, to cooperate and contract with other local governments for the joint exercise of land use planning and regulation, and to regulate designated matters of state interest. The state has also provided counties with broad authority to plan for and regulate land use matters of specific local concern that are not otherwise addressed by state law. Many Colorado counties have been innovative in utilizing this broad grant of authority, in conjunction with their other land use powers, to regulate in such nontraditional land use areas as merger by continuity, growth management, transmountain water diversion projects, utility location, development of federal and state lands, moratoria, transfer of development rights, impact fees, overlay or floating zones, and oil and gas development and operations. A county's enactment of these more novel land use approaches is not without statutory limitations and requirements.

Planned Unit Developments

PUD regulations may be separate regulations or they may be part of the county's zoning regulations, subdivision regulations, or both.[45] PUDs are based on the premise that a county can offer some flexibility in its zoning and subdivision standards in exchange for a developer's adherence to a master development plan previously approved by the county. Their hallmark is the integration of diverse uses and density patterns within the tract commensurate with the needs and welfare of the public.

Because PUD regulations vest broad discretion in the county, such regulations are required to contain sufficient standards against which the county's action may be measured. At a minimum, PUD applications must meet all the standards, procedures, and conditions of the county's zoning regulations.[46] The primary requirements for the establishment of a PUD are that the PUD will be compatible with the existing zones from which it is carved, will be in harmony with the surrounding neighborhood, will not jeopardize or reduce zoning standards in the area, and will promote the general welfare of the community.[47] A PUD cannot be established without the written consent of all of the property owners to be included within the PUD. Furthermore, a county cannot limit development exclusively to PUD districts.

Vested Property Rights

A vested property right is, in simple terms, the right to complete land use development or construction in accordance with the terms of previous governmental approvals, regardless of the subsequent enactment of land use regulations precluding or otherwise altering such prior land use actions. A statutory vested property right shall be deemed established in Colorado with respect to any real property upon the approval, or conditional approval, of a site-specific development plan, following notice and public hearing, by the local government in which the property is situated.[48] A site-specific development plan is a plan that has been submitted to the county by a property owner describing with reasonable certainty the type and intensity of use for a single parcel or parcels of property. The determination of what constitutes a site-specific development plan basically rests in the discretion of the board of county commissioners, with the exception that a variance, sketch plan, preliminary plan, final architectural or construction plans, public utility filings, or zoning in and of itself cannot constitute a site-specific development plan.

A statutory vested property right is generally valid for a period of three years, unless further extended by county approval or development agreement. This right runs with the land and confers upon the property owner the right to undertake and complete the development and use of his property under the terms and conditions of the approved site-specific development plan. Failure to abide by such terms and conditions can result in a forfeiture of the vested property right.

Once a statutory vested property right is established, a county cannot zone or impose any land use action that would alter, impair, prevent, diminish, or otherwise delay the development or use of the property as set forth in the site-specific development plan except: (1) upon consent of the property owner; (2) upon discovery of natural or humanmade hazards on or in the immediate vicinity of the property that could not reasonably have been discovered at the time of plan approval and that pose a serious threat to the public health, safety, and welfare; or (3) if the property owner is paid for all his costs, expenses, and liabilities. Some land use regulations that are general in nature and applicable to all properties subject to land use regulation by a county may be applied without compensation to properties that have been vested.[49]

Joint Planning and Land Use Regulation

Counties are authorized to cooperate and contract with other units of government for the purposes of joint land use planning or regulation.[50] Through an intergovernmental agreement, local governments can jointly adopt, after notice and hearing, mutually binding and enforceable comprehensive development plans for areas within their jurisdictions. These plans may include master plans; zoning plans; subdivision regulations; and building-code, permit, and other land use standards, which, if set out in specific detail, may be in lieu of such regulations of the local governments. In the event that a comprehensive development plan is silent as to a specific land use matter, existing local land use regulations shall control.

Matters of State Interest

Under a Colorado law commonly referred to as H.B. 1041, counties are authorized to designate and regulate any of the following as an "area or activity of state interest": mineral resource areas; flood-plain hazard areas; wildfire hazard areas; geologic hazard areas; historical or archaeological resources; natural resources (wildlife and shorelands); areas around key facilities (airports, public utilities, highway interchanges, and mass-transit facilities); major new domestic water and sewage treatment systems; major extensions of existing domestic water and sewage treatment systems; major solid-waste disposal sites; site selection of airports, rapid- or mass-transit facilities, and major highways and interchanges; site selection and construction of major facilities of a public utility; site selection and development of new communities; efficient utilization of municipal and industrial water projects; and the conduct of nuclear detonations.[51] Upon designation and regulation by the board of county commissioners in its quasi-legislative capacity, any person desiring to engage in development in a designated area of state interest or to conduct a designated activity of state interest is required to apply to the board of county commissioners, in its quasi-judicial capacity, for a permit. The county board must deny the permit application if it does not comply with the county's H.B. 1041 regulations and may impose reasonable conditions on the issuance of a permit.

A county has greater authority and flexibility in regulating under H.B. 1041 than under its traditional land use powers. A county can regulate municipal and quasi-municipal entities, other political subdivisions of the state, and the federal government in designated matters of state interest. A county is not accorded this regulatory authority in the state zoning and subdivision enabling statutes.[52] Subsequent to designating a matter of state interest, a county is expressly authorized to impose a moratorium pending consideration and final enactment of regulations. There is no comparable statutory provision in the zoning or subdivision context.

Implementing, administering, and enforcing H.B. 1041 regulations can be time consuming and complex. As such, H.B. 1041 is more conducive to those major projects and activities that do not otherwise fall within the scope and provisions of a county's general land use regulations.

Land Use Act

Colorado has enacted what is commonly referred to as H.B. 1034, or the Land Use Act, which provides, in general terms, broad grants of authority to local governments to deal with such land use matters as regulating development and activities in hazardous areas; protecting lands from activities that would cause immediate or foreseeable material danger to significant wildlife habitat and would endanger a wildlife species; preserving areas of historical and archaeological importance; regulating, with respect to the establishment of, roads on public lands administered by the federal government; regulating the location of activities and developments that may result in significant changes in population density; providing for phased development of services and facilities; regulating the use of land on the basis of the impact thereof on the community or surrounding areas; and otherwise planning for and regulating the use of land so as to provide planned and orderly use of land and protection of the environment in a manner consistent with constitutional rights.[53] H.B. 1034 does not prescribe any statutory restrictions, conditions, or procedures for the enactment of H.B. 1034 regulations with the exception that where other procedural or substantive requirements for the planning for or regulation of the use of land are provided by law, such requirements shall control.[54] In this respect, H.B. 1034 is generally utilized by counties in conjunction with other statutory land use powers.[55]

IV. Conclusion

Counties are not uniform in the control and regulation of land uses within their respective unincorporated boundaries. Initial consultation with the county planning department is crucial in determining whether the county even regulates the proposed land use and, if so, its applicable land use procedures and requirements. The county planning department can be either an important friend or foe in assisting a property owner through the county's land use review and hearing processes.

In pursuing or reviewing a land use proposal, a property owner should inquire as to whether the county has the statutory authority to so regulate and whether there exist any statutory restrictions to the county's exercise thereof. A review of the county's land use regulations should also be conducted to ascertain the review standards and conditions applicable to the land use proposal. The "Let's Make a Deal" syndrome is no longer an acceptable practice in the land use context. Case-by-case negotiations are discouraged and should be employed only in the application of clearly delineated standards, which entails minimal discretion on the part of the county.

Bibliography

Colorado Chapter of the American Planning Association, *Colorado Land Planning and Development Law, 4th Edition* (1992).

Colorado Counties Inc., "Land Use Workshop—1041 Powers" (October 28, 1994).

Whittier, Beth A., "A Primer on Colorado Counties' Land Use Powers" (revised April 1998). *See* note 1 *infra* for information on obtaining a copy.

Whittier, Beth A., "General Overview of H.B. 1041" (April 1997). *See* note 1 *infra* for information on obtaining a copy.

Notes

1. A more detailed and comprehensive analysis, including case law citations, can be obtained by contacting Whittier, Shupp and House, LLC, telephone: (888) 640-5010 or fax: (303) 526-5508, and requesting a copy of the paper prepared by the author of this article titled "A Primer on Colorado Counties' Land Use Powers." Copying costs and postage will be requested in advance.

2. *See generally Board of County Commissioners v. Bainbridge, Inc.,* 929 P.2d 691, 699 (Colo. 1996); *Hibbard v. County of Adams,* 900 P.2d 1254, 1259 (Colo. App. 1994), *aff'd in part, rev'd in part,* 918 P.2d 212 (Colo. 1996).

3. *See generally Bainbridge, supra,* note 2 at 710–13; *Board of County Commissioners v. Bowen/Edwards Associates, Inc.,* 830 P.2d 1045, 1055-60 (Colo. 1992); *C and M Sand and Gravel Company v. Board of County Commissioners,* 673 P.2d 1013, 1016–18 (Colo. App. 1973).

4. *Wilkinson v. Board of County Commissioners,* 872 P.2d 1269, 1275-76 (Colo. App. 1993).

5. *Board of County Commissioners v. Conder,* 927 P.2d 1339, 1348 (Colo. 1996), *citing Beaver Meadows v. Board of County Commissioners,* 709 P.2d 928, 936 (Colo. 1985); *see generally* C.R.S. §§29-20-201, *et seq.* (1999).

6. *See generally Jafay v. Board of County Commissioners,* 848 P.2d 892, 897- 898 (Colo. 1993).

7. *See generally Wilkinson, supra,* note 4 at 1276.

8. *See Tracy v. City of Boulder,* 635 P.2d 907, 910 (Colo. App. 1981).

9. *Jafay, supra,* note 6 at 897–98.

10. S.B. 99-218, codified at C.R.S. §§29-20-201, *et seq.; see generally City of Monterey v. Del Monte Dunes,* 119 S.Ct. 1624 (1999); *Nollan v. California Coastal Commission,* 483 U.S. 825 (1987); *Dolan v. City of Tigard,* 114 S.Ct. 2309 (1994). For cases on the judicial standards of review, *see generally Powell v. Colorado Public Utilities Com'n,* 956 P.2d 608 (Colo. 1998); *Board of County Commissioners v. O'Dell,* 920 P.2d 48, 50 (Colo. 1996); *Ace West Trucking, Inc. V. Public Utilities Com'n of Colorado,* 788 P.2d 755 (Colo. 1990); *Alexander v. Colorado Dept. Of Personnel,* 952 P.2d 814 (Colo. App. 1997).

11. *See Jafay, supra,* note 6 at 899; *Leonard v. Board of Directors,* 673 P.2d 1019, 1022–25 (Colo. App. 1983); *Soon Yee Scott v. City of Englewood,* 672 P.2d 225, 227 (Colo. App. 1983).

12. *See generally Jafay, supra,* note 6 at 899; *Sundheim v. Board of County Commissioners,* 904 P.2d 1337, 1345–46 (Colo. App. 1995), *aff'd* 926 P.2d 545 (Colo. 1996); *Russell v. City of Central City,* 892 P.2d 432, 437–38 (Colo. App. 1995).

13. *See Save Park County v. Board of County Commissioners,* 969 P.2d 711 (Colo. App. 1998), *cert. granted* Jan 4, 1999; *Anderson v. Board of Adjustment,* 931 P.2d 517, 520 (Colo. App. 1996); *Abbott v. Board of County Commissioners,* 895 P.2d 1165, 1167 (Colo. App. 1995).

14. *See generally Kohn v. City of Boulder,* 919 P.2d 822, 824–25 (Colo. App. 1995); *Lehman v. City of Louisville,* 857 P.2d 455, 457 (Colo. App. 1992); Freirich, *Estopping Local Governments in Colorado,* 18 Colo.Law. 2113 (Nov. 1989).

15. C.R.S. §§30-28-101, *et seq.*

16. C.R.S. §§30-28-201, *et seq.*

17. C.R.S. §§30-28-106 through 109.

18. *Bainbridge, supra,* note 2 at 705; *Theobald v. Board of County Commissioners,* 644 P.2d 942, 948-49 (Colo. 1982).

19. *Conder, supra,* note 5 at 1345.

20. C.R.S. §§30-28-111 through 116.

21. *King's Mill Homeowners Association v. City of Westminster,* 557 P.2d 1186, 1190 (Colo. 1976); *Carron v. Board of County Commissioners,* 976 P.2d 359 (Colo. App. 1998); *Applebaugh v. Board of County Commissioners,* 837 P.2d 304, 309 (Colo. App. 1992).

22. *Elam v. Albers,* 616 P.2d 168, 169 (Colo. App. 1980).

23. *See Western Paving Construction Co. v. Board of County Commissioners,* 506 P.2d 1230, 1231–32 (Colo. 1973); *C and M Sand and Gravel, supra,* note 3 at 1018.

24. *See Sherman v. City of Colorado Springs Planning Commission,* 763 P.2d 292, 296–97 (Colo. 1988).

25. *See generally Holcomb v. City and County of Denver,* 606 P.2d 858, 862–63 (Colo. 1980); *Bitts v. Board of Adjustment,* 765 P.2d 1077, 1079 (Colo. App. 1988).

26. C.R.S. §§30-28-117 through 118; *see also Board of County Commissioners v. Moga,* 947 P.2d 1385, 1390 (Colo. 1997).

27. *See generally Levy v. Board of Adjustment,* 369 P.2d 991, 995–96 (Colo. 1962); *Murray v. Board of Adjustment,* 594 P.2d 596, 597–98 (Colo. App. 1979); *Landmark Universal, Inc. v. Pitkin County Board of Adjustment,* 579 P.2d 1184, 1185 (Colo. App. 1978); *Monte Vista Professional Building v. City of Monte Vista,* 531 P.2d 400, 402 (Colo. App. 1975).

28. C.R.S. §30-28-120; *see generally Anderson, supra,* note 16 at 519.

29. *Anderson, supra,* note 13 at 519–20.

30. *See generally Hartley v. City of Colorado Springs,* 764 P.2d 1216, 1224–25 (Colo. 1988); *Anderson, supra,* note 16 at 519–20.

31. *Town of Lyons v. Bashor,* 867 P.2d 159, 161 (Colo. App. 1993).

32. C.R.S. §§30-28-101 and 133.

33. *Pennobscot, Inc. v. Board of County Commissioners,* 642 P.2d 915 (Colo. 1982); *but see Wilkinson, supra,* note 4 at 1273–75.

34. C.R.S. §§30-28-101(10)(d), 30-28-301, *et seq.,* and 30-28-401, *et seq.*

35. *See generally Bainbridge, supra*, note 2 at 701; *Shoptaugh v. Board of County Commissioners*, 543 P.2d 524, 526–27 (Colo. App. 1975).

36. C.R.S. §§30-28-133 and 136.

37. C.R.S. §30-28-133.5; *see also Conder, supra*, note 5 at 1348; *Beaver Meadows, supra*, note 5 at 936; *Save Park County, supra*, note 13.

38. C.R.S. §30-28-133.5.

39. C.R.S. §§30-28-101(11) and 137.

40. *See generally Bainbridge, supra*, note 2 at 698–99 and 702–03; *Beaver Meadows, supra*, note 5 at 935–39; *Bethlehem Evangelical Lutheran Church v. City of Lakewood*, 626 P.2d 668, 672–74 (Colo. 1981).

41. C.R.S. §30-28-110(1); *but see* C.R.S. §24-65.1-501; *City of Colorado Springs v. Board of County Commissioners*, 895 P.2d 1105, 1117–18 (Colo. App. 1994).

42. C.R.S. §§30-28-201, *et seq.*

43. *Bainbridge, supra*, note 2 at 704.

44. *See generally Gramiger v. County of Pitkin*, 794 P.2d 1045, 1048 (Colo. App. 1989); *Winters v. City of Commerce City*, 648 P.2d 175, 177 (Colo. App. 1982).

45. Planned Unit Development Act of 1972, C.R.S. §§24-67-101, *et seq.*

46. *Applebaugh, supra*, note 21 at 307.

47. *Moore v. City of Boulder*, 484 P.2d 134, 135–36 (Colo. App. 1971).

48. C.R.S. §§24-68-101, *et seq.*, as amended by House Bill 1280 (1999).

49. *See Villa at Greeley, Inc. v. Hopper*, 917 P.2d 350 (Colo. App. 1996).

50. C.R.S. §29-20-105.

51. C.R.S. §§24-65.1-101, *et seq.*

52. *See generally City and County of Denver v. Board of County Commissioners*, 782 P.2d 753, 761–63 (Colo. 1989); *City of Colorado Springs, supra*, note 45 at 1116–18.

53. C.R.S. §§29-20-101, *et seq.*

54. *See generally Bainbridge, supra*, note 2 at 707; *Pennobscot, supra*, note 33; *Oborne v. Board of County Commissioners*, 764 P.2d 397, 400 (Colo. App. 1988), *cert. denied*, 778 P.2d 1370 (Colo. 1989).

55. *See generally Bowen/Edwards, supra*, note 3 at 1056; *Wilkinson, supra*, note 4 at 1274.

22

Takings, Exactions and Impact Fees, Eminent Domain, and Growth Management Tools

Erin J. Johnson, *Attorney at Law, Planning Consultant*

Many disputes in Colorado stem from misunderstandings of various land use regulatory tools employed by governmental entities. These disputes are frequently precipitated or fueled by differences between deeply rooted Colorado traditions and the expectations of people who have lived in other states where growth and development long ago required greater exercise of the police power by governmental entities. A basic understanding of some of the land use tools is needed so that rational discussions can take place as citizens and local governments face the challenges of growth. This chapter provides an overview of some of these fundamental concepts.

I. Takings

The underlying principle of a "taking" is derived from seventeenth- and eighteenth-century English legal traditions that developed along with the advancement of private rights associated with real property. Based on principles of fairness and justice, the traditions were developed to prevent kings from confiscating or using a subject's property without due process or just compensation. This protection of private property rights is balanced by the responsibility of private landowners to refrain from using their land in a manner that might harm the public or other landowners. These rights and duties are governed under the "police power," or the authority of a government to make regulations to secure the health, safety, and welfare of all its citizens.

In the United States, the drafters of the Constitution included the "just compensation" or "takings" clause in the Fifth Amendment (it is applied to actions by the states in the Fourteenth Amendment), establishing a fundamental individual right to own property free of the threat of seizure by the government unless the government pays for it. The intent of the constitutional principle is to balance the rights of the individual with the governmental need to utilize some land for the benefit of the general public. The Colorado Constitution also embodies these principles in Article II, §§14, 15 and 25.

Modern situations giving rise to legal analyses using takings concepts and cases often do not involve physical confiscation or seizure of property. The legal principles still apply in modern regulatory contexts that seek to balance individual and governmental rights. However, the evolution of real property regulation has brought about many challenges regarding whether a particular situation is in fact a taking.

Although the fundamental concept is easy to understand and the legal principles remain unchanged, the interpretation of the constitutional principles through case law can be very difficult to grasp. There is no clear statement of the modern takings law because the application of the constitutional principle is highly dependent on the individual circumstances of each case. Additionally, case law represents the constant evolution of defining the boundaries of the underlying legal principles. Several landmark cases illustrate the legal principles, provide a historical perspective of modern takings law, and provide a context for comparison to new situations.

In a 1908 case in Maine (*In re Opinion of the Justices*, 69 A. 627 (Me. 1908)), the state wanted to regulate the cutting or destruction of trees on private property for several purposes, including soil erosion control, without compensating the owner of the land. The U.S. Supreme Court made a very clear statement about the limits of private property rights: "We think it is a settled principle, growing out of the nature of a well-ordered society, that every holder of property, however absolute and unqualified may be his title, holds it under the implied liability that the use of it may be regulated so that it does not injure the rights of the community."

Regulatory takings evolved in the 1920s. In a case involving Pennsylvania Coal (*Pennsylvania Coal Co. V. Mahon*, 260 U.S. 393 (1922)), the Supreme Court determined that regulations can cause a taking even if there is no actual physical invasion of the property. In this case, the state of Pennsylvania had passed a law forbidding coal mining that would cause things on the surface to sink into the mine shafts. The court found that even though the regulation served a valid public purpose, the law itself constituted a taking. In this case Justice Holmes made the famous statement, "The general rule is that while the property may be regulated to a certain extent, if a regulation goes 'too far,' it will be recognized as a taking."

Determining how far is "too far" has challenged governments and courts and has been the measuring stick for cases ever since the Pennsylvania Coal case. In 1926 the Supreme Court supported the use of zoning ordinances by local governments to control land use conflicts in *Village of Euclid v. Ambler Realty*, 272 U.S. 365 (1926). In this case a landowner argued that the town's zoning regulations reduced the value of his property by 75 percent, but the validity of the ordinance was upheld by the court.

Although each potential takings situation needs to be evaluated on an individual basis, there are three general areas of questions that courts use to determine whether a taking has occurred. The first area is analyzing the economic impact of the regulation on the property owner. The loss in value must be almost total to find a taking, and to determine this courts ask if there is a reasonable economic use left for the property. A regulation that denies the property's "highest and best use" is not a taking. Courts also ask if there is a reasonable investment-backed expectation involved in the property ownership and look at the timing of the investment in comparison to the timing of the regulations.

The second area of questions addresses the public pur-

poses being served by the regulations. In certain situations, increasingly broad purposes have been upheld in takings challenges, including aesthetic considerations, view corridors, and wetland and wildlife habitat protection. The courts usually exhibit a high deference to a local government's determination of its regulatory needs. However, the regulations must be fair and cannot be used to exclude certain segments of society.

The last general area of a takings analysis concerns the character of the government action by asking what the government entity is trying to accomplish with the regulation. In 1988 the Supreme Court struck down a greenbelt ordinance that was enacted by a city after it had run out of funds for acquisition of open space (*Allingham v. City of Seattle*, 109 Wash. 2d. 947, 749 P.2d 160 (Wash. 1988)). The city had taken the property for public use by resorting to a regulatory method to "take" property instead of paying for it, as had been done prior to the regulation.

II. Exactions and Impact Fees

Exactions are specific requirements placed on new developments, and impact fees are charges assessed against new developments in lieu of the requirements. Local governments have increasingly employed these tools in response to the demands for public services created by the development itself. Historically these fees or requirements were applied to provide appropriate water and sewer facilities, but recent application has been expanded to public safety needs such as police and fire stations, school needs, and parks and trails.

Although many impact fees and exactions are valid, several legal questions are raised by these practices. It is important to understand that impact fees are intended for the construction of new facilities necessary to accommodate growth and not for maintenance of either existing or new facilities. To establish a valid impact fee, the government needs to show that the facilities to be constructed are required to serve the new development and that those who pay the fees will receive a benefit in return.

The analysis of an impact fee or exaction challenge involves a series of questions regarding four general issues. The first question is whether the local government has the authority to make the requirement or impose the charge. Local governments operating under the home-rule powers granted by the state constitution can exercise broad powers that can be preempted by the state only in very limited situations. Additionally, specific enabling legislation directly authorizes all local governments in Colorado to impose requirements and fees for certain improvements. Finally, court decisions have shown that there is implied authority for governments to make certain requirements. In *Beaver Meadows*, 709 P.2d 928 (Colo. 1985), the Colorado Supreme Court held that counties in Colorado can condition development approvals on the provision of adequate facilities and that the authority was embodied in zoning and planning enabling laws.

The second question is whether the charge or requirement is actually a disguised tax. Impact fees based on the value of the property are particularly vulnerable to this type of challenge. There are several important differences between an excise tax and an impact fee. The authority to tax is derived from the taxing powers of the government, and impact fees are authorized by the police power. A public vote is required for a tax but is not required to establish an impact fee. Excise taxes are imposed on people; impact fees are imposed on property. Unlike excise taxes, funds generated by impact fees cannot be commingled with other funds and cannot be used for operation and maintenance purposes.

The third issue is whether the requirement or fee has a reasonable relationship to the need for improvements created by the new development. The leading case in this area is *Nollan v. California Coastal Commission*, 482 U.S. 304 (1987), where the U.S. Supreme Court held that a government regulation must "substantially advance legitimate government interests" in order to avoid a taking. In this case, a one-home beachfront development project was required to allow the public to cross the beach above the high-tide line. The court invalidated the land dedication requirement because it found no rational relationship between the condition and the original purpose of the building restriction.

Two philosophies are used by courts to determine whether there is a rational relationship. A few courts allow impact fees and exactions only to the extent that they specifically benefit the development in question. Most courts employ a proportionality or fair-share analysis that allows impact fees and exactions to the extent necessitated by the development. The developer generally must pay for his fair share of the improvement based on some supportable theory or formula. In *Dolan v. City of Tigard*, 512 U.S. 374, 114 S.Ct. 2309 (1994), a city required a land dedication for a drainage easement and bicycle path as a condition for approval of expansion of a hardware store. The court struck down the requirement as a taking, holding that the city must make some sort of individualized determination that the required dedication related both in nature and extent to the impact of the proposed development.

The final legal issue is whether the fees or requirements have been properly calculated and whether revenues have been properly managed. Generally, fees must be based on intelligible standards and must be apportioned fairly and equitably. In Colorado, impact fee funds must be properly accounted for and segregated from general revenues. They also must be spent for the facilities and services that they were assessed against within a reasonable amount of time.

III. Condemnation and Eminent Domain

Powers of condemnation or eminent domain are utilized when a government has a substantiated need to purchase property for a public purpose and the landowner does not wish to sell. This is the greatest civil power possessed by governmental entities, and it is authorized by the government's right to take private property under the federal and state constitutions, statutes, and case law. The legal principles used in modern law and statutes were developed based on principles of fairness and the protection of private property rights. If an owner and a government cannot voluntarily agree on a fair price to be paid for the land that the government needs to use, then the government entity may file a petition for eminent domain with the district court, and the court establishes the fair price to be paid.

The cost analysis for the condemnation process is based on modern appraisal techniques. A central issue in a condemnation action is balancing the needs of the public and the rights of the landowner—it would not be fair for the landowner to receive less than the fair market value for the property taken, nor would it be fair for the landowner to receive a windfall profit at the expense of the public. The condemning entity must prove the necessity of the public use. Usually courts find that what the government entity wants to do provides the greatest public good with the least private injury.

After the government has proved the public need to take a property or a portion of a property, the court establishes the just compensation that is due to the owner. Just compensation is the fair market value, or the amount that the property would bring on an open market between willing buyers and willing sellers, acting without coercion and for their own benefit, after the property has had sufficient exposure to the market. The techniques used are not totally objective—the fair market value is an opinion derived from the marketplace. Statutes and case law addressing condemnation adopt definitions and principles that mimic the marketplace in order to make the proper analyses.

Just compensation does not mean that the owner is entitled to all damages that might occur as a result of the governmental action. Generally, compensation is limited to the value of the real property and does not compensate the owner for personal or consequential damages. Statutory provisions sometimes extend just compensation to cover loss of goodwill, business damages, attorney fees, court costs, appraisal fees, and other related items that are not part of the constitutional provisions.

Many condemnation actions involve only a partial taking. In this situation, the measure of compensation is based on the value of the property actually taken, plus damages to the part not taken, less improvements to the part not taken. Some condemnations are based on a "before and after" analysis—a valuation of the entire tract before the taking and the market value of the remainder parcel after the taking. A highest-and-best-use analysis is typically part of the market research but is not a part of the compensation owing to the danger of speculation in the analysis. Previous unaccepted offers are generally excluded from evidence unless there was a bona fide offer from someone financially able to carry through with the deal. Standard appraisal practices require the use of comparable sales from a relevant area within a relevant time frame and reflecting genuine market trends.

Income received by the landowner from a completed condemnation is taxable, similar to any other sale, gain, or income. Actual damages are based on the individual circumstances of the case and are difficult to predict.

IV. Growth Management Tools

The need to manage the growth that many Colorado towns and counties have experienced has brought about the implementation of "growth management tools" by local governments. Some of these sound simple and straightforward, and really are, whereas others are conceptually basic but are legally very complex. To some Colorado citizens these management tools invade private property rights, and to others they are a necessary part of continuing to enjoy our beautiful state as our population grows. Whatever your perspective is, a quick summary of some of these tools will help you get started in supporting or opposing a local government growth management effort.

One important thing to keep in mind is that local governments really do try to address the problems at hand, many being created by growth, in a way that is fair to all of the citizens. When all is said and done, the local government won't do anything that is opposed by a majority of the citizens, regardless of whether the issue is progrowth or antigrowth. If you have an opinion about a growth issue

and you do not make your opinion heard, you had better be prepared to accept the actions taken by the government as being in the best interests of the community.

The following is a list of some of the growth management tools that might be used in your community.

Master plans
Master plans are technically not a growth management tool in that they are policy or advisory documents. Depending on how communities have organized their planning efforts, the term "master plan" may be interchangeable with "comprehensive plan," or these may be functionally very different. Make sure you understand the purpose of all of the planning documents of your community.

Master plans are the philosophical backdrop against which land use decisions are made. They can be frustrating because they contain a lot of vague and fuzzy language. You should try not to abuse them or let others abuse them by stretching a point, but remember their intent: to make a statement about a community that can be used on a long-range basis so that decisions are not made on a whim or in response to a matter of apparent immediate concern. Evaluate the credibility of the document itself: How long has it been since it was adopted? Even if it is relatively new, has the area changed drastically, or have many new citizens moved in? Was it done in a fair manner and with an adequate budget? You may need to do some research to answer these questions.

Zoning
Believe it or not, many rural areas in Colorado do not have zoning. Zoning establishes allowable-use restrictions in various areas, or zones. Within a particular zone, similar restrictions should be applied to similar uses. Part of the reason that some areas do not have zoning is that traditional zoning concepts may not translate well to rural and agricultural areas, especially if there has not been significant growth in recent years. Newcomers from areas with well-established zoning systems will be very uncomfortable in areas without these tools. Remember that zoning does not have to be everywhere—it usually makes sense for defined areas that need it, but it doesn't have to be the whole county. If there is zoning, assess the validity of the decisions made and whether they still apply under current circumstances.

Intergovernmental agreements
Any government entity can make a written agreement with another government entity. This tool is becoming widely used in the context of planning and growth management. Usually the impetus is based on common sense—many

times jurisdictional boundaries do not follow geographic or functional boundaries, and there is a need to combine rather than duplicate planning efforts. If your community is pursuing an intergovernmental agreement, make sure you know what the issues are, and try to make the government conduct the negotiations in public. Negotiations sometimes get away from the public dialog when they shouldn't, so it is the responsibility of the citizens to keep things in the open all the way through the process. Colorado has open-meeting laws intended to protect the rights of the public.

Annexation policies

In Colorado, towns and cities are the primary providers of services such as water and sewer. Many counties do not wish to be in the business of providing utilities, so they tend to encourage the annexation of new high-density growth by nearby municipalities. Sometimes this policy is set forth in a written agreement or embodied in planning documents. Some counties can accommodate a lot of growth, depending on the circumstances. When growth gets to the point where municipalities are near each other, there may be annexation policies within or between the towns. Written policies usually address the funding of utility extensions by the new development and can help neighboring jurisdictions promote orderly growth. Be aware of situations where a town is aggressively pursuing annexation of adjacent lands—it may be in the interests of the community to increase the potential tax base, but the town may take on more than it can handle for some time.

Extraterritorial jurisdiction

Colorado law provides some planning authority to municipalities that extends beyond their actual boundaries. This allows them to formally address certain extraterritorial issues that may affect them. However, the success of exercising that authority really depends on the general nature of communication and cooperation between the jurisdictions. If different local governments get into a battle over the nature of their respective areas of authority, the concerns of affected citizens may get lost in the fray.

Adequate public facility ordinances

This type of ordinance requires the presence of utility infrastructure or specified levels of public services in an area prior to the issuance of development approvals. In this way, planning efforts can anticipate future growth, but "leapfrog" development is prevented. This tool encourages growth in areas where service delivery is cost effective but does not necessarily address service deficiencies. It requires

a sophisticated system of data collection and management and requires constant staffing and updating that some areas may lack adequate budgets to provide.

Urban growth boundaries

Some jurisdictions establish specific extraterritorial boundaries where urban-level growth is appropriate through annexation. This tool requires a high level of intergovernmental and citizen cooperation to be successful. These efforts are typically very emotionally charged because some landowners will benefit and others will be negatively affected.

Development caps and growth-rate systems

These types of tools set an absolute limit on the amount of development within a community or specify an allowed rate of growth. If they are not very carefully established, these tools are subject to constitutional challenges. They are best used as temporary measures or moratoriums in emergency situations when the ability of one or more service providers is beyond its capacity and cannot easily expand.

Density transfers

This is a tool that sounds like a simple and great idea but is really very complex. A certain area is protected from development by transferring the development "rights" to another area. With many different landowners in both areas, it is very difficult to identify the rights and more difficult to transfer them. After much ado, the original objectives may not be met.

"Designer" zoning

There are many innovative zoning techniques, including planned unit developments (PUDs), "overlays" for various purposes, cluster allowances, and density incentives. If the zoning system foundation is effective, these tools are typically useful "refinements" of the community's land use objectives. It can get out of hand if too many designer techniques are applied, so question your community's motives if there are more than two or three "layers" in any one area, and be aware of potential constitutional or other legal challenges if the regulations seem unreasonably restrictive.

Large-lot zoning

This tool establishes large minimum size lots such as 80 or more acres, primarily in agricultural areas. This approach may cause conflict with private property rights supporters and be subject to other challenges, but it has been implemented in some areas to effectively achieve community objectives.

Conservation easements

Municipalities can support and encourage private land conservation in areas that support their established planning objectives. This approach may protect specific parcels, but it is hard to implement to an effective regional level.

Acquisition tools

If a government really desires that development is prevented in a certain area, and it has public use objectives for that area, the government can purchase, or arrange to purchase in the future, land in that area. This can be a very effective method of achieving planning objectives if the government has an appropriate budget and the citizens continue to support the acquisition objectives.

V. Conclusion

As shown, there are many ways to approach problems associated with growth. Before you either support or oppose any type of tool being implemented, make sure you fully understand the objectives and the implementation. Remember that most management objectives begin as a sincere effort to address a problem, and your analysis should begin with looking at those original objectives. Next, consider whether the resulting regulation meets the objectives, goes way too far, or falls short of the intended outcome. If the outcome doesn't relate to the objectives, or you have other questions, read the minutes of the proceedings and newspaper articles from the time of the adoption of the ordinance. Then it is your responsibility as a citizen to communicate your views and suggestions to the local government entity.

Bibliography

American Planning Association. "APA's Position on Takings." April 11, 1995.

Clarion Associates of Colorado, LLC. "Colorado Growth Management Toolbox, Smart Growth and Development White Paper." Governor's Smart Growth Summit, January 1995.

Clarion Associates of Colorado, LLC. "The Evolving Law of Development Impact Fees in Colorado." 1997.

Duerksen, Christopher J., Clarion Associates. "Development Impact Fees, Linkages, and Exactions: A National Overview." 1994.

Duerksen, Christopher J., and Richard J. Roddewig. "Takings Law in Plain English." American Resources Information Network, 1994.

Hart, Valerie E., and Christopher J. Duerksen. "Development Impact Fees in the Rocky Mountain Region." Rocky Mountain Land Use Institute, 1995.

Malizia, Emil, AICP, Richard Norton, and Craig Richardson. "Reading, Writing, and Impact Fees." *Planning Magazine*, September 1997, p. 18.

Townsend, Jean C., Coley Forrest, Inc. "Impact Fees: Demonstrating Rough Proportionality." Prepared for the Smart Growth and Development "Best Practices" Workshop, 1997.

Recreation, Public Lands, and Tribal Lands

Whether at Home, Work, or Play, There Are Many "Neighbors" in Colorado

When people think "Colorado," many of the images that pop into their minds are of majestic mountains, forests, rivers, canyons, and other natural features. In fact, a majority of the land in Colorado is "owned" by the public and managed by various governmental agencies. These public land resources are a primary component of the economy of Colorado, and they are why Colorado is such a desirable place to live, work, and play. Because of the natural beauty of the state and the value of the public resources, many conflicts arise based on recent growth and development trends that result in competing land use demands and increased levels of recreational use.

With more residents and tourism activity in Colorado, the "great outdoors" is becoming a little crowded. Our public resources offer recreational opportunities for every skill and fitness level; every day new sports, recreational "toys," and vehicles that you have never heard of before are developed and show up in Colorado. This ever-increasing recreational activity results in more people in campgrounds, on back roads, and around water resources—and makes it more difficult to have the high-quality outdoor experience we all want and expect from our public resources.

The first two chapters in this section focus on how to be a responsible "neighbor" on the trail. **Anne Rapp**, one of the best-known and most experienced guides in Colorado, describes how you can get the most out of your backcountry experience by respecting the land and trying to use the forests and fields in a way that will make your use invisible to others. This chapter describes the "rules of the road" for those trails used by hikers, horses, mountain bikes, and all-terrain vehicles (ATVs). This chapter also discusses how to be a considerate and safe hunter.

Respect for other people's viewpoints and a genuine willingness to share Colorado's beauty go a long way toward fostering attitudes that make sharing the "wonderfulness of it all" a joy instead of a chore. **Ed Zink** offers thoughtful insights on "being a good recreational neighbor." His chapter identifies common pitfalls and effective tools that can be used to maintain good recreational neighbor relationships. He also addresses the important need for generating funds to accommodate the increased demand for public recreational facilities and services. This need has sparked considerable controversy because it strikes at the heart of most Americans' concept that public lands belong to the citizens of this country and, therefore, should be free. However, the realities of increased demand for and use of our natural resources make continued free access an impossibility, especially if the resources themselves are to be maintained or improved to support increased use. The sources of the necessary funding and how it is allocated are among the most difficult issues that the American public will face in coming decades. This important chapter helps us understand these issues and sets the stage for productive and rational discussions regarding recreational management.

The next chapters deal with how to be a responsible user of the public and tribal lands in Colorado and what rules you need to keep in mind if your "neighbor" is a governmental entity such as the U.S. Forest Service, a State Trust parcel, or a sovereign Native American tribe.

Public lands in Colorado are held and managed by many different entities. In order to maintain the quality of the resources and recreational opportunities on these lands, management agencies find that they have to institute increasingly stringent rules and regulations. In this section representatives of a number of land management entities describe their purpose, philosophy, management methods, and general rules governing use.

Thea Rock explains the basics of how to be a good recreational neighbor when using Colorado state parks and the Colorado Trail System. Kate Jones outlines the purposes and uses of Colorado's State Trust Lands, which were given to the state by the federal government primarily for the support of "common schools" when the state was created. Pat Tucker discusses lands managed by the Colorado Division of Wildlife.

Roger Alexander highlights the things you need to know when using lands managed by the Bureau of Land Management. This chapter also includes a short history of public lands and some of the federal laws that affect many public lands. Linda Martin's chapter explains how to be a responsible visitor to national parks and archaeological sites. Matt Glasgow tells us about issues related to U.S. Forest Service lands in Colorado.

As in many states, when you buy property, your neighbor could be a state or U.S. federal entity, or it could be a Native American sovereign government. In Colorado the Southern Ute Indian Tribe and the Ute Mountain Ute Indian Tribe control considerable land in the southwestern part of the state. These governments are a hybrid of many levels of local government administration. They have communities that are managed as municipalities, and they have landholdings and resources that are managed using processes that are more like those used by county governments. However, they operate separately from nontribal municipal and county governments and, in many respects, separately from the state government because they are, in many ways, sovereign nations governed by tribal and federal law. The chapters by the Southern Ute and the Ute Mountain Ute tribes present general information to help nontribal members respect tribal property and rules in order to be good neighbors to these governments.

This section illustrates the good neighbor concept in the context of respect and consideration for other recreational users, for Mother Nature, and for government agencies and entities that are responsible for protecting our natural resources. Following the basic principles in this section will help each one of us learn to be more considerate of all the other people who are out there trying to enjoy nature in their own way. If we all do our part to share the beauty that really does belong to all of us and make recreation fulfilling as well as fun for ourselves and others, the value of our natural resources will be protected for generations to come.

23

Being a Good Neighbor on the Trail

Anne Rapp, *Outfitter and Backcountry Guide*

Did you know that Colorado has over 22 million acres of public lands? Doesn't that just make you feel like getting out and exploring? In order to get the most from your outdoor experience, you need a plan. First, you need to think about what you'd like to do. You might choose rock climbing, hunting, horseback riding, four wheeling, hiking, biking, llama trekking, etc. Second, you need to focus on an area suitable for the activity you plan. Once you've decided on an area, you are ready to begin planning your exploratory trip.

All backcountry excursions should be thought of as exploratory because no two experiences are alike. Some trips will be better than others. For example, on one trip you may be drenched by downpours and pummeled by hail. That's Mother Nature for you, and maybe it taught you to bring better raingear along. Every trip is different, but the lesson in every trip is to be prepared.

How well you plan is an important element of a successful outing. Go to a local outdoor-equipment store to purchase maps of the area you plan to explore. Look for the roads, trails, and natural or historical features in the area. Think about how much time you have to spend and try to realistically estimate how much time it will take you to do what you'd like to accomplish. If the land you'll be exploring belongs to the federal government, you might contact the administrative agency, usually the U.S. Forest Service or the Bureau of Land Management, and request a copy of their maps and rules for that area if they have them. These agencies may have particular "designated uses" in some areas; this means that those areas may be used only for certain kinds of activities. If it may be necessary to cross private property, contact the landowner to request permission. Be sure to choose your gear and clothing for safety and comfort; local outdoor stores or hiking clubs can be wonderful sources of information about what conditions to expect and the appropriate gear. There are many different climates in Colorado, and weather is subject to change (even on the same day, especially as you change elevation). The ruggedness of the terrain should also be a big consideration in your planning.

I. Trail Sense: Getting the Most out of Your Outdoor Experience

So you're prepared for the temperature swings, you know where you're going, you've checked out the designated uses, and you've finally made it to the trailhead. *Stop.* Resist the urge to rush past that signboard at the trailhead. Read it before you start out. The information is usually interesting and could give you tips that you haven't thought about, such as:

- trail closures
- fire bans or fire danger ratings
- designated trail uses
- special events
- fishing regulations
- tips on bears and other wildlife
- information on lost persons or equipment

After all that preparation, relax and enjoy your day in the backcountry.

If you're planning to stay in the great outdoors overnight, at the end of your day of outdoor activity you need to thoughtfully plan for the best campsite. Camp location is vital to the success of your trip if comfort, practicality, and not damaging the land are important to you. There are a number of excellent books on low-impact camping or horsepacking. Several are listed in the references at the end of this chapter.

After years of experience on my own trips and of guiding others in their backcountry experiences, I have come up with a short list of suggestions for locating your campsite.

- If possible, pick a location off the trail and out of view of others. You're there for the wide-open spaces, so give yourself some space and respect the privacy of others.
- Pick a fairly level area with some trees and fairly hard ground.
- Think about orienting your campsite toward the direction of the morning sun for warmth.
- Camp near water if you can, but never in the area right next to the water. The area by the water is usually cold and damp. Worse, you could damage sensitive riparian habitat.
- To avoid damaging the riparian zone, water livestock away from the water in a rocky area some distance from camp.
- Get your drinking water from the clearest-running part of the stream and purify it.
- Use a campfire only if trailhead regulations permit open burning. In dry years and in areas with a lot of trail usage, it's doubtful that fires will be allowed. If you do have a campfire, douse the fire thoroughly when you are finished and, to the best of your ability, restore the campfire area to the way it looked before you came.
- If you have pack animals with you, you'll need a campsite with grasses and legumes that will keep the animals happy. The best "fence" is good grass.
- Picket your animals in an area that has the least impact on the land (away from trees, brush, and stumps). The lowest impact is not to tie your animals at all, but you might have to spend outdoor quality time searching for strays. My plan is usually to picket the lead horses in good grass and turn the rest loose with bells on. I unconsciously listen for the bells in my sleep and know that if I don't hear bells, we may be late out of camp the next morning.
- If you tie your animals, use a "high line," a large-diameter rope (or lash ropes) tied between two or more large trees in such a way as to keep the livestock from damaging the base of trees and their root systems.
- Don't tie an animal with a history of pawing or restlessness when tied. Know the personalities of your animals and accommodate their quirks.

In addition to knowing where and how to camp, it is ab-solutely essential that you think carefully and in advance about safety.

First, always take along a well-equipped first aid kit for stabilization of injuries. Second, if you learn how to use them properly, a good topographical map and compass (or one of the new GPS units if you're technically inclined) can save your life by helping you find the way back to "civilization." The U.S. Geological Survey quadrangle maps (called "quads") are available in many outdoor stores and in addition to planning are valuable for knowing your location and safety. If you don't know how to read and use a map, think about taking a course in map skills or orienteering. Third, *respect Mother Nature*. She is powerful and unpredictable, and I've always believed that if you don't show some respect she'll probably teach you a very uncomfortable or even fatal lesson. Self-preservation is a serious responsibility. Proceed with respect for the changing weather and terrain—altitude sickness and hypothermia can kill you. Do not press on and challenge the elements.

If you are not accustomed to the elevations through which you travel and you get a bad headache or feel dizzy or tired, consider heading back down immediately. There are no specific factors such as age, sex, or physical condition that correspond with each individual's susceptibility to altitude sickness. Altitude sickness can impair your ability to think clearly, and you need to be sharp every minute you're in the backcountry. Proper acclimation over a few days will allow your body to adjust to accommodate lower barometric pressures at higher elevations.

Hypothermia means that your body temperature has dropped below the normal 98.6°F. As the body temperature falls, shivering, poor coordination, and slurred speech occur. Eventually your body temperature drops to a level that will not sustain life. What can you do to avoid hypothermia? Dress in layers so that if you're too hot hiking you can take off a sweater and then easily put it on again if the pace slows down or the wind starts to blow. Use breathable gear such as polypropylene so that your sweat is wicked away from your body and dries quickly. Always wear a hat. This is useful to avoid sunburn but is also vital to avoid the considerable loss of body heat through your scalp.

Trail sense means just that: Be sensible. If you get into trouble you endanger not only yourself but also those who may need to find and rescue you.

II. The Rules of the Road

One of the most important concepts to grasp when you think about being a "good neighbor" in the outdoors is that you're not the only one out there. Maybe there's not another human in your field of view, but these days we share the outdoors with many, many other people. And these people are having fun doing lots of different activities; that's what multiple use is all about.

Respect your fellow outdoors folks. The forests are, or should be, a place to cleanse the spirit. Some choose to do this by hiking in peace and solitude; others challenge their bodies on mountain bikes; some find the best medicine is riding a horse; still others need the wind in their face while riding their ATV. Try to remember that every user group shares the common interest of seeing remarkable country at a pace and in a way they enjoy. So relax and respect other people's needs. If the traffic on a trail doesn't suit you, try another in a more restricted or remote area; seek out the road less traveled.

I've spent twenty years exploring the backcountry of southwest Colorado on horses, afoot, on mountain bikes, and even on ATVs. What I've learned is that being considerate of others on the trail, "trail etiquette," can be summarized in a few commonsense rules.

1. If you encounter horses or mules on the trail, if at all possible, move off the trail on the *low side*. It's far more dangerous for a horse to bolt downhill than uphill. Maybe nod a friendly "hello," but be careful about sudden movements. Horses are wonderful, but many of them spook easily. And if the rider doesn't return your greeting, don't take it personally. He or she may be having trouble keeping the mount under control, or a packer may sense that the animals are on edge. Under those conditions, being pleasant isn't tops on the list of things to think about. Some horses and mules are accustomed to strange sights on the trail, such as bikes, llamas, or people carrying backpacks. Other animals will bolt at seeing their own shadows. Act conservatively and be as considerate as you can.

2. If you're riding an ATV on a trail designated for ATV use, by all means ride at a reasonable speed. If your sight distance is limited, please slow down for your own safety as well as that of others sharing the trail. ATVs are required to stay on the trails because of the damage they can do off trail in short periods of time. Therefore hikers, horseback riders, and others need to move off trails to let ATVs pass. Other trail users should remember that ATV users can't hear very well because of their engines, so shouted instructions won't do much good. If you're riding the ATV, travel at a reasonable speed. Be a good trail neighbor.

3. And then there are llamas. These New World cousins of the camel are being used more and more frequently as pack animals on the trails of Colorado. For the safety of all, when horses and mules meet llamas on the trail, somebody's got to move. Generally, it is safer for a llama handler to move, and llamas have less off-trail impact. Horses and mules and llamas are distrustful of each other, so the farther apart, the better. In other areas such as trailheads where the three quadrupeds may have to be together, the animals need to be kept on short leads and watched closely.

4. Be considerate of hikers carrying heavy loads or mountain bikers moving up steep slopes. Move off the trail if you can. When somebody moves off the trail for you, let them know that you appreciate it.

5. Don't allow your dog to run loose or bark at or disturb wildlife or other people on the trail.

6. If anyone comes up behind you moving faster than you are, be considerate and move off the trail to let them pass.

7. Don't cut switchbacks, as they cause erosion that can start gullying and can quickly ruin a trail.

8. Pack out all trash.

9. In short, use common sense and common courtesy.

III. Being a Considerate (and Safe) Hunter

Every year the state of Colorado is host to more than 220,000 deer and elk hunters. Big-game hunting is a rich but normal experience for state residents who may have an annual tradition, but for many out-of-state visitors, it is the experience of a lifetime. However, that amounts to a lot of people sharing the forests during a limited period of time in the autumn.

Most of the big-game hunting in Colorado is on federal land, but with permission of the landowner, big-game hunting may also take place on private land. Sometimes permission is granted in the form of a "lease" for which hunters pay a negotiated fee. Many hunters carry maps to show the boundaries between public and private lands, and under no circumstances may hunters (or nonhunters, for that matter) cross private land to get to public land beyond without the permission of the intervening landowner. Some landowners have strong feelings against hunting, and hunters should respect those feelings and hunt and walk only where allowed.

To hunt in the state of Colorado you must first take a hunter safety course and receive a certificate. The local Division of Wildlife office or a local gun club can usually advise you where to take the course. If you were born before 1949, the state gives you credit for acquiring more sense with every passing year, so you are not required to take the course. However, it may be worth your while to take it anyway.

Every year the state issues several *Game Proclamations*, which are inserted in newspapers or are separately available at newsstands, that describe the rules, regulations, and penalties for violations for each type of game. The *Big Game Proclamation* is issued in March each year. Pick this up early because sometimes it is necessary to enter a lottery to get a tag to hunt in special management units or to take a specific gender.

Hunters might be able to improve their collective image if they learned to show more respect for the land and for the animals they harvest. When a hunter takes an animal's life, nothing should be wasted. The meat should be kept clean while in the field waiting for retrieval. It can be a big job packing an animal out, and you may want to plan ahead for a local registered outfitter to retrieve your game. Outfitters are registered with the state to accept payment for this service when working on public lands. They will cost you some money, but they are usually quick and efficient, and they are the only legal way to hire someone to provide these services on federal land.

Your animal should be field dressed immediately for cooling, and under no circumstances should there ever be a whole deer or elk on top of your vehicle to be paraded around town. This kind of display is extremely offensive to nonhunters and to ethical hunters. Your meat should be promptly taken to a processor or packed into coolers to take home.

Although you may feel great pride in the accomplishment of bagging an animal in the backcountry, particularly if the meat goes to feed your family or is donated to others, try to remember that not everyone shares your sense of accomplishment. Show others in any way you can that you respect the land, the animals, and the opinions of nonhunters.

IV. Summary

The Queen of Soul said it best: *respect.* That's what a backcountry experience is all about. Sharing the backcountry of Colorado starts with respecting each other's interests and passions. Our interests may not always be the same, but that doesn't mean any higher value should be placed on one use over another. There are many forest user groups in Colorado, and they can get into some pretty heated discussions about trail use, but that's okay and can be constructive. When so many people compete for backcountry resources it's natural to feel like protecting your favorite uses lest you lose your rights to others. However, if we all learn to respect other people and their competing land uses, we can go on using the trails and forests for many purposes and everyone can continue to share, enjoy, and nurture our precious backcountry resources.

References and Additional Information

Back Country Horseman Guidebook
P.O. Box 597
Columbia Falls, MT 59912

Packing In on Mules and Horses
Smoke Elser and Bill Brown
The Mountain Press Publishing Company
283 West Front Street
Missoula, MT 59801

Wilderness Medicine Beyond First Aid
William Forgey, M.D.
ICS Books Inc.
1370 East 86th Place
Merrillville, IN 46410

"Leave No Trace" leaflets and brochures available at all U.S. Forest Service and Bureau of Land Management offices

24

On Being a Good Recreational Neighbor

Ed Zink, *Outdoor Recreation Specialist*

Being a good recreational neighbor may have more to do with emotion and perception than with logic and laws. In managing successful recreational relationships with our neighbors, we need to consider both aspects. This article offers some of these perspectives.

I. Common Myths Regarding Recreation

History starts with me

Most of us view the world in short time frames rather than on a historic continuation. We believe that "reality" starts in a neighborhood the day we arrive. Therefore, we believe that the way things are on that day is not only how they always have been but also how they always should be. Unfortunately, we all arrive on different days and have very differing perceptions. As you might expect, there will be extreme differences in perception between folks who have lived in a neighborhood for years, and have seen many changes occur, and the recent arrival. Identifying and understanding these differences is crucial to maintaining good recreational neighbor relationships.

I was here first, so it's mine

Somewhere in our genetic history is a territorial gene. Each of us stakes out our territory and resents others invading our space. Legally we mark our territory with fences and walls. Frequently we also have emotional territories that are less clearly marked, like our favorite fishing hole on a public stream. It is important to recognize both our own and our neighbor's territories, whether they are marked by fences or by memories.

I worked hard to earn my recreational reward, and I deserve it

Each of us feels fulfillment when we attain our recreational goals. We feel pride in overcoming either physical or emotional obstacles in our quest to continually reestablish our recreational self-image. Unfortunately, we often resent anyone who can do the same thing more easily or faster.

There ought to be a law

When we want or expect things to be a certain way, we often assume there is a law somewhere to ensure that we can control the situation to our own liking. Before we get too worked up about anything, we need to seek out good factual information. It is usually emotionally costly to accept as fact everything we hear. It is especially costly when we have selective hearing—and hear just what we want.

II. Tools for Good Recreational Neighbor Relationships

Look and listen

In maintaining good recreational relationships with our neighbors, we need to identify and consider the points of view of both ourselves and our neighbors. Good communication is the essence of being a good recreational neighbor.

Education is more effective than anger

Seldom does anyone intentionally do something they think is wrong. Even if someone is doing something you believe is wrong, you can assume they think it is okay or they wouldn't be doing it. Education is much more effective than anger in modifying behavior.

Be considerate

Each of us has an equal right to life, liberty, and *the pursuit of happiness*. Conflict often arises when someone else's pursuit of happiness infringes on our own path to happiness. Be considerate of their point of view.

There are rules

Although the primary issues in being good recreational neighbors are emotional, there are often a few rules and laws that give guidance to our recreational interaction. A clear understanding of these rules and laws is essential for good neighbors.

We're all different

We need to accept each other for who we are. Think how boring life would be if we all got up at the same time, went to bed at the same time, and did everything else the same too.

Whose land is it?

This is sometimes hard to know. It is advisable to take the time to search out the information, especially if you plan to be in an area repeatedly or often. People should always know whose property they are on. If it is public, then there will undoubtedly be some rules by the land manager about proper uses of the area. Sometimes travel is restricted to designated trails in heavily used areas. Usually dogs must be on a leash or at least under constant control. Frequently there are restrictions about firearms, fires, trash, overnight camping, or travel closures to protect sensitive environmental or wildlife issues. Always watch for signs giving information about the area. The appropriate land managers will also have maps and pamphlets in their offices. With 60 percent to 70 percent of the West being managed by either the U.S. Forest Service or the Bureau of Land Management, there is a very good chance that backcountry recreation is taking place on federal land. *Know before you go!*

Traveling on private property without permission is trespassing. Private landowners are *not* required to post or fence their property to keep people off. If you are found by a landowner to be trespassing, the old "I didn't see any signs" defense won't help the situation a bit. A prompt apology and request for good information to prevent any unwanted trespassing in the future is the best approach. Even if you suspect that you are within your rights to be there, it is a good idea to avoid a confrontation until you can research the situation. Federal agency maps, county

ownership records, or knowledgeable neighbors are good sources of information about landownership.

In many cases private landowners will grant permission for you to travel on their property if they are asked in advance. Good neighbors offer to assist private landowners in exchange for permission to use their land. This can be as easy as picking up some trash as you travel through. Or maybe something more like helping the landowner one afternoon a year if the benefit you gain for being on the land is worth it to you. It has become common for private landowners to charge for hunting rights on their property.

III. How Are We Going to Pay for the Facilities We Need to Have Fun?

As our utilization of the land intensifies, so does the management. When the West was settled, public land was open to any and all recreation uses. Well into the 1900s only a few of the premier spots, and areas of obvious damage, had any recreational restrictions. Times have changed. Recreation on public lands now must adhere to travel management plans, wilderness management profiles, special-use permits, National Enviromental Policy Act (NEPA) processes, and siltation gradients, to name a few restrictions. This intensified management of the recreational activity is coming simultaneously with a reduction of activity by the historical extractive uses. With a loss of extractive-industry activity on our public lands, there is a corresponding loss of funding available to manage those public lands. Previously the extractive industries paid substantial amounts into the national treasury and had powerful lobbies to insure that the money was reinvested in managing the public lands. Now the lobbies are weaker and the management budgets are leaner. As the recreational demands on the public lands increase, there are increasing challenges to fund the necessary facilities and management needed to protect them. In the past, recreation has been the beneficiary of trail building, road development, mapping, etc., that was being done by the extractive industries. Things are changing, and recreational users will be called upon to fund facilities and management for their own activities.

Various recreational factions conduct fund-raising activities in order to influence developing policies. The most established recreational lobby is the Sierra Club, and there are constituencies developing for every recreational use, from horseback riding to four-wheel driving. There are even strong lobbies developing in support of no human use, with an emphasis on preventing fragmentation of wildlife habitat. Even though the lobbies exist, there isn't much funding coming along to pay for the necessary evaluation and subsequent management necessary to accommodate all these points of view.

There is only one source of funds: us. The real question is, When and how do we allocate the funds to manage recreation? Shall we raise taxes and trust that the political process will deliver these increased funds to this use? Do we apply political pressure to reallocate existing tax funds to this management use, and if so, at what cost to which existing programs? Or do we develop some kind of fee system by which the users would pay for the management of their use? None of these will be effective until the recreationalists view each other as partners and work together to find funding solutions. This may well be the most difficult issue facing recreation on our public lands for the next decade: where to get the money. In the spirit of this book, good neighbors should work together to insure adequate funding to protect the values each of us cherish about the public lands.

IV. Specific Recreational Activities: How to Be a Good Neighbor

Walking or hiking

Walking or hiking is the most common recreational activity in America. Usually we are walking for the sake of walking. Our pace is suited to our own needs. Some of us want a social experience and speak to every one we meet. Others are searching for quiet time and prefer to keep to themselves. Usually we can observe walkers for only a few moments to get some clues about their expectations from their walk. Then it is easier to be a good neighbor if you help them achieve their goals.

Remember, we noted that people often resent others who are faster or travel with less effort. Walkers often resent and are intimidated by folks who are using bikes, motorcycles, horses, or automobiles to get places faster and more easily. Sensitive walkers should choose their routes wisely and make some effort to avoid areas where they may be negatively impacted. Wilderness areas are a good choice for walkers who wish to avoid conflict with mechanical activity.

The faster travelers need to recognize that they may be intimidating to the walker and be extra considerate when passing the walker. The walker may be offended by speed, noise, and dust. There are all types of plans about who should yield to whom when meeting on the trail. The best rule of thumb is—whoever can yield with the least inconvenience should be considerate and do so. Unfortunately for a walker on a busy bike trail, this means that they may be yielding every few minutes. By the twentieth time,

they may be getting a little tired of always being the one to step aside. Faster travelers should be extra polite to walkers who yield, greet, and thank them.

Mountain biking

The newest member of the recreational family is the mountain biker. Unlike walking, which has been around for millions of years, the etiquette of mountain biking is just developing. For the most part, mountain bikers can be divided into two groups: those who ride for the thrill of speed and those who ride for the pleasure of exercise and the chance to escape into a backcountry experience. Either way, they are new, and as a group they haven't "paid their trail dues." Oftentimes more established trail user groups resent the newcomers with their bright clothing. However, the popularity of mountain biking will ensure that cyclists will soon be a very important faction of the overall recreational coalition. Mountain biking is destined to take a prominent place in the future of public recreational policy.

Walkers are intimidated and often angered by the speed of mountain bikers. This is especially true if a group of mountain bikers is riding aggressively, trying to outdo each other. Even though the mountain bikers may seem to be out of control, they seldom run into trees. If they can avoid the trees, they can avoid other trail users as well.

Equestrians and their horses are often startled by mountain bikes, especially when the cyclists ride up from behind. Since the bikes are quiet, they are often fairly close before the rider or the horse is aware. The best thing a mountain-bike rider can do is to call out, or have a little bell on the handlebars, to give the horse rider adequate warning that they are approaching. When the bike is coming from behind, the horse rider will need time to find a wide place in the trail to allow for passing. The bike rider should wait until the horse rider selects the safe passing place and then proceed slowly.

In the case that the bikes and horses are going opposite directions, the bike riders should yield to the horses. It is safer for the bike rider to be on the downhill side of the trail and at least 4 or 5 feet from the trail. A courteous greeting by everyone involved goes a long way toward being a good neighbor.

Mountain bikers can travel a long way in a day. This adds to the popularity of the sport, and also the risk. Lost mountain bikers are often hard to find because they can go so far. It is especially important for mountain bikers to gather good route information before going out for a ride. They also need to give someone good information about where they are going and their expected return time. Unfortunately, a simple mechanical failure can reduce the 15-mile-an-hour bike to a 25-pound impediment to walking back. Mountain bikers should always keep their bikes in good operating condition and carry enough tools to repair the most common mechanical failures, especially flat tires.

Motorized recreation

The number one recreational activity in the West is windshield tourism: driving a car. Our national fascination with motors has found its way into off-road recreation as well. Four-wheel drives, motorcycles, and ATVs are carrying their owners on many great adventures. Sometimes the thrill of speed and power is the recreational goal. Other times the objective is to get to some particular location faster and more easily than by more natural means. The proliferation of roads made by the extractive industries, such as logging or mining, has provided a wealth of motorized recreational opportunities. The reduction in extractive activity will shift the burden of funding those roads to recreation.

Motorized recreationalists may be thought of as at the top of the food chain. They are not usually bothered by any other user groups. They have more mobility, more power, more speed, and more volume than any other group. They are also more tolerant of other user groups because they feel less affected by anyone else. However, they have the most impact on other user groups. They travel farther in a day and can have an impact on more miles of country. In addition to the direct ecological impact of the vehicles, there is the noise pollution that can affect other user groups and wildlife. Motorized recreational users have a high responsibility to understand how they affect other users and to mitigate that impact as much as possible. Their recreational future will depend on their ability to work with the other users for an amicable coexistence.

It is especially important that motorized users are well informed about approved uses and that they apply peer pressure to ensure compliance. Staying on the designated routes is essential for motorized users to be viewed as good neighbors.

25

Colorado State Parks: Our Pride and Joy

Thea Rock, *Former Public Information Specialist*
Colorado State Parks

Although we claim the lands we use for public recreation as our own, we should remember that we are only visitors. We have entrusted management of those lands to specially trained staff charged with caring for the land and the wildlife and with fostering the enjoyment of visitors today and in the future.

As a manager of outdoor recreation on public lands, Colorado State Parks provides a variety of opportunities to play and to satisfy the human need to connect with our surroundings. The programs of Colorado State Parks offer guidelines for good neighboring while enjoying outdoor recreation.

I. Things We Do

When you think state parks, often the first thing that comes to mind is camping or hiking. However, though these are important activities administered by Colorado State Parks, many other statewide programs are also administered by the division, including boating safety, education, and law enforcement; river and flat-water patrols; boat and off-highway vehicles (OHV) registrations; snowmobile programs; and the Colorado Natural Areas Program (sustaining and registering unique, endangered, or threatened wildlife, plants, and geologic formations). Partnerships with agencies such as the Colorado Division of Wildlife, the federal Bureau of Land Management, the U.S. Army Corps of Engineers, the U.S. Forest Service, and others allow Colorado State Parks to provide a variety of outdoor experiences for the public.

II. Organization

The division is divided into four regions (South, West, North and Metro), each of which boasts a variety of outdoor offerings. Parks range from a prairie oasis such as Bonny Lake State Park on the eastern plains of Colorado to the world-famous rugged rock-climbing site at Eldorado Canyon just south of Boulder. The West Region's Ridgway State Park is an alpine paradise, and the Arkansas Headwaters Recreation Area is famed for white-water rafting. A list of state parks, by region, is included at the end of this chapter.

Good Neighboring

With the growth of population in Colorado, public lands are crowded with adventurers and citizens trying to get away from it all. Whenever entering state parks or any public lands, be a good neighbor and keep these principles in mind:

- Golden Rule—Treat other users as you would have them treat you.
- Leave No Trace—In order for the natural beauty of our public lands to be maintained, pack out what you bring into the park. Use only established trails and campsites. Don't leave your mark on the park!
- Park staff members are charged with protecting the land and the natural resources on and in it, providing for public safety, and fostering stewardship.
- Know the rules. Park staff members will give you a copy of the rules and regulations if you ask.

Getting There

There are currently forty great Colorado state parks in which to play; you can almost certainly find a Colorado park within a reasonable drive. All vehicles entering state parks are required to have a parks pass. You may select an annual vehicle pass that allows you entrance to all state parks for one calendar year or a daily pass good for a single park for a single day (expiring at noon the following day). Some parks also charge an individual fee for users who enter on foot, bicycle, or other nonmotorized conveyance.

Get Out and Explore

State parks have a variety of trails for visitors. Almost all of the trails may be used for hiking. However, because hiking trails are not made to withstand vehicles, not all hiking trails may be used for motorized vehicles such as all-terrain vehicles (ATVs) and motorcycles. Use ATVs, motorcycles, snowmobiles, etc., only on trails marked for such use. These trails are built and maintained by volunteers and staff to minimize the impact of motorized vehicles on the land. Rules apply to all vehicles, whether they are cars, four-wheel-drive vehicles, recreational vehicles, snowmobiles, motorcycles, or ATVs. Park only where parking is provided. Although we have a "trail-blazer" spirit, it's the user's responsibility to keep on the trails, allowing public land managers to keep recreation opportunities available.

Tread-itors

Even when you're on foot, bike, or horseback, there are rules of courtesy. Bicyclists should give the right-of-way to all other trail users. People on foot should yield to horseback riders or people with other livestock. Trail users are always responsible for their actions. When using a trail, stay to the right except when passing another trail user. Look ahead as well as to the rear before attempting to pass on the trail, and stay on the trail as much as possible to lessen your impact on the habitat. Always respect private property—do not cross fences. Although you may be tempted to take home a wildflower or an unusual rock as a souvenir, remember that these objects may be food or shelter for some wildlife. Never litter. Carry a trash bag with you and pick up food scraps, empty containers, cigarette butts, and other debris. Litter is unsightly and could pose a danger to wildlife.

Meeting Wildlife

One of the wonders of hiking, biking, or using off-highway vehicles is the chance to view wildlife. Keep in mind that these creatures are not cute, cuddly pets but fiercely protective wild animals. The Colorado Division of Wildlife produces materials on wildlife encounters; highlights from these publications are provided below. Take the time to obtain these brochures and read them. It could save your life.

All wildlife

Be constantly aware of your surroundings, and if you encounter a bear, mountain lion, or moose, stay calm. Don't allow children to run or scream. Make sure you are not separating the animal from its young.

Bear

Stay calm. Stop and face the bear, but avoid direct eye contact. Give the bear room to escape. Don't run—slowly leave the area. Speak softly, reassuring the animal that you mean it no harm. If a black bear attacks you, fight back with rocks, sticks, even your bare hands.

Mountain lion

Stay calm. Stop and make yourself appear larger by raising your arms over your head or opening up your jacket like a boat's sail. Yell and shout at the animal, throw rocks, and slowly move out of the area. If you run, the animal will consider you prey and attack. If the lion attacks, fight back with a walking stick, rocks, or your bare hands.

Moose

Moose have keen senses of smell and hearing. They are big, and they know it. The size and nasty temper of a moose leaves it with few natural enemies. Be alert to the possibility that a moose is nearby. Never approach a moose; view them only from a distance. If a moose becomes alarmed or angered, the heavy mane on its thick neck will stand up. If you see this sign, retreat immediately. This display of aggressive behavior will most likely come from a cow protecting her calves or during the mating season, from mid-September to mid-October. Hold still, blend into the background, and get a barrier (such as a tree) between you and the animal. A moose's long legs allow it to run fast and cover lots of ground, so outrunning a moose is highly unlikely.

Water Wise Guys

On the water, even more care must be taken to be a good neighbor. On lakes and reservoirs you may be enjoying an afternoon of water-skiing, but your activities may annoy nearby anglers trying to land a trophy fish. Be considerate. Colorado State Parks has a set of water use plans for different bodies of water that explains which activities are allowed in different areas of the water. Understand buoy markings and navigational rules before you launch. Know the rules. Always wear life jackets. Don't drink and boat. Watch out for the other guy (including personal-watercraft users and downed skiers). Be alert to "boating hypnosis" brought on by wind, waves, sun, and the drone of the boat motor. Take responsibility for your actions.

It's also important to be considerate of other users when you use rivers. White-water rafting, canoeing, and kayaking are very popular in Colorado. Numerous commercial outfitters provide thrilling experiences, but remember that the adventure isn't a controlled amusement-park rollercoaster ride. It's a potentially dangerous experience controlled by Mother Nature. The way to ensure white-water safety is to realistically assess the skill level of the participants. Many people overestimate their skills and find themselves dealing with more river than they can handle. Make an honest assessment of your limitations.

If you or your group take a break from the river, be a good neighbor. Respect private property and do not trespass. Pack out any trash you create and any you find. Camp or picnic only in established takeouts or campsites. Alert rangers to potential hazards in and out of the water. Keep vehicles on existing roads and parking areas.

Fido's Folly

Although your pet is one of the family, you may need to think twice before bringing your pet to a park. Dogs must stay in areas in which they are allowed and must be on a leash no more than 6 feet long. They are not allowed at beaches where people swim or water-ski. These rules are necessary for at least four good reasons. First, not all park users like pets; they may not appreciate a cold nose on their knee and may react with fear or anger. Second, other park users may have dogs that are not as well trained as your dog or may be aggressive; you wouldn't want your dog hurt in a fight. Third, trail users don't appreciate stepping in any kind of animal scat—always clean up after your pet. Fourth, it's against state law for dogs to harass wildlife; you need to have your dog under control.

Camper Capers

Most of Colorado's state parks provide campgrounds for tent or recreational vehicle (RV) camping. Campgrounds are busy places these days, and you should reserve your site in advance (a reservation fee and nightly camping fees apply) in order to assure that you have a space once you get to the park. Contact the campground reservations unit at 1-800-678-CAMP or (303) 470-1144. Camping is allowed only in established campsites, and fires are restricted to fire rings or grills provided. Camping "ABCs" are "Always Be Considerate" of others within the campgrounds. Quiet hours are observed between ten P.M. and six A.M. Don't overload the campsite with too many people and too many vehicles. Pick up your trash; keep lights low; always tend campfires and be sure they are completely extinguished when retiring or leaving the campsite. Secure your pets so they don't disturb your neighbors or wildlife. Don't leave food or even empty coolers unattended; bears or mountain lions may not be able to resist your unintended invitation. Resist the temptation to feed squirrels and other small animals. Be considerate with power generators that can disturb neighboring campers. If you choose to consume alcohol, do it responsibly. Never drink when boating, using off-highway vehicles, or swimming.

Home Sweet Habitat

As Colorado's population continues to grow, housing developments are swallowing up open spaces. Many developers know that an attractive selling point is a location next door to a state park. However, if you are considering purchasing land or an existing homesite that borders a state park, you need to realize that these areas may have special problems.

Parks shelter wildlife of all kinds. You will suddenly be a neighbor to the wildlife in the area, including endangered and protected species. Your neighbors may include foxes, raccoons, skunks, bats, geese, deer, prairie dogs, snakes, squirrels, bears, mountain lions, and elk as well as many birds. Your wild neighbors need to eat, so if you plant a lush vegetable or flower garden, remember that it will be seen as an open invitation to feasting wildlife. Never leave pet food outside or an animal tied up unattended. Consider native plant species for landscaping. Keep fencing to a minimum.

These days long-range fire management techniques in public forests sometimes include the use of prescribed burns that are intentionally set and controlled fires that burn the tinder off the forest floor. Periodically your home may be in the smokepath. It's not a bad idea to keep firefighting tools handy.

Homeowners close to public land need to be even more vigilant than most homeowners about the unchecked growth of noxious weeds that can displace the native plants that wildlife need for fodder. Check with your county weed-control district or with the Cooperative Extension office at Colorado State University. It's okay not to mow areas of native grasses.

Often boundaries between parklands and developed property are not clearly marked. Be prepared to confront hunters and hikers who may wander onto your property as a good neighbor.

Consideration and common sense are the keys to having a good experience while using the state parks. These principles also guide the stewardship of the Colorado State Parks staff as they manage and protect the beautiful public lands we all share.

Resources

For more information on trails across the state or within Colorado State Parks, contact the State Trails Program at the Colorado State Parks address below or check out the Colorado State Parks website and select the "Trails" option.

Colorado State Parks Division Office
1313 Sherman Street, Room 618
Denver, CO 80203
Phone: (303) 866-3437
Fax: (303) 866-3206
Website: www.coloradoparks.org

Colorado State Parks North Region Office
3842 S. Mason, Room 202
Fort Collins, CO 80525
(970) 226-6641

Colorado State Parks West Region Office
361–32 Road
Clifton, CO 81520
(970) 434-6862

Colorado State Parks South Region Office
2128 N. Weber
Colorado Springs, CO 80907
(719) 471-0900

Colorado State Parks Metro Region Office
13787 S. Highway 85
Littleton, CO 80125
(303) 791-1957

Colorado State Parks Registration Unit (Boats, Snow-mobiles, Off-Highway Vehicles)
13787 S. Highway 85
Littleton, CO 80125
(303) 791-1920

Colorado State Parks Campground Reservations
Statewide: (800) 678-2267
Denver metro area: (303) 470-1144

Colorado State Parks "Boating Safely in Colorado" education programs
(888) 593-BOAT or (303) 791-1954

Colorado Department of Natural Resources
1313 Sherman Street, Room 718
Denver, CO 80203
(303) 866-3311

Division of Wildlife
6060 Broadway, Denver, CO 80216
(303) 297-1192

Publications

Colorado State Parks Regulations, published annually
Colorado State Parks Boating Statutes and Regulations, published annually
Colorado State Parks "Park Pointers," topical brochures for park visitors. Titles include "Top 10," "Pets in Parks," "Life's a Beach," "Climate Clues," "Camping with Kids," "Camping Kindly," "Sharing the Trail"
Colorado State Parks Guide, "40 Great Places to Play"
Individual park brochures

State Parks by Region

Metro
Barr Lake State Park
Castlewood Canyon State Park
Chatfield State Park
Cherry Creek State Park
Eldorado Canyon State Park
Golden Gate Canyon State Park
Roxborough State Park

North
Barbour Ponds State Park
Boyd Lake State Park
State Forest State Park
Jackson Lake State Park
Lory State Park
North Sterling State Park
Pearl Lake State Park
Picnic Rock State Park
Stagecoach State Park
Steamboat Lake State Park
Yampa River Legacy

South
Arkansas Headwaters Recreation Area
Bonny Lake State Park

Eleven Mile State Park
Lathrop State Park
Mueller State Park
Lake Pueblo State Park
San Luis Lakes State Park
Spinney Mountain State Park
Trinidad Lake State Park

West
Colorado River State Park
Crawford State Park

Harvey Gap State Park
Highline Lake State Park
Mancos State Park
Navajo State Park
Paonia State Park
Ridgway State Park
Rifle Falls State Park
Rifle Gap State Park
Sweitzer Lake State Park
Sylvan Lake State Park
Vega State Park

26

Colorado's State Trust Lands

**Kate Jones, *Public Information Officer*
Colorado State Board of Land Commissioners**

Often when people buy property, they like to know a little bit about the neighbors; in Colorado it's possible that one of your "neighbors" might be the state of Colorado itself. There are 3 million acres of land in Colorado that are considered State Trust Land. This chapter will explain where those lands are and how they're managed by the state. Many of these tracts are off limits to the public, but some are managed by other agencies, such as the Colorado Division of Wildlife (DOW), for public use.

I. What Are State Trust Lands?

Colorado's 3 million acres of State Trust Lands were given to the state by the federal government in 1876 for specific purposes such as the support of "common schools." To this day these lands are leased for ranching, farming, mineral and oil and gas production, and other uses in order to produce income that is put into eight trust accounts. The largest trust is managed for the benefit of kindergarten through twelfth grade education in the state. All trust lands are managed by the Colorado State Board of Land Commissioners (also known as the State Land Board, or SLB), a division of the Department of Natural Resources. This agency is overseen by a five-person citizen board and has a staff of twenty-nine people and a budget of around $2 million a year.

In November 1996, Colorado voters passed a constitutional amendment that changed the structure and mission of the SLB. The amendment did a number of things:

• Reaffirmed that the School Trust (93 percent of the State Trust Lands) is an intergenerational trust that is managed for the long-term benefit of public schools

• Set the revenue benchmark as "reasonable and consistent income over time." (Prior to the amendment, the Constitution had been interpreted as directing the SLB to maximize revenue)
• Mandated that the SLB place a high priority on good stewardship of State Trust Lands so that they can benefit future generations of Colorado schoolchildren
• Created a 300,000-acre Stewardship Trust of lands that are to receive special stewardship attention and are protected from sale or development unless four of the five SLB members vote to take them out of the trust

II. Where Are State Trust Lands Located?

If you look at a map that shows state trust ownership (most often shown in dark blue), you will notice that many parts of the eastern plains look like a blue checkerboard pattern. In other places, especially the far western portion of the state, the blue blotches are bigger and there are large areas where there are no blue squares at all. The basis of these patterns is that the federal government granted Colorado sections 16 and 36 in each township, except in areas where there were already claims to those lands. There are examples of already claimed land in Costilla County, which was subject to a Spanish land grant; Montrose and Delta Counties, which were then part of the Ute Indian Reservation; and Summit County, where there was already a lot of mining activity. In areas with preexisting claims, the federal government ceded larger blocks of land to the state than in areas where there weren't prior claims.

III. How Are State Trust Lands Managed?

Because the SLB has a very small staff, State Trust Lands are managed through leases to individuals, companies, and government agencies that pay for the privilege of using State Trust Lands in specific ways. Common uses that lands are leased for include grazing, farming, mining, and oil and gas production. The board also issues rights-of-way, easements, and road access permits.

In the early 1990s the SLB also began leasing land for recreation and other uses. So far the biggest customer is the CDOW, which leases more than 400,000 acres of trust land throughout the state for hunting, fishing, and other wildlife-related recreation. These recreation leases are "stacked on top of" other existing leases for grazing and other activities, and all the lessees work together to create an access plan to ensure that they can peacefully coexist and that the natural values of the state land are conserved. The DOW can provide information about recreation on these lands. In recent years the SLB has begun to diversify its portfolio of assets to include commercial properties in Denver and other urban areas.

IV. How Much Money Does the SLB Make for Schools?

In fiscal year 1996–1997, the agency earned about $23 million in revenue from uses including grazing fees, oil, gas and coal royalty payments, and rents from office buildings. A second source of annual dollars for schools is interest income from the School Permanent Fund, which contains nearly $275 million earned over the years by the SLB—mainly from land sales and mineral royalties. When this interest is added, total benefits to schools in Colorado amounted to more than $30 million. The agency also manages seven other smaller trusts that benefit the University of Colorado, Colorado State University, Colorado State Parks, Fort Lewis College, the Department of Corrections, and Public Buildings. The total revenues of these seven trusts in fiscal year 1996–1997 were over $650,000.

V. Can I Hike, Mountain Bike, or Bird-Watch on State Trust Lands?

Because the SLB's first responsibility is to its trust beneficiaries, State Trust Lands are not "public" in the same way that lands owned by the U.S. Forest Service and the Bureau of Land Management are. Unless a local or state agency or private individual has come forward and offered to pay for the right to have recreational use of a particular piece of State Trust Land and taken responsibility for managing that recreation, the land is just as off limits to the public as a piece of private land.

Some large blocks of State Trust Land are open for recreation. For example, the SLB's 72,000-acre Colorado State Forest west of Fort Collins in Jackson County is managed for recreation by Colorado State Parks.

For Additional Information

The SLB's main office is located at 1313 Sherman, Room 620, Denver, CO 80203; the phone number is (303) 866-3454, ext. 320. Also check out the SLB website at: www.dnr.state.co.us/slb.

The agency also maintains five district offices:

Craig Office (970) 824-2850
577 Yampa Ave. (P.O. Box 1094)
Craig, CO 81626
(Delta, Eagle, Garfield, Grand, Gunnison, Jackson, Mesa, Moffat, Montrose, Ouray, Pitkin, Rio Blanco, Routt, and Summit Counties)

Greeley Office (970) 352-3038
800 8th Ave., Suite 219
Greeley, CO 80631
(Adams, Arapahoe, Boulder, Clear Creek, Denver, Douglas, Elbert, Gilpin, Jefferson, Larimer, Morgan, and Weld Counties)

Sterling Office (970) 522-0975
301 Poplar, Suite 3
Sterling, CO 80751
(Cheyenne, Kit Carson, Lincoln, Logan, Phillips, Sedgwick, Washington, and Yuma Counties)

Alamosa Office (719) 589-2360
422 4th St. (Box 88)
Alamosa, CO 81101
(Alamosa, Archuleta, Conejos, Costilla, Dolores, Hinsdale, Huerfano, La Plata, Las Animas, Mineral, Montezuma, Rio Grande, Saguache, San Juan and San Miguel Counties)

Pueblo Office (719) 543-7403
201 W. 8th, Suite 307
Pueblo, CO 81003
(Baca, Bent, Chaffee, Crowley, Custer, El Paso, Fremont, Kiowa, Lake, Otero, Park, Prowers, Pueblo, and Teller Counties)

27

Colorado Division of Wildlife Lands and You

Pat Tucker, *District Wildlife Manager*
Colorado Division of Wildlife

Much of Colorado is owned by the public. In many ways we are fortunate that there is so much land under federal, state, and local government jurisdiction and management. Although these lands may be enjoyed by all, try to think of the agencies that manage these lands as neighbors who are trying to keep the property in good condition for the benefit of all—for that reason, there are some restrictions on use.

One of your governmental neighbors may be the Colorado Division of Wildlife (CDOW). The Colorado state legislature has declared that "wildlife and their environment are to be protected, preserved, enhanced, and managed for the use, benefit, and enjoyment of the people of this state and their visitors. It is further declared to be the policy of this state that there shall be provided a comprehensive program designed to offer the greatest possible variety of wildlife related recreational opportunity to the people of this state and its visitors" (C.R.S. §33-1-101).

The CDOW is the state agency within the Department of Natural Resources that is charged with fulfilling this mandate. Policy and regulatory decisions are made by an eight-member Wildlife Commission whose members are appointed by the governor. Meetings are held around the state throughout the year as a way for public input and comment to be received.

The Colorado DOW is one of the few agencies with a true statewide presence. There are numerous programs that (1) assist landowners in creating habitat and solving wildlife-related problems, (2) provide hunting and fishing opportunities, (3) conduct biological studies and research projects, (4) locate and maintain wildlife viewing sites, (5) coordinate with federal, other state, and local entities about projects that may affect wildlife or its habitat, and (6) develop educational programs for schools and private clubs. In addition, there are a host of other activities conducted on a daily basis by the DOW's nearly six hundred employees.

Unlike most governmental agencies, your neighbor, the DOW, does not receive any general-fund tax funding. Instead, a nearly $75 million annual budget is derived from the sale of hunting and fishing licenses, a federal excise tax from the sale of hunting and fishing gear, a voluntary state tax checkoff for nongame and endangered species, and state lottery proceeds for specific projects.

The Colorado Division of Wildlife manages approximately 675,000 acres of state land (November 1997 figure). These areas are called State Wildlife Areas (SWAs) and are acquired for wildlife habitat protection or wildlife recreation (hunting, fishing, photography, observing). The division does not follow the doctrine of "multiple use" for land management that is implemented by the U.S. Forest Service and the Bureau of Land Management. Owing to federal and state laws regulating the use of DOW properties, wildlife is the top-priority emphasis, and other uses are allowed only if they don't conflict or interfere with the protection of habitat or wildlife recreation. A permit from the Wildlife Commission is needed for most nonwildlife activities that take place within an SWA.

These areas exist for wildlife first and for people second. Consequently, statewide and area-specific restrictions are in place to control people and reduce any impacts they may have on wildlife. Motorized (trail bikes, ATVs) and non-motorized (mountain bikes) wheeled vehicles are allowed only on designated roads within SWAs. Dogs must be leashed. Camping is generally not allowed or is allowed only within designated areas. Many SWAs are closed at certain times of the year to protect wildlife. The most typical example is during the winter for big game or during the spring and early summer for nesting or breeding wildlife.

If the idea of owning land next to a SWA is attractive to you, be sure you've thought about the activities that the DOW does allow in these areas. Hunting and fishing are allowed in most SWAs. Adjacent landowners must recognize that many activities, not just the ones they approve of, may be taking place. You may not agree that hunting is a legit-imate recreational activity, but if your neighbor is a DOW SWA, you may have no choice but to live next to land on which hunting is allowed. During the fall, these lands receive heavy use from hunters.

Although owning land next to governmental open space may seem attractive and an inexpensive way to have a piece of those wide open spaces, think long and hard about the activities that will take place next door.

Regardless of whether you are a hunter or fisherman, plan to visit your local DOW office and get to know your neighbor. These offices have much interesting and free information about the wildlife in Colorado that you can take with you. The locations and phone numbers can be found in the telephone book blue pages.

28

Wide Open Spaces:
The Bureau of Land Management

Roger Alexander, *Public Affairs Specialist*
Bureau of Land Management, Colorado

In Colorado, the Bureau of Land Management (better known as BLM) manages more than 8.3 million acres of public lands and an additional 27.3 million acres of subsurface (mineral estate). Most of the public lands are located on the Western Slope, although the San Luis Valley, North Park, and areas northwest of Canon City have substantial public land acreage.

What exactly are "public lands"? For the purposes of this chapter, public lands refer only to the lands held in the public trust by the U.S. government and administered by BLM.

Why is it important to know that BLM is your next-door neighbor? Well, most people like to know a little about their neighbors: Do they take care of their property? What kind of activities do they allow on their property, and what are the potential future uses of that property? If you're not comfortable with those uses, what recourse do you have?

If you know the answers to these questions *before* you use or buy property, then you can make an informed decision. But even if you've already scheduled recreation or bought your dream property in Colorado, it's not too late to learn a little about your new neighbors—the public lands and BLM.

I. A Very Short History of the Public Lands and BLM

BLM's roots go back to the founding of the United States. After the Revolutionary War, the state of Maryland proposed that the "backcountry," those lands between the Ap-

palachian Mountains and the Mississippi River, which were claimed by seven of the newly formed states, be held in "common stock" by all the citizens of the United States.

Although there was resistance to this proposal by the land-claim states, eventually Maryland's proposal was accepted, thus creating the first public lands. Since then, every state admitted to the Union, with the exception of Texas, has ceded its claims to all vacant and unappropriated lands within its boundaries to the U.S. government. Of course, the lands weren't really vacant; the native peoples who lived in North America at the time had no choice but to accept the states and federal governments' claims to the land, which were based on European concepts of discovery and conquest.

Land acquisitions such as the Louisiana Purchase and the 1850 purchase of the northwest portion of Texas (what is now central Colorado) contributed to the growing public domain. At the same time that the U.S. government was acquiring new lands, it also embarked on its policy of "manifest destiny" and actively encouraged the settlement of the western United States by making the newly acquired lands available for private use. The General Land Office (GLO) was created in 1812 to ensure the orderly disposal of the public domain.

Various land disposal laws, the best known being the Homestead Act of 1860, provided a way for individuals, corporations, and states to acquire their pieces of the public domain. Other acts of Congress set aside large portions of the public domain for military and Indian reservations, the national park system, and the national forests.

Eventually the rapid westward expansion of the United States slowed as the arable and otherwise desirable lands in the public domain were claimed, purchased, or granted. The remaining public lands were considered leftovers, good only for livestock grazing and mining.

In response to range conflicts and growing public and congressional concerns about grazing on the public domain, the Taylor Grazing Act was passed in 1934. The Secretary of the Interior created the Grazing Service to administer the new law. In 1946, the GLO and Grazing Service were combined to form the Bureau of Land Management.

On October 21, 1976, the Federal Land Policy and Management Act (FLPMA) was passed and signed into law. After thirty years, BLM finally had an official mandate to manage the public lands for multiple uses. Congress used FLPMA to identify the "principal" uses of the public lands: "domestic livestock grazing, fish and wildlife development and utilization, mineral exploration and production, rights-of-way, outdoor recreation, and timber production."

So now that you now a little bit of the history of BLM, it's time to visit the neighborhood.

II. Bringing the Cows Home

The majority of public lands in Colorado are grazed by livestock. If you live next door to the public lands, you will probably get to meet the neighborhood livestock herd before too long. In Colorado, seasonal grazing on the public lands is the rule: late-spring, early-summer, and fall grazing at the lower elevations and summer grazing at the higher elevations.

Is your property fenced? If you don't want your neighbor's livestock grazing on your land, Colorado law puts the burden for financing and constructing the fence on you, the neighbor—that's what it means when you hear the expression "Colorado is an open-range state." The boundaries of many cattle-grazing allotments are already fenced, but if your land is surrounded by BLM land, the BLM grazing allotment is less likely to have an existing fence around your property. Sheep-grazing allotments are usually not fenced because most sheep grazing is conducted under the watchful eye of a sheepherder.

III. Where Do the Deer and the Antelope Play?

Next door! The public lands provide habitat for an incredible variety of wildlife species, and BLM has the responsibility to manage that habitat. However, based on the European concept of sovereign ownership of game animals, the state of Colorado (or the two Ute tribes with reservations in Colorado) own the wildlife, and the Colorado Division of Wildlife has responsibility for managing the state's animals. Of course, the animals couldn't care less about management responsibility or landownership, so don't be too surprised when some of the "real" locals decide to have dinner at your place.

IV. Timber!

Got a fireplace or wood-burning stove? Do you cut your own firewood? Many public lands in Colorado support scrub oak and piñon-juniper woodlands at the lower elevations and ponderosa pine and Douglas fir at higher elevations. Every year thousands of Colorado residents cut their firewood in specially designated areas on the public lands. Firewood permits are required, and they can be purchased at any BLM office and various vendors throughout the western half of the state.

Commercial timber operations on public lands in Colorado are relatively uncommon these days, and most are conducted to support a broader land management goal such as habitat improvement or to salvage bug-killed or diseased trees. Thousands of Christmas trees, primarily piñon pine, are harvested from Colorado's public lands each year.

V. They're Moving a Drilling Rig Next Door?

Generally, the public lands are available for oil and gas leasing, exploration, and development unless they have been withdrawn from operation of the mineral leasing laws or closed to oil and gas leasing through BLM's land use planning process. If you live in an area with little or no oil and gas potential, the odds are that you'll never see a drill rig on the public lands. But if you live in the southwest or northwest corners of the state, where oil and gas potential is high, don't be surprised if a drill rig sets up operations down the road a bit.

Whenever an oil and gas lessee or operator files an application for a permit to drill (APD) on public lands, BLM is required to notify the public. APDs are posted at BLM's Colorado state office in Lakewood and at local offices with responsibility for processing the applications. If you live in an area with high oil and gas potential and are concerned about exploration and development activities, you should visit the local BLM office public room on a regular basis.

VI. Honey, Are the Neighbors Digging a Swimming Pool or Is That an Open-Pit Mine?

One day you're walking around the neighborhood and notice some white PVC pipe sticking out of the ground on the adjoining parcel of public lands. So you walk over to check it out and find that somebody has filed a mining claim! How can they allow somebody to do this?

The General Mining Law of 1872 allows an individual or business to claim the locatable minerals (gold, silver, zinc, platinum, etc.) on public lands. Other laws provide for the leasing of geothermal resources and solid minerals such as coal, sodium, and potassium. Still other mineral materials such as sand and gravel can be sold to individuals or businesses, or in some situations provided free of charge to local governments.

Public lands are open to locatable mineral claims unless specifically withdrawn from the operation of the General Mining Law. In addition, the public lands generally are available for mineral leasing and the sale of mineral materials such as sand and gravel unless withdrawn or closed through BLM's land use planning process.

Does this mean that somebody could develop a mine next door? It's possible. But in reality, most locatable mining claims never go to production. If you live in a coal-producing area and the public lands are leased, the likelihood of development is higher, though if it's an underground operation, you may not even be able to see any mining-related activities.

Probably the most likely scenario for mining activity on the public lands is the development of a gravel pit. The demand for construction and road materials has increased dramatically as Colorado's population has exploded during recent years. The public lands provide a ready source of sand and gravel, and local governments can obtain those mineral materials free of charge from the public lands. If you live in a high-growth area, you should be aware that the public lands may be the best source of gravel for local governments and the construction industry. Generally, adjacent landowners are provided an opportunity to comment on these types of actions as part of BLM's environmental analysis process.

VII. A Road Runs over It

Many federal and state highways, county roads, and other roads and vehicle trails cross public lands. Many of these routes merely pass through public lands on their way to other destinations, whereas others terminate on the public lands. It is quite common for private access roads to pass through public lands, and in some cases, a new road is needed or desired. In that situation, a right-of-way to use and occupy the public lands is required.

In order to obtain a right-of-way to cross public lands, you must file an application with the BLM office that has jurisdiction for the area in which you live. An application fee is required to offset the cost for BLM to process the application. If a right-of-way is granted, an annual right-of-way rental fee is assessed. If you think you will need a right-of-way to cross public lands, check with the local BLM realty specialist as soon as possible to avoid future "roadblocks."

VIII. Can't They Put That Power Line Someplace Else?

Utility and communication companies find public lands to be desirable locations for water, gas, and oil pipelines as well as telephone, electrical, and fiber-optic lines. In addition to cross-country linear rights-of-way, microwave, radio, and television communication sites can be found on public lands at strategic high points throughout Colorado. The procedure for obtaining a utility right-of-way is generally the same as obtaining a right-of-way for a road.

IX. The Neighbors Are Selling? There Goes the Neighborhood!

Prior to 1976, it was national policy to dispose of the public lands. With the passage of the FLPMA, however, Congress expressly stated that the public lands were to remain in public ownership unless their disposal (via sale or exchange or other method) could be shown to be in the public interest. This was a radical change in perception regarding the value of public lands; for the first time, public lands were officially recognized as having public value.

But settlement patterns and previous disposal efforts have left a mosaic of public and private lands throughout the Western states. In many cases, isolated tracts of public lands ranging in size from less than 40 acres to over 1,000 acres are entirely surrounded by private lands. Unless private landowners in the area have granted an easement to BLM or other appropriate government entity, the public cannot legally cross private land to use the isolated public land parcels. In these types of situations, retaining the land in public ownership has to be questioned even though the land may have natural or cultural resource values.

Congress provided BLM with the authority to dispose of public lands if the disposal can be shown to be in the public interest. Although there are a number of different ways to dispose of the public lands, exchanges, and occasionally sales, are the primary methods used in Colorado.

BLM's disposal process requires public notification, and the public is invited to participate throughout the process. Public lands available for sale must be identified during BLM's land use planning process, which provides for public participation during the scoping and commenting phases. If an exchange proposal is received, BLM must first decide whether to pursue the exchange; if it appears that the exchange would be in the public interest, then BLM issues a Notice of Exchange Proposal, which is published in the *Federal Register* and the legal notices section of local newspapers; notifies adjoining landowners; and issues a news release to inform the general public of the proposal.

Because people's ideas of what constitutes the "public interest" may differ, public land disposal can often be a controversial and emotional issue. Almost everybody has a certain amount of uneasiness when we find out the neighbors are moving; we wonder what the new neighbors are going to be like and how we'll get along with them. When your neighbor is a tract of undeveloped public land and you're the only one who has had access to the area for the last ten years, then the level of apprehension can be very high. By participating in the public scoping and comment process, you can help ensure that your interests are considered along with other public interests.

X. Looking for a Little Culture in Your Life?

The New World was "new" only to Europeans; native peoples lived in North America for thousands of years before the Vikings and Columbus sailed the Atlantic. Evidence of these native peoples' lives can be found at thousands of cultural resource sites on public lands throughout Colorado. These sites and the artifacts (arrowheads, points, pottery shards, etc.) associated with them are protected by federal law. What should you do if you find cultural resources on the public lands? First, do not pick up or remove anything. Not only is it illegal, but you may be destroying the context of the site by altering the location and position of the artifacts. If the context of a cultural resource site is destroyed, most, if not all, of the scientific value is lost. Second, report your finding to the BLM so an archaeologist can investigate the site and take steps to protect it. And last, but not least, you might want to use your discovery as a starting point to increase your knowledge of the native people who once made their home where you now live.

XI. Why Do the Neighbors Have to Party All the Time?

Outdoor recreation: It seems like everybody in Colorado is doing it, and chances are they are doing it right next door! Hunters, hikers, horseback riders, mountain bikers, motorcyclists, all-terrain-vehicle riders, snowmobilers, four-wheel-drive enthusiasts, nature photographers, trail runners, rafters, kayakers, fishermen (and women!), cross-country skiers, snowshoers, lovers looking for a secluded spot, New Agers seeking the spiritual center of their universe, and people just trying to get away from the hustle and hassles of everyday life—you can find them all on Colorado's public lands. And if you're like most Coloradans, whether or not you were born here or moved here last week, you're an outdoor recreationist yourself.

If you use the public lands for recreation, you should expect primitive conditions with few amenities. Recreationists in undeveloped areas need to accept responsibility for their personal well-being by being informed and knowledgeable about the area they are visiting.

- Buy and learn how to read and use maps.
- Become skilled in your chosen activity and basic outdoor survival techniques.
- Be prepared for unexpectedly awful weather.
- Know which county you're in—the county sheriff has primary responsibility for search-and-rescue operations. Even with cellular phones, global (geographic) positioning systems, air ambulances, and skilled, dedicated search-and-rescue teams, it's not that hard to find yourself miles from the nearest paved road and hours from medical care.
- Be aware of potential hazards you might encounter on the public lands: open mine shafts, mine tailings, narrow, twisting roads with vertical drop-offs, unstable slopes, lightning, flash flooding, predator-control devices and activities, target shooting, and in some areas poisonous plants and animals.
- Purchase a $1 hiking certificate from the state of Colorado; it helps fund search-and-rescue operations if you should be unlucky enough to need them! You can purchase the hiking certificate wherever hunting and fishing licenses are sold.

When you're on the public lands, your safety and well-being is *your* responsibility; play smart and play safe.

Outdoor recreation is not new to Colorado; it was here long before the "New West" arrived. But increasing population and changing demographics of Colorado ensure that it's a rare parcel of public land that hasn't seen the print of a hiking boot or mountain bike tire. When you move into your dream house next door to the public lands, you need to remember that there are many "old-timers" out there who have been recreating on the public lands since long before many of the newcomers were even born. Your dream house may be located right next to the best elk-hunting spot in the whole county, or the public road that runs along your property line might provide the only access to the most popular four-wheel-drive trails in the area. Unfortunately, the "Old" and "New" West sometimes clash along property lines, but if everybody takes a neighborly attitude toward the problem, it can usually be worked out to everybody's satisfaction.

There are many groups, organizations, and governmental entities that have developed user ethics for the public lands. Tread Lightly and Leave No Trace are two of the most widely recognized, and they have been very successful in promoting proper use of the public lands. But no matter how the message is said or who the target audience is, the essence of public land ethics is simple: Treat the public lands as you would want somebody to treat your private land—and treat other public land users as you would like to be treated.

XII. Isn't There Some Kind of Zoning on the Public Lands?

In a way, yes, the public lands are "zoned." BLM is required to manage the public lands in accordance with approved land use plans; these plans are known as Resource Management Plans (RMPs) in Colorado. The RMPs express decisions regarding land use allocations (e.g., areas open to livestock grazing), resource condition objectives (e.g., vegetative cover), and management direction for major programs (e.g., the lands in Management Unit 17 will be managed for primitive, nonmotorized recreational and natural values).

Many of these plans contain maps indicating the surface ownership of the land and in some cases ownership of the subsurface (mineral estate). Even if you can't describe your property by legal subdivision, it's fairly easy to determine your location in relation to the public lands. Correlating the map information with the text of the plan, you can then determine what kind of land use planning decisions apply to the public lands adjoining your property. Once you have this information, you will be able to anticipate what kinds of uses might go on next door and, conversely, what kinds of uses will probably not be occurring next door.

XIII. Isn't There Some Way for the Little Person to Be Heard by Big Government?

You bet! It's known as the National Environmental Policy Act (NEPA), and one of its two guiding philosophies involves public involvement, participation, and disclosure. (The other guiding philosophy of NEPA is interdisciplinary review of proposed federal actions.) The most commonly known product of NEPA is the environmental impact statement (EIS), but NEPA also allows for other types of environmental analysis documents. On a regular basis, BLM prepares NEPA documents known as environmental assessments that are used to analyze relatively small-scale federal actions that typically will not have a significant impact on the human environment.

If an EIS is being prepared, there are regulatory requirements for public participation in determining the scope of the environmental analysis and for public comment on the process and products. The process for environmental assessments is much less formal and provides for case-by-case flexibility. Either way, the beauty of the NEPA process is that it allows for public participation *before* the action is approved by BLM. This allows you to voice your concerns regarding any and all aspects of the proposed action, to suggest alternatives that should be considered, and to help develop mitigating measures that may lessen or avoid adverse impacts. Check with your local BLM office and let them know you're interested in participating in the NEPA process.

XIV. So How Can You Be a Good Neighbor to BLM and the Public Lands?

Even though the scene from your four-wheel-drive vehicle or front porch may look idyllically unspoiled, the public lands can prove to be a very busy place.

First, scope out the neighborhood. Don't assume that just because an advertisement states that a given parcel "borders BLM," the lands will always remain in public ownership or never be developed. Visit the nearest BLM office and ask to review a copy of the approved land use plan. Find out if the public land next door is open to mining or oil and gas leasing, or if it's identified for disposal, or if it's a Wilderness Study Area or an off-highway-vehicle play area.

Second, get to know your local BLM personnel. The area manager and his or her staff are the folks who actually manage the public lands; their decisions and actions directly affect the public lands and public land users. Let the BLM know you're interested in the public lands in general, and especially the public lands next to your property; they will appreciate your views, concerns, and interest.

Third, find out who your local representatives are on BLM's Resource Advisory Councils (RACs). There are three in Colorado: the Southwest, Northwest, and Front Range RACs. Each RAC has fifteen appointed citizen members who represent public land uses and users and who provide advice and recommendations to BLM managers. Meetings are held on a regular basis and are announced in the *Federal Register*, through the local news media, and in most cases on the World Wide Web.

And last, but perhaps most importantly, *get involved in public land management.* Tell your local BLM manager that you want to be on the mailing list for environmental assessments, environmental impact statements, and planning documents—and then respond with your comments. If the public lands adjoining your property are open to livestock grazing, feel free to request that you be allowed to participate in decisions for that grazing allotment. Attend BLM meetings, open houses, and workshops. Check BLM Colorado's web pages (http://www.co.blm.gov) for current information and activities. If you have information that BLM should be aware of, let the area manager know.

XV. Living Close to the Public Lands

If you follow the advice in this chapter, will you be able to influence management on neighboring tract of public lands? Yes and no. Some decisions may have been made long before you moved into the neighborhood, and some of those would literally take an act of Congress to change. Others may require a land use plan amendment, and still others may require a change in national policy. To paraphrase part of an old saying, may you have the grace to accept those things you cannot change and understand that even the things you can change may not be changed easily or quickly.

However, many of the decisions and actions that affect the public lands can be influenced at the local level. Become informed, get involved, keep an open mind, and recognize that BLM must constantly try to balance local needs with national interest. Like many neighborhood disputes, a friendly discussion between neighbors can resolve the problem to the satisfaction of both parties. And if neighbors can't talk to each other, it's not really a neighborhood, is it?

For Additional Information

BLM national website: http://www.blm.gov

BLM Colorado's website: http://www.co.blm.gov

Mulin, James, and Hanson R. Stuart. "Opportunity and Challenge: The Story of BLM." 1988. Check with local BLM office to obtain a copy.

29

Being a Responsible Visitor to National Parks and Archaeological Sites

Linda Martin, *Interpretation and Visitor Services*
National Park Service

When people make plans to visit a national park or monument, the first thing they want to know is: "What is there to see?" It is the rare visitor who also asks questions about the rules that apply to visiting that area. Most people assume that visiting a typical park is like visiting a government building: You just walk in and go where you want to go. However, parks are not like buildings; there are many different rules and regulations necessary to protect the land and the historical and cultural artifacts that belong to all the people of the United States.

Just because you happen to know the general rules that apply to other kinds of federal lands, for example, the national forests or Bureau of Land Management (BLM) management areas, you can't assume that the rules in a national park will be the same. For example, in a national forest or on BLM land, you may hunt or fish, but that is not true of national parks or monuments.

In order to be a good neighbor to our national park system, you need to read about restrictions that may apply to a specific area before you go to visit that area. Write or call a National Park Service office before deciding to take a vacation or go on a recreational adventure. Well-informed visitors have a better appreciation of why national parks exist and why we need to protect them.

Most people realize that simply paying the entrance fee does not entitle them to go wherever they please to do whatever they want. Although there may not be extensive rules, all areas have some regulations or a code of conduct.

It is each individual's responsibility to find out what these regulations are and abide by them. Just as you cannot indiscriminately run a red light or a stop sign, you cannot do whatever you might like when you visit federal lands. These areas were set aside for the protection and enjoyment of all people, and each individual accepts certain responsibilities along with the privileges and rights every citizen has. Using a little common sense can make your visit a much more rewarding experience as well as saving you the embarrassment of violating the law.

There are varying guidelines for visiting the national parks and monuments of Colorado. Because these guidelines are so different, it is difficult to give general guidelines.

National parks and monuments have been created by Congress for many different reasons. Some were set aside for their unparalleled natural beauty, some for their historical significance, others for their ethnographic and archaeological sites. Depending on the purpose for which the park was created, there may be different rules in each park. Consider the distinction between a natural area such as Rocky Mountain National Park and a cultural area such as Mesa Verde National Park. Yes, there is beautiful scenery in both places, but the scenic beauty is secondary to the cultural values of Mesa Verde. A place such as Bent's Old Fort National Historic Site offers a reconstructed trading center along the Santa Fe Trail. The guidelines used for the fort's reconstruction may involve completely different legislation than that which applies to the Black Canyon of the

Gunnison National Monument, which includes a large area of designated wilderness. Such wilderness areas have restrictions about the maintenance of roads and trails based on the way the land was managed before the wilderness designation occurred. There is no way that the same guidelines would apply for the Bent's Old Fort, Black Canyon of the Gunnison, Mesa Verde, and Rocky Mountain parks.

Whether you live in close proximity to a National Park Service area or visit an area only on vacation, the easiest way to find out what laws apply is simply to contact the park itself. A list of addresses and phone numbers for all of the National Park Service areas in Colorado is included at the end of this chapter. Address your inquiry to the superintendent of the area, and a staff member will answer your questions. You can also contact the National Park Service through the Internet at www.nps.gov.

For questions requiring a legal reply such as surface mining on land adjoining a National Park Service area, a superintendent may refer the question to an authority in the regional office or in Washington, DC.

I. Cultural and Archaeological Sites: The Special Case of Mesa Verde

Mesa Verde was established by an act of Congress on June 29, 1906. It is quite unusual for a cultural and archaeological site to have the special protection offered by national park status. Although some national monuments, historical sites, historic landmarks, and other special areas have been created by presidential proclamation to protect cultural heritage, these areas do not have the level of federal protection inherent in national park status.

In 1906 Congress decided that if the destruction of Mesa Verde by natural forces, vandalism, and looting was to be slowed or halted, a high degree of federal protection needed to be put in place quickly in order to conserve the remaining artifacts and buildings. Therefore, Mesa Verde National Park has some rules that do not generally apply in the national park system.

To protect the many archaeological sites within the park and to prevent vandalism and looting, Congress decided to prevent visitors from freely exploring the park or leaving designated roadways or trails. The backcountry of Mesa Verde National Park was closed to the public from the beginning. Legislation also prohibited public access to cliff dwellings unless there was a uniformed ranger present. Both of these regulations are strictly enforced, yet most people have no idea that these rules even exist. Frequently visitors enter the park, see an interesting feature or ar-

chaeological site, and immediately stop to explore the area. Many may not be caught, but those who are apprehended often tell park rangers that they had no idea they were breaking the law. Although there are no signs posted at the entrance to the park that specifically outline these rules, the color brochure given to visitors as they enter the park does include information about these restrictions. These regulations are included in the superintendent's compendium of laws applying to the park. They are also listed in the Code of Federal Regulations published by the Government Printing Office in Washington, DC, and are available for any federal area.

Once visitors realize that they need to stay on designated roadways and trails and that they can't explore the backcountry as they can in other parks, is there anything else they need to know to be a good neighbor to the park service and to other Mesa Verde visitors who share the site? Absolutely. Basically the rules of park etiquette involve courtesy and consideration for other visitors and care that artifacts and cultural sites remain as they were when you found them.

Visitors tend to focus on looking at the cliff dwellings to the exclusion of their everyday world. If your children run ahead on the trail, looking for lizards or other interesting critters and checking out nooks and crannies that catch their eye, that's fine, but keep an eye on them and don't let them leave the trail to look at archaeological sites or to cut across switchbacks. When adults or children leave the trail, it is a violation of federal regulations; when you cut across switchbacks you create erosion gullies that can ultimately destroy a section of trail or require costly repair. Such activities may seem like minor violations, but consider that 650,000 visitors enter the park yearly. A small problem multiplied by 650,000 is a major problem.

It is a good idea to remember the saying, "Take nothing but pictures, and leave nothing but footprints." It may be trite, but following the simple creed will help visitors remember the importance of protecting fragile areas.

One mental trick that may help visitors remember proper archaeological-site visitor etiquette is to imagine that you are visiting a stranger's home or the home of someone you do not know well. Obviously, you would not want to harm or damage anything in that person's home and would be on your best behavior. You would be careful not to disturb their possessions or walk into rooms you have not been invited to enter. You would know that you need to treat their home as you would want them to treat yours. You would naturally respect their privacy without questioning why. Your children would be told to ask before playing with toys in a stranger's home, and you would remind them that they should be careful not to break or damage these toys. Just as you would not want your children to damage the walls of your own house, you would expect them to refrain from writing on the walls or carving their initials into furniture. And clearly, you would not do that yourself. You would not remove any of the occupants' possessions because that would be stealing. These same rules apply to archaeological sites. The purpose of these rules is to protect the dwellings and to show respect for the individuals and families who once lived there.

As you walk into a cliff dwelling, notice the signs requesting that people "Please Do Not Sit, Stand, or Climb on Walls." Although that request may be clear enough in a modern context, it is not always clear at an archaeological site. Sometimes the "walls" are below ground level within a site, for example, around a kiva, or sometimes "walls" may be at ground level as a retaining wall. Walls at ground level are still walls and need protection from 650,000 pairs of feet walking over them every year.

Children cannot be expected to completely understand that the signs mean to stay off all masonry unless it is directly in the designated path. Parents should discuss the rules with their children or ask a ranger to do so. He or she will be happy to explain about where you can go and what you can do.

In general, there are rope or chain barriers to keep visitors from climbing over walls or going into the back areas of sites. Humans are a curious species, and it's perfectly natural to want to see what is beyond a barrier. Resist the temptation. Such exploring is against regulations meant to protect the site for the thousands of visitors who want to see the site just as much as you do. Even though you intend no harm, exploring restricted areas can damage original walls and plaster. Guide booklets often describe what the off-limits areas are like, and rangers can answer questions about special features. Children can understand the need for these rules if you talk to them about what the site would look like if all the visitors climbed all over the place. They understand quickly that thousands of people climbing on walls would destroy the site and leave nothing for future visitors to see. Your children would not want strangers to walk into their room at home and start opening drawers or playing with toys or removing their possessions. The plants, animals, and artifacts within the park are the possessions of the park, and they should not be touched or taken. Children may be disappointed initially, but they soon learn that there's a lot to see without entering the back areas or removing objects.

Try looking at a cliff dwelling for evidence of visitor use. Look around the edges of a doorway where visitors lean into a room to see what it looks like inside. A glance at the stones on the sill or at either side of the doorway clearly shows a discolored area caused by the oils of people's hands as they touch the walls. It may seem insignificant, but that darkened texture can never be removed. Oddly enough, people tend to pick mortar out from between building stones. After hundreds of people have wedged their fingers into a crack, the mortar loosens and falls out. Then the stones may break away from the surrounding material and may pull out other stones in the process. Pretty soon walls begin to crumble.

Never try to climb down into a kiva unless there is a reconstructed roof with a sign telling you that visitors may enter. Inevitably, when people climb into an unroofed kiva, they disturb the plaster and mortar; the stones loosen and eventually the kiva collapses. If there is original plaster present, the material is so fragile that one kick can chip pieces out. Once that original plaster disappears, it cannot be recreated in its original condition. A stabilization crew can patch the area, but the original material is gone and researchers have no idea what it looked like or how it was made.

Despite the temptation, avoid crawling through doorways or other small spaces in rooms of cliff dwellings. You may damage the wall or knock out stones nearby. In Mesa Verde, you seldom have a chance to crawl anywhere in a cliff dwelling, but make it a habit to treat all archaeological sites the same no matter where you may be. Whether a site is excavated or unexcavated, human activity takes a toll as time passes. The pressure of people walking over middens (Ancestral Puebloan trash dumps) in front of cliff dwellings or around the edges of surface sites may harm artifacts that may still be located there. Potsherds on the ground are crushed under people's feet. Textile remnants are disturbed and destroyed. If you pick up a potsherd, put it back where you found it. Do not make a pile of potsherds in one place. You change the provenance of such artifacts and make it difficult for researchers to learn anything from the location of the artifacts.

Rules and regulations may seem complicated and dull, but the reason they exist is to allow a maximum number of people to enjoy these national treasures without destroying them in the process. The purpose of setting aside U.S. National Park Service properties is to protect them so that they can be enjoyed by future generations. The treasures may be scenic, historical, cultural, or archaeological, and you can learn a great deal about the natural world as well as about the everyday lives of earlier cultures. Think of your national park system as a vast network of outdoor museums where your children, grandchildren, and great-grandchildren can have the same experience in the future that you have today.

For Additional Information

The following is a list of addresses and phone numbers for all of the National Park Service areas in Colorado:

Bent's Old Fort National Historic Site
35110 Highway 194 East
La Junta, CO 81050-9523
(719) 384-2596

Black Canyon of the Gunnison National Park
102 Elk Creek
Gunnison, CO 81230
(970) 641-2337

Colorado National Monument
Fruita, CO 81521
(970) 858-3617

Curecanti National Recreation Area
102 Elk Creek
Gunnison, CO 81230
(970) 641-2337

Dinosaur National Monument
4545 Highway 40
Dinosaur, CO 81610-9724
(970) 374-3000

Florissant Fossil Beds National Monument
P.O. Box 185
Florissant, CO 80816-0185
(719) 748-3253

Great Sand Dunes National Monument
11500 Highway 150
Mosca, CO 81146-9798
(719) 378-2312

Hovenweep National Monument
McElmo Canyon Route
Cortez, CO 81321-8901
(970) 529-4461

Mesa Verde National Park
P.O. Box 8
Mesa Verde, CO 81330-0008
(970) 529-4465

Rocky Mountain National Park
Estes Park, CO 80517-8397
(970) 586-1206

See also:

Office of Public Affairs and the Division of Publications, National Park Service. The National Parks: Index 1997–1999. Washington, DC: U.S. Government Printing Office, 20402-9325.

30

Your *Big* Neighbor: National Forests in Colorado

**Matt Glasgow, *Public Information Officer*
U.S. Forest Service**

So, you're thinking about buying your dream property in Colorado and the real estate agent tells you that the best feature of this land is that it's right on the edge (or in the middle) of a national forest? There's no doubt about it, it is wonderful to live near or adjacent to a national forest. Depending on where your land is located, you may be able to watch deer and elk graze from your back porch. You may see chubby marmots or lean coyotes or even bears fattening themselves for the winter. You'll enjoy magnificent sunrises and Hollywood-style sunsets. You'll smell sage and pine trees and wildflowers.

But even paradise has a few thorns, and if you're thinking of moving in next to a national forest there are a few things you'll want to know about your neighbor.

I. Access and Easements

In Colorado, often the biggest thorn of all is simple access to your land. Under Colorado law you cannot be land-locked by your neighbors, but it may be very costly to get a right-of-way across another private landowner's property. If your property is completely surrounded by public land managed by the federal government, you can get a special use permit for "reasonable access to property as long as that use doesn't unnecessarily damage public lands and resources, or reduce federal land management options." If your land is outside federal boundaries and you wish to use federal lands as part of your access, the permit will be approved only if it is in the public interest and no other access exists. The permit process may be lengthy.

If you are granted an access permit, remember that na-tional forest roads are not plowed in the winter. In order to use a snowplow to access your land, you need a special use permit and may have to post bond to cover any damage to the road that may occur.

Before you buy, make sure that you know what easements have been granted across your property and what easements you may have across neighboring properties. Sometimes new owners may be dismayed to discover that former owners sold public-access easements right down the middle of the property. If that's true, it could be illegal for you to try to control who or what travels over your land. Before you buy, go to the closest U.S. Forest Service office. Check for easements, and if you find any, discuss the meaning of those easements with the public land manager for that area. Discuss these types of easements with your title company.

II. Property Boundaries

The second biggest thorn for folks buying land next to a national forest is the need to know exactly where their property begins and the public lands end. Even though it can be expensive, it's a good idea to hire a state-certified surveyor to check the property boundaries and to put in survey "monuments" that can be relocated if there is any question in the future. Over the years in Colorado, many boundaries have become questionable. Mining claims, which are often the basis of private land inholdings in the national forests, were often staked over other claims. West-ward expansion brought land-hungry settlers who may or may not have been careful about putting fences on correctly surveyed boundaries. Tales abound about land deals in the 1800s that were "surveyed" without leaving the bar where the deal was struck. Many of the problems created in the 1800s can turn out to be unfortunate surprises for the unwary. Today, most state-certified surveyors are reputable and reliable.

III. Development

Potential buyers who come from more heavily populated areas don't always consider what might be required to provide water, power, telephone service, wastewater disposal, and other utilities needed to develop the property. This process can be very expensive and time consuming, and sometimes it is simply not possible to bring in all the utilities that a buyer may need.

If you need to cross your neighbor's property with utility lines, you need their consent. The same is true if your neighbor is a national forest. It will require a permit that can be granted to the utility company only after full environmental assessment work has been completed. That process can take two or more years, and in the end it is possible that the permit would not be granted.

IV. Will the National Forest Next Door Remain Unchanged?

If you're considering purchase of property next door to a national forest, you may think that the land will always remain as it is and will guarantee you quiet, serenity, and privacy. Maybe; maybe not.

America's national forests are working forests. Timber is harvested. Cattle and sheep may be grazed. Minerals are mined. Oil and gas wells may be drilled. Any of the multiple uses of the forests can create problems for the adjacent landowner. There may be noise. That tall stand of aspen that you admire from your living room window could be part of a timber sale needed to improve forest health. There might be heavy truck traffic on local roads. Hunters and fishermen may use the forests near your land.

In fact, it is even possible for the U.S. Forest Service to exchange a parcel of public land near yours for another parcel that may make it more efficient to manage the forests or may be more desirable for recreation. In other words, just because you buy land next to a national forest, there is no guarantee that the land will always be public land.

In addition, living in heavily timbered country carries the risk of fire. Wildfire, started by lightning, campfires, or cigarettes, can be devastating. It can endanger your home or your family. It can change the landscape or your view for many years to come. Even prescribed burns, which are set by the Forest Service to remove the buildup of tinder under trees in order to prevent serious wildfires, can be inconvenient as smoke billows from the burn site.

In short, the forests are not static. They are used, and they do change over time.

V. Public Recreational Use of the National Forests

These days there are almost as many kinds of recreational use as there are people using the forests. In the summer they will arrive on foot, ATVs, mountain bikes, horses, mules, llamas, or in four-wheel-drive vehicles. In the winter they will arrive on snowmobiles, skis, or snowshoes. They may camp or hunt or fish. Although most will respect your private-property boundary markers, some will not be aware of your boundaries or your rights.

A smile and a kind word are usually all that's needed to set them straight. In the rare case of criminal trespass, it's best to call the sheriff's department.

VI. Other Uses

National forests are managed to benefit the American public as a whole and to maintain sustainable resources for the future. Therefore, people who remove natural resources such as rocks, firewood, or tree transplants are required to get a permit from the Forest Service office. Christmas tree permits usually go on sale the third week in November. Firewood permits are on sale from spring through fall. Sapling transplant permits may be granted. Commercial permits are required for the removal of any items you plan to sell. Check with your local Forest Service office before you remove anything from a national forest.

VII. Summary

Living next to a national forest can be wonderful because as a member of the public you can make use of huge tracts of beautiful land without having to buy it for yourself or sometimes even having to get in your vehicle to drive there. But look before you leap. Although being a next-door neighbor to the national forest may, on balance, be just what you want, be sure to be well informed about road access, utilities, boundaries, forest uses, and recreational pressure before you put down that earnest money. National forests can be wonderful neighbors, but remember that these days the forests can be very busy places.

For Additional Information

The U.S. Forest Service welcomes your interest and involvement in decisions that may affect you or your land. Please go to the Forest Service office nearest you to discuss how you and the National Forest Service can be good neighbors. Some other useful contacts are:

U.S. Department of Agriculture
U.S. Forest Service
201 14th Street SW
Washington, DC 20250

Rocky Mountain Regional Office
740 Simms Street
Golden, CO 80401
(303) 275-5350

Grand Mesa, Uncompahgre, and Gunnison National
  Forests
2250 Highway 50
Delta, CO 81416
(970) 874-6600

San Juan and Rio Grande National Forests
1803 West Highway 160
Monte Vista, CO 81144
(719) 852-5941

Pike and San Isabel National Forests
1920 Valley Drive
Pueblo, CO 81008
(719) 545-8737

Arapahoe and Roosevelt National Forests
240 West Prospect
Fort Collins, CO 80526
(970) 498-1212

White River National Forest
Old Federal Building
9th and Grand, Box 948
Glenwood Springs, CO 81602
(970) 945-2521

31

Being a Good Neighbor to the Southern Ute Indian Tribe

Southern Ute Indian Tribe

There are currently two federally recognized Indian tribes in the state of Colorado. Both are located in the southwest part of the state. The eastern boundary of the Ute Mountain Ute reservation is the western boundary of the Southern Ute Indian Tribal Reservation. The Southern Ute reservation is 75 miles long and 15 miles wide and located in an east-west band along the northern New Mexico border. For those familiar with southern Colorado landmarks, the reservation lands run from Red Mesa to Highway 160 to Pagosa Springs to Archuleta Mesa. It is a "checkerboard" reservation in that the tribal lands are not all contiguous but are interspersed with privately held properties. Within the exterior boundaries of the reservation are approximately 308,948 acres of tribally owned land, approximately 308,285 acres of land that is privately held (in fee), and approximately 56,579 acres of public land.

Within the exterior boundaries of the reservation are complex jurisdictional issues that were largely created by establishment of the reservation in 1868 and by federal legislation such as the Homestead and Allotment Acts of 1895. There are both Indian and non-Indian residents within the reservation, and therefore, tribal, federal, and state entities all have some role. Today the Southern Indian Tribe is very cognizant of its sovereignty in that only tribal and federal laws apply to Indians within the tribal boundaries, whereas tribal, state, or federal laws can apply to non-Indians. It is important for neighbors to tribal lands and for tribal members to remember that their neighbors may be governed by a different set of rules and laws.

For generations the Southern Ute Indian Tribe has worked to be a good neighbor in southern Colorado. It is

helpful to keep the following information in mind if you are not a tribal member and are living, working, or vacationing within the reservation:

1. All nonmembers need authorization from the Tribe to cross or use any lands held in trust for the Tribe as a whole. In addition, it is essential to get the permission of individual tribal allotment owners to cross or use their property in any way. Tribal allotments are lands held in trust for individual tribal members, and just as anyone needs the permission of any private landowner to cross or use his or her lands, it is important to get permission from individual allotment holders.

2. All lands owned by the Southern Ute Indian Tribe are regularly posted with red "no trespassing" signs to help nonmembers identify tribal lands.

3. The Southern Ute Indian Tribe regularly patrols its lands with its own law enforcement personnel.

4. The Southern Ute Indian Tribe does not assume any liability for damage to property caused by wildlife.

5. The Southern Ute Indian Tribe legally owns all wildlife on tribal lands within the boundaries of the reservation.

6. The Southern Ute Indian Tribe has a Tribal Court that handles cases involving tribal members, other Indians, and civil matters involving all residents within the reservation.

The Southern Ute Indian Tribe has its own government, which operates many programs that benefit the Southern

Ute people and that also may be beneficial to neighbors of the Tribe. Phone numbers for Southern Ute offices may be found in the blue pages (government) of your phone book in the federal government section.

Fence agreements. If you share a boundary with Southern Ute tribal land, you can contact the permit and right-of-way coordinator for the Tribe to negotiate an agreement to fence the common boundary. Often these agreements are for the Tribe to provide the fencing materials and for the other party to supply the labor.

Pasture leases. These are short-term (six month) leases of tribal lands for the purpose of utilizing the range for pasture. Contact the Southern Ute natural resources Ute Range conservationist.

Utility services. If it is necessary for utilities to cross Southern Ute lands, contact the permit and right-of-way coordinator for the Tribe.

Custom farming. This service provides farming services such as disking or plowing or baling to Southern Ute tribal members and to other members of the community if the tribal need has been met. Contact Southern Ute Custom Farms.

Business leases. If you would like to locate a business or commercial enterprise on Southern Ute lands, you may contact the Lands Division of the Tribe. The lease is the joint responsibility of the Tribe and the federal Bureau of Indian Affairs.

Hunting and fishing opportunities. Contact the Southern Ute Division of Wildlife for current information. In some years the Tribe does not issue hunting licenses to nonmembers. Fishing licenses are required for all nonmembers fishing designated tribal waters. There are different prices for those under twelve years of age and for different time periods (two- or five-day or season). The following vendors sell tribal fishing licenses:

- Sky Ute Thriftway, 15051 Highway 172, Ignacio, Colorado
- Duranglers, 501-B Main Avenue, Durango, Colorado 81301
- ZIA Sporting Goods, 500 East Main, Farmington, New Mexico

Crossing permits. If you would like to "cross" tribal land for any reason, for example, to service a well or for recreation, you need to apply to the Lands Division for a "crossing permit."

Rights-of-way and easements. If for any reason you believe that you or your company needs to negotiate a right-of-way or easement agreement with the Tribe, you should contact the tribal permit and right-of-way coordinator.

For more information, please contact the Southern Ute Indian Tribe Department of Information Services at (970) 563-0100.

As a general rule, if you are not sure what to do or how to proceed when dealing with your neighbor, the Southern Ute Indian Tribe, please call and ask. The Tribe feels that providing you with the answers you need is one of the best ways to be a good neighbor.

32

The Ute Mountain Ute Indian Tribe

Ute Mountain Ute Indian Tribe

The Ute Mountain Ute Indian Tribe is one of two federally recognized Native American tribes in the state of Colorado. The tribal lands are located in southwest Colorado, with portions extending to White Mesa, Utah, and northwest New Mexico. It is the homeland of the Weminuche Band, with a population of approximately 1,960 tribal members, and covers 553,008 acres, or 993 square miles; the land is held in trust by the U.S. government.

The Tribe holds fee patent to 40,922.24 acres in Utah and Colorado; this land is divided into twelve ranches. These lands are not necessarily contiguous to the main area of reservation land. However, these lands also are subject to the same restrictions and rules as other tribal trust lands.

The tribal seat, Towaoc (pronounced Tow-yok), Colorado, is located at the base of Sleeping Ute Mountain in Montezuma County, Colorado. This area is commonly referred to as the "Four Corners" region, where Colorado, Utah, Arizona, and New Mexico meet at a single point. The boundary lines are at right angles and form a + sign. To the south, southwest, and west, the Ute Mountain Ute Reservation shares a boundary with the Navajo Reservation in the states of New Mexico, Arizona, and Utah. To the north and northeast the reservation borders private lands and the federal lands of Mesa Verde National Park. To the east the Ute Mountain Ute Reservation is adjacent to La Plata County, Colorado, and the Southern Ute Indian Tribal Reservation.

In Colorado, the Ute Mountain Ute Reservation does not have any allotted or assigned lands controlled by tribal members. The Tribe must expressly authorize (in writing) all access to any tribal lands by nonmembers.

Historically, the Ute Nation roamed throughout Colorado, Utah, and New Mexico. Members of the hunter-gatherer society moved with the seasons to the best hunting grounds and locations for harvesting native plants.

Dealings with the U.S. government did not benefit the Tribe when, in the late 1800s, the United States forced the Ute Nation into southwest Colorado. The Ute Mountain Ute Reservation was established in 1868. As with all "Indian country," the Tribe is very cognizant of its sovereignty and protects it with all available resources. Today the government-to-government relationship between the Tribe and the U.S. government provides many opportunities, such as leases, between the Tribe and its neighbors. The federal Bureau of Indian Affairs (BIA) must approve any leases signed with the Tribe for the protection of both parties. The BIA also provides law enforcement services on reservation lands. The county sheriff provides law enforcement to nonmembers on private fee lands.

In general, these guidelines apply to all tribal lands:

- All nonmembers need written authorization from the Tribe to cross or use any lands owned by the Tribe.
- All lands owned by the Tribe are posted "no trespassing" to help identify the boundaries.
- Boundaries are patrolled by tribal wildlife officers and Tribal Employment Rights Ordinance (TERO) compliance officers in conjunction with BIA law enforcement.
- The Ute Mountain Ute Tribe claims ownership of all wildlife on tribal lands within the exterior boundaries of the reservation.

The Ute Mountain Ute Tribe operates its own government with many different divisions, departments, and programs that benefit the Ute Mountain Ute people. Typically, telephone numbers can be found in the governmental blue pages of any telephone book. The main tribal information number for the Ute Mountain Ute Tribe is (970) 565-3751.

Frequently Needed Information

Fence Agreements

The Tribal Natural Resources Division maintains all boundary fences on the reservation. If you share a fence with tribal land, please contact the Resources Division at (970) 565-3751, ext. 315.

Right-of-Way Agreements and Easements

All rights-of-way and easements are controlled through the BIA Division of Realty, (970) 565-8473, and the Ute Mountain Ute Justice Department, (970) 565-3751, ext. 239.

Hunting and Fishing

Currently the Tribe does *not* grant any hunting or fishing privileges to nonmembers. Tribal members may also be issued special Brunot hunting licenses by the Tribal Brunot and Wildlife Department; these licenses allow tribal members to hunt in a 6,000-square-mile area outside the reservation boundaries without state hunting licenses or permits. Areas closed to hunting, for any reason, by the Colorado Division of Wildlife are closed to all persons, members and nonmembers alike.

Crossing Permits

If you need to "cross" tribal land for any reason, for example, to survey a boundary or a fence line, apply to the Bureau of Indian Affairs Realty Office, (970) 565-8473, for a "crossing permit."

Business and Commercial Licenses

If you would like to locate a business or operate a commercial enterprise on Ute Mountain Ute lands, you need to contact the Tribal Economic Development Division, (970) 565-3571, ext. 230, in order to acquire a written lease approved by both the Tribal Council and the Bureau of Indian Affairs.

Working on the Reservation

All contractors working on the reservation are subject to TERO, which promotes employment of tribal members. All contractors must contact the TERO office, (970) 565-3751, ext. 344, and pay a 1 percent (of the contract) fee in order to work on the reservation.

Non–tribal members are authorized to work on the reservation through the terms of their employment agreement. The Tribe operates many tribal enterprises and is the largest employer in Montezuma County, Colorado. Approximately 50 percent of all tribal employees are non–tribal members.

Oil and Gas Permits

Oil and gas companies must apply for an annual permit in order to work on the reservation by contacting the Energy Department, (970) 565-3751, ext. 212. *All* operators, large or small, must apply for this permit and comply with all TERO laws.

In general, if you are not sure what to do or how to proceed when dealing with the Ute Mountain Ute Tribe, please call and ask. For more information, contact the Ute Mountain Ute Tribe at (970) 565-3751.

Protecting Our Western Heritage

A Modern "Code of the West"

As growth and development continue to change Colorado and all Western states, many people are concerned about preserving important elements of our heritage such as freedom, individuality, personal integrity, a rural lifestyle, agricultural viability, and helping others when help is needed. These are strong values that have always been part of the American tradition but are particularly important in Western living. As the West becomes more populated and suburbanized, people who live in that region watch these values being changed in ways they often do not like and do not understand. Why, when the traditional lifestyle is romanticized and sought-after, do Westerners find that the harsh realities of the new West challenge their very existence?

The many voices in this section describe not only the underlying values but creative and very modern ways of preserving those values.

In order to accurately present some of the fundamental Western values of Colorado citizens, we interviewed "Colorado Red," the oldest old-timer we could find. Words of wisdom from Red capture the essence of living in the West and illustrate the true "Code of the West." Preserving these traditions is now such a hot topic that there are a number of booklets and short publications, for example, various "Rural Living Handbooks" prepared by local Soil Conservation Districts, that discuss Western values and how to preserve them. Colorado Red (a.k.a. **Erin Johnson**) shares with us a list of some age-old values from his own perspective.

Ranching and farming have always been fundamental occupations of the Western population. The West was settled in order to take advantage of vast areas of land that people could not afford back East. Now, at the state level, Colorado and many other states have recognized that changing land use patterns in Colorado often place farms and ranches adjacent to residential development. In order to protect agricultural land uses and operations from lawsuits, and for carrying out normal and necessary farm and ranch tasks, Colorado enacted strong "right-to-farm" laws. In fact, Western values have many strong voices in most legislative processes. **Michael Preston** discusses the practical side of right-to-farm laws and other issues concerning being a rural neighbor, and **Randall Feuerstein** discusses the future of right-to-farm laws in Colorado.

Life in rural Colorado just wouldn't be "rural" without a good disagreement over fences and whether they appropriately keep animals either in or out. You might be sunning in the garden when the neighbor's prize bull strolls through on his way to the river. Your dog may develop a taste for your neighbor's chickens. Although Colorado is a "fence-out" state, it is pretty easy to get tangled up in the barbed wire. **Peter Holton** and **Nancy Greif** outline the basics of fencing responsibilities in Colorado.

Whereas the right-to-farm laws are a legal approach to the preservation of Western values, the practice of "sustainable agriculture" is a modern method of protecting the old rural value of taking care of the land. The practice of agriculture itself is changing in many ways. Suburban development in rural Western states often fragments agricultural land and increases land values to the point that the economic viability of agricultural operations may be threatened. Although conventional agriculture calls for bigger and bigger operations in order to remain competitive, many farmers and ranchers are applying concepts of sustainable agriculture as an opportunity for compatibility with other growth trends. Sustainable agriculture involves restoring and maintaining ecosystem health, providing a healthy return on investment, and building and restoring community vitality. **Bill Kinney** brings us the latest on these issues and examples of successful sustainable agriculture.

Another creative approach to land stewardship is the growing trend in Colorado to use conservation easements for long-term protection of the land and for valuable tax breaks to preserve some of the "classic" ranches and other lands with special values. **Katherine Roser** outlines the basics of conservation easements, and **Donald Moore** illustrates some of the major conservation easement efforts from a number of areas in Colorado.

However, no matter how creative farmers and ranchers are about caring for their land, it may all go to Uncle Sam in the end if they do not properly plan to transfer the property when they die. A major problem for farmers and ranchers is that the family may not be able to, or may not want to, continue the farming operation, or only one family member may be willing to take on the task. With all of the family assets tied up in the land, how do you pass it on from one generation to the next without destroying the viability of the operation? **Donald Kelley** describes several ways to approach this problem.

The new Code of the West also involves recognizing that the West has long had a multicultural heritage and that there are increasingly strong ethnic groups in the West that deserve respect and consideration. In order for the prevalent cultures to get along better together as neighbors, we all need a healthy understanding of the various cultural components in Colorado. **William Harrell** brings us a unique perspective about resolving cultural problems in the form of a radio talk-show discussion by a group of migrant farm workers.

Some newcomers in Colorado ask, "What is the big deal about agricultural tax classification?" Land is taxed according to its use in Colorado, and historically agricultural lands have been taxed at a low rate. As more development occurs, landowners moving to many land uses that are not really agricultural try to seek or maintain an agricultural tax classification. **Craig Larson** sets out the ground rules for the assessment process and describes how citizens can discuss their concerns with local assessment offices.

The chapters in this section provide valuable information about Colorado's most fundamental asset—our agricultural and Western heritage. The Code of the West is alive and well—but just a little more complicated than it used to be.

33

Tips for Rural Living:
Interview with "Colorado Red"

Erin J. Johnson, *Attorney at Law, Planning Consultant*

The *Good Neighbor Guidebook* is intended to present important topics and legal principles that are broadly applicable throughout Colorado in a way that can be understood by the general public. However, one important Western saying is that "if you can say it in fewer words, please do so." To make sure that we captured the true essence of the "Code of the West" for the guidebook, we interviewed the oldest "old-timer" we could find, "Colorado Red," who lives out near Egnar somewhere. ("That's 'Range' spelled backward," says Red.) From him we learned certain nuggets of Western wisdom and other illustrations of the Western lifestyle.

Colorado Red has a few things to say, in a few to-the-point words, to anyone in Colorado who might claim to be a "local." You might get a chuckle out of Red's manner of communication, but don't brush it off—everything he says has quite a bit of truth to it. "Outsiders" and "newcomers" beware: If you can remember all of these, you might be mistaken for a local.

I. Access

Things are farther apart in the West than in some other places. It might take longer to get where you are going, especially if you are an ambulance or fire truck.

Even if you have a road on your property, you may not have access. On the other hand, you might have a public highway on your property that is invisible.

Sometimes those county plows and road graders stop right before they get to your property for no apparent reason. Had to get my own tractor out the other day and grade my own road.

The mailman came all the way out to my house just to tell me that he couldn't deliver the mail to the mailbox I put on *my* side of the road.

My friend built his wife a house just where she wanted it up in the trees, but it burned plumb down last summer because the fire truck couldn't get up the driveway. He was real sorry he didn't think about the trees being a fire hazard and all, but I told him it really didn't matter because the fire truck never could have gotten across that dinky little bridge he built where his driveway takes off from the county road.

You know that story Grandma always tells about having to walk miles and miles to get to school when she was a kid, and how good the kids have it now? She's been eating crow since my daughter moved to the country—her kids have to walk quite a spell just to get to the bus stop, and boy, does Grandma hear about that!

In nasty weather, roads get worse than you think. Cars built for high speeds and paved roads sometimes don't do so well on narrow gravel roads with sharp corners, especially when they are wet and slippery.

Every year when I pay my taxes I tell the county that all those ruts and potholes and stuff in the roads are *dangerous*, and every year they ignore me.

You better hope that little gal you plan to marry is a good duster. My wife hates to dust more than she hates the dirt roads—the other day we couldn't even find the refrigerator.

I like to laugh at all those superfast delivery-service commercials—and I love to watch the FedEx guy try to stay on schedule when he brings me a package.

II. Utilities

That new guy who moved in next door didn't even know what a "party line" is—he went and got a cell phone after a few days of trying to make calls when my grandkids were on the phone.

Funny thing, that guy from the state told me I couldn't use all the water in my well.

That couple I sold the 40 acres to aren't real happy right now. They just found out that property out here doesn't necessarily come with sewer and water attached. They had to pay more than they paid me for the land just to get their utilities in.

Have you noticed the price of propane lately? Not to mention gasoline. I guess I won't be buying any of that high-octane stuff anymore.

You know the power company won't put lines just anywhere anymore. Cost me my retirement savings to have them put a line to that mobile home I set up for my daughter to get those screamin' grandkids away from here.

Mabel, the new neighbors want me to *pay* for driving across their pasture—you know, the one that Mr. Hanson let me use for years for *nothing* before he sold it!

Boy howdy! That new guy says he is a "lone eagle," whatever that is—anyway, he got his computer and a bunch of other fancy electronical stuff set up in his house, then we had our regular Thursday-afternoon power outage. Would you believe that his house is already for sale again?

After my neighbor's trash bags got real piled up in his driveway and then tore up all over by some raccoons or skunks, I went and asked him about it. He said he was going to come over and ask me when in heck they picked up trash around here. I told him he had to contact the trash company himself, and that he would maybe have to pay extra for all of that trash pile. I had some extra time the next day and helped him take it to the dump in my pickup. I showed him the trash container area I built myself that seems to work in keeping critters out of the trash.

III. Land

My new neighbor just doesn't understand that the survey stakes for his land are on the inside of my property's fenceline.

That guy from California is going to build his house right on the top of that mesa over there. Shall I tell him there's

solid rock about 4 feet down and how bad the spring winds blow over there? Lots of guys buy land thinking of their dream or some movie they saw, and then find out all kinds of reasons why they can't build on their property.

A fella came up the other day and said he had an easement to build a road and put a power line across my land—had a piece of paper with my granddaddy's signature on it to prove it. Guess I'll have to let him do it, but I never knew about it.

When all of my uncles sold off their ranches many years back, they severed the mineral rights and put them in my name. I'm getting ready to do some exploratory drilling on some of them, and I know that there is some gravel I can sell off of that one mineral right I own up the river.

I told those new people that their dog might not live long if I catch it chasing my cows one more time.

I went to town and learned a new word the other day—"zoning." I'm not real clear on it, but I think it's a disease or something that spreads out of towns and cities and ruins your land.

That new subdivision down the road has a thing called "covenants." My neighbor told me it means that you have to build your house in a certain way and in a certain place, and you can't even have horses or cows! What kind of developer would make something that nobody will buy?

You know, some of these newcomers aren't all that bad. I went and talked to the guy I sold 40 acres to about how much I love to watch Colorado sunsets, and he agreed to change his plans to build his house so it wouldn't block my view. I might even could like the guy if I can get him to understand that the water in the ditch isn't his just because the ditch is on his land. He didn't ask to buy any water rights, so I didn't sell him any.

IV. Mother Nature

If you build in those trees without clearing some of them, I guarantee a fire will get you sooner or later.

Some of the dirt in this country is real funny—it swells up like a spring toad when there's a lot of water around, then shrinks up and gets cracks all over it. I found some over where I wanted to build my barn, so I don't guess I'll do that now.

That new cabin won't last long seein' that it's built at the base of that snowslide area.

Rivers get real big in the spring. Watch your kids.

Last year my neighbor dug out a part of a hillside above his house to build a garage. I guess he didn't think about the grading too much because this spring the whole first story of his house got flooded with mud.

You know, I've known people that have frozen to death up in the mountains, *in the middle of the summer.*

Last Fourth of July we went to the mountains. First we got snowed on, then couldn't get back across that creek we forded because of a flash flood. Had to turn around and go the other way—we didn't get home till midnight.

It's really nice to see a bald eagle now and then. Until just recently, I haven't seen one since I was a kid.

I was getting ready to go hunting the other day, and my friend had all the food packed up in a big cooler. We left the cooler outside overnight and planned to leave early in the morning. Wouldn't you know, before morning a dern bear came by and had himself a big picnic on us!

We moved here in the fall, and my wife and I really enjoyed watching the deer and elk graze for most of the winter. When spring came my wife planted a wonderful garden and tulips and things all over—and then some deer came through and ate *everything.*

Most critters are fun to watch if you are lucky enough to see them. They need their space and protection just like you need yours, so don't mess with vegetation and other things that provide cover for the wildlife.

Both wild and farm animals can be dangerous and can attack humans. Make your kids aware of natural reactions in animals, and teach them about places where predators can pounce from. Also, be especially careful about protective mothers with babies.

If you can't respect Mother Nature and help her do the things that should be done, you might as well head on back to the city.

V. Agriculture

If you don't like the smell of cow perfume or burning grass in the spring and you sneeze a lot when the hay is cut, maybe country life isn't for you.

Last summer, my new neighbor actually called the cops and told them he thought he saw a UFO when I was harvesting my crops at night.

My old neighbors all used to know when I was spraying chemicals because they were all doing it at the same time I was. Now I try to be real neighborly and tell the new folks so they can protect their dogs and kids and stuff. Some of those chemicals are downright nasty.

I bought a copy of that movie *City Slickers* and took it over to the new neighbors. I told them they might want to fix a few of their fences before I drive my cattle to the summer range next week. I also asked them if they wanted to help with the cattle drive, but told them to watch the movie first.

If you are a newcomer and you want to be treated neighborly by others, it would be a good idea to go down to the county offices and educate yourself a little about noxious weeds, why they are an important problem, and what your responsibilities are concerning your own land.

You know, that highway noise is getting so loud that the other day I couldn't even hear the water I was putting in that gopher hole.

VI. Living in the West

Things change.

Hunters aren't as smart as they used to be.

Watch out for wildlife and domesticated animals on county roads and highways. Most times the animals are killed when they are hit, but the more serious damage can be to you or your car. However, don't overreact to try to save an animal—you might be risking your own life.

If you come up on a stock drive on the highway, slow down to the speed of the animals and do what the cowboys motion to you or tell you to do.

Pull off the road to let emergency vehicles pass you safely. It is also common courtesy and considered respectful to pull off and stop when a funeral procession goes by in either direction.

If you happen to be a large, slow vehicle and the cars are piling up behind you, find a good place to pull over for a minute until they get by.

You can spot a city driver a mile away—it used to drive me crazy when these people would get right up behind me. Then I went to a big city and learned that everyone drives that close to everyone else there. Now I figure if they can't watch out for their own safety when they are out here, it's their problem, and I go about my business at my regular pace.

Like the song says, "Throw away the TV and feed your kids peaches"—the country life is a great thing to teach to your kids, but please warn them about the very real dangers associated with farm and other equipment, ponds, storms and lightning, mysterious holes in the ground or hillside, and a whole host of other potential hazards. It breaks my heart to have to go out on a search-and-rescue for a perfectly good kid who didn't know what he was getting into.

Don't take emergency services for granted. In most rural areas, the services are volunteer and operate on very limited budgets. When there is an emergency call, these people have to leave their jobs or get up in the middle of the night. Be thankful for whatever assistance you get.

Don't trespass on the property of others without permission. Leave gates exactly as you find them, either open or closed. Last week a fella come waltzin' down the middle of the river looking for trout. Said he thought the rivers belonged to everyone. Had to explain to him that I owned and paid taxes on the riverbed out to the middle of the river. He was standing on my property just as much as if he'd crossed my fence.

If you treat others in a friendly, neighborly way, they will probably treat you the same. One of the best assets that Colorado has is that the people are friendly and honest, almost too much so for some folks. If we want Colorado to stay friendly, we have to teach new people to be friendly instead of reacting to them like folks who don't know how to say "hello" or "welcome to the West."

You never know when you might need some help from your neighbors. You just hope they are of a mind to pitch in when the time comes. If you are a good neighbor, they probably will be.

For Additional Information

Many counties in Colorado have published their own version of the Code of the West. These are usually very helpful, short documents that have a very serious intent but might also contain a sprinkling of Western humor.

Many Soil Conservation Districts in Colorado have compiled "Rural Living Handbooks" that go into significant detail about rural living and small-scale agriculture, tailored to local information.

Another publication, the result of a cooperative effort between federal and state agencies and other entities titled "Landowning Colorado Style," is an excellent presentation on the basics of soils, weeds, water, water quality, riparian areas, grazing, trees and forests, wildlife, and homesite planning. It's available from the Natural Resource Conservation Service, and other state agencies.

34

Living Next Door to a Farm or Ranch

Michael Preston, *Director, Office of Community Services*
Fort Lewis College

I. The Golden Egg: Agriculture and the Quality of Life in Rural Colorado

There's nothing quite like irrigated pastures, alfalfa fields, and waving rows of grain nestled against canyons, wooded areas, streams, and irrigation ditches. The flowing contours, the ever-changing colors, the sounds and movements of livestock, game animals, and birds are a feast for the senses. Add to these pastoral qualities the social attractions of friendly small towns, limited traffic, and low crime rates, and it's no wonder that urban and suburban people are relocating to rural Colorado in search of the golden egg commonly referred to as "rural quality of life."

New neighbors are taking up residence in rural areas that have historically been exclusively agricultural. These new neighbors offer the prospect of renewed prosperity, wide-ranging talents, and long-desired opportunities for economic diversity that can help rural Colorado adapt to the social and economic challenges of the twenty-first century.

Don't Kill the Goose: Protecting the Viability of Family Farms and Ranches

It is critical to recognize that behind the scenic vistas and pastoral sounds that are attracting new neighbors to rural Colorado are hardworking farm or ranch families with their livelihoods on the line. Sustaining the rural quality of life that new neighbors are seeking involves protecting an interwoven fabric of productive agricultural landscapes, viable agricultural livelihoods, and cultural values that have developed from generations of people working the land. If this fabric unravels, everyone—"old-timers" and "newcomers" alike—will lose something irreplaceable.

The challenge for new neighbors is to contribute prosperity, diversity, and opportunity to rural Colorado without unraveling the traditional fabric that has created the attraction in the first place. This means learning how to become a constructive part of a working landscape.

Being Part of a Working Landscape

In the past most rural landowners were farm or ranch families living on large agricultural parcels. Absorbing new neighbors was relatively simple. The current proliferation of smaller residential subdivision lots, with families that don't rely on agriculture for a living, involves new challenges in developing neighboring ethics capable of dealing with this increased diversity.

New neighbors must be aware that the creation and maintenance of these beautiful agricultural landscapes involves intensive periods of clearing, burning, spraying, plowing, bawling livestock, and the operation of farm machinery—at times on an around-the-clock basis. In agriculture, timing is critical. Performing the right operations at the right time can make the difference between prosperity and economic failure.

New neighbors must also be prepared to assume responsibility for the impact that their presence can have on working farms and ranches. The failure of rural residents to do their part to control weeds, pests, domestic pets, and trespassing can undermine economic productivity and social harmony. Living next door to a farm and ranch involves a combination of legal obligations, land stewardship responsibilities, and a commitment to open communication, hard work, and constant learning.

II. Laws, Land Use Regulations, and the Right to Farm

Under Colorado's Right-to-Farm Law (C.R.S. §§35-3.5-101, 102, 103), existing farm and ranch operations are protected from nuisance liability lawsuits. This law was passed to prevent new residential landowners from curtailing or pushing out established agricultural practices. Colorado also has an "open-range law" that puts the burden on landowners to fence livestock out.

New rural residents should also be aware that their farm and ranch neighbors are typically not very fond of land use regulations and restrictions. Agricultural families are used to a lot of "elbow room" and see little need for the level of land use controls that cities and towns adopt to address circumstances where people are living at close quarters. They often supplement farm earnings with full-time jobs and side occupations such as welding or dirt work and want to be able to pursue these activities without a lot of restrictions. As a result, rural counties tend to have relatively relaxed land use standards in agricultural areas.

Agricultural families are also very protective of their right to divide and sell land. Land equity, which is most often a result of generations of hard work, is critical to addressing financial obligations and emergencies as well as retirement and family inheritance. Agricultural landowners generally don't mind providing "open space" as long as they choose to continue farming, but they don't want their land to be "locked into" agriculture should the need arise to sell some or all of their land. To protect these rights, Colorado law gives landowners the right to create parcels of 35 acres or larger without having to submit to county subdivision regulations.

Agricultural landowners tend to describe the above issues in terms of "the protection of private property rights." By way of review, some of these rights include:

- the right to farm without the threat of nuisance liability suits
- the right to divide land into parcels of 35 acres or larger without having to comply with most land use regulations
- a great deal of flexibility concerning a wide range of land uses that can be conducted on agricultural property in many rural counties

Respect for these rights will help establish positive relations between new neighbors and agricultural families. These rights also support the economic viability of agricultural operations. It is important to realize that if an ag operation can't make it economically, the land may well end up being developed.

There are some cases where agricultural families are willing to join with their new neighbors in seeking regulation. An example that has received a lot of attention in the late 1990s is the proliferation of large industrial-scale hog operations, where the smell and the potential for water pollution go well beyond traditional agricultural practices. If new neighbors avoid polarization over the "small stuff," there is more potential for cooperation when big issues come along.

Although understanding these legal parameters is important, it is even more important for new neighbors to understand their responsibilities to their farm and ranch neighbors. Agricultural families are much more comfortable handling neighbor relations in a cooperative, informal manner than they are with legal and regulatory approaches, which they view as a last resort.

III. Tolerances and Stewardship Responsibilities Associated with Being a Farm and Ranch Neighbor

Some of the basic tolerances and land stewardship responsibilities essential to being a good farm and ranch neighbor are summarized below:

Tolerance for Agricultural Practices

To remain viable, your agricultural neighbors are going to need to continue engaging in a wide variety of land management practices. Rural residents need to be prepared to tolerate the following activities:

- burning fields and vegetation along irrigation ditches
- cleaning irrigation ditches, some of which may run through residential property
- chemical spraying
- plowing, planting, harvesting, and otherwise using farm equipment (early in the morning and at times through the night)
- weaning and moving livestock, which can result in a lot of loud bawling over extended periods of time

Land Stewardship: Taking Care of Your Own Backyard in an Agricultural Setting

New neighbors have a responsibility not to harm the viability of their agricultural neighbor. Here are some of the fundamental stewardship responsibilities:

- Control weeds and pests on your property so they don't invade the property of your agricultural neighbors.
- Limit and control your pets, especially dogs. If your dogs run loose and harass livestock, they may be shot.
- Don't go on a neighbor's property without permission.
- Leave open gates open and closed gates closed.
- Don't take down boundary fences, and work with your neighbors to keep them in good repair.
- Don't take down your roadside fences. Roads are used as stock drives, and landowners are responsible for fencing cattle out to protect landscaping and avoid the inconvenience of straying livestock.
- If an irrigation ditch or pipe goes through your land to serve other properties, don't block access needed for cleaning and maintenance.
- Don't take water out of an irrigation ditch unless you are legally entitled to do so, and take only your entitled amount.
- Don't plow or disturb your land unless you have a solid plan for how you will revegetate and maintain it. Disturbed land invites weeds, erosion, and runoff that can invite problems for you and your agricultural neighbors.

Thinking Through Your Options

People thinking about becoming farm and ranch neighbors should carefully consider the tolerances and the land stewardship responsibilities outlined above and consider the options outlined below:

- Buy or build a house in town and use the free time you'll gain to drive, take bike rides, and hike out in the countryside.
- Buy a small lot in a rural housing cluster or a parcel in a nonagricultural area and leave the farming to others. Respect and tolerate your neighbor's right to farm.
- Make a conscious decision that you want to take the responsibility for managing a piece of agricultural land and plan on spending a substantial amount of time and money being a good steward of your land and preserving the productive harmony of your agricultural neighborhood.

Communication, Cooperation, and Good Information: Key Ingredients to Being a Good Farm and Ranch Neighbor

Learning the ethics and methods of being a good farm and ranch neighbor is no simple matter.

Good communication, cooperation, and information are critical:

- Maintain open communication with your agricultural neighbors. When you see a conflict arising, you will gain your neighbors' respect by coming forward and openly addressing the problem. If you are not sure how to do something, your agricultural neighbors are generally glad to advise you or tell you where to get help.
- Contact your county extension agent. Most counties in Colorado have an extension agent who is there to help you get the information you need to take proper care of your land. Extension agents can also advise you on how to be a good farm and ranch neighbor.
- Contact your county planning office. If you have a question about the rules, or whom you need to contact to solve a particular problem, someone in your county planning or administration office can usually help.
- A friendly wave or visit to your neighbors will keep up good relationships. Take every opportunity to slow down and get to know your neighbors. Agricultural neighbors tend to be pressed for time during the production season but tend to be more relaxed and able to visit during the winter.

IV. Conclusion

The "golden egg" in rural Colorado is agriculture. To share the golden egg without killing the goose involves being part of a working agricultural landscape in a way that allows your farm and ranch neighbors to remain productive and economically viable. There are laws that protect your neighbors' right to farm as well as flexibilities built into many county land use codes intended to prevent damaging agricultural viability by overregulation.

Farm and ranch neighbors should be prepared to tolerate a variety of intensive land management practices on the part of your agricultural neighbors while assuming stewardship responsibility for their own land. There are other options, such as living in town or in nonagricultural rural areas, that allow for enjoyment of the countryside without the more intensive tolerances and responsibilities associated with living in an agricultural area. For those who decide that being a farm and ranch neighbor is for them, communication and cooperation with neighbors and good information are essential. There is no substitute for taking the time to visit with your neighbors and getting to know them.

35

The Future of Right-to-Farm Laws in Colorado

Randall J. Feuerstein, *Attorney at Law*

As Colorado's rural landscape begins to be challenged by the encroachment of urbanization, conflicts between property owners have developed and will continue to emerge. The stark reality is that farming and ranching operations create dust, odors, and noise that new residents living on the fringe of an agricultural operation may find objectionable. Conflicts can arise when a landowner's domesticated pets chase livestock or when a farmer's or rancher's livestock gets out onto the road or into the neighbor's property. Other conflicts may exist because of the movement of livestock and farm implements on highways and country roads or as a result of the use of fertilizer and other chemicals as part of agricultural production. Other similar issues include weed and pest control, trespass, and negligence in conducting a farming operation.

A right-to-farm law may take the form of a statute, a county or city ordinance, or a precedent-setting decision issued by an appellate court. This chapter will focus on the state statute denominated as Colorado's Right-to-Farm law. The Iowa example of right-to-farm legislation being invalidated by a court will also be addressed. Right-to-farm law can be broadly defined to include provisions that protect an agricultural operation and its owners from complaints about legal and non-negligent agricultural activities or that promote and encourage farming, ranching, and associated agricultural activities and operations.

I. Colorado's Right-to-Farm Statute and Amendments

The Statute

In 1981 Colorado enacted its version of a right-to-farm law. This statute is codified at 10 C.R.S. §35-3.5-101 *et seq.* (1998). The statute establishes the policy of Colorado "to conserve, protect and encourage the development and improvement of its agricultural land for the production of food and other agricultural products" (*id.* at §101). Further, the General Assembly recognized "that, when nonagricultural land uses extend into agricultural areas, agricultural operations often become the subject of nuisance suits." The General Assembly recognized that the consequence of nuisance suits could lead to a number of agricultural operations being forced to cease and many others being discouraged from making investments in farm improvements. The purpose of Colorado's Right-to-Farm statute is to reduce the loss to Colorado of its agricultural resources by limiting the circumstances under which agricultural operations may be deemed a nuisance.

An agricultural operation is defined to be the science and art of production of plants and animals useful to humans, including, to a variable extent, the preparation of these products for humans' use and their disposal by marketing or otherwise, and includes horticulture, floriculture, viti-culture, forestry, dairy, livestock, poultry, bees, and any and all forms of farm products and farm production (*id.* at §35-1-102(1)). Livestock includes cattle; sheep; goats; swine; mules; poultry; horses; alternative livestock as defined in §35-41.5-102(1); such domesticated animals as foxes, minks, martens, chinchillas, beavers, and rabbits; and all other animals raised or kept for profit (*id.* at §35-1-102(6)).

The statute provides some protection against nuisance lawsuits by providing that an agricultural operation is not, nor shall it become, a private or public nuisance by any changed conditions in or about the locality of such oper-ation after it has been in operation for longer than one year if the operation was not a nuisance at the time the oper-ation began, except that the protection from a nuisance is not available in the case of a negligent operation or when a change in the operation would result in a private or pub-lic nuisance or when a substantial increase in the size of the operation occurs.

The Right-to-Farm law also voids any ordinance or res-olution of any unit of local government such as counties, cities, or towns that makes the operation of any agricul-tural operation a nuisance or provides for the abatement of an agricultural operation as a nuisance under the cir-cumstances provided in the statute. This subsection of the statute voiding such ordinances does not apply to an agri-cultural operation located within the municipal limits of a city or town on July 1, 1981, or located on property that the landowner voluntarily annexes to a municipality on or after July 1, 1981.

Reported Decisions

Interestingly, there are no reported decisions from Col-orado appellate courts that have yet construed Colorado's right-to-farm statute. Colorado courts have, however, ad-judicated nuisance and trespass cases against agricultural operations. For example, in *Miller v. Carnation Co.*, 516 P.2d 661 (Colo. App.), *cert. denied* (1973), neighboring home-owners brought an action against the owner of a chicken farm for injunctive relief, compensatory damages, and ex-emplary damages, alleging that the agricultural operation constituted a nuisance, depriving them of their use and en-joyment of their own property, and a trespass on their own property. The trial court granted the defendant's motion to dismiss at the conclusion of its case. The Colorado Court of Appeals reversed the decision of the trial court.

It is interesting to note from this case that the plaintiffs purchased a home on land abutting the egg ranch after the egg ranch was already in place and had been operated by the existing owner for two years prior to the plaintiffs mov-ing into the area. The plaintiffs complained about an-noying odors and a large number of flies caused by the fail-ure of the egg ranch owners to adequately remove chicken manure from underneath the chicken houses. The accu-mulation of chicken manure caused the breeding of flies and produced a home for mice and rats. Even though the defendant sprayed the chicken houses and the plaintiffs' house with insecticides, the problem persisted, and owing to cost considerations, the defendant did not remove the manure from under the chicken houses.

The trial court ruled that since the plaintiffs sought in-junctive relief, the suit was essentially equitable in nature and granted a motion to dismiss based upon the court's determination as the trier of fact that the plaintiffs' evi-dence was insufficient to support either injunctive relief or an award of monetary damages. The Court of Appeals re-versed that finding on the basis that the complaint alleged claims essentially legal in nature and sought both money damages, a legal remedy, and injunctive relief, an equitable remedy. The Colorado Court of Appeals held that because monetary damages were sought and the complaint was primarily seeking a remedy at law, the plaintiffs were en-titled to a jury trial on the legal issues. On the issue of whether a private nuisance was established, the court noted that the essential question is whether the defendant has un-reasonably interfered with the plaintiff's use and enjoy-ment of her property. Because the defendant failed to re-move the chicken manure from underneath the chicken houses, that failure to act resulted in a breeding ground for flies. The flies, in turn, annoyed the plaintiffs and damaged their property.

The court also held that a reasonable jury could con-clude that the flies constituted an unreasonable and sub-stantial interference with the plaintiffs' use and enjoyment of their property. The court also held that the plaintiffs es-tablished a prima facie case for trespass. It adopted the Re-statement (Second) of Torts that establishes liability where one, irrespective of whether he causes harm to any legally protected interest of the other, intentionally enters land in the possession of the other or causes a thing or third per-son to do so. The court noted prior holdings that a landowner who sets in motion a force that, in the usual course of events, will damage property of another is guilty of a trespass on such property.

Finally, on the issue of exemplary damages, the court held that a jury could find that despite repeated complaints by the plaintiffs over a period of five years, the defendant, while making some attempts to control the fly problem, may have failed to take the only action that would clearly remedy the situation—removal of the chicken manure. The failure of the defendant to remove the chicken manure could be construed by a jury to be a wanton or reckless disregard of the plaintiffs' rights. The only portion of the trial court's ruling upheld by the Court of Appeals was the trial court's decision not to award an injunction to the plaintiffs.

Four years later, the case went again to the Colorado Court of Appeals and is reported as *Miller v. Carnation Co.*, 564 P.2d 127 (Colo. App.), *cert. denied* (1977). The trial court, based upon a jury verdict, awarded approximately $86,000 in compensatory damages and $300,000 in exemplary damages against the Carnation Company, the owner of the Brighton Egg Company, a poultry ranch or egg farm. The court held that damages for both loss of use and enjoyment of property, on the one hand, and for annoyance and discomfort, on the other hand, are not duplicative. Damages attributable to the use and enjoyment of land are to compensate for a proprietary interest, and damages to compensate for annoyance and discomfort are to compensate for personal interests.

With respect to Carnation's claim that the exemplary damage award was excessive, the Court of Appeals held that it was not the province of the trial court to disagree with a jury and grant a motion for new trial even though the trial court may disagree with the verdict. The court held that in the face of conflicting evidence, the trial court may not substitute its view for that of the jury. The plaintiffs were entitled to have exemplary damages considered by the jury since there was evidence to support it.

Moreover, the Court of Appeals reversed the trial court's decision denying interest on the award from the complaint filing date to the date of judgment. The Court of Appeals held that interest on the portion of the award attributable to annoyance and discomfort should have been included from the date of the complaint. Both Carnation cases were heard and decided before enactment of Colorado's Right-to-Farm law in 1981. Although this legislation would now provide a defense to a cause of action based upon public or private nuisance, the statute likely would not help to shield against claims for either negligence or trespass.

Staley v. Sagel, 841 P.2d 379 (Colo. App. 1992), is also an interesting case involving an agricultural operation nuisance. It should be noted that this case was decided eleven years after enactment of Colorado's Right-to-Farm law, but curiously no mention of the statute is made in this decision. In *Staley*, a nuisance case was brought against a hog farm. In that case, neighboring landowners brought a lawsuit against the owner of a hog farm alleging nuisance and requesting both monetary damages and an injunction to close the operation. The trial court split the case and submitted the damages claim to a jury, which returned a verdict of $40,000; $20,000 was attributable to the reduction in value of the property, $10,000 was attributable to past impairment of the quality of the plaintiffs' lives, and $10,000 was for future impairment of the quality of their lives. After a trial to the court on the equitable injunction claim, the trial court entered a limited injunction requiring the hog-farm owner to make changes in the hog operation designed to lessen the effects of dust, smell, and disposal of wastes and dead animals of which the plaintiffs had complained.

The first issue dealt with by the Court of Appeals was the wording of the jury instruction. The Court of Appeals held that the jury instruction, as approved by the trial court, was satisfactory. The jury instruction provided that to find that plaintiffs had proven their private nuisance claim, the jury was required to determine that the hog facilities operation "unreasonably and substantially interfered with plaintiffs' use and enjoyment of their property" (841 P.2d at 381). The court also instructed the jury that interference is unreasonable and substantial only if the activity is disturbing to a person of ordinary temperament and sensibility (*id*). The Court of Appeals held that the substantive instructions were, cumulatively, a reasonable statement of the prevailing law regarding a private nuisance.

The court recognized that a landowner is generally not entitled to both a permanent injunction terminating a nuisance and an award of damages for the nuisance's injury to the market value of the landowner's property. It held that if the nuisance is abated by injunctive relief and there is no permanent damage to the property resulting from the nuisance, then the proper measure of damages for any prior adverse effect upon the land's value is the loss of the property's rental value for the period during which the nuisance continued. The court further held that the plaintiffs were entitled to damages only for the activities that constituted a nuisance and were not entitled to recover for any claimed diminution in the value of their property caused by the defendants' actions that do not constitute a nuisance or other actionable wrong. Therefore, the Court of Appeals reversed the judgment awarding $20,000 in damages based upon the property's permanent loss of value because the injunctive relief was designed to prevent such future loss. The Court of Appeals remanded to the trial court for a new trial the issue of the plaintiffs' economic loss suffered during the existence of the nuisance. As noted above, the curious aspect of this case is the fact that the Right-to-Farm law was not utilized as a defense in the case, which was clearly brought under a private nuisance cause of action.

II. Legislative Amendments to Right-to-Farm Statute

First Amendment

Colorado's Right-to-Farm law was first amended in 1996. That amendment added a provision to encourage local governmental units to adopt regulations or ordinances consistent with the state's right-to-farm policy. A subsection was added to the statute providing that "nothing in this article shall be construed to prohibit a local government from adopting an ordinance or passing a resolution that provides additional protection for agricultural operations; except that no such ordinance or resolution shall prevent an owner from selling his or her land or prevent or hinder the owner in seeking approval to put the land into alternative use."

This amendment was added by S.B. 96-36, effective May 2, 1996. The original Right-to-Farm law was enacted in 1981 as H.B. 1099, effective July 1, 1981. The Right-to-Farm statute, including this first amendment, is attached as Appendix A at the end of this chapter.

Second Amendment

In 1999 the General Assembly enacted S.B. 43 as an amendment to Colorado's Right-to-Farm law. The amendment was introduced by Senator Ken Chlouber and, innocently enough, proposed a new subsection (1)(b) to award expert fees, court costs, and reasonable attorneys' fees as follows: "The court shall award expert fees, court costs and reasonable attorney fees to the prevailing party in any action brought to assert that an agricultural operation is a private or public nuisance" (S.B. 99-043, §1) (as introduced).

It was apparently intended by the drafters of this amendment that if a farmer or rancher prevailed in litigation of a public or private nuisance lawsuit, then the farmer or rancher should be made whole by the award of expert fees, costs, and attorneys' fees. The language, however, could be construed as a double-edged sword imposing more costs and expenses upon a farmer or rancher who did not prevail in a nuisance lawsuit.

With respect to the award of attorneys' fees, Colorado common law follows the "American Rule." The American Rule provides that attorneys' fees generally are not recoverable absent an agreement between the parties, or as authorized by statute or court rule (*e.g., Bernhard v. Farmers Insurance Exchange*, 915 P.2d 1285 (Colo. 1986)). The proposed amendment, therefore, was in response to this American Rule.

Also, with respect to attorneys' fees, it could be argued that there are adequate provisions in both the Colorado Rules of Civil Procedure and in Colorado Revised Statutes that could provide for the potential to award attorneys' fees in a nuisance action brought against an agricultural operation. For example, the most common of these provisions is Rule 11 (Colo. R. Civ. P. 11), under which attorneys and parties can be sanctioned for signing or filing a pleading where the signatory did not reasonably inquire into the relevant facts; the pleading was not well grounded in fact; the pleading was not based on existing legal principles or a good-faith argument for the modification of existing law; or the pleading was filed for the purpose of causing delay, harassment, or an increase in the cost of litigation.

Colorado's frivolous and groundless statute authorizes an award of attorneys' fees where an action lacks substantial justification, which means that it is substantially frivolous, substantially groundless, or substantially vexatious. An action is frivolous if the proponent cannot present a rational argument based on the evidence or law. An action is groundless if the allegations in the complaint are not supported by any credible evidence at trial (5 C.R.S. §13-17-101 *et seq.* (1998)). Awards of attorneys' fees are common where there has been misconduct by an attorney or a party, there is a failure to conduct a prelawsuit investigation of the claim, or actions are taken in the case that are spurious or attendant with significant delay.

Given that background, it should be noted that the amendment as proposed would, however, take away the judicial discretion that is ordinarily applied by judges when they consider either Rule 11 or the substantial justification statute. Thus, the amendment as proposed would benefit farmers and ranchers to the extent that they were the ones most likely to prevail in a public or private nuisance case. The disadvantage for a farmer or rancher would be his or her liability in the event that the farmer or rancher was not the prevailing party in such an action.

Certain constituent groups requested that the language be "softened" so that an award of expert fees, costs, and attorneys' fees was not mandatory. For example, it was proposed that the word "shall" be changed to the word "may." The version as enacted does, in fact, utilize the word "may" and includes references to the frivolous, groundless, or vexatious actions statute, §13-17-102, and also to Colorado's costs in civil actions statute, §13-16-122. In addition, the word "reasonable" was added prior to the words "court costs."

Finally, the constituency opposed to large confined feeding operations wanted to make sure that their statutes involving potential actions against a housed commercial swine-feeding operation (C.R.S. § 25-7-138(5) (1999) and §25-8-501.1(8) (1999)) remained unaffected by the Right-to-Farm law. Hence, the second sentence of Section 1 of the amendment was also added. This Second Amendment, as enacted by the Colorado General Assembly and as signed by Governor Owens on April 16, 1999, is attached as Appendix B.

Future Amendments?

What might the General Assembly consider in the year 2000 for strengthening Colorado's Right-to-Farm law? Perhaps the defense against nuisance suits could be expanded to include trespass or other torts. Another proposal might involve narrowing the exceptions to application of the statute. For example, an exception exists in the case of a negligent agricultural operation or when a change in operation would result in a private or public nuisance or when a substantial increase in the size of the operations occurs. If the public policy of the state of Colorado is indeed the promotion of farming as a continued permitted business, then one would think that a change in the operation should not be prohibited from taking advantage of the statute. By the same token, a substantial increase in the size of the operation should also not be prohibited from taking advantage of the protection of the statute. It remains to be seen whether future legislation is proposed and enacted in this respect to increase the scope of Colorado's Right-to-Farm statute.

III. The Iowa Experience

In 1998 the Iowa Supreme Court in *Bormann v. Board of Supervisors* (584 N.W.2d 309 (Iowa 1998)) decided that Iowa's Right-to-Farm law resulted in a taking of private property for public use without just compensation in violation of both the federal and Iowa constitutions. In that case, property owners sought to include 960 acres comprising their land and the land of neighbors in an "agricultural area." The application was initially denied by the Kossuth County Board of Supervisors because the board found that there were no present or foreseeable nonagricultural development pressures in the area for which the designation was requested. Apparently some neighbors of the applicants opposed the designation and the nuisance protections provided by the designation because they would have a direct and permanent impact on the existing and long-held private property rights of adjacent property owners.

A subsequent application to include the property in an agricultural area was approved by the board. The neighbors who opposed the application challenged the board's

actions in court, alleging that the board violated their constitutionally inalienable right to protect their property under the Iowa Constitution, deprived them of property without due process or just compensation under the federal and Iowa constitutions, and denied them due process of law. The trial court agreed with the neighbors but determined only that the board's action was arbitrary and capricious. By obtaining the agricultural area designation, the applicants were granted immunity from nuisance suits.

The neighbors argued to the Iowa Supreme Court that approval of the designation including the nuisance immunity resulted in a taking of private property without the payment of just compensation in violation of the federal and state constitutions. The neighbors further argued that the nuisance immunity provision gives the applicants the right to create or maintain a nuisance over the neighbor's property, in effect creating an easement in favor of the applicants. The neighbors concluded that this action results in an automatic taking under a claim of regulatory taking. The board and the applicants responded that an automatic taking occurs only where there has been a permanent physical invasion of the property or where the owner has been denied all economically beneficial or productive use of the property.

The Iowa Supreme Court focused on the Fifth Amendment to the U.S. Constitution, which provides that "no person shall be … deprived of life, liberty, or property without due process of law; nor shall private property be taken for public use, without just compensation." The Fourteenth Amendment of the U.S. Constitution prohibits a state from "depriving any person of life, liberty or property without due process of law." The Fourteenth Amendment makes the Fifth Amendment applicable to the states and their political subdivisions. The Iowa Constitution at Article I, §9 provides that "no person shall be deprived of life, liberty or property without due process of law." Further, §18 of that article states that "private property shall not be taken for public use without just compensation first being made, or secured to be made to the owner thereof, as soon as the damages shall be assessed by a jury."

The nuisance immunity contained within the agricultural area designation provided that "a farm or farm operation located in an agricultural area shall not be found to be a nuisance regardless of the established date of operation or expansion of the agricultural activities of the farm or farm operation. This paragraph shall apply to a farm operation conducted within an agricultural area for six years following the exclusion of land within an agricultural area other than by withdrawal as provided in §352.9."

The immunity does not apply to a nuisance resulting from a violation of a federal statute, a regulation, state statute, or rule. Nor does the immunity apply to a nuisance resulting from the negligent operation of the farm or former operation. Additionally, there was no immunity from suits because of an injury or damage to a person or property caused by the farm operation before creation of the agricultural area. In addition, there was no nuisance immunity from suit or injury or damage sustained by pollution or change in the condition of waters of a stream, overflow, or excessive soil erosion.

Because the court concluded that the property interest at stake here was that of an easement in that the right to maintain a nuisance is an easement, the court concluded that there was a constitutionally protected private property interest at stake. The court also concluded that easements are property interests subject to the just compensation requirements of the federal and state constitutions. In concluding that the easement resulted in a taking, the court discussed many physical invasion cases that dealt with cable television transmission facilities; water flooding; low-flying aircraft; an easement for access; and smoke, dust, cinders, and vibrations from railroad operations. The court concluded that the state cannot regulate property so as to insulate the users from potential private nuisance claims without providing just compensation. The court determined that the agricultural-area classification would permit the creation of noise, odor, dust, or fumes. Immunity from nuisance was deemed to deprive the neighbors of a property right without just compensation. Accordingly, the court held unconstitutional and invalidated the portion of the Right-to-Farm statute that provided for immunity against nuisance suits. The court added that it thought the statute was both plainly and flagrantly unconstitutional. The decision was unanimous among all justices except two justices who took no part in the case. The Iowa position, apparently, would strike down all right-to-farm legislation as unconstitutional if it provided a nuisance immunity.

Appendix A

Colorado Revised Statutes, Title 35: Agriculture

Article 3.5: Nuisance Liability of Agricultural Operations
Section:
35-3.5-101. Legislative declaration.
35-3.5-102. Agricultural operation deemed not nuisance.
35-3.5-103. Severability.

35-3.5-101. Legislative declaration.

It is the declared policy of the state of Colorado to conserve, protect, and encourage the development and improvement of its agricultural land for the production of food and other agricultural products. The general assembly recognizes that, when nonagricultural land uses extend into agricultural areas, agricultural operations often become the subject of nuisance suits. As a result, a number of agricultural operations are forced to cease operations, and many others are discouraged from making investments in farm improvements. It is the purpose of this article to reduce the loss to the state of Colorado of its agricultural resources by limiting the circumstances under which agricultural operations may be deemed to be a nuisance. It is further recognized that units of local government may adopt ordinances or pass resolutions that provide additional protection for agricultural operations consistent with the interests of the affected agricultural community, without diminishing the rights of any real property interests.

History.—Source: L. 81: p. 1694, 1. L. 96: Entire section amended, p. 675, 1, effective May 2.

35-3.5-102. Agricultural operation deemed not nuisance.

(1) An agricultural operation is not, nor shall it become, a private or public nuisance by any changed conditions in or about the locality of such operation after it has been in operation for more than one year, if such operation was not a nuisance at the time the operation began; except that the provisions of this subsection (1) shall not apply in the case of a negligent operation or when a change in operation would result in a private or public nuisance or when a substantial increase in the size of operations occurs.

(2) As used in this article, "agricultural operation" has the same meaning as "agriculture," as defined in section 35-1-102 (1).

(3) Any ordinance or resolution of any unit of local government that makes the operation of any agricultural operation a nuisance or provides for the abatement thereof as a nuisance under the circumstances set forth in this section is void; except that the provisions of this subsection (3) shall not apply when an agricultural operation is located within the corporate limits of any city or town on July 1, 1981, or is located on a property which the landowner voluntarily annexes to a municipality on or after July 1, 1981.

(4) This section shall not invalidate any contracts made prior to July 1, 1981, but shall be applicable only to contracts and agreements made on or after July 1, 1981.

(5) Nothing in this article shall be construed to prohibit a local government from adopting an ordinance or passing a resolution that provides additional protection for agricultural operations; except that no such ordinance or resolution shall prevent an owner from selling his or her land or prevent or hinder the owner in seeking approval to put the land into alternative use.

History.—Source: L. 81: Entire article added, p. 1694, 1, effective July 1. L. 96: (5) added, p. 675, 2, effective May 2.

35-3.5-103. Severability.

If any provision of this article or the application thereof to any person or circumstances is held invalid, such invalidity shall not affect other provisions or applications of this article which can be given effect without the invalid provision or application, and to this end the provisions of this article are declared to be severable.

History.—Source: L. 81: Entire article added, p. 1695, 1, effective July 1.

1999

SENATE BILL 99-043

BY SENATORS Chlouber, Andrews, Musgrave, Owen, Powers, and Tebedo;
also REPRESENTATIVES Miller, Paschall, Pfiffner, Scott, Stengel, and Tochtrop

CONCERNING THE AWARD OF COSTS IN ACTIONS FOR NUISANCE AGAINST AGRICULTURAL OPERATIONS.

Be it enacted by the General Assembly of the State of Colorado:

SECTION 1. 35-3.5-102 (1), Colorado Revised Statutes, is amended to read:

35-3.5-102. Agricultural operation deemed not nuisance - attorney fees. (1) (a) An agricultural operation is not, nor shall it become, a private or public nuisance by any changed conditions in or about the locality of such operation after it has been in operation for more than one year if such operation was not a nuisance at the time the operation began; except that the provisions of this subsection (1) shall not apply in the case of a negligent operation or when a change in operation would result in a private or public nuisance or when a substantial increase in the size of operations occurs.

(b) THE COURT MAY, PURSUANT TO SECTIONS 13-16-122 AND 13-17-102, C.R.S., AWARD EXPERT FEES, REASONABLE COURT COSTS, AND REASONABLE ATTORNEY FEES TO THE PREVAILING PARTY IN ANY ACTION BROUGHT TO ASSERT THAT AN AGRICULTURAL OPERATION IS A PRIVATE OR PUBLIC NUISANCE. NOTHING IN THIS SECTION SHALL BE CONSTRUED AS RESTRICTING, SUPERSEDING, ABROGATING, OR CONTRAVENING IN ANY WAY THE PROVISIONS OF SECTIONS 25-7-138 (5), C.R.S., AND 25-8-501.1 (8), C.R.S.

SECTION 2. Effective date - applicability. This act shall take effect July 1, 1999, and shall apply to all actions commenced on or after said date.

SECTION 3, Safety clause.

Approved April 16, 1999

Capital letters indicate new material added to existing statutes; dashes through words indicate deletions from existing statutes and such material not part of act.

36

How to Corral Critters in Colorado

Peter A. Holton, *Planning Consultant*
Nancy S. Greif, *Attorney at Law*

I. Colorado Fence Law

Colorado is an "open-range," or "fence-out," state. Generally, this means that livestock owners have the right to turn their animals loose to graze without constructing a fence to confine them to the owner's property. Under Colorado law, the neighboring landowners, if they do not want the stock to roam about on their property, must construct fences sufficient to keep the unwanted stock out. If you're not from the West, this responsibility may come as an expensive surprise. In most of the Eastern and Midwestern states, stock owners must fence their animals in rather than the neighbors fencing them out.

Colorado open-range law dates back to 1880, when the Colorado Supreme Court heard a fence-law case and decided that it would cripple the growing livestock industry, which was a significant contributor to the tax base of Colorado, to require that stock owners fence in their animals. The court reasoned that because the croplands tended to be located in semirestricted linear belts along watercourses, it would be much more practical to require that these areas be fenced rather than the vast arid rangelands.

Colorado statutes decree that if a landowner constructs a fence and gates sufficient to "turn" ordinary stock, and somebody else's animals still manage to get onto a landowner's property and damage the grass, crops, gardens, or vegetable products, then the landowner may sue in civil court for damages based on the trespass. Generally, the county sheriff has no jurisdiction to cite a stock owner for trespass and damage by his or her stock. You have to go down to the courthouse and file a civil complaint, or you can write or talk to your neighbor and see if you can "set-

tle up" without going to court (see Chapter 42, "Solving Problems Without Litigation").

Even if you have not put up a fence to keep animals out, you may be able to obtain compensation for damage done if the rancher has turned out a larger number of stock than his or her land can reasonably support. The theory is that if there is adequate pasture on the home ranch, the stock will not be as likely to roam.

Keep in mind that the fence-law statutes apply only to liability for damage related to agriculture. If your horse gets loose and kicks a neighbor's kid, you may still be liable for the injury even if the neighbors chose not to construct a fence. So you may want to fence your animals in even though it is not required by state law.

A "lawful fence" is defined as a well-constructed, three-barbed-wire fence with substantial posts set approximately 20 feet apart, or any comparably sturdy fence. The livestock referred to in the statutes are cattle, mules, donkeys, goats, sheep, pigs, buffalo, and cattelo. The statutory definition does not include commercially raised wild animals such as elk and fallow deer; this means that if your neighbor has an elk farm, you do not have to fence the elk out. Because they are not covered by the statute, the elk rancher would have to fence them in.

If you and your neighbor have agricultural and grazing lands and either one or both of you would like to fence the boundary line, Colorado Statute §35-46-113 states that "partition fences between agricultural and grazing land shall be erected and also kept in repair at the joint cost of the owners of the respective adjoining tracts, except as otherwise agreed by such owners."

If your land abuts a highway that was constructed using

federal highway funds, you may be able to get some help from Uncle Sam in constructing a fence along the highway so that your stock will not constitute a safety hazard to the motoring public.

General Colorado fence law can be found in the Colorado Revised Statutes from §35-46-101 through §35-46-114.

II. Varmints, Vermin, and Other Not-So-Cuddly Wild Things

According to the dictionary, a varmint is a bird or animal that is considered undesirable or troublesome, and vermin are small animals or insects that are destructive, annoying, or injurious to health. Obviously, prior to the presence of people these wild things were just that—wild. But as humans encroach more and more on the habitat of the wild things, humans may define the wild animals as varmints or vermin. Depending on your point of view, one person's wildlife may be another person's pest. Skunks, raccoons, squirrels, bats, snakes, foxes, and other small animals are sometimes called nuisance wildlife. In any case, many of these small animals are as much at home in the city as in the country, and we need to know how to live near them without having them become too annoying.

The best reason for trying to keep these creatures out of the areas you inhabit is that some diseases present in animal populations may be transmitted to humans. One serious danger is hantavirus, which is usually fatal to humans and contracted primarily by handling feces of deer mice. Many outbreaks of disease in animal populations seem to be a response to stress such as overpopulation. In other words, disease is nature's way of reducing the population to a level that the available habitat can support. Rabies can be transmitted directly through breaks in the skin. Distemper may be transmitted to your pets, and bubonic plague may be transmitted to your pets and to you. Make sure that your pets are up-to-date on their vaccinations, and if you happen to be bitten by a wild animal, contact your doctor immediately. The most important action you can take to control the presence of unwanted small animals is to eliminate food sources and housing sites.

1. Never intentionally feed wild animals of any kind.

- Animals can transmit diseases to humans, and eating human food can cause nutritional problems or diseases in the animals. The animals, if left to cope on their own, will almost certainly be able to find their own food.

2. Never unintentionally feed wild things.

- Store your garbage in animal-proof containers and in a closed garage or shed if possible. Periodically clean garbage cans with hot water and chlorine bleach to remove any odors. Or splash a little ammonia into the can after each new addition of garbage.
- Never leave pet food outside. You'll end up with more "pets" than you counted on.
- String bird and hummingbird feeders on wires between trees or take them in at night. Many small creatures love birdseed, and bears love sugar water.
- Don't put fruit, melon rinds, corn cobs, etc., in compost bins or mulch piles.
- Fence garden areas as securely as you can afford.

3. Don't allow wild animals to gain entry to your attic, basement, the space under your mobile home, crawl space, garage, etc. Skunks, raccoons, snakes, squirrels, birds, bats, etc., are always looking for places to nest and live. The following guidelines should help:

- Put screening over chimneys, furnace and dryer vents, and attic vents.
- Seal all cracks and holes larger than 1 inch.
- Discourage access to rooftops by removing overhanging branches and tacking sheet metal at least 3 feet square to the corner edges of buildings.
- Discourage the residence of Colorado's only poisonous snake, the rattlesnake, by storing firewood in a container or shed, by not landscaping with large flat rocks, and by reducing rodent populations.

What can you do if an unwanted animal does decide to take up residence? Before you do anything, check with the local Division of Wildlife office and with city and county officials to find out what you are allowed to do by state and local law.

Raccoons, skunks, squirrels, and bats can be driven out of attics or crawl spaces by playing loud voices, such as a talk-radio station, and by flashing lights. Apparently you can get a flash attachment for an ordinary light bulb at hardware stores. The removal of skunks and squirrels can be facilitated by putting a plastic owl near the flashing light. Owls are predators for many nuisance animals and will scare them away. Move the owl daily so they don't become accustomed to it.

When you think that the animal has left, cover the entrance with a sheet of plastic for a day or two, and if the plastic remains undisturbed, permanently seal the opening.

Rags soaked in ammonia may assist in the removal of skunks, and sprinkling naphthalene flakes may get bats out of your belfry. Use 1 pound of flakes per 400 square feet of attic space. If a squirrel has fallen into your chimney, he is probably trying to get out. Lower a thick rope or knotted sheets down the chimney, and he will climb out.

Live trapping and relocation is very limited for most of these animals, and generally they must be destroyed after capture. In Colorado, it is illegal to capture and release skunks, so they must be killed if trapped. Released animals frequently find their way back to the source of food or shelter, so live trapping and release may not be a reasonable solution anyway. Preventing problems from the start is the best approach.

The Colorado Division of Wildlife and the local animal control agency may provide advice on the removal of unwanted animals from your home, but in most areas they do not perform the actual removal. Commercial pest-control exterminators or professional trappers may be hired to remove your unwanted wild guests.

For Additional Information

"Fences for Man and Beast," a booklet sponsored by the San Juan Habitat Partnership Committee, the U.S. Forest Service, the Colorado Division of Wildlife, and the Bureau of Land Management. These booklets can usually be obtained from the Public Affairs offices of any of the three agencies.

Hygnstrom, Scott E., Robert M. Timm, and Gary E. Larson. 1994. *Prevention and Control of Wildlife Damage*. University of Nebraska Cooperative Extension.

"Too Close for Comfort: How to Avoid Conflicts with Wildlife in the City," available at Colorado Division of Wildlife Offices throughout the state (addresses given below).

Division of Wildlife Offices

Central Region
6060 Broadway
Denver, CO 80216
(303) 291-7327

Northeast Region
317 West Prospect
Fort Collins, CO 80526
(303) 484-2836

Southeast Region
2126 North Weber
Colorado Springs, CO 80907
(719) 473-2945

Northwest Region
711 Independent Avenue
Grand Junction, CO 81505
(303) 248-7175

Southwest Region
2300 South Townsend Avenue
Montrose, CO 81401
(303) 249-3431

Main Headquarters
6060 Broadway
Denver, CO 80216
(303) 297-1192

37

Sustainable Agriculture: A Proven Method of Conserving Farm and Ranch Lands

Bill Kinney, *Resource Management Specialist*

I. What Is Sustainable Agriculture?

The irony of growth in the Western United States is that it undermines the very attributes that attract people to this part of the country. People move here because they like the majestic scenery and vast open spaces of this region. However, urbanization usually occurs on private agricultural lands, filling those open spaces with houses, shopping malls, and businesses. More importantly, this growth creates a host of pressures and difficulties for agricultural producers, which, when combined with the economic problems they face, can accelerate the loss of agricultural lands to development.

Other chapters in this section discuss many factors that contribute to the urbanization of Western farm and ranch lands. These factors include increasing agricultural land values, which make it more difficult for young farmers to enter this profession as property and estate taxes increase, and young farmers cannot afford to buy agricultural land to get started. In addition, the fragmentation of agricultural lands, which tends to undermine agricultural support businesses, makes it harder for farmers to buy supplies or sell agricultural products.

For the past two decades or more, state and local governments, universities, and nonprofit organizations have tried to ameliorate these pressures in various ways. Several chapters in this section discuss some of these measures. However, if farm and ranch operations cannot remain profitable, farmers and ranchers cannot afford to leave their land undeveloped. This chapter discusses how a num-

ber of agricultural producers have turned adversity into opportunity by approaching the practice of agriculture in a different way.

U.S. agriculture in the twentieth century has shown a steady and precipitous drop in the number of farms, accompanied by increasing farm size and decreasing farm employment.[1] This trend resulted from the increasing mechanization of agricultural production and the substitution of energy for farm labor.[2] And while farm productivity has soared, conventional agriculture is trapped on a treadmill, requiring the increasing use of high-cost inputs (fuel, fertilizer, pesticides, and machinery) to survive. This dependency creates an economic squeeze as production costs go up while producer prices go down because world agricultural production continues to grow faster than overall demand for food and fiber products.

This apparent dependency on technological solutions, and the harmful ecological costs associated with them, has encouraged a variety of alternative approaches. These alternative approaches to the practice of farming and ranching are known as "sustainable agriculture." To be sustainable, we must be able to continue practicing an agricultural activity indefinitely, without harmful side effects. That is, we must account for all of the impacts of an activity on future generations.

To really qualify, agricultural activities must ultimately be socially and economically, as well as ecologically sustainable. More specifically, they must provide a quality of life and community vitality that keeps families together and willing to continue their efforts from one generation to the next. They also must generate sufficient wealth to support that quality of life and to reinvest in the agricultural enterprise. Finally, and perhaps most importantly, sustainable agriculture must restore and maintain the health of the ecosystems upon which these activities depend.

In the industrial model of conventional economics and agriculture that is widely taught in our major universities, these goals, or criteria, for sustainability are seen as conflicting.[3] However, a small but growing minority of farmers and ranchers is recognizing that these goals are mutually interdependent and synergistic. For example, a farmer could use the following "suite" of strategies to produce more sustainably:

- use a leguminous cover crop ("fixes" nitrogen, controls undesired plants, provides habitat for beneficial insects, and reduces erosion significantly)
- avoid cultivation by using "no-till" planting (preserves cover crop, soil microbes, and worms)
- "harvest" a crop with livestock, grazing at high densities for short periods (converts harvested sunlight to valuable products without high input costs; recycles minerals)
- avoid using chemical fertilizers and pesticides (saves worms and beneficial bugs)
- use young family members to help produce and harvest products because of increased safety—fewer dangerous chemicals and machinery, etc. (builds family "ownership" of the farm business)
- market a diverse line of farm products directly to consumers, at higher prices (increases profitability and promotes self-sufficiency by diversifying product lines)

This chapter discusses these and other strategies for sustainable agriculture in more detail and provides examples of how they are being applied in Colorado and neighboring states. We will then examine some guidelines for the practice of sustainable agriculture and review some simple rules of thumb for getting started and succeeding with this approach. Finally, I provide some information resources for those who want to learn more about sustainable agriculture.

II. Sustainable Agriculture: A Closer Look

As agricultural land is developed for other uses in any area, it becomes increasingly difficult for the remaining farmers and ranchers to continue producing, for several important reasons. Perhaps chief among these is a breakdown

of the traditional support infrastructure that producers need to continue their business. This infrastructure includes both vendors of agricultural supplies and buyers of agricultural products.

Conventional farming and ranching in the United States has become increasingly specialized since World War II as farms have become bigger and more mechanized. Instead of running a variety of crop and livestock enterprises, producers increasingly focused on only one or two products and on larger and larger farms or ranches. This increasing concentration of farms encouraged the growth of larger supply businesses that could provide and deliver large quantities of the seeds, fertilizers, and pesticides that were needed for these enterprises. It also allowed the development of large feedlots, processing or packing facilities, and other businesses requiring a large volume of agricultural products to justify their larger scales of operation.

As urbanization occurs and land is taken out of agriculture, the total production in a region is reduced. Then the economic viability of these support businesses is threatened, and eventually they relocate or quit operating. This in turn makes it more expensive for conventional, large-scale producers to continue to compete in their markets, so they are in turn encouraged to sell their land to developers, and the cycle accelerates.

Sustainable producers have to be more adaptable and flexible in the face of urbanization than their more conventional neighbors by taking advantage of the increasing population of their area while relying less on traditional channels for marketing their products. By marketing directly to the public and focusing on "niche markets" (specialty products marketed to a narrow spectrum of the public), producers can achieve higher profits. Even if they continue to use many conventional production strategies, when they bypass the marketing middlemen, they can garner a greater share of the final retail price.

For example, by selling directly to restaurants, specialty stores, or even local grocers, farmers and ranchers can charge the same prices that previously went to the processor or wholesale distributor. If they sell directly to the consumer at a farmers' market or roadside stand, they get 100 percent of the retail price. However, producers must be willing to "add value" to their products by processing, sorting, grading, or packaging them to meet consumer desires for a consistent, high-quality product.

Ecological and Economic Interdependencies

Perhaps the most important aspect of sustainable agriculture is its relationship to the environment. Modern, conventional agricultural production often sacrifices the long-term health of agricultural ecosystems for short-term profits and high yields. Although not apparent at first, the continued use of high-cost inputs impairs the ability of a natural system to function in a productive way. The problem is that many producers have failed to recognize that their dependency on these high-cost technologies is hurting them economically in the long run, as their economic well-being is ultimately tied to the health of their agricultural ecosystems.

One of the core principles of sustainable agriculture is the idea that increasing biological diversity is not only beneficial but economically essential for any agricultural producer. This idea is in direct contradiction to historical thinking, which is based on the strategy of monocultures. In a monoculture, any species of plant or animal except the target crop or livestock species is viewed as a threat. Thus, the producer tries to eradicate these "weeds," "pests," or predators. These strategies contribute to the escalating spiral of increasing costs for conventional producers while preventing many natural ecosystem synergies from occurring.

In sustainable agriculture, we recognize that this strategy is self-defeating because in creating a monoculture, one is always fighting Mother Nature. Nature abhors a vacuum—she will always try to fill it. That is, any time humans try to simplify an ecosystem by eradicating certain species, they in fact create ideal conditions for reinvasion by the same or other species. An example of this principle is the phenomenon of increasing resistance to pesticides. As we try to eliminate an undesirable species (weed, bug, or predator), natural selection operates to fill that ecosystem with the members of that or some other species that has resistance to the pesticide. Thus, the producer will face increasing costs over time trying to maintain the monoculture.

Besides the costs of maintaining monocultures, it has become apparent that conventional, high-input agriculture is increasingly vulnerable economically in its dependency on expensive technology for survival.[4] As farms and ranches increase in size and mechanization, the cost of ownership and operation increases as well. Even for the largest producers, specialized equipment often sits idle for large portions of the year, tying up capital that could otherwise be used more productively. This recognition has led some producers to get rid of most, if not all, of their expensive machinery, and to rely on alternative strategies for planting and harvesting crops or feeding livestock.

These simple ideas, so often ignored in conventional thinking, can be used to reduce the costs of production and increase profitability. By choosing the right combination of enterprises, a producer can dramatically increase the "productivity" of the land by allowing and promoting natural synergies among the species used. Let's look at some real-life examples.

Small-Scale Crop and Livestock Production

Steve Groff farms on 175 acres in Lancaster County, Pennsylvania. Working with USDA scientists who have experimented with sustainable production practices, Steve developed a system of cultivation that dramatically decreases his need for herbicides, synthetic fertilizers, and pesticides, lowering his overall production costs and increasing his profits.[5] There are three important elements in this strategy that work together synergistically (the combined impact is greater than the sum of each element if used alone):

1. use of a cover crop that is established before his "cash crops" are planted
2. long-term "no-till" production practices
3. proper crop rotations

Steve has been using no-till practices since the early 1980s and began using cover crops in 1991. Working closely with scientists and engineers from the USDA and Virginia Polytechnic Institute, Steve has developed a more profitable system for the no-till transplanting of vegetables as well as for the direct seeding of corn, pumpkins, and soybeans.

The first step in this process is the planting of the cover crop. After this crop is established, it is rolled over and lies dormant as mulch, into which the cash crop is planted. In the fall, Steve uses no-till seeding to establish this cover crop, either a mixture of clover, vetch, and winter rye or just the vetch or rye by itself, depending on the cash crop.[6] In the spring, this cover is standing 5 feet tall and has contributed to soil health and productivity by reducing soil erosion, increasing soil organic matter and microbial action, and "fixing" nitrogen naturally in the soil. Steve then lays this cover crop down flat on the ground and crimps it by dragging a modified cornstalk chopper over it, which suppresses further growth for the season. He then transplants or seeds his cash crop directly into the cover residue, again using a "no-till" planting method. The heavy mulch on the ground creates an environment that drastically reduces competing vegetation, conserves soil moisture, provides habitat for beneficial insects, reduces incidence of pests and diseases, and increases the yields of many of his cash crops.

There are other environmental benefits that are economically important. Steve has significantly reduced his use of herbicides for weed control because the cover crop dramatically reduces the factors that promote weed growth. He has also increased soil organic matter and microbial activity, thereby improving overall soil health and productivity, which in turn improves his yield and product quality. In side-by-side test plots with conventionally produced tomatoes, the new approach had a much lower incidence of pests (Colorado potato beetle) and disease (early blight), thereby reducing his production costs. Finally, product quality is as good or better as under the conventional approach.[7]

Livestock Systems

Joel Salatin and his family started out raising a small herd of grass-finished beef for direct market to consumers in Virginia. In the next section, we will examine the operations of the Salatin farm in more detail. Here, let's just look at one example of how to increase biodiversity and profitability at the same time. The Salatins use a high-density, time-controlled grazing system in which the herd is moved frequently (often daily) to fresh grass, allowing each paddock to recover sufficiently for continued plant health before it is grazed again.[8] This system, which mimics the patterns of wild grazing ecosystems, has been used by thousands of livestock producers worldwide in recent years to dramatically improve the health and productivity of their grassland ecosystems and to reduce the costs of controlling animal pests and parasites.[9]

The Salatins then developed another enterprise that mimics the way natural grazing ecosystems work and in the process increased the amount of free solar energy they were harvesting into usable agricultural products. In trying to prevent heel fly infestation in their cattle, they invented an "eggmobile," a movable roost for egg-laying hens, which follows two days behind the cattle as they are moved from paddock to paddock. As the hens search for various bugs and larvae in the cow manure, they also accelerate its decomposition.

Since they began this "pasture sanitization" process, the Salatins have not had any heel fly problems. The system also increases the recycling of nutrients stored in the manure because they are returned to the soil, thereby increasing pasture productivity. With higher gains per acre of pasture, the Salatins get higher returns on their investments and in the process sell the by-product (organic eggs), netting another $2,000 or more per acre.[10] By reducing parasite problems in their cattle, they reduce their beef production costs even more, further contributing to higher profits.[11]

III. Common Themes in Sustainable Agriculture

From these examples, we can see some of the principles of sustainable agriculture at work. Rather than increasing farm size and mechanization, these producers focus on specialty products that require a more management-intensive approach. Instead of simplifying their agricultural ecosystems, they promote a rich diversity of synergistic species, which combine to capture a higher amount of free solar energy in products that can be harvested and sold at premium prices.

This increased biodiversity promotes better soil health, thereby increasing yields, and reduces or eliminates expensive inputs such as herbicides, pesticides, and antibiotics. These production strategies can often be accomplished without owning expensive equipment and processing facilities, further reducing the costs of owning and operating the businesses. Finally, by marketing directly to a smaller target group of consumers, these producers gain a greater share of the premium retail price that these consumers are willing to pay.

In the following section, we will look at how a larger-scale operation has successfully adapted these ideas to its operations, thereby increasing its profitability and restoring the health of its ecosystems. We will also look more closely at the Salatin farm to illustrate these concepts more clearly. Finally, we will look at the James Ranch, an example of the Salatin approach in southwest Colorado.

Woodruff Unit of the Deseret Ranch

The Deseret Ranch in Northeast Utah is made up of 200,000 acres of private land, with an additional 50,000 acres of BLM inholdings that form a checkerboard ownership across the ranch. In the early 1980s, while the ranch still belonged to a Hong Kong investor, Greg Simmonds was hired as the new ranch manager, with the understanding that the ranch needed to start showing a profit in the very near future. Simmonds began implementing a holistic resource management (HRM) approach and, with his management team, focused on lowering costs of production, increasing profits, and diversifying their sources of income.[12]

Through experimentation and the application of the HRM decision model, the Deseret team was able to lower their beef production costs 50 percent by the early 1990s. They accomplished this reduction through a variety of changes to their operation, including how they store the hay they produce for winter feeding. Instead of baling and stacking hay in the conventional way, the Deseret leaves the hay loosely piled in small mounds, or "hills." In the winter, when these mounds are covered with snow, microbial action inside the mound begins to produce heat, which tends to melt the snow on top of the mound. When the cattle are turned into the meadow, they can easily find the hay and will uncover the rest of the mound in the process. This change significantly reduces the cost of providing winter feed, as the usual costs of baling the hay, hauling it to the barn, stacking it, and hauling it back to the winter feeding area are eliminated.

Many conventional ranchers time their breeding so their cows will calve in the late winter in order to maximize the weaning weights of their calves in the fall, when they are shipped to market. High weaning weights are supposed to fetch a higher price per pound, not to mention the bragging rights associated with this measure of ranching performance. However, the mother cows experience considerable nutritional stress just after calving, so many ranchers have to feed their cows supplemental hay throughout the winter and early spring until their range forage has sufficient volume and nutritional value to meet these demands.

By delaying calving until spring, the Deseret matched the peak nutritional demands of the cows with the peak producing months of the ranch's range. The calves are then weaned onto irrigated pasture in February, where they gain weight at one-third of the cost before weaning. And though their weaning weights are lower, the costs of a gain of a pound of beef in these yearling calves are now one-sixth of their former level, boosting the ranch's profits dramatically. In addition, because the cows were under less overall stress while nursing their calves, they went into the next winter in better shape to weather the cold.

By using the time-controlled grazing system that is part of the HRM model, the Deseret improved its rangeland ecosystem health and productivity to the point where its wildlife population levels began increasing significantly. Because the ranch developed a sizable trophy elk population, it could charge premium prices for guided hunts on the ranch as well as offering a high-quality hunting experience for other game animals. The Deseret Ranch now has a full-time wildlife biologist on its management team, and the wildlife populations are managed as an integral part of the ranch, as important to its success as livestock production. In fact, in 1996, fully 60 percent of the Deseret's income came from hunting fees and associated services.[13]

The Deseret management team realizes that the diversity of habitat and wildlife on the ranch not only improves its overall ecosystem health and productivity but also provides economic security by diversifying its sources of income. Wildlife species include elk, deer, antelope, eagle, sandhill crane, waterfowl, and mountain lion. In fact, the ranch has become a favorite site for nature groups and bird-watchers as well as for game hunting.

The Salatin Farm—A Closer Look

The Salatins farm about 95 acres in the Shenandoah Valley of western Virginia, with another 400 acres of woodlands that they selectively harvest. In addition to beef and egg production, the Salatins have developed some other innovative production practices. They raise "pastured poultry," which they grow in specially designed, bottomless cages that can easily be moved through the pastures. A lot of this work can be done by their children, as the system is extremely clean and safe to work around, primarily because of the composition of the bedding.[14] They also dress these chickens at the farm, where they sell most of their other value-added products to about four hundred families who visit from within a 200-mile radius of their farm. Their pastured-poultry enterprise nets an additional $20,000 to $25,000 over their six-month summer season.[15]

In the winter they use their "rackinhouses" to combine their rabbit and chicken production. The rabbits go on the top layer, and their droppings fall through to the second layer, where the chickens scratch through the waste, composting the bedding below. Again, owing to the thoughtful design and construction of this system, it is extremely safe, clean, and pleasant for the Salatins' children to work around. In fact, their son Daniel manages the rabbit business completely on his own. The Salatins use the wood chips from their firewood and lumber business for bedding material, which they combine with manure and the inedible parts of their chickens to create compost.

One of the Salatins' most innovative enterprises is their brush-clearing operation. After harvesting a small section of woodland where they needed to clear small saplings and brush from the area, they fenced the area, put some hogs in, and let them root out the brush and create a seedbed for grass. Not only does this practice avoid the use of expensive equipment for clearing the land, but they also sell the hogs after the work is done, pocketing a profit for an activity that is normally an expense on most farms. Keeping the hogs for ninety days, they spent $25 for each on feed and then sold the hogs at a profit of $400 apiece. The Salatins paid $.30 per pound for their brush-clearing "equipment," which is lot cheaper than the cost of heavy machinery.

The Salatins also believe in the diversity of wildlife on their farm to create a healthier ecosystem that is more in balance and resistant to drought and other climatic extremes. They strive to achieve a high diversity of grasses in their pastures, and they keep a balance between their grassland and woodland ecosystems. They have reforested 60 acres to break up their pastures as well as clearing 60 acres to create new pasture areas within their woodlands to provide a diversity of habitat for deer, small mammals, birds, and natural predators. Not only does this wildlife diversity help to prevent predator loss among their chickens but the wooded strips keep the hens roosting on the eggmobile rather than running back to the farmhouse.

The James Ranch in Durango

The James family has a 400-acre ranch located a few miles north of Durango, Colorado. David and Kay James began ranching this property in the 1960s. As their children grew, married, and had children of their own, they needed to find a way to support this extended family on such a small ranch. They have used the HRM and Salatin models to find additional sources of revenue from this land and so keep their family together and continue their rural lifestyle. At this time, three out of their four children are living at the ranch, and they hope to lure their youngest son back home in the near future.

Like the Salatins, the Jameses raise grass-finished beef that is cut and packaged by a small, custom butcher who lives nearby. They also raise pastured poultry following the Salatin model. Another key source of income in a rapidly growing area like Durango is their nursery, where they have a diverse collection of native trees up to thirty-five years of age. As new homes are built in the Durango area, the Jameses find that homeowners are quite willing to pay for "instant landscaping" in order to have full-grown trees in their yard. They also provide a tree-moving service in the Four Corners region for anyone who wants trees moved from one location to another.

One of the Jameses' daughters has begun an organic produce operation, and she sells the produce at the local farmers' market and at the ranch. The family sees this as not only another source of income but also another marketing tool to bring new customers to the ranch for their other products. They also have a grass-seeding service that they hope to expand in the near future.

IV. Guidelines for Sustainable Agriculture

From these examples, we can glean several core principles or operating guidelines for practicing sustainable agriculture. These principles, or guiding concepts, include the idea that one should adapt agricultural enterprises to "get in sync with nature." This approach relieves the producer

of the high costs of fighting the natural tendencies of agricultural ecosystems. More importantly, it allows her to maximize the percent of free solar energy that she harvests and converts into high-value products and services.

For example, rather than continuing to treat their heel-fly problem with conventional practices, the Salatins found a system that more closely approximates how nature keeps parasites in balance. The corollary to this idea is that you must adapt your enterprises to fit your unique situation— what works in Virginia or Utah may not work exactly the same way in Colorado.

As Joel Salatin likes to point out, when one is planning a sustainable agricultural activity, "nature is always the pattern." That is, we should ask ourselves, "How does nature do this?" Just as the wild birds of Africa follow herds of large herbivores, so too can chickens follow domesticated livestock. You should look for these "natural" synergies between enterprises and view every by-product (manure, offal) as a resource. The Salatins have created a virtual "closed system" on their farm, where nothing is thrown away. They strive for biological diversity, or "perennial polyculture," because they recognize that their farm is most resilient (i.e., sustainable) when it has a high diversity of plant and animal species.

Holistic Management

One of the fastest-growing approaches to the practice of sustainable agriculture is HRM, or holistic management (HM). In the HRM decision model, families are first advised to form a long-range "holistic goal," or vision of what they want for their future.[16] This goal should encompass everything that is important to them. To form such a goal, a family must first assess or inventory their resource situation and determine how this set of resources ("the whole under management") is unique. Then they create a vision of what they want for their lives and their landscape one or more generations in the future.

The HRM model provides a set of decision-making guidelines to assist the producer in making sound, sustainable decisions in the operation of her farm, ranch, or other enterprise:

- Decisions should be driven by your long-range visions, not by trying to solve short-run problems.
- Diversity is beneficial when managed properly; the key is to learn to take advantage of natural synergies available through biological, economic, and human diversity.
- The quickest and least expensive path to achieving

your long-range goal is to focus on your "weak link," that is, focus only on that part of your whole enterprise that is your current bottleneck.

- Choose enterprises or activities that give you the highest return for your effort; that is, get the "biggest bang for your buck" (e.g., the Salatins' use of hogs for clearing brush).
- Always plan for and assume that the unexpected will occur—nature is dynamic, complex, and unpredictable; plan and monitor for adverse outcomes and then adjust when necessary.
- Decisions should be made by looking at the health of the whole system rather than just the parts in isolation; the whole is greater than the sum of parts— ecosystems are synergistic when healthy.
- Find the true cause of the problem instead of just treating the symptoms.

HRM has given many farmers and ranchers an invaluable tool in starting and maintaining the change toward more sustainable agricultural practices. A key component in the model is the recognition that grazing animals play several critical roles in ecosystem health when managed properly. To manage grazing animals sustainably, they must mimic the behavior of wild herbivores in a natural system that includes their natural predators. In an agricultural setting, however, we can substitute management and planning for the natural movements of wild herbivores and achieve sustainable production. The farmer or rancher must be willing to monitor her ecosystem carefully to ensure that it is indeed moving in the right direction.

Getting Started in Sustainable Agriculture

Farmers and ranchers practicing sustainable agriculture offer several suggestions for those who might want to pursue this direction in agricultural production.[17]

- Start small—don't try to change your entire operation at once; experiment on a small scale.
- Learn as much as you can from others who have already tried a new idea, but don't be afraid to try something new yourself.
- Adapt activities to your own situation—most sustainable production practices are not recipes, like conventional agriculture, but rather are as much art as science; be flexible and adaptable.
- Try to diversify your enterprises over time to spread your risk and add sources of income.

- Look for opportunities to add value to your products, and focus on niche markets where you don't have to compete with large, conventional producers on price and volume.
- Find the kind of customers you can enjoy dealing with and develop personal relationships with these people based on quality, customer satisfaction, and filling a genuine need.

There is a growing body of practitioners in sustainable agriculture, so it is possible to get help and support from those who are already doing it. At some point, however, the would-be practitioner needs to just begin, as part of the fun is learning how much is really possible in one's own situation as we experiment with the art of sustainable agriculture.

This chapter has provided a brief overview of the practices and philosophy of sustainable agriculture. There are many farmers and ranchers in Colorado who could also serve as excellent examples of this approach but were not included simply for lack of space. The bibliography provides several sources of information for locating sustainable producers in your area. These people are perhaps the best resources for someone trying to start in sustainable agriculture because they already know the local markets and have some experience with what works and what doesn't. However, in the long run, there is no substitute for the firsthand experience of learning the art and science yourself.

Notes

1. Kinney 1981.
2. Ibid.
3. Kinney 1980. The standard models of conventional economics and business are unable to deal with the kind of synergistic behavior of complex ecosystems that we examine here.
4. Joel Salatin speaks of the tremendous economic, ecological, and emotional costs of trying to maintain a monoculture (Salatin 1995).
5. See Groff 1997 for a video demonstration of this system.
6. No-till planting uses a seed drill to plant seeds without turning the soil over.
7. Groff 1997.
8. See Savory 1988 for a detailed discussion of high-density, time-controlled grazing.
9. See *The Stockman Grass Farmer*, various issues; for example Nation 1996 and Jost 1996.
10. Salatin 1991.
11. Ibid.
12. For a complete discussion of HRM, see Savory 1988. The official title is now holistic management (HM) in order to gen-

eralize the decision-making process to nonagricultural situations. The Center for Holistic Management, located in Albuquerque, New Mexico, is the official source of information about this decision-making model.

13. Bill Hopkins, Deseret Ranch manager, and Rick Denver, wildlife biologist, personal communication, 1996.

14. Salatin 1996. The bedding is a mix of dry carbonaceous material (wood chips, sawdust, etc.) that chemically binds the nitrogen compounds in animal dung, urine, and other by-products. When the carbon and nitrogen are in the proper balance, there is no smell or toxicity to these materials.

15. Salatin 1993.

16. Savory 1988.

17. See Salatin 1998 for a list of suggested behavioral guidelines for getting started.

References

Groff, S. 1997. *No-Till Vegetables* (videotape with supplemental materials). Holtwood, PA: New Generation Cropping Systems/ Highland Productions.

Jost, J. 1996. "Kansas Grazing Study Shows Benefits of Management Intensive Grazing." *The Stockman Grass Farmer*, 53:30–31

Kinney, W. C. 1980. *Land-Use Conflict in Wildland Watershed Management: A Multiple Objective Economic Analysis.* Davis: Department of Agricultural and Resource Economics, University of California.

1981. "U.S. Agriculture Faces Major Changes." *Washington Farmer-Stockman* 106:2–10.

Nation, A. 1996. "High Stock Density Grazing Improves Pastures." *The Stockman Grass Farmer*, 53:1–10

Salatin, J. 1996. "Family Farming and Ranching." Ridgeland, MS, SGF North American Grazing Conference.

1995. "Managing for Diversity." Ridgeland, MS, SGF North American Grazing Conference.

1991. "Pastured Egg Production." *The Stockman Grass Farmer*, 48:1–3

1993. *Pastured Poultry Profits* (videotape). Swoope, VA: Polyface, Inc./Five Star Video Productions.

1998. "10 Commandments for Succeeding on the Farm." *The Stockman Grass Farmer*, 55:23–25.

Savory, A. 1988. *Holistic Resource Management.* Washington, DC: Island Press.

For Additional Information

The Stockman Grass Farmer is a monthly journal covering practitioners of management-intensive grazing across the United States and throughout the world. It also sponsors an annual grazing conference as well as selling a variety of books, videotapes, and audiotapes of past conference speakers.

The Stockman Grass Farmer
P.O. Box 2300
Ridgeland, MS 39158-2300
(800) 748-9808

The Colorado Department of Agriculture publishes a booklet titled "Farm Fresh Directory" that provides information about farmers' markets in the state, including times and days of operation. To order, call (800) 886-7683.

The Center for Holistic Resource Management is the official source of information about this decision-making model. They can be contacted at:

The Center for Holistic Resource Management
1007 Luna Circle NW
Albuquerque, NM 87102
(505) 842-5252

The National Farmers' Union works to support small family and organic farmers, and it is a source of information about farmers in your area. It is headquartered in Aurora, Colorado.

National Farmer's Union
11900 East Cornell Avenue
Aurora, CO 80014
(303) 337-5500

The Sustainable Agriculture Research and Education Program (SARE) of the U.S. Department of Agriculture provides numerous resources through the Sustainable Agricultural Network (SAN) for producers wanting to learn more about sustainable production practices. These include:

Sustainable Agriculture: Directory of Expertise, 3rd Edition, $18.95
Source Book of Sustainable Agriculture, 1997, $12.00

SARE also has other publications, a website (www. sare.org), and an e-mail discussion group. *Sustainable Agriculture: Directory of Expertise* provides information on 1,000 individuals and 200 organizations that have knowledge of sustainable agricultural practices. The Source Book identifies 559 resource materials, including print, video, and electronic media. Order SAN publications from:

Sustainable Agriculture Publications
Hills Building, Room 10
University of Vermont
Burlington, VT 05405-0082

Also, see the References section for specific audio, video, and printed materials cited in this article.

38

Conservation Easements

PART A: BECAUSE THEY'RE NOT MAKING LAND ANYMORE
Katharine Roser
Executive Director, La Plata
Open Space Conservancy

Another minute, another 3 acres of America's productive farmland lost to development. In Colorado alone, more than 270,000 acres of prime agricultural land and more than 200,000 acres of critical wildlife habitat are ripped up each year, moved around, paved over, and removed from our inventory of resources necessary to sustain life as we know it. As our open lands go, so go our food supply, clean water and air, effective aquifer recharge, natural flood control, biological diversity, scientific opportunity, and so on and on. The lands will never be reclaimed (when did you last see a subdivision being bulldozed to make way for a farm?), and the amenities those lands once provided for free will now cost billions of taxpayer dollars to try to replace or duplicate.

Why the wanton destruction? Greed, of course, is an enormous factor. Many people are willing, even eager, to trade in tomorrow for dollars in their pockets today. Another factor is ignorance. There are many people who don't think much beyond the grocery store when they think of food supply. But an overlooked factor in the loss of our open lands is poor public policy. State property taxes and federal estate taxes are structured so that many families will lose their lands to the forces of development unless they take active steps, including private land conservation, to prevent that loss.

Of course landowners have the right to develop their land. But they have just as much right to permanently protect it from harmful development. By doing so, they can benefit their land, their families, and their communities. Many tools are available to use either alone or in combi-

nation to permanently protect land. By far the most popular tool, and a "must do" for landowners as part of effective estate planning, is the conservation easement.

I. What Is a Conservation Easement?

When a person owns land, he owns a "bundle" of rights or interests. He owns the right, for example, to farm, to timber, to mine minerals, to subdivide, to construct buildings, and so on. He has the right to sell or give away his land (in which case he would transfer all of his rights or interests). He also has the right to sell or give away just some of the rights or interests. In a conservation easement, a landowner gives up, in a legal deed of conservation easement, his rights to use the land for purposes that might harm identified natural features. He spells out the restrictions that are necessary to protect his land and then conveys the rights that he never wants to see exercised to a qualified conservation organization (a private land trust or a government agency) that is bound by law to enforce the restrictions. The "dangerous" rights are essentially extinguished, but the landowner retains all other rights to use his land. A conservation easement is a "deed restriction," but unlike simple deed restrictions it is (1) conveyed for conservation purposes and (2) held by a conservation organization that has the right and the obligation to enforce it.

Conservation easements may be either donated or sold by the landowner. Easements donated to qualified organizations are considered charitable gifts and can result in significant tax benefits to the donors.

II. How Long Does a Conservation Easement Last?

A conservation easement can be written to last a period of years (a term easement) where state law allows, or it can be written so that it lasts forever (a perpetual easement). Only gifts of perpetual easements, however, can qualify the grantor for income and estate tax benefits. Most conservation organizations will accept only perpetual easements.

Whether term or perpetual, conservation easements run with the land. Easement restrictions bind not only the landowner who executes the easement but any future owners of the land as well. Because conservation easements are recorded in the official records of the county where the land is located, future owners will learn about the easements when they obtain title reports. In addition, most easements require the landowner to notify the easement holder when a transfer of the property is pending so the easement holder can contact the new owner and inform him of the easement restrictions.

III. What Lands Qualify for Conservation Easements?

There are federal and state laws that govern the types of land that qualify for conservation easements. To be tax deductible, easements must be given "exclusively for conservation purposes" that benefit the public by protecting land for purposes including (1) public outdoor recreation or education, (2) significant natural habitat, (3) scenic enjoyment, (4) agriculture and forestry, and (5) historic preservation.

In addition, each land trust will have its own criteria for conservation easements it accepts. These criteria spring from the goals of the land trust and are based on (1) the type of property the trust was created to protect, (2) the quality of each particular parcel, (3) whether an easement is the best tool for protecting that parcel, and (4) whether the land trust is capable of monitoring and enforcing the easement forever. Some land trusts, such as the Colorado Cattlemen's Agricultural Land Trust (CCALT), were created specifically to protect agriculture. Thus, CCALT will only accept an easement on a producing farm or ranch, and its easements will be written to reflect its single purpose of protecting the landowner's ability to farm or ranch. Other land trusts have different goals, which are reflected in the lands on which they choose to hold easements and the content of those easements. The Nature Conservancy focuses mainly on lands with threatened or endangered plant and animal species, necessitating very specific easement restrictions to protect those species. Many land trusts, such as La Plata Open Space Conservancy (LPOSC), are of the "generic" variety, accepting a variety of easements with a variety of conservation purposes and tailoring restrictions appropriately. For example, LPOSC holds easements to protect agriculture that simply prevent the breakup and development of the land, allowing the owner to continue farming or ranching as he sees fit. Other LPOSC easements protect sensitive riparian habitat and are considerably more restrictive. LPOSC also holds easements that protect scenic views by preventing development in the view shed and easements that protect watershed by preventing development and the use of harmful herbicides and pesticides and limiting human activity near a municipal water supply.

IV. Just How Restrictive Is a Conservation Easement?

Most land trusts use a model conservation easement that contains necessary legal "boilerplate" that protects the land trust and the landowner, but land trusts do not impose restrictions upon the land or the landowners. The restrictions placed and rights reserved in each easement are negotiated between the landowner and land trust and are unique to each parcel, each landowner, and each set of circumstances. Each conservation easement restricts development and other land uses as necessary to protect the specific natural values of the land. Sometimes all construction is prohibited, and sometimes it is not.

If the landowner's goal is to protect a pristine natural area, he will probably want to restrict all development as well as other activities, such as motorized recreation or logging, that would change the land's natural condition. However, if his goal is to protect agriculture, he may only want to prevent subdivision and development while allowing for construction of buildings and continuation of activities necessary for and compatible with agriculture. He may wish to reserve the right to grow new crops and engage in new, as well as historical, methods of agriculture.

It is important to remember that the land trust does not tell the landowner what to do with his land. Landowner and land trust work together to determine what restrictions are necessary to meet the stated purpose of each conservation easement. Sometimes landowners desire restrictions that are greater than the land trust's ability to enforce, and sometimes land trusts feel landowners must give up more rights than they wish to in order to meet the stated conservation purposes. Where landowners and land trusts cannot agree, conservation easements don't happen.

V. Do Conservation Easements Give the Public the Right of Access?

In general, landowners who give conservation easements do not have to open up their land to the public. If the purpose of a conservation easement is to protect land for public recreation, then public access to the land must be granted. If the purpose of an easement is to protect a scenic resource, then the public must have visual access to the land (i.e., be able to see it from a public roadway or trail). In no other cases must a conservation easement grant public access, although landowners are free to convey certain public access rights if they wish.

VI. Who May Grant a Conservation Easement?

Any landowner may grant a conservation easement to a qualified organization. If land is owned by more than one person, all owners must consent to encumbering the land with the easement. If there is a mortgage on the property, the lender must agree to subordinate its rights in the property to the rights of the easement holder to ensure that the easement will not be extinguished in the event of foreclosure.

Most experienced land trusts have educated local lenders about conservation easements and the mortgage subordination requirements and have developed relationships with the lenders that enable quick and painless compliance with the subordination requirement.

VII. Who May Accept a Conservation Easement?

A conservation easement may be accepted and held by a public agency or a conservation organization (generally a land trust) that qualifies as a public charity under Internal Revenue Code 501(c)(3) and that is set up specifically to hold, monitor, and enforce conservation easements. There are more than thirty local, statewide, and national land trusts operating in Colorado.

In areas where there is a local land trust in operation, the local trust is generally the best choice because the easement is more likely to receive regular attention and the land trust more likely to take immediate action in the event of an actual or threatened violation of the easement. Statewide and national land trusts work mainly in areas where there is no local land trust, or to meet special needs. In addition, statewide and national trusts sometimes work in partnership with the local trusts to leverage resources. In any case, holding conservation easements is an enormous responsibility, and a landowner should make sure that the intended easement holder has the willingness and ability to shoulder that responsibility.

VIII. What Are the Responsibilities of the Land Trust or Public Agency Easement Holder?

As explained above, conservation easements must be given exclusively for conservation purposes. It is up to the land trust when negotiating an easement to ensure that one or more of these purposes are met by the easement. In addition, each land trust should have its own criteria for evaluating and accepting conservation projects, and the land trust should be sure that each project meets these criteria.

Although the landowner and land trust negotiate the specific easement restrictions to their mutual satisfaction, it is the land trust's responsibility to draft a conservation easement that is understandable and enforceable.

Once a conservation easement has been negotiated, drafted, given, and accepted, the real work begins. The land trust or agency that holds a conservation easement is required by law to ensure the effectiveness of the easement. To do this, the easement holder must monitor (inspect) the easement property on a regular basis—once a year or more. Ideally, the landowner should accompany the land trust inspector on each monitoring visit to point out and explain any changes that have taken place on the land since the last visit. If a visit reveals that the easement is about to be or has been violated, the land trust is obligated to prevent or cure the violation and restore the property to its condition at the time the easement was conveyed.

IX. What Does It Cost to Give a Conservation Easement?

In the big picture, private land conservation using conservation easements is very inexpensive, costing the taxpayers little or nothing in exchange for enormous public benefit. But it is not entirely free. The landowner can expect to incur costs for some or all of the following:

- legal and financial advice
- an inventory documenting the condition of the property at the time of the grant of easement. This "baseline report" consists of maps, photos, verification of resource values from public agencies or knowledgeable consultants, and other pertinent documentation.
- a survey of the land to be encumbered by the easement (When an entire property is encumbered, a survey may not be necessary, but an accurate legal description is needed.)

- an appraisal of the land assessing values prior to and after the encumbrance to establish the value of the conservation easement for tax purposes
- title report and title insurance
- a stewardship donation to the land trust to enable the trust to monitor and enforce the easement in perpetuity in accordance with the landowner's wishes. A responsible land trust will calculate the annual cost of easement stewardship and ask for a donation to a restricted fund of an amount that will generate enough earnings to cover the annual cost.

Because every easement is different, it is impossible to give an estimate of landowner costs. It is safe to say that they can range from a few thousand dollars to $20,000 or more. Landowner financial benefits, discussed below, can range from a few thousand dollars to hundreds of thousands or even millions of dollars. Although most landowners will realize financial benefits from their easements that will more than offset their costs, this is not always the case. When landowners cannot afford the costs of executing conservation easements, land trusts will look to alternative sources of funds rather than leaving the land unprotected.

X. Why Should a Landowner Give a Conservation Easement?

A conservation easement involves giving up rights, and it can cost money, so why do it?

Because, though a landowner may have no intention of ever developing his land, he isn't going to live forever. By giving a conservation easement, a landowner who cares about his land can ensure that its natural, scenic, agricultural, recreational, and historical values will be protected in perpetuity for the benefit of his children and their children, and for the benefit of the general public.

Why must a landowner take action when he just wants his land to stay as it is? Because (1) without a conservation easement, he has no assurance that future owners will honor his wishes, and (2) federal estate taxes, which can be as high as 55 percent of the value of the estate, may force his heirs to sell part or all of the land for development just to pay the taxes.

XI. What Tax Benefits Are Associated with Conservation Easements?

Tax benefits that can result from conservation easements fall into three categories: property tax, income tax, and estate tax. The following is a general overview of existing tax benefits. Easement donors are encouraged to seek professional tax and estate planning advice.

Property Tax Benefits

Although conservation easements limit uses of land and therefore generally decrease the land's value, Colorado does not yet recognize this fact with a property tax category for restricted property. Colorado's property tax provision for conservation easement–encumbered properties does not decrease the land's valuation or the tax but instead splits the tax liability between the easement holder (liable for tax on the value of the easement) and the landowner (liable for tax on the remainder). In theory, this decreases the tax burden on the landowner by shifting some of the burden to the land trust (which can then apply for exemption based on its tax-exempt status). In practice, however, the assessment is rarely split automatically when a property is easement-encumbered, and it is generally up to the landowner to request that the assessment be split, or to otherwise argue that his property's value has decreased and his tax should be decreased accordingly.

A relatively new Colorado property tax provision does offer an incentive to owners of agricultural land to protect their land with conservation easements. Generally when the county assessor determines that land is no longer in productive agriculture, for whatever reason, the land is bumped into the "vacant land" category. The result can be a fiftyfold or even a hundredfold increase in the property tax bill. A classic example in La Plata County bumped a parcel of mountain grazing land, taxed at $400 per year in the agricultural category, into the vacant land category. The result: a $21,000 tax bill. Owners of bona fide agricultural land of greater than 80 acres who choose to protect the land with a conservation easement are assured that their land will stay in the agricultural tax category even if they should retire or take the land out of production for any reason.

Income Tax Benefits

Federal income tax.

When a landowner donates a perpetual conservation easement exclusively for conservation purposes to a qualified conservation organization or public agency, the IRS considers the donation a charitable gift, the value of which is deductible from federal income tax. The value of the easement, determined by an appraisal, is the "highest and best" use value of the property before it was restricted minus the price the property can bring subject to the easement restrictions.

A landowner can deduct the value of his gift at the rate

of 30 percent of his adjusted gross income each year for a total of six years. A higher-income donor may deduct all of the value of his gift in a shorter time, while a lower-income donor may not be able to deduct the full value of his gift. Easement donors often give their easements in the same year that they sell capital gain property and are thereby able to offset much of the capital gains tax.

State income tax.

A Colorado taxpayer may follow his federal income tax deduction with a similar deduction against Colorado income. But for easements granted in the year 2000 or after, taxpayers may substitute a new tax benefit that is generally far more valuable than the deduction. The tax credit may be taken for the first $100,000 of value of a donated conservation easement, and any unused portion of the credit may be carried forward for up to twenty years.

Federal Estate Tax Benefits

The most significant tax benefit resulting from conservation easements, particularly for families with highly appreciated land, is the estate tax benefit. Conservation easements can make the difference between land staying in families and heirs having to sell family lands just to pay estate tax. When land use is restricted by means of a conservation easement, the land can be valued only for its remaining uses for purposes of estate tax. For example, a 2,000-acre ranch that might be valued at millions of dollars for development can be valued only at a fraction of that for ranching if it is restricted to ranching by a conservation easement. A conservation easement removes value from the estate and thereby reduces estate tax.

The conservation provisions of the Taxpayer Relief Act of 1997, P.L. 105-34, make an even greater difference. Some important provisions of this law include:

1. A partial exclusion from estate tax of certain land that is subject to a qualified conservation easement. The exclusion, to be phased in over a five-year period and capped at $500,000, will exclude from tax up to 40 percent of the value of the land and is in addition to the initial estate tax benefit resulting from the easement's effect on land value and in addition to the $1.3 million exclusion for family-owned businesses described below. Some geographic restrictions apply, but much of Colorado's important open land will qualify for the exclusion.
2. A postmortem election whereby the heirs or executor of an estate may grant a conservation easement to take advantage of the new tax benefits.
3. An increase in the estate and gift tax exclusion, previously $600,000 per individual, to $625,000 for 1998 and increasing annually until the exclusion reaches $1 million in 2006.
4. An exclusion of $1.3 million for family-owned businesses, including farms and ranches, that meet certain criteria. (This exclusion includes but is not in addition to the general estate tax exclusion.)

These and other favorable provisions of the new tax law went into effect on January 1, 1999. The law will enable many families to keep land that would otherwise have to be sold for development to pay estate taxes, and it will provide for permanent protection of that land. The new law does not lower estate tax rates, however, which underscores the importance for families who own land to include conservation easements in their estate planning.

PART B: SIGNIFICANT CONSERVATION EASEMENT EFFORTS IN COLORADO
Donald E. Moore
Douglas County Planner

XII. Real-Life Examples

Most conservation easements involve a landowner who grants the easement and an easement holder who oversees and manages the easement. In this situation the owner retains the ownership of the land, uses it according to the terms of the conservation easement, and uses the resulting tax benefits to make this type of conservation affordable for himself and his family. These transactions are between two parties and do not require purchasing funds.

There are also many conservation easements that are more complex and may involve local governments, non-profit organizations, or private parties. These persons or entities raise funds to enable conservation easements to be placed on the lands. The following summaries describe several of these types of easements that have been successfully completed in Colorado.

L-Cross Ranch

A partnership of the Nature Conservancy and public and private organizations will ensure the long-term protection of the L-Cross Ranch in the San Luis Valley, which has outstanding natural, agricultural, and historical resources.

With funds from the Great Outdoors Colorado Trust Fund (GOCO) and the Colorado Division of Wildlife (DOW) as a partner in GOCO's Wetlands Initiative, the Nature Conservancy purchased a conservation easement on over 6,200 acres of the ranch. The Rocky Mountain Bighorn Sheep Association and Trout Unlimited also helped to finance the easement.

The 8,000-acre L-Cross Ranch controls more than 55,000 acres of grazing leases on public land. In addition to purchasing the conservation easement, the Conservancy also purchased a 1,700-acre parcel of the ranch and plans to convey it to the Bureau of Land Management (BLM). The BLM is interested in acquiring this 1,700-acre parcel to ensure better access to the federal lands that surround the ranch and help to protect the ranch's ecological values.

What makes the L-Cross Ranch so exceptional? The ranch is home to numerous raptors such as golden eagles and bald eagles as well as a nesting pair of short-eared owls, a species that is rare in Colorado. Deer, elk, pronghorn, bighorn sheep, and moose winter on the ranch; it is very unusual to have even three of these species wintering in the same location, let alone five.

Carnero Creek, a perennial stream that bisects the ranch, supports important riparian vegetation and a healthy native fish population of Rio Grande cutthroat trout. The DOW considers Carnero Creek to be critical foraging habitat for the peregrine falcon. Both Carnero Creek and La Garita Creek, which also flows through the ranch, feed important wetlands on the valley floor, including the Nature Conservancy's Mishak Lakes Preserve.

The L-Cross provides habitat for several plant species of concern, including the rock-loving neoparrya, a globally rare plant in the parsley family. Excellent examples of montane grassland and woodland communities are also found on the ranch.

From a historical perspective, the Native American rock art etched on the cliff walls in Carnero Creek has earned the ranch a listing as a National Significant Archaeological Site. These pictographs have become a source of hands-on learning for the local school districts.

One of the San Luis Valley's premier cattle ranches, the L-Cross has been recognized by the Colorado Cattlemen's Association and the DOW for its excellent management. Ranch manager Mike Spearman has received numerous awards for the ranch's agricultural excellence and wildlife management.

Edwards Ranch

By devising an innovative solution to a conservation challenge, the Nature Conservancy was able to protect one of the most biologically significant sites on the Yampa River.

The 430-acre Edwards Ranch includes an important reach of the Yampa River where its meander bends and broad floodplain support mature cottonwood forests, gravel bars with dense stands of young cottonwood saplings, oxbow sloughs, and cattail marshes. In addition, the river area is a major roosting site for threatened greater sandhill cranes. The ranch, which is immediately downstream of the Conservancy's historical Carpenter Ranch, also has important agricultural open space values.

This critical site was on its way to being subdivided before the Conservancy stepped in, bought it, placed a conservation easement on it, and then sold it to a local ranching family. The easement will protect the ranch and its ecological values as well as allowing for fencing of the entire riparian area to manage cattle grazing.

As a result of this creative deal, an additional 1.5 miles of the Yampa River are now protected, and a ranching family will be able to maintain their livelihood in the Yampa River Valley. To date, the Conservancy has protected 6 miles of the Yampa River.

Preservation of a Highway Corridor: Douglas Heights

Located in southern Douglas County, a 1,632-acre parcel of land commonly called Douglas Heights was proposed for development as 35-acre residential homesites. This property consisted of a highly visible long ridge of open grasslands located in the heavily traveled Interstate 25 corridor. This property is part of a very important highway viewshed and open space area separating the Colorado Springs and Denver metropolitan areas. The Conservation Fund, a nonprofit land conservation organization, with support from Douglas County, sought to preserve this property.

Recognizing that to purchase the entire property for open space would be economically infeasible, the Conservation Fund worked with Douglas County and the landowners to cluster the residential homesites in one area of the property that would not affect the highway views of the mountains; in return, the homes would not be adversely affected by the view or the noise of the interstate. To accomplish this, a grant was applied for and received from GOCO to purchase a portion of the property while the remainder of the open space was acquired by giving a density bonus for additional clustered homesites. The Douglas Heights property now consists of 1,075 acres of open space now owned by Douglas County and fifteen 10- to 23-acre residential homesites located on approximately 250 acres.

Legislation approved by the Colorado General Assembly in 1996 (H.B. 1364) makes it easier for county governments to cluster development by amending water-well permit rules. A number of county governments, including Routt, Douglas, and Larimer, have specific regulations by which rural residential clustering of homesites can be done.

To meet a requirement that open space purchased with GOCO grant monies be preserved in perpetuity, a conservation easement is held by the Douglas County Land Conservancy, a local land trust. As part of the Douglas County Land Conservancy holding the conservation easement, the Douglas County Land Conservancy was paid $5,000 to cover its costs to monitor and maintain the easement.

Estes Valley Land Trust: Scenic Entrance to Estes Valley and Rocky Mountain National Park

The historical Meadowdale Ranch, 1,200 acres adjoining the Highway 36 entrance to the Estes Valley, was held in a trust whose beneficiaries wished to maintain the open space values of the property.

In return for approximately one-half of its appraised value regarding its development potential, the ranch owners granted a conservation easement on the ranch to the Estes Valley Land Trust. Funding for the purchase of the easement was secured by a successful local fund-raising drive and a matching grant from GOCO.

Cooperation in working out the details of the transaction was secured from the town of Estes Park, Larimer County, the U.S. Forest Service, Congressman Wayne Allard, and many local residents. The purchase price of the easement was $325,000 plus eight future residential sites on not more than a total of 40 acres.

Cherokee Ranch

The Cherokee Ranch is an important 3,200-acre ranch located in Douglas County, Colorado, with numerous his-

torical buildings, including a home patterned after a Scottish castle, and important wildlife habitat. The owner, Mrs. Tweet Kimball, wished to preserve this land in perpetuity for the benefit of wildlife, maintain the historical working ranch operations as an educational demonstration facility, develop an outdoor education center, and create a museum within the Scottish castle.

These ambitious preservation and education plans needed a large infusion of money and a legal mechanism to ensure that the ranch would be well maintained and left in a natural state. This was accomplished by the cooperation of Mrs. Kimball, Douglas County, and a private, nonprofit, tax-exempt foundation. To ensure the overall long-term care and management of the property, the ownership of the ranch was placed in the hands of the Cherokee Ranch and Castle Foundation, of which Mrs. Kimball was a member until her death in 1999. To ensure the perpetual preservation of the ranch, Douglas County purchased a conservation easement over all of the ranch property with the exception of areas including and immediately surrounding existing and planned buildings, such as the proposed education center. Needed monies to upgrade and maintain the ranch and buildings were provided by the purchase of the conservation easement by Douglas County for $2 million, to be paid in ten annual payments of $200,000.

XIII. Now What?

This chapter is intended as an overview of conservation easements and how they work, not only to protect land but to benefit landowners, their families, and their communities. If a conservation easement is an attractive option to you or to someone you know, you should contact the Colorado Coalition of Land Trusts for information about the land trusts that work in your area: Colorado Coalition of Land Trusts, 710 10th Street, Golden, CO 80401. Phone: (303) 271-1577; Fax: (303) 271-1582; E-mail: janeh@sopris.net.

39

Farm and Ranch Estate Planning to Avoid Unintended Breakup for Taxes

Donald H. Kelley, *Attorney at Law*

I. The Basic Problem

A farm or ranch operation consists of the land on which crops are grown or livestock raised and the related production assets. The production assets include farming machinery, tools, livestock, and working capital.

A typical farm or ranch family may involve both a child or children who are working in the farm or ranch operation and want to continue as the operators after the retirement or death of the parents and children living off the place who are not interested in involvement in the operation. The off-farm heirs sometimes desire to have an ongoing ownership participation, but usually want their share of the family inheritance in nonfarm property.

The child likely to succeed to management of the family operation is primarily concerned with (1) economic security as to the ability to own the land and production assets necessary to farm or ranch operation and (2) participating in the growth of net worth taking place during his or her working life. The best assurance as to both is an arrangement for funding the parents' retirement, as they desire, and buying out the off-farm heirs or satisfying their inheritances with nonfarm property.

Fundamental to a successful transition of the family farm or ranch property into the next generation is that the operation not be burdened with excessive debt charges. Such debt arises primarily from three major sources. They are (1) commercial debt, both long term and operating, (2) federal and state estate taxes, and (3) payments designed to be made by the operating heirs to the nonoperators for the purpose of equalizing inheritances.

The estate-planning goals of farm- and ranch-owning parents are typically to preserve their hard-won operation into the next generation while treating all their children fairly. In many situations the cash flow of the farm or ranch is not sufficient to discharge commercial debt and estate taxes and to fund a fully proportionate inheritance to the off-farm heirs. The parents may be forced to make difficult decisions if they desire their operation to pass intact to the next generation. There are financial and tax planning tools available that may ease this problem in some instances, but it remains the most challenging aspect of planning for succession of farm or ranch ownership. The parents should consider the following factors:

- They have worked long and hard to create the operation, and its basic economics may dictate that exactly equal inheritances for their children are inconsistent with its preservation into the next generation.
- Cash to the off-farm heirs in an amount less than the proportionate value of the farm or ranch may produce as much income to the off-farm heirs as the successors will receive from the operation. For example, if the operation generates a return on the fair market value of 4 percent and the off-farm heirs can earn 8 percent on money, an inheritance of one-half the value passing to the operating successors may be equitable from the income generation standpoint.
- Equality is not always equity. An equitable or fair inheritance need not necessarily be an equal one.

II. Basic Financial and Tax Factors Affecting Transition Planning

Family Debt

The level of both long-term and operating debt may limit the available choices for transition of ownership. Given the reverse leverage of farm debt, that is, interest rates substantially exceeding the earning power of agricultural assets, debt reduces the flexibility in funding inheritance to off-farm heirs and the likelihood of successful operation by the operating heirs.

The federal estate tax is a potential addition to family debt. Avoiding the estate tax or, if necessary, planning effectively for its payment is necessary to assure a successful transition of the farm operation to the designated heirs.

Transition to the Next Generation Through Lifetime Sales

Lifetime installment sales are inhibited by the potential capital gain tax where relatively low-basis assets are involved. Many families own land with a very low historical cost, or basis from family inheritance, which causes a built-in capital gain problem.

Gain may be planned for with regard to the sale of production assets to the successor operator by selecting relatively high-basis assets, such as breeding cows and relatively new machinery, to be purchased by the successor. Again, the income tax on capital gain becomes a problem to the parents if too much gain is involved in such sales. Furthermore, assets as to which depreciation has been taken may suffer a recapture of that depreciation at ordinary income rates.

The step-up in basis of assets at the death of the owners is an important tax consideration. In the estate of an active operator, all property owned, including grain and livestock (but not the amount receivable on contracts for the sale of assets) and inventory held for sale, receives a new basis equal to date-of-death fair market value. As a result, (1) such property may be sold after death with no income tax cost as to the date-of-death value, and (2) all income tax that would otherwise flow from the sale of raised grain and calves is eliminated to the extent of their value at the date of death. The overall tax cost to the family of succession in ownership may thus be lower when assets are held by the parents until death. In some circumstances, a scaling down of the operation by sale after the parents' deaths of assets not essential to the operating unit passing to the successor operator may be appropriate as a means of funding inheritance to off-farm heirs. The step-up in basis of estate assets permits such a sale without capital gain tax.

The Federal Estate Tax

There is a small credit from the federal estate tax payable to the state of Colorado, but the amount of estate taxes is primarily governed by federal law. The estate tax is computed at a percentage of your net worth. You are first entitled to deduct an amount called the "Unified Credit" that is equal to the estate net values, called the "Applicable Exclusion" for deaths in the years shown in Table 39.1.

TABLE 39.1 Unified Credits and Applicable Extension Amounts

Year	Unified Credit	Applicable Extension Amount
1997	198,200	600,000
1998	202,252	625,000
1999	211,300	650,000
2000	220,550	675,000
2001	220,550	675,000
2002	229,800	700,000
2003	229,800	700,000
2004	287,300	850,000
2005	326,300	950,000
2006	345,800	1,000,000

The estate tax is then computed according to the federal estate tax rate table with the beginning bracket being 37 percent of the value in excess of the Applicable Exclusion amount, less debts and the expenses of your estate (the "taxable estate"). The brackets graduate upward depending on the amount of your estate to a maximum of 55 percent at a taxable estate of $3 million.

It may be seen from the above discussion that transition planning arrangements should not be entered into without a careful computation of the income tax and estate tax consequences of the various methods of property transmission to the next generation that you are considering.

III. The Marital Deduction

The key to federal estate tax planning for married couples is the proper use of the federal marital deduction. The marital deduction is a feature of the federal estate tax law that allows a deduction from the value of your estate for everything that passes from you to your spouse. The deduction is limited to the type of property holding that is taxable in your spouse's estate. On the other hand, property left in a trust that pays the income to your spouse for life and then distributes the trust property to your children is not deductible because it is not taxable to your spouse's estate. Such a trust (typically referred to as a Family Trust or Credit Trust) may even grant your spouse the ability to withdraw property for his or her support, maintenance, medical expense, or educational expense and a power to appoint the trust property to members of your family at your spouse's death without being taxable in your spouse's estate.

The important thing is to take advantage of your Applicable Exclusion amounts for both spouses. This can be done while still having a zero tax in the first estate by leaving property equal to the Applicable Exclusion amount to the children outright, or to a Credit Trust, with the balance to the surviving spouse. The property left to the surviving spouse may also be in the form of a trust called a Qualified Terminable Interest in Property Trust (QTIP). In a QTIP the surviving spouse receives all the income, but the principal goes at his or her death to persons so directed in the trust, with the first spouse's estate making an election on its estate tax return for the trust to be taxable in the surviving spouse's estate. This procedure generally looks like Figure 39.1 (using the husband's estate first as an example).

IV. The Effect of Gifts on the Federal Estate Tax

It is possible to begin the transfer of property during your life through a gifting program. An individual may address specific family needs in this manner or may simply be re-ducing estate values through such gifts. Each individual may give tax free up to $10,000 (or the amount adjusted for inflation in years after 1997) to as many other individuals as they desire. This amount is called the "annual exclusion." Thus, couples can give each child up to $20,000 per year gift tax free. The annual exclusion will be adjusted for the cost of living beginning in 1998.

If the parents' estates are likely to generate substantial estate tax, a consistent program of annual gifting to their children may be needed for estate tax control. Such gifting may be efficiently done with shares in family business organizations, as discussed below. Giving by assignment or cancellation of installment contract amounts receivable is no longer feasible, since such gifts now are considered to be a payment of the gift amount for purposes of taxing sale gain.

V. Federal Estate Tax Valuation and Payment Elections

You should be aware of the following federal estate tax elections that, if available to you, will affect the impact of federal taxation on your heirs:

1. If your actively operated farm real estate exceeds 25 percent of your estate and your total actively operated farm and business property exceeds 50 percent of your estate, your qualified heirs (children or grandchildren) may elect to have your real estate valued by dividing its fair rental

Figure 39.1

Marital Deduction Estate Plan
Example of Husband's Estate First

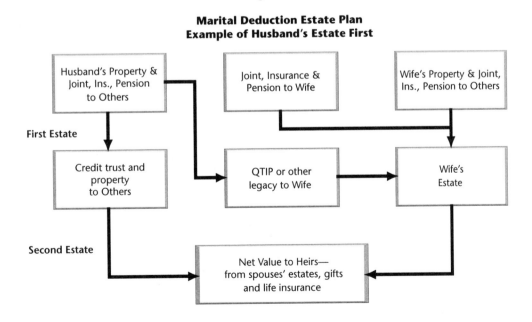

value (as established by comparison with cash leases in your vicinity) by the average Federal Land Bank interest rate. Typically, this will reduce the value of your real estate from 40 to 60 percent. The price for this reduction is: (1) Your heirs must hold the land for a period of ten years following the date of your death, and (2) they must apply it to active business operation managed by at least one of their number. This value is generally referred to as "farm special use value."

2. If land elected for the farm special use value is sold within the ten-year period, the tax saving must be repaid (without interest). This repayment amount is secured by a lien filed against the land that is elected for farm income value. Not all of the land need be elected, however. The filing of the federal lien does not occur until your estate tax has been agreed upon with the Internal Revenue Service following audit.

3. The Taxpayer Relief Act of 1997, P.L. 105-34, added a new provision (§2057) that will allow an additional value reduction to estates of which 50 percent consists of active farm or business property. The value reduction is $1.3 million less the Applicable Exclusion amount. This provision has a ten-year recapture period similar to that of farm special use value.

4. If 35 percent or more of your estate consists of actively operated farm or business property, your estate tax may have the payment deferred on the basis of interest only being paid for the first four years following the date of your death, with principal repayment thereafter, together with interest, at the rate of 10 percent of the tax principal amount per year.

5. For deaths in years after 1997 the law provides for a rate of 2 percent on the "2 percent portion." This portion of the estate is defined to be the tentative tax computed on the amount of $1 million, plus the Applicable Exclusion amount in effect for the year of death less the applicable credit amount in effect. The result is that the 2 percent portion is approximately the first $400,000 of federal estate tax. This portion of the allowable estate tax deferral is adjusted for inflation. The balance of the estate tax deferred bears interest at a current rate, presently 9 percent.

VI. Alternate Methods of Intergenerational Transition

Production Assets

The successor may be worked into the ownership of production assets over time through the purchase of machinery and vehicles and the retention of raised livestock.

The successor may acquire a separate operation over time involving land leased from the parents or purchased land. Often the successor will negotiate a profit-sharing arrangement or partnership to compensate for owned production assets. Usually the goal of the successor is to obtain security for the future by acquiring at least ownership or control of a core amount of production property.

An arrangement may be developed whereby the successor may gradually, or by a single purchase, acquire the minimum machinery and livestock to operate in the future and may run these assets on land leased or purchased from the parents.

Contract Sales

In some instances the tax consequences may not be severe enough to inhibit simple and direct sale arrangements. If a price can be agreed on that can be handled from the cash flow of the operation, the parents could sell the production assets and the land to the successor through appropriate time payments. The proceeds of the sale and the right to unpaid installments could then be left to the off-farm siblings as their inheritance. The successor receives a break on the sale constituting the successor's inheritance, and the successor owns any increase in value from the date of sale to the date of the parents' deaths.

If the parents accept the need for retirement but are unwilling to part with ownership, or if the tax cost of time sale to the successor is prohibitive, the lease alternative could be used.

Lease Arrangements

In some instances the cash flow of the operation, whether from problems of debt service or otherwise, will not fund a purchase of the parents' land. In other instances, tax problems or parental reluctance may inhibit lifetime sale arrangements.

Lease arrangements from the parents to the successor, which fund the parents' retirement while giving the successor a commitment, may be an alternative. Although a lease alone is not a permanent solution, a lease may be a long-term one binding on the off-farm heirs, or may be so directed in the parents' wills. Such a lease could, additionally, contain purchase options protecting the right of the successor to purchase the land if the economics of the situation improve in the future.

In another configuration, the lease could extend for the lifetime of the parents and be coupled with an option in the parents' wills for the successor to buy the land from the estate or the heirs on time payments. The price and interest rate in all such options should be carefully considered, as they affect the ability of the successor to fund the payments. What might otherwise be a lifetime contract sale arrangement may be easily converted into a lease with a contract or option to buy and achieve the same result, while saving taxes. The tax saving will enhance the amount that the successor can afford to pay and may make the difference in the feasibility of the arrangement.

If the estate is large enough to be taxable and the making of the farm special use value election is likely, the option should always provide for purchase from the estate, not from the heirs, to avoid taxable gain to the selling heirs.

Business Organizations

Business organizations that may be useful in agriculture include corporations, partnerships, and limited-liability companies. These organizations may serve as practical tools when needed to accomplish specific objectives. Business organizations help people operate together in structured and defined economic and working relationships as well as facilitating the transmission of ownership in the property held by the organization. They also help in estate tax control through facilitating gifting and assisting in reducing the value of interests in the organizations retained by the parents.

For example, a partnership between the parents and the successor operator may facilitate movement of production asset values to the successor through gifts or serve as a vehicle for the successor to buy such assets.

A partnership or corporation may enable routine annual gifts to be made more easily. If a partnership or corporation is used to make annual exclusion gifts to non-operating children or grandchildren, it should be accompanied by agreements that allow the successor to buy the gifted stock. Such purchase options could be triggered by the death of the parents along with provisions in the parents' wills giving the successor the right to buy the parents' stock.

Generally, interests in partnerships or corporations are subject to value adjustment for lack of marketability and lack of control of the underlying operation. Such an adjustment may assist in the reduction of estate taxes and provide value leverage in the making of gifts. For example, adjustment of the value of a gift of a partnership ownership interest by 35 percent for lack of marketability and control would enable the donor to take a significant amount out of the donor's estate.

Locking successors and off-farm heirs together in a business organization, as is often done, may be no better than any other form of common inheritance. Sooner or later the tensions that may develop between each heir's disparate goals will jeopardize the operation. Any placement of agricultural assets in partnership or corporate form should be accompanied with the same provisions for ultimate consolidation of the ownership interests by the successor as would be the case in the absence of an organizational form.

VII. Funding the Buy-Out Among Heirs

Installment Sales

In one way or another the funds for the retirement of the parents and the inheritance for the off-farm heirs comes from the cash flow of the operation, after debt service. The initially apparent method to divert the necessary portion of the business cash flow to the parents and subsequently to the heirs is the installment sale to the successors. Whether the sale is entered into during the lifetimes of the parents or after their deaths is only related to the timing of payments. The same quantity of cash outlay will be necessary in either event, unless adjusted for the retirement needs of the parents. The capital gain problems, discussed above, inhibit lifetime intergenerational sales.

Life Insurance

An alternative method of diverting cash from the operation to the off-farm heirs is through the purchase of life insurance for the parents. Life insurance premiums may involve a smaller actual outlay of dollars than installment payments starting at the same time. An appropriate life insurance product to consider is joint life coverage on both parents. Normally the funds to pass to the off-farm heirs will not be needed until the death of the last surviving parent. The premiums may be substantially less than insurance on one or the other of the parents.

Life insurance proceeds may be payable to the estate of the surviving parent and dealt with in the will or may be made payable directly to the off-farm heirs. In either event the amount of the coverage should be related to the amount of inheritance desired to be passed to nonoperating heirs.

If the choice is made to allow the farm assets to pass through the estates of the parents and commence funding for the off-farm heirs only after their deaths, insurance may be the best option. The premium payments must be made during the lifetimes of the parents, however, which may inhibit retirement funding. The timing of death may, however, be hedged, and the desired amount of cash will be immediately available at the death of the insured. If desired, some diversion of cash to the successor may be built into the life insurance contract. The successor is thus left with a reduced debt burden, which will help to assure the viability of the ongoing operation.

The insurance approach may be further helpful if substantial estate taxes are anticipated, which would enhance the debt-service burdens on the successor, or if there is substantial long-term debt. Life insurance may be made nontaxable in the estates of the parents if it is owned by the children or by an irrevocable trust for their benefit. Insurance trusts have complex rules regarding the gift tax annual exclusion for premiums paid through trusts, however, that you should thoroughly understood before entering into such a trust.

VIII. Summary

There is no one universal or simple solution to the problems of assuring operating continuity of a farm or ranch on the part of the successor. An approach that may be the best thing for one family may be disaster for another. The same degree of thoughtful consideration and effort that goes into the day-to-day operation of the farm or ranch should go into planning for its passage to members of the next generation.

For Additional Information

For an in-depth treatment of estate planning and business organization matters of concern to farmers and ranchers, see Neal E. Harl, *Farm Estate and Business Planning*, Century Communications Corp., 6201 Howard Streed, Niles, IL 60714-3435.

As a guide for general tax matters, see Internal Revenue Service, *Tax Guide for Farmers.*

Your Land Is Your Legacy, an estate-planning guide for farm and ranch families, is available from American Farmland Trust, P.O. Box 96982, Washington, DC 20077-7048.

Descriptions of various estate-planning techniques by American Farmland Trust and an order form for its estate planning guide are available at its website: http://www.farmland.org/Farmland/files/protect/estatecov.html.

The Mississippi State University Extension Service furnishes an excellent guide to estate planning for farm and ranch families at its website: http://ext.msstate.edu:80/pubs/pub1742.htm and http://ext.msstate.edu/pubs/pub1373.htm

For a listing of a number of websites with estate-planning information for the layperson, see http://www.findlaw.com/01topics/31probate/index.html.

The Province of Alberta, Estate Planning, maintains a very useful study website that, although the tax information is not relevant to U.S. citizens, contains a good overview of economic and family matters involved in farm and ranch estate planning at http://www.agric.gov.ab.ca/ruraldev/homestdy/farmesta.html.

40

Understanding Neighbors from Different Cultures

William Clark Harrell, *Attorney at Law*

Radar: Welcome to this evening's program, *Community Talk/Charla Comunitaria*, brought to you each week here on Radio KMTY, Radio Community. I'm your host, "Radar" Goodman. Tonight's guests are workers from the Bright Sun Carrot Company. Bright Sun has been operating here in the valley for two decades. It employs over two hundred members of this beautifully diverse community. We have had a number of unfortunate occasions to report on the strife and discontent at Bright Sun. But tonight the program will take a different flavor. As our guests will tell us tonight, there was a breakthrough at the plant this week in terms of the working conditions there. We will also hear from the plant's general manager, Phil Farmer, and the workers' legal counsel, Justina Chavez. They will be joining us by phone later in the program. First let's hear from our guests here in the studio. We have with us here Pedro Martinez, Ramiro Choc, and Chafa Gaspar. Present here at the studio is also José Carretera, who is not a regular worker at Bright Sun. José is a migrant worker passing through the valley. He has worked a couple of short stints at the plant and brings a slightly different perspective to tonight's *charla*. Pedro, tell us what came about this week at Bright Sun.

Pedro: First, let me thank you for having us on your program tonight. Our success as workers at Bright Sun is a success for the whole community. It is important we have a chance to explain it to the whole valley, *a todo el pueblo. Muchas gracias.* I have worked at Bright Sun pulling carrots for almost twenty years, almost since the day it opened. I have seen a lot of things and I have witnessed a lot of struggle, *o sea mucha lucha.* This week ends many

years of anger and conflict at the plant. We have come together, all the workers, Guatemalans working with Mexicans, and we have reached an agreement with management that will make all of our lives better. All of our families will live healthier and happier.

Radar: Please tell us exactly what was achieved.

Pedro: For one, we will get paid more for every crate of carrots we fill. Also, we will not be told we have to work on our day of rest. We will now have a meeting every month with management to discuss problems we have. I have worked there for a long time, and I was making the same amount of money last week as I was the day I started, *ni centavito más.* I have more children now, and everything is more expensive. We needed more money. My children are getting older, and so am I, and I want to spend more time with them while I still can. Now I am guaranteed a day off from work to spend with them. We are also really optimistic about the future because management has agreed to meet with us each month to discuss problems. We have opened the door to meaningful dialogue. That was missing all along—*desde siempre.*

Radar: Why did it take so long to accomplish this?

Pedro: We were never able to agree between ourselves, the workers. We never got along. We had our groups, and our groups stuck together and didn't get along with other groups. We never tried to trust each other. *Una falta de confianza total!* So we defeated ourselves.

Radar: José, I understand that as a migrant worker you've seen workers divided and workers united all over the country. Could you compare what happened at Bright Sun to some of your other experiences?

José: *Con mucho gusto!* I have been in the migrant stream for about five years and have migrated up through Colorado most of those years on the way northwest for the apple harvests in Washington. I worked a couple of times at Bright Sun—I have family there. But usually I do melon and onion work here. This is great news what happened at Bright Sun, and that sort of thing is happening all over the country. Down in Texas, where most of us migrant workers return after the harvests, I have heard all kinds of stories. But these *compas* in the valley got it easy. They have a stable community. Its harder for us migrants to organize ourselves because we work different farms with different crews all the time. But on the other hand, rolling stones gather no moss. In a place like the valley where people live for generations, old feuds and personal stuff can get in the way of collective progress. Every year we migrants start anew. We start with a clean slate and an understanding that the next *compa* is in the same *rollo* with you. You gotta get along to go along in the migrant stream. But the *onda* at Bright Sun is really different now. When I was here last year—*Dios mio que frio!* People didn't even talk to you on the streets if you were from another group. Now things are more open, more friendly.

Radar: Ramiro Choc, thank you for coming in tonight. Ramiro, why do you think you Bright Sun workers were not able to work together before? Is that why the workers were not able to solve the problems at the plant long before now?

Ramiro: *Si pues, cabalisimo mano!* That's exactly why we were not able to better our situation at the plant. I haven't been here as long as Pedro. My family came here only in 1983—we had to flee the war in Guatemala. The Guatemalan army burned our whole village to the ground and killed many of us. José is Mexican; he has been here a long time. Some of the Mexicans have ancestors who were here a long time before Colorado was a state. Colorado means colored red in Spanish. Where do you think the U.S. got that name? Anyway, that was our biggest problem. You see, they didn't like that we were coming here and taking jobs. But they don't like us anyway even back in our home countries. Our cultures are very different; we have different words and food. Even our tortillas are different. They make 'em with flour. We make 'em with corn. *Somos hombres de maís.*

Radar: So how did that change in a week? How did you come together and work together despite those differences?

Ramiro: It did not change in a week. It's just that it took us a long time to realize that we are not so different after all. At least not anymore. You see, the Mexicans and the Guatemalans here are all refugees in a way. We all had to flee what we call home because we could not stay there,

even though we wanted to. For us it was war that forced us to leave. For the Mexicans who came here, especially since the 1950s, it was poverty. War and poverty both kill the innocent. We are here to live and so that our children can live. The Mexicans just want to survive, just like us.

Chafa: May I speak?

Radar: Please, tell us what you think, Chafa Gaspar. How did the workers unite finally?

Chafa: Well, there was not only division between the Mexicans and the Guatemalans, there were divisions between the Guatemalans too. Those divisions started at home, and we brought them here. Some of us supported the military and others supported the guerrillas in the Guatemalan civil war. In Guatemala you had to choose sides. The other side was your mortal enemy. Many people in their family might have killed people in my family. Ramiro could have killed me, or I could have killed him. So we never talked; we never trusted each other; we never were friends.

Radar: So how did you overcome that and work together?

Chafa: Things got really bad at the plant. We had to do something. The only way to succeed was to work together. José Carretera told us stories of things he has seen all over the country, and we were convinced that we had no choice but to unite. It was hard at first, but we had to do it. For us that was harder than joining with the Mexicans. But once we started, we realized that we are not enemies. We realized that the war was far away and we both had to leave our homes—for the same reason—the war. We realized that here we are together in a strange land and we both suffer in the same ways. We are the same here. *Todos somos iguales aca!*

Radar: We have on the line Phil Farmer, general manager of Bright Sun Carrot Company. Phil, would you like to comment on the week's development at your plant?

Farmer: Certainly, Radar. I too want to thank you for airing this program tonight because as Pedro said, this is a community matter, not just a Bright Sun matter. Bright Sun is based here as it has been for two decades and as it will be for many decades to come. It is from this very community that Bright Sun draws its workers. Bright Sun is this community, and this community is Bright Sun. I want to emphasize that this is not just a victory for the workers but a victory for the community. And it is a victory for us, the management at Bright Sun.

It is a victory for us in two ways. First, an unhappy work force is an unproductive work force. But really, Radar, I want to say this. I live in this community too. My parents and their parents lived here. This is where my children have grown up, and I hope they will stay here. I do not want to be hated and shunned by my neighbors. I see my workers on the street, in the store, at church. I know what they think when they see me in public. It's the same thing they think when we are in the plant. I always thought that it was possible to be two people: Phil Farmer the general manager and Phil Farmer the neighbor. But I can't. I can't be a businessman in a vacuum. Rather, I am also a person who lives in a community full of his workers. I decided that I cannot just treat these people as chattel at my disposal but as human beings living in my community, my neighbors. I had to think not only of the profit margin I hoped to reach by the quarter's end but also of the livelihood of my neighbors.

Radar: But Phil, you will be paying more in wages, and you will not be able to call your workers to work on their day of rest when you have a last-minute order to fill. Won't you lose money?

Farmer: Perhaps. Perhaps not. There are many market studies out there that demonstrate that underpaid, overworked workers lose their efficiency, become ill, or simply leave the job. An inefficient, unhealthy work force means profit loss too. Many of my workers have been here long enough to become really good at the job, really skilled. If they leave we have to train new ones. But again, I am prepared to take a decrease in profit if it means I will not be shunned by my own community. I am not just talking about my employees. I am talking about community leaders who care about everyone who lives here. I am talking about health services workers, religious figures, social workers, and even students who come from outside the valley to help people and who are now themselves part of the community too.

Radar: Thank you for calling in, Phil. We appreciate your comments, and congratulations on, as you call it, the victory for the community and the workers and management of Bright Sun Carrot Company. Now we have on the line Justina Chavez, legal counsel for the workers. Justina, thanks for joining us all the way from Denver, and congratulations on the victory this week at Bright Sun.

Justina: Thank you very much, Radar, but honestly the congratulations go the valley community, to the united workers of Bright Sun, and also to the Bright Sun management. I'm merely a lawyer, and the law had nothing to do with the agreement reached between Bright Sun workers and management. *Nada que ver!* Everyone needs to understand that we never had to go to court. Victory was achieved through the willingness of both sides of this dispute to negotiate a settlement suitable to both parties. I simply facilitated that dialogue. Also, you see, all I have to

work with is federal law drafted and promulgated far away from the valley. Those laws do not necessarily reflect the reality of life in the valley. These laws reflect much more accurately the brute political strength of the big-money agro-industry's effective lobby efforts on Capitol Hill. Federal laws offer only *de minimis* protection for workers against exploitation, which, in my opinion, is not enough. This agreement goes beyond the minimal protections offered by the law. It is important to recognize that workers can only advance their collective interest if they are united and prepared to stand up for their rights and assert their needs. The workers of Bright Sun are to be commended for overcoming their differences and working together. Mr. Farmer too is to be commended for recognizing that his business interests are inextricably intertwined with the level of content of his workers. But more than anything, I am moved by the power of community reflected by this whole scenario. People from different cultures and different political and economic backgrounds have come together to make life better for each other so as to make their own better. That is the power of community, and that is how our society will survive.

Radar: Thank you for calling in and sharing your reflections on this positive development. Now for a last word from our guests here in our studio. What is the future of interworker relations at Bright Sun?

Pedro: It's not just Bright Sun we are talking about. It's about the whole communal lifestyle. This is one victory that has been a long time waiting to happen. But the future was being told before we workers even began to unite. The story of our future was being told by our children. Like Ramiro and Chafa said, we all come from different cultures and experiences, and that made it hard to come together. But our children were born here and are United States citizens. They are growing up together, Guatemalans, Mexicans, and Anglos all together. They share the same experiences and will make their own traditions. They are the future, and they are united. *El futuro es brillante, porque un pueblo unido jamás sera vencido!*

Radar: Well, I want to thank you all for coming. This has been a lesson to us all. When we drop our prejudices and overcome the barriers of distrust, we can begin to work together. If we work together, we can help to better the lives of our neighbors. In the process, we better our own lives. Please join us here next week at the same time for *Community Talk/Charla Comunitaria.* This is your host, Radar Goodman, signing off.

41

Agricultural Use Valuations and Property Taxes

Craig Larson, *Assessor, La Plata County*

Many people fall in love with Colorado because of the seemingly untouched mountain beauty that is either just out their window or over the fence. The initial reaction to all this open space is awe, but the realities of maintaining open space are serious and economic. Most of the mountains themselves are federal or state lands and as such pay very little directly to local taxing entities, such as counties, school districts, water districts, and towns, for the impacts caused by the attraction of visitors and newcomers. This simple fact means that local governments must provide service amenities from the local private property tax base, with little help from the larger state and federal governments.

Some of the property tax–exempt state and federal lands do provide direct economic impact through their use by farmers and ranchers as leased summer pastures and hay fields and as a watershed storage for summer irrigation. The local food providers are able to supplement their private farm and ranch holdings with leased lands, which aid grazing rotations while allowing for the harvesting of irrigated crops from their lower elevation holdings. This cycle of "lease and farm" once made all the economic sense in the world for large pieces of land that had little use other than as a farm or ranch.

Even with rapid residential growth and changing local economies in all areas of Colorado, agriculture remains a key factor in the state's economy. Agriculture is the third largest industry in the state; it provides an estimated 86,000 jobs. Farms and ranches generate about $10 billion annually in gross income. Colorado is the leading sheep- and lamb-feeding state in the nation and ranks fifth in cattle feeding.

However, times have changed, and as urban and sub-urban growth cycles have made rural land more valuable as residential or commercial property, the farmers and ranchers have asked for tax assessment protection. During the 1970s, a number of laws were passed to protect agricultural interests from the booming values of their lands, which local entities perceived as tax base. The laws that were then formulated are more or less still in place and provide for the valuation of land based on its use.

I. The Use Valuation Method

Property taxes throughout Colorado are based on the "use valuation" method. This means that how a property is used determines how it will be valued for tax-base calculations. Agricultural lands qualify for that use if the primary purpose of the land is to make a profit from the agricultural productive capacity of the land. The law used by county assessors to classify properties is specific about a two-year prior and current agricultural use requirement but is somewhat general in the interpretation applied to a viable agricultural operation. The law directly addresses the fact that the land must be used for food production or animal grazing and that the use of animals must be for food, draft, or profit.

All improvements to a farm or ranch are appraised as part of the valuation process. Improvements include buildings, other structures, fixtures, fences, and water rights associated with the land. Water rights, fences, windmills, and sprinkler systems are all improvements that are appraised and valued as a unit with the land. Some agricultural property that does not meet the definitions of farm, ranch, or forest land, such as dairies, feedlots, or greenhouses, is valued according to its use on the assessment date, and the assessment is generally based on a market-value appraisal method. Agricultural equipment is exempt from property taxation if it is used on the farm or ranch for planting, growing, and harvesting agricultural products or for raising or breeding livestock. Other personal property, such as livestock, livestock products, agricultural products, and supplies are exempt from property taxation.

Residences on farm, ranch, or forest lands are valued using only the market approach to value. The market approach compares sales of similar properties and adjusts for the differences from the property being assessed to arrive at the market estimate of value. Other assessable agricultural buildings and improvements are valued using the appropriate consideration of the three methods of establishing value: the market approach, the cost approach, and the income approach. The cost approach estimates the replacement cost of the buildings and deducts the accrued depreciation to arrive at the cost estimate of the actual value. The income approach capitalizes the income stream produced by the improvements into a value estimate.

In general, the assessment offices will require physical agricultural use of the land for an agricultural use classification. In marginal cases, the county appraisers may request proof in the form of sales and expense receipts for the crops raised or the animals sold. If the land is leased to an agricultural operator, proof of a monetary relationship between the landowner and the operator, in any form of active lease, is usually requested for verification.

The land valuation method itself is strictly an economic calculation. The process is as follows:

1. The land type and crop capacity is determined using U.S. Soil Conservation maps and description books that detail the amount of tons, bushels, or, in the case of grazing lands, animal-carrying capacity typical for the soil and water combination.
2. The assessor then applies a ten-year commodity average price to the crop raised, based on the production amounts and prices reported to the Colorado Department of Agriculture by county farmers and ranchers.
3. Typical acceptable agricultural expenses are then gathered from the local agricultural community, and a net income per acre per soil type is determined.
4. This is then capitalized just like any other investment to determine the agricultural value of the land for the assessment period based on the production capacity. The capitalization rate is established by law and is currently 13 percent.

5. The assessed value is then calculated by multiplying the actual value established by the assessor by the statutory assessment rate for agricultural uses of 29 percent. The assessor revalues agricultural property types every two years, thereby accounting for changes in commodity prices and farming and ranching practices.

II. Special Concerns

A recently added provision in the law addresses forestry lands as agricultural lands if the land is being managed under an approved forest management plan. Forest land that has been designated as agricultural land is classified and valued in the same way as comparable surrounding agricultural land. If there is no agricultural land surrounding a forest land parcel, the land is valued according to similar soil types.

In mountain counties experiencing recreational or resort development, the agricultural valuation of land is usually far less than the market value of the land for other purposes. This is the main reason that yesterday's hay field becomes not only a housing development but in very real terms the farm family's retirement plan. You can't blame anyone for these economic realities, but you may be able to work with your neighbors to preserve the best agricultural lands while protecting for the owner the right to make his or her own choices of passing down an economically viable farm or ranch or selling the property for other uses.

There is currently one legal mechanism that mandates agricultural use valuation on conserved lands of 80 acres or more where there is a residence, or on less land if the land is vacant. This agricultural classification applies to lands that had been in agricultural production but now have transferred certain development rights to a nonprofit trust for perpetual preservation. Contact a local land trust representative for more information.

Open space is one of the most impressive amenities of Colorado. To truly be an asset it must be maintained as either an economic agricultural unit or as a managed natural setting. Both configurations take time and effort by the individuals in a community to ensure long-term success and vitality for both the economic and the natural uses.

For more information, contact your local county assessor's office, where you can obtain brochures on several different topics regarding property taxation, or contact the Division of Property Taxation in Denver at (303) 866-2371.

Avoiding and Resolving Problems

Tools for Avoiding Lawsuits, Shootouts, and Financial Ruin

The general theme of this book is to provide in-depth information for longtime residents and newcomers alike that will allow everyone to live and have fun in Colorado without doing things that upset each other. As we have seen in the chapters in this book, "neighbors" exist in many forms, shapes, and sizes. Good neighbors try to respect each other and try not to do things that lead to bad feelings. Practical advice suggests that if your neighbor is upset about something you did or didn't do, you should listen to them and hear them out. Don't get defensive. Try to find a solution that works for you and for your neighbor.

Sometimes, however, neighborliness is a fragile flower that needs careful handling and care to survive, blossom, and grow. There is bound to come a time, no matter how hard you and your neighbor try, when you grit your teeth and start thinking downright hostile thoughts. Instead of calling your lawyer at one of those moments, we suggest that you read this section, take a deep breath, and call your neighbor.

In the first chapter in this section, **Nancy Greif** provides a "how-to" guide for resolving neighbor problems without lawsuits. Sometimes just doing nothing is better than litigation—it is certainly less expensive, and if you give yourself time to cool off, you may realize that the problem may not be as important as it once seemed to be. Sometimes you and your neighbor can sit down one on one and negotiate a solution. Sometimes you might need a neutral third party to help you mediate the conflict. If the case has already gone to court and you want to find out your chances if you do take the case to trial, you might consider early neutral case evaluation. Finally, if you have an arbitration clause in a contract that you're upset about or if you want your case decided by a real expert in a particular field rather than a generalist judge, you may choose arbitration. All of these

methods are considered alternative dispute resolution (ADR) because they are "alternatives" to litigation. However, a better way to think of ADR is "appropriate" dispute resolution because each method has its advantages and disadvantages with respect to particular kinds of disputes.

Some serious problems experienced by rural residents in Colorado, especially regarding financial situations, may really be more a matter of avoidance than a matter of resolution. Although the Western lifestyle may seem pretty attractive, it is sometimes not as easy as it appears. For example, many newcomers can't wait to get that "hobby farm" started, but many of the folks who have been here a while operate a farm or ranch because it takes three or four jobs and businesses just to make ends meet. Careful accounting of agricultural operations is necessary not only to keep people like bankers happy but for your own assessment of the viability of the operation. With more and more people trying to use farm and ranch operations as a tax shelter, IRS employees have sharpened their pencils; if you get audited they will look into your financial management with a fine-toothed comb. **Patricia Murray** provides information about what IRS auditors are looking for with regard to agricultural accounting. Her chapter can help you avoid tax problems so you can continue to contribute to agricultural viability in Colorado.

Some problems are unavoidable and cannot be resolved through knowledge or neighborliness. A jar of home-canned pickles or chokecherry jelly won't send the tax man away, and knowing about the laws of nuisance will not prevent nuisances from occurring. If you have a problem that can't be resolved by your own efforts, you need professional advice about what your next steps should be. Keep in mind that advice is as common as bindweed and most of it is just about as desirable. Additionally, the old adage that advice is worth what you pay for it is not always true. Be sure you talk to the right expert and one with appropriate experience in your area of concern.

If all else has failed and you decide that you really need the coercive power of a lawsuit in order to resolve the conflict between you and your neighbor, **Nancy Greif**'s chapter on Colorado courts and procedures will help prepare you to understand these legal procedures. Our overburdened courts need to operate as efficiently as possible, so citizens need to understand their functions and procedures and know what to expect if they do end up in one of the various courts in the formal judiciary system.

42

Solving Problems Without Litigation: How to Avoid the Shootout at the Neighborhood Corral

Nancy S. Greif, *Mediator, Attorney at Law*

Have you ever been irritated by something your neighbor has done or maybe something not done that you think they should do? Although the title of this chapter may seem a bit humorous and extreme, the police blotters are full of real incidents in which neighbors, for a huge variety of reasons, decided to take the law into their own hands and settle a conflict with a neighbor by intimidation or violence. Conflict happens; it's a very normal part of the human experience, and conflict that isn't allowed to get out of control isn't always bad. Sometimes conflicts bring important issues to the surface that need to be addressed. Avoiding conflict isn't always desirable or possible. But when conflict does occur, neighbors need to know how to solve the problem peacefully. Obviously, violence is neither politically correct nor socially acceptable. Even worse, it could land you in jail. So if you're not going to punch your neighbor's lights out, what to do? Do you call the cops? Do you turn your neighbor in to the county? Do you get a lawyer and write a threatening letter? Do you file a complaint at the courthouse and serve your neighbor with a summons? Think about it. Do any of these ideas sound like they would lead to greater neighborhood peace, much less solve the underlying problem? Of course not. All of those actions escalate the conflict, and that's exactly what a good neighbor would not want to do. You need a method of getting the problem solved and improving neighborhood relationships.

Collectively, the methods that may be used to solve problems without resorting to the law enforcement and legal systems are referred to as "alternative dispute reso-lution," or ADR. Perhaps an even better way to think about ADR is "appropriate dispute resolution." These days there are professional "neutrals" who are trained to analyze your situation and help you decide the most appropriate way of resolving the problem. Often the most appropriate method is mediation, but it could be mediation and arbitration, arbitration, or even resorting to litigation.

This chapter discusses a number of ADR methods for resolving conflict between neighbors. Use the facts of a particular conflict to decide what the most appropriate method of resolving the conflict is likely to be. Conflict avoidance, direct negotiation, mediation, neutral case evaluation (settlement conference), and arbitration will be discussed.

A brief set of guidelines is included for resolving conflicts with your neighbors so that you'll have a clear idea of the actions to take "before the shooting starts."

I. Using Appropriate Dispute Resolution to Solve Problems

Conflict Avoidance

Often conflict avoidance is the most commonsense response to conflict between neighbors. One way to avoid conflict is to decide that the problem really isn't so bad after all. When you really try to objectively look at the problem, you may decide that you may be overreacting just a bit or you may be expecting urban or suburban behavior in a rural environment.

In addition to deciding not to pursue a perceived problem, an even better way to avoid conflict is to do what you can to anticipate things that might be expected to cause conflict and eliminate those issues as a source of conflict before they become problems; in other words, be a good neighbor. Remember that the Golden Rule of neighborhood peace is: Treat Your Neighbor as You Would Like to Be Treated.

Let's look at some examples. If you see your neighbor out spraying or pulling up weeds, why not go out and offer to help in exchange for an agreement to have your neighbor help you get rid of the weeds on your property. Talk about the different methods used to control weeds and come up with a plan for your own property.

If you want your neighbor to haul away the assorted deceased vehicles from the land adjacent to your yard, you might try getting rid of the old tractor behind your own barn. Set a good example and be sure that your property is cleaned up before you ask your neighbors to clean up their property.

The best part about being neighbors is being neighborly. Invite your neighbors for dinner. Bring them produce from your garden. Offer to help them prune their orchard, and while you're at it, prune your own trees that hang over the fence into the neighbor's yard. Think of all the things you could work on together that would benefit both of you.

However, conflict avoidance isn't always the best course of action. If keeping quiet about a perceived problem is starting to get under your skin, it would be better to discuss the problem with your neighbor. Irritation is cumulative, and you don't want anger to simmer under the surface and boil over.

Neighbor-to-Neighbor Negotiation

As soon as a disagreement arises in your neighborhood, what's the first thing you should do? Even though it seems intuitively obvious, it is surprising how many people do not simply call or invite their neighbor over to talk about the perceived conflict. It seems so obvious, and yet pride seems to be involved. It's the age-old complaint: "If they don't know what's wrong, I'm not about to tell them." People can't be expected to read your mind. Frequently something that you've noticed and don't like may not even be on the radar screen of the person you perceive to be responsible for the problem; even though the problem is obvious to you, you do need to let your neighbor know how you feel. It's also possible that you may be mistaken about the person responsible for the action that irritates you; it would be a waste of time to be mad at the wrong person.

It is important that you initiate a discussion as soon as possible after you notice that you feel angry over a particular issue. Delay and procrastination usually allow the problem to fester, and additional incidents may make a small initial problem larger.

As soon as you realize that there is an issue that you want resolved, call or go over for a visit or invite your neighbor to your home. Try to find a time that is convenient for everybody involved and tell them that you need to talk to them before a little problem becomes a bigger problem.

When you meet, it helps to do so over a meal or with refreshments of some kind. We can learn from Native American groups, who have always known that in order to settle differences it can be useful to feed your guests or "smoke a peace pipe" while you talk. That approach can work in your neighborhood too.

What do you need to know to make that face-to-face encounter a successful problem-solving session? First and foremost, be as objective as you can possibly be, and really listen to your neighbor when you discuss the problem. There may be some pretty good reasons for their action or lack of action, and if you can work on the underlying reasons, maybe you can eliminate the real source of contention.

Remember that the way to persuade someone else to do what you want them to do is to think of at least one good reason why it is to their direct and personal advantage. In recent books on negotiation, this kind of reasoning is often called "interest-based negotiation." Interests are the motivators behind people's positions. A position is what a person says they want; an interest is the reason they want it. And there's almost always more than one way to accommodate a person's underlying concerns.

Let's look at an example. One neighbor has an old refrigerator and some other "junk" piled close to the lot line and behind a lot of screening vegetation. The next-door neighbor, trying to avoid direct confrontation, calls the county and tries to get all the "junk" removed as a health hazard. This causes a lot of hassle for their neighbor, who finds out who reported them, and the war is on. None of that had to happen if the next-door neighbor had negotiated using interest-based negotiation. As it turns out, the next-door neighbor has an adventurous seven-year-old, and her mother is worried sick that, despite warnings, in her games of hide-and-seek she will climb into the old refrigerator, close the door, and suffocate. That's a motivation the first neighbor could have understood, and, at the very least, they could have agreed to get rid of the refrigerator or remove the door. The position was: Get rid of all the junk. The interest or goal or motivator was: safety.

When you negotiate, think long and hard about the reasons behind what you think you want. It may turn out that there are alternative ways of meeting your concerns that work better for the person with whom you're negotiating.

And never try to "motivate" neighbors through threats and intimidation. For example, would you rather hear your neighbor say, "I had no idea that all those junked cars are piling up behind your barn because your wife is very ill and you don't have the money to have the cars taken away" or "Those old junked cars behind your barn are a rat-infested eyesore and are ruining my property values. If you don't cart them away by the end of the month, I'm going to sue you." Which approach would make you feel more like trying to find a solution to the problem?

So, how does it work? Once you and your neighbor are face to face, try as objectively as possible to describe your underlying concern or problem. Then let your neighbor talk about that concern and how they see it. Listen carefully. Make casual eye contact; don't try to stare them down. Ask helpful questions that show you understand their point of view.

Many disputes result from simple misunderstandings. One neighbor may be upset at some perceived affront when the other neighbor didn't mean it as an affront at all. This frequently happens when two individuals are from different cultural backgrounds. Listen and learn; try not to jump to conclusions. Ask clarification questions such as, "I want to be sure that I understand what you mean; do you mean that …" Professional neutrals, such as mediators, often ask such questions and call this approach "restatement." The purpose is clarity of communication. Use this technique in direct negotiation even if you think you understand what the other person is saying.

If your neighbor says something you agree with, let them know. Say that you agree with them. Positive reinforcement makes everybody feel good about the relationship.

Once the two parties are sure that they understand the immediate problem and issues, then use your knowledge of each other's underlying concerns to develop a list of alternative ways of solving the problem. This is usually called "brainstorming." Don't try to filter the list of ideas yet; just spit out ideas to solve the problem. Then talk about the pros and cons of each idea until the two of you select an alternative that works for both of you. That is what's meant by a "win-win" solution, and that is the goal of any successful neighbor-to-neighbor negotiation.

It sounds like a lot to remember, but it's really a short list:

- As soon as you perceive a problem, try to meet with your neighbor.
- After a little small talk about families, jobs, etc., say

that you've noticed "——," and the reason you're concerned is that "——."
- Ask for your neighbor's ideas on the subject, and really listen to what they have to say.
- Work together to identify alternative ideas for solving the problem.
- Together discuss the pros and cons of each alternative and select the one that works best for both of you.

Isn't that better than legal fees and a summons?

Neutral Third-Party Mediation

Occasionally, neighbors aren't able come up with a solution that works for both of them. Don't get angry. There are lots of reasons that direct negotiation may fail. Maybe one of you wasn't able to communicate your underlying interest or concern. Maybe you mistook your position (what you say you want) for the real problem; this is easy to do. Maybe the two of you could use some outside help in coming up with alternatives that may help to resolve the problem. Maybe one neighbor still thinks that they've got a legal slam-dunk and refuses to budge from what they think they could get in court. Typically these situations are also characterized by escalated emotions, which makes it even harder to address them.

Don't give up and feel that litigation is the only answer. What you need is the assistance of a person who is absolutely neutral and unbiased, someone who has no stake in the outcome. You need a mediator.

If negotiations don't work, maybe you can agree to split up the task of finding a mediator who will work with the parties to find a solution. Phone interviews are a useful way of deciding on a mediator. Your neighbor might agree to call mediators whose last names begin with A–M, and you might call mediators from N–Z. Look in the telephone directory under mediation services; call attorneys for recommendations; ask mediators for names of other possible mediators.

Be aware that in the state of Colorado there is no such thing as a "certified mediator." Some mediators may have been to various mediation training sessions and received a "certificate" or other designation, but that's not the same thing as having a state program with uniform standards of training and conduct. There is no certification or licensing of mediators in the state of Colorado, so when you call each one, ask lots of questions. Ask about any mediation and legal training. If the mediator is an attorney, ask if they have ever represented the other party or if they have previous knowledge or opinions about the situation. Ask whether they've had experience with the kind of conflict that you'd like resolved. Ask about their fees. Then you and your neighbor can compare notes and select a person whom you both respect to work with you to resolve the problem.

The mediator's job is to facilitate effective negotiation between the parties. Good mediators are particularly skilled at understanding the motivations, sometimes unspoken, underlying a conflict. Two very practical motivators are the expense and time involved if the issues have to be resolved by a court. The mediator will assist the parties to broaden the range of alternatives considered and to understand the relationship of each alternative to the real concerns. This approach usually, but not always, results in agreement.

The mediator will write up the points of agreement in a Memorandum of Understanding (MOU) that the parties, and their attorneys, if any, will review and sign. The signed MOU is a contract that should be kept on file. Even though you should file a copy, it would be very unusual to have to get it out again unless the agreement were very complex. Because the parties have developed the solution themselves, they know what they have to do and why. It's much more agreeable to retain the power over the actions you need to take than being ordered to do something by a court. Most people would rather comply with a mediated agreement in which they participated than comply with a court order.

Neutral Case Evaluation, or "Settlement Conference"

As part of the normal litigation process, most attorneys are familiar with the process known as a moderated settlement conference. At some point during the litigation of a dispute, the trial judge may require the attorneys and possibly the parties to meet with a neutral evaluator to determine if there is a reasonable way to settle or end the case. Attorneys are most accustomed to having the neutral evaluator be another sitting judge or a retired judge, but in fact any legally trained and objective person can help the two sides to evaluate the strengths and weaknesses of a particular case (for example, an essential witness who has lousy credibility, or a legal precedent to the contrary) and give an opinion as to probable outcome should the case go to court. Settlement conferences in many areas of the state are frequently conducted by professional neutrals who are also lawyers. Typically, settlement conferences occur fairly close to the trial date, and many do find ways to end cases.

However, an ADR method that can be used earlier in a case and may save more money, anxiety, and aggravation than later-stage settlement conferences is called early neu-

tral evaluation. It is much like a settlement conference but usually occurs after partial or full discovery but before trial preparation. This method hasn't been used much in rural settings, but if you and your neighbor have a serious dispute and cannot resolve the issues using a mediator, you may want to consider using a neutral third party or parties to impartially listen to both sides of the story and to evaluate the strengths and weaknesses of your position and your neighbor's position.

The usual context for early neutral evaluation (or for moderated settlement conferences) is that either you or your neighbor has filed a lawsuit. However, that doesn't necessarily have to be the case. There is no reason why a party to a dispute can't say to their lawyer, "I have to live next to this guy for the rest of my life; I'd like to get this settled sooner rather than later. If we can reach agreement on a respected knowledgeable person or persons to listen to our essential arguments and to give us a nonbinding evaluation of the strengths and weaknesses of both sides, then it may shed light on the best way to settle this."

Both moderated settlement conferences and early neutral evaluations are confidential and nonbinding. The moderator or neutral is usually an attorney who is selected by both parties. In both techniques, one or more neutrals is selected to hear the case. Then, in a rather informal proceeding, both sides present their essential arguments and facts to the moderator or panel; this presentation is usually followed by questions to both sides and possibly by closing arguments.

Either immediately after the presentations or at some agreed-upon time, the neutral or panel summarizes their opinion of the strengths and weaknesses of each case to the parties and their attorneys and may give an opinion regarding the probable outcome of the case if it goes to court. The primary difference between the two methods is that early neutral evaluation often takes place prior to substantial discovery or fact finding backed by the power of the court. For some cases this may be appropriate and may result in significant cost savings.

This process is basically a reality check on your chances if you do wind up in court. Frequently, in the heat of the moment, parties may say, "I won't give in; it's the principle of the thing." But it may be that the legal system views the facts differently; it would be more cost effective to know that before you've spent all the money it takes to be heard in court. This is especially true if your side turns out to have serious legal flaws. So think about the idea of realistically assessing your risks in this way before you proceed very far with a serious legal dispute.

Even if you decide to proceed with litigation, time spent

on early neutral evaluation or a moderated settlement conference isn't wasted. These methods provide useful information about the parts of your case that need to be strengthened before presenting the case in court. It is a logical technique to use before your attorney files a document known as a case management order in a lawsuit.

Arbitration

Arbitration is more like litigation than the other methods of ADR. It is more formal in that attorneys are almost always used to present the case to the arbitrator, and the rules of civil procedure and evidence are usually more courtlike. However, unlike litigation, it can usually be scheduled within a few weeks of the "demand" for arbitration, and it usually costs the disputants considerably less than the preparation for a full-blown trial.

Arbitration can be binding or nonbinding. In its nonbinding form it may be used to "practice" the organization of the case and to test the credibility and admission of evidence. The nonbinding arbitration decision may be an indication of the kind of damages that a court could conceivably award in a trial.

Naturally, if both parties evaluate the award by the arbitrator and decide that the hope of a marginally more favorable result in court doesn't justify the additional expense of actually taking the case to the judge, then the parties may agree to accept the nonbinding decision of the arbitrator or panel of arbitrators.

Binding arbitration is more common and is the method chosen contractually by many parties. It begins when one of the parties informs the other party that they would like to arbitrate their dispute. If the other party agrees or has contractually consented to settle disputes using arbitration, the most common procedure is for each party to select an arbitrator and then for the two arbitrators to select a third arbitrator. If the parties are able to select a single arbitrator that they both agree is neutral with respect to the case, then they may proceed with only one arbitrator.

If the contract specifies that the arbitration be conducted by the American Arbitration Association (AAA), or if the parties agree to a AAA arbitration, the first step is for one of the parties to submit what is known as a "demand for arbitration" to the AAA in Denver. Arbitrators are then selected from the national panel of the AAA. The advantage of this process is that the AAA has been arbitrating cases since 1926; the AAA, a not-for-profit organization, has an excellent reputation for integrity and neutrality as well as a specifically defined process.

In any case, once the arbitrator or panel of arbitrators is selected, a few decisions have to be made with regard to discovery and the rules of evidence and civil procedure that will be used at the arbitration hearing. These prehearing issues are usually argued in writing to the arbitrator or panel. Once prehearing issues are settled, a hearing is scheduled.

The hearing is more like a court proceeding than the other forms of ADR. It usually is quite formal, with opening statements, presentation of evidence, and testimony by both sides as well as closing arguments. Most people choose to be represented at arbitrations by an attorney.

Despite the formality of arbitrations, the advantages to the parties are: (1) An arbitration can almost always be scheduled much sooner than a trial, and (2) preparing for an arbitration almost always costs considerably less than preparing for a trial.

The arbitration award is issued very soon after the hearing and is binding on the parties. For a limited range of reasons, the parties may appeal to the District Court to vacate the award or to temporarily reinstate the authority of the arbitrator or panel for the purpose of confirming a consent award that is a settlement agreement reached between the parties by negotiation or mediation.

II. Guidelines for Resolving Conflicts

- Be considerate and help your neighbors when you can.
- Set a good example.
- If something is bothering you, call or visit immediately to talk about possible ways of resolving your concern.
- Don't be defensive if neighbors bring up a problem. Work together to find a solution.
- If you don't find a solution directly, consider working with a mediator to solve the problem.
- If you are unable to solve the problem in mediation, consider arranging for a legal professional to listen to and evaluate the situation and recommend a settlement.
- If you want a neutral third party to listen to both sides and actually make a decision, then arbitration is the method you need. Arbitration is a private, relatively fast, and lower-cost alternative to lawsuit.
- If you become a party to a lawsuit, consider neutral case evaluation early in the litigation process or a moderated settlement conference closer to trial; it can save a lot of time, money, and anxiety if you are able to assess the realistic legal risk if you have to go to court.
- If the case is in litigation and you have not tried mediation, ask the judge to refer the case to mediation. Judges usually consider this a positive move. Cases solved without the anxiety and expense of trial tend

to facilitate better neighborhood relations than lawsuits between neighbors.

For Additional Information

Check at your local library under keywords like "mediation," "ADR," "alternative dispute resolution," "arbitration," etc.

Call the American Arbitration Association in Denver, (800) 678-0823, to request materials on mediation or arbitration.

Call the Colorado Council of Mediators and Mediation Organizations (CCMO) in Denver, (800) 864-4317, to request information about ADR.

Call the Office of Dispute Resolution (ODR), a state program in the Judicial Branch, in Denver at (800) 888-0001 to find out if there is a local ODR office near you.

Look in the yellow pages of the phone book under mediation services and call a couple of the local providers. Ask if they are giving any talks locally about ADR and if they have mediated neighborhood issues.

43

Agricultural Accounting: What IRS Auditors Look For

Patricia K. Murray, *Accountant (M.T., C.P.A.)*

Farming and ranching may be a great way of life, but most of us pay a precious price for the privilege. It seems like the horses get new shoes before the children do, and all the animals get fed before the family. Nonetheless, the Internal Revenue Service keeps a sharp eye on farm and ranch operations. It is important to keep good records, practice good accounting, and know what IRS agents look for if you get audited.

IRS agents use standardized guidelines called Market Segment Specialization Program (MSSP) guides that are published for several special areas. Prior to the MSSP guides being issued, IRS agents were not very well informed about specific industries. Unless an agent had a prior background in agriculture, they had no idea how to audit a farm tax return. Now IRS agents study these guides prior to an audit so that they are very familiar with the segment they are auditing. This chapter is based on the grain farming MSSP, but much of the information generally applies to most farm and ranch operations.

I. First Things First

There are several reasons why farm and ranch operations might result in underreported income:

Most income is received from non–information return sources; that is, no 1099s ("Miscellaneous Income" reports) are issued. Crops can be sold at harvest or held into another year.

Income is received in an irregular manner.

The books maintained may be elementary, a basic check system or a spreadsheet.

There is no internal control; the farmer sells, receives, records, and deposits checks, sometimes with no supple-

mental or confirmatory documentation or any other documentation.

The MSSP guide explains the risks, both on the income side and the inability of the farmer to control costs of inputs, to the IRS auditors. They are informed that agriculture is very capital intensive. The guide explains the production cycles of winter wheat, spring wheat, corn, milo, sorghum, soybeans, and alfalfa. The agents are informed about possible double-cropping, and they are given information about soil preparation and planting for wheat, corn, alfalfa, soybeans, etc. They are also given information on the fertilization, harvesting, storage, and marketing of the various crops.

II. Farm Records

The IRS agent will give you a list of all farm records that they wish to review. They will review canceled checks and deposit slips; they will ask to see receipts, weigh slips, and invoices. They will not compile the farm records for you. If the receipts or invoices are missing, they will require that you go to third parties to obtain them. The agent will do an on-site initial interview and a visual inspection.

The initial interview is one of the most important steps of an audit. The agent will try to put the farmer at ease and ask pertinent questions to lead the taxpayer to talk freely. In this way the agent will secure a lot of information through casual conversation. During the initial interview, the agent will allow the farmer time to discuss himself or herself, the family, farming operation, style of living, successes, failures, hobbies, financial history, and sources of income, including those of other family members. If casual conversation doesn't work, they will resort to a list of interview questions as an aid.

If the initial interview is with the taxpayer's representative, the agent will schedule a field inspection shortly after or possibly before the initial interview. The agents review different types of farm record books and bookkeeping systems prior to the meeting so that they are prepared to know how farmers categorize income and expenses and what they should be looking for. At the field inspection, they are instructed to observe everything, including:

- Types of buildings, machinery, and vehicles and their state of repair.
- Is there livestock; what kind and how many?
- What is the style of living, and what other people live on the farm?
- Does the income reported substantiate the standard of living?

III. Employment Taxes

Agents will check to see if all employment forms have been properly filed, including 943 (Employer's Annual Return), 940 (Employer's Annual Federal Unemployment Tax Return), 945 (Annual Return of Withheld Federal Income Tax), and 1099s.

Reportable payments for Form 1099 information returns include interest, rent, royalties, commissions, and non-employee compensation. Rent includes cash rent and the fair market value of crop rent. These forms need to be issued by the farmer to veterinarians, attorneys, accountants, mechanics, custom harvesters, and chemical applicators who provide their own equipment. If a contractor who is not a dealer in supplies performs services for which he also provides the supplies needed, the farmer must report the entire payment for supplies and services on the Form 1099 issued to the contractor.

The farmers should obtain W-9s with social security numbers prior to paying for any of the above. 1099s do not need to be issued to corporations. The agents will review expense accounts to see if 1099 requirements have been complied with, including labor, machine hire, legal fees, rent, and interest to individuals. If there are no 1099s, backup withholding of 31 percent needs to be collected and remitted with Form 945.

IV. Accounting Methods

The agent will determine whether the correct fiscal year is followed. Most individual farmers must use a calendar year. Corporations can elect a fiscal year. The agent will de-termine whether income and expenses are recorded in the proper tax year.

A farmer is the only producer/manufacturer who can adjust taxable income by accelerating or deferring expenses between years. Expenses of a cash-method farmer are generally deductible only in the tax year paid. In the case of a farming syndicate, as defined in I.R.C. Section 464(c), a deduction for prepaid supplies is deductible only in the year the supplies are actually used or consumed.

Cash-basis farmers are not required to use inventories to determine income taxes. However, a cash-method farmer cannot deduct commodities, such as livestock or grain held for resale, in the year acquired unless the purchase and sale occur in the same year.

I.R.C. Section 447 requires farm corporations, with certain exceptions, to use the accrual method of accounting. Sub S corporations and corporations with less than $1 million in gross receipts for the prior taxable year are exempted from the accrual method along with specified family corporations.

The hybrid method of accounting allows the farmer to combine cash with accrual under I.R.C. Section 446(c). Farmers can use the accrual method for purchases and sales and the cash method for all other items of income and expenses.

Grain farmers (cash or accrual), with or without livestock, are generally not required to capitalize inventory costs under I.R.C. Section 263A. All farmers must use 150 percent depreciation if not using the uniform capitalization rules.

Noncash wages are exempt from social security taxes if they qualify. The payment of compensation with commodities if structured properly can help avoid some payroll taxes. Remuneration paid in any medium other than cash for agricultural labor is generally excluded from "'wages" for FICA, FUTA, and income tax withholding under Sections 3121(a)(B)(A), 3306(b)(11), and 3401(a)(2). The services provided must be "agricultural labor" within the meaning of Section 3121(g) of the code.

V. Income

The agent is instructed to look for all the sources of possible income. Income to the farmer consists primarily of sales of grain, livestock, produce, or other products of the farm. Other sources of farm income can include miscellaneous income from farm labor or custom work, government benefit checks, rents, royalties, and other similar activities.

I.R.C. Section 1231 assets include buildings; machinery

and equipment; livestock held for draft, dairy, and breeding; etc. The sale of these assets are initially reported on Form 4797, then carried to Schedule D. Other assets that do not fit I.R.C. Section 1231 treatment (draft, breeding, dairy, or sporting animals held less than one year) are reported in Part II of Form 4797.

Capital assets (farmhouse, stocks and bonds, personal automobile, etc.) are usually reported directly on Schedule D. The gain from the disposition of farmland is regulated by I.R.C. Section 1252. The gain is reported on Form 4797.

The gross profit percentage for farming can be misleading because there is generally no income pattern among individual farmers. Due to the variation in the size of farms and marketing methods, the IRS has a difficult time applying any set of norms or standards.

The agent must determine that all products produced and sold have been included in income. The net proceeds from the sale of a crop by someone acting as the farmer's agent must be included in gross income for the year the farmer's agent receives payment. The agent is given details on when all crops are normally harvested. They will inquire of the farmer regarding whether the crop was sold at harvest or stored until a later year. Be prepared to provide contracts, weigh slips, etc. to the agent.

Potential areas of abuse that the agent will look for include:

1. Alternative minimum tax (AMT) adjustments when the installment method of reporting income is used.
2. Checks received from the sale of livestock or crops in December, held and not deposited until January.
3. Sales made on December 31 so that there is no way the check will be received until January.
4. Sales in which the agreement to defer payment occurs after the farmer obtains the right to receive payment.

Other sources of income include:

1. Income received from granting rights-of-way or easements is either income or may be used to reduce basis in the asset.
2. Fuel tax credits and refunds, machine work, and commodity future transactions (see the "Hedging Farm Commodities" section below).
3. Machine work or work performed by the farmer on someone else's farm. The farmer may be paid in cash, check, services, or merchandise. This income is taxable, but you will not always find it reported on Schedule F, where it belongs. The omission from Schedule F results in understating self-employment income.

The revenue agent is given a detailed summary of the U.S. Department of Agriculture and its agencies, how their organizations provide support to the farmers in many areas, and how this potential income should be reported. They are informed about the functions of the old Agricultural Stablization and Conservation Service (ASCS) and the Soil Conservation Service (SCS), as well as and how the Farm Service Agency (FCA) operates now. The agents are informed as to what payments are reported on the CCC-1099-G and which ones are not. They are informed as to the different methods of handling loans, etc.

In the interview, the agent will review prior returns for elections to defer crop insurance proceeds, then confirm that those amounts were reported as income in the year under examination. Form 1099-Misc is used to report the gross amount of insurance proceeds. The 1099-Misc can be reconciled to deposits.

VI. Farm Product Marketing Methods

Crop shares are rental payments made to a farmer-landlord based on a percentage of the yield of the crop, usually payable in kind. The regulations state that the crop share rents are to be treated as income by either a cash-basis or an accrual-basis farmer only when the shares are reduced to money or its equivalent.

If the landlord receives crop shares and uses them as feed in his or her farming operation, he or she must include the fair market value (FMV) of the crop shares in gross income. At the same time, under I.R.C. Section 162, the landlord will be entitled to a trade or business deduction for livestock feed if engaged in a trade or business.

If the farmer donates crops, then the farmer recognizes FMV income at the time of the donation, not when the crop shares are converted to cash or cash equivalent. He can then take a deduction on Schedule A as a contribution.

The crop share income is not subject to self-employment taxes unless the landlord materially participated in the growing of the crop. Material participation is necessary to build a social security base and may be necessary if current use valuation is to be used for federal estate tax purposes.

Material participation may cause social security payments to be decreased for a person eligible to receive such payments. If the person receives crop share, this is not earned income. Therefore, it has no effect on current social security benefits.

The agent will verify whether active income is classified as passive income and whether income earned by the farmer is reported as income by another family member. This is done so that social security payments will not be affected. The revenue agent will look at all pricing contracts to see if they are being handled properly.

If the farmer has sold grain, livestock, or other products on the installment basis, there should be a contract stating the selling price and the dates the payments are to be made.

In a "price later" contract, title to the product passes upon delivery to the buyer; however, the price is fixed on some date in the future. A farmer executing a "price later" contract cannot use the installment sale provisions of I.R.C. §453.

A cooperative is an enterprise owned by and operated for the benefit of those using it. A patronage dividend is a refund of purchase price and gets reported on Schedule F. The dividend is usually paid part in cash and part in stock; the entire dividend is subject to income inclusion.

Per-unit retain certificates evidence an obligation from the cooperative to the farmer. An important consideration is whether this scrip is qualified or nonqualified. If it is qualified, the farmer has consented to include the amount in income upon receipt of the scrip. Nonqualified scrip is included in income when redeemed.

The revenue agent will look to see if the dividends are reported on Schedule F, as they are subject to self-employment tax. They look to see if the entire dividend is reported, not just the cash portion received.

VII. Hedging Farm Commodities

Hedging is a common technique used by businesses to reduce risk resulting from certain assets, liabilities, or foreign currencies. Farmers, cattle feeders, and feedlots generally enter into hedging transactions to reduce the risk of price changes with respect to inventory and noninventory supplies.

Gain or loss from such a transaction will qualify as ordinary gain or loss only if it satisfies the definition of a hedging transaction in Treas. Reg. §1.1221–2(b). Under the Treasury Regulation, a hedging transaction is a transaction entered into in the normal course of the taxpayer's trade or business primarily to reduce risk of price or interest rate changes or currency fluctuations.

There are various marketing tools that can be used to protect the price of a commodity. The futures market is used frequently because it offers actual futures contacts and futures options. The most popular are the actual futures. The options market is gaining popularity because of the reduced risk, but, as in futures contracts, the temptation to speculate is present.

The revenue agent is given a brief overview of hedging, futures, and options trading. Hedging losses should be entered as negative amounts under "other income" on Schedule F. Some losses are erroneously deducted as separate items in other expenses and are occasionally found in either the cost of the product or in cost of goods sold. When auditing these transactions, the agent will ask for all broker statements.

VIII. Cancellation of Indebtedness

A discharge of indebtedness takes place when a creditor reduces, in whole or in part, the amount owed. As a general rule, the debtor realizes ordinary income from the discharge of indebtedness equal to the difference between the amount due on the debt and the amount paid for its discharge. Taxable income includes discharge of indebtedness income; however, there are several important exceptions in the law to this rule. These exceptions involve the cancellation of a deductible debt, the reduction of a purchase-money debt, and the cancellation of a debt intended as a gift.

A farmer does not recognize income from the discharge of indebtedness if the payment of such debt would have entitled him to a deductible expense. If interest is discharged and would have been deductible, then it is not included in income.

IX. Exclusions from Income: I.R.C. §108(a)(1)

Debtors who are in bankruptcy or insolvent and (in certain circumstances) farmers are exempted from recognizing income from discharge of indebtedness. They are required instead to reduce certain tax attributes such as net operating loss, general business credits, minimum tax credit, capital loss, basis in property, passive activity loss, credit carryover, and foreign tax credit. (I.R.C. §108(b)).

If the debt discharge occurs in a bankruptcy case under Title 11 of the U.S. Code, I.R.C. §108(a)(1)(A) provides that income from the discharge of indebtedness is excluded from gross income.

I.R.C. §108 (a)(1)(B) provides that income from the discharge of indebtedness is excluded from gross income if the discharge of debt occurs when the farmer is "insolvent" outside of bankruptcy. The insolvency exclusion under I.R.C. §108 applies only to income from the discharge of indebtedness.

Under I.R.C. §108(a)(1)(C), gross income does not include income from the discharge of indebtedness if the debt discharged is qualified farm indebtedness and the discharge is made by a qualified person. Form 1099-C, Cancellation of Debt, should be issued.

The debt of the farmer is qualified if:

1. the farmer incurred the debt directly in the business of farming, and
2. for the three taxable years preceding the taxable year in which the discharge of indebtedness occurs, 50 percent or more of the farmer's total gross receipts is attributable to the business of farming.

A qualified person discharging the debt is any federal, state, or local government, or any agency or instrumentality thereof, or a person who actively and regularly engages in the business of lending money and is *not:*

1. a person related to the farmer,
2. a person from whom the farmer acquired the property securing the debt, or
3. a person who receives a fee with respect to the farmer's investment in the property securing the debt.

If the discharged debt exceeds the sum of the adjusted tax attributes and the adjusted basis of the qualified property, the excess is included in gross income.

Unless the farmer makes an election to first reduce basis of depreciable property, the excluded debt-discharged income is applied to reduce the farmer's tax attributes, in the following order (I.R.C. §108(b)(2)):

1. net operating loss
2. general business credit
3. capital loss
4. basis of depreciable and non-depreciable property
5. foreign tax credit

The tax attributes are generally reduced dollar for dollar of excluded income realized from the discharge of indebtedness. However, credit carryovers are reduced only 33.33 cents for each dollar.

The discharge of indebtedness of a shareholder by a corporation is treated as a distribution of property. A solvent shareholder whose debt to a corporation is forgiven realizes dividend income to the extent of the corporation's earnings and profits available for distribution.

Income from the discharge of indebtedness can arise in a wide array of circumstances. Audits have produced sizable adjustments in the following areas:

1. Solvent partners incorrectly exclude debt-discharged income owing to the insolvency of the partnership.
2. When debtors perform services in payment of labor,

no income is realized from the discharge of indebtedness. The debtor is considered to have received taxable compensation equal to the amount of the debt canceled.
3. Farmers incorrectly reduce attributes by the earliest year of any attribute instead of reducing attributes in the prescribed order.
4. The election to first apply any portion of the excluded income to reduce basis of depreciable property must be made on Form 982 in the taxable year of discharge.
5. Farmers incorrectly consider land as depreciable when making the election under I.R.C. §108(b)(5).
6. Farmers excluding debt not issued by a qualified lender.
7. Disputes may arise in determining the extent of a farmer's insolvency.

X. Foreclosures, Repossessions, and Abandonments

A farmer who transfers property in satisfaction of a debt may realize a gain or loss and, in some cases, income from the discharge of indebtedness. A farmer who transfers property, voluntarily or by foreclosure, in full or partial satisfaction of a debt is treated as having sold or exchanged the property.

If the debt satisfied by the transfer of the property is recourse (personal liability), Treas. Reg. §1.1001–2(a) treats the property as if it were sold by the debtor at fair market value.

If the debt satisfied by the transfer of the property is nonrecourse (no personal liability), the full amount of the canceled debt is treated as proceeds from the sale or exchange of the property, even if the value of the property is less than the unpaid balance of the debt.

The discharge of a recourse or nonrecourse debt without a corresponding transfer of property results in income from the discharge of indebtedness whether or not the debt exceeds the value of the property (Rev. Rul. 91-31).

If the property securing payment of a debt is the sole means of paying that debt, the abandonment of that property results in the debtor realizing income from the release of debt.

How the auditor sees it:

1. A gain on a property transferred due to repossession or abandonment is sometimes incorrectly characterized as income from discharge of indebtedness.
2. The revenue agent should review information returns (Form 1099-A) issued to the farmer to ascertain that the farmer has correctly reported all transactions.

XI. Farm Business Expenses

I.R.C. §162 and Treas. Reg. §1.162-12 provide for the deduction of ordinary and necessary expenses paid or incurred in connection with the operation and maintenance of a farm.

The revenue agent will examine expenses paid at or near the end of a year to determine if they are deposits or payments. A deposit is applied against future expenses and is not currently deductible. For a disbursement to be considered a payment, the farmer must prove that:

1. The payment was not refundable.
2. The payment was made under an enforceable sales contract.

I.R.C. §464 limits the allowable deduction for prepaid farm supplies. If the cash method is used, no deduction is allowable for advance payments of supplies that will be used or consumed in a later tax year unless each of the following conditions is met:

1. The expense is a "'payment" for the purchase of supplies, not a deposit. Factors that show a expense is a deposit rather than a payment include:
   a. A specific quantity wasn't stated in the contract or in the invoice.
   b. The farmer was entitled to a refund of any unapplied payment.
   c. The seller treats the amount received from the farmer as a deposit and not a sale.
   d. The right exists to substitute other goods or products for those specified in the contract.
2. The prepayment is not merely for tax avoidance but has a specific business purpose.
3. The deduction does not result in a material distortion of income. Some factors they will use to consider if there is a material distortion of income are:
   a. the farmer's customary business practices in conducting the farming operation
   b. the amount of the expense in relation to past purchases
   c. the time of the year the purchase is made
   d. the amount of the expense in relation to income for the year

Feed expense for livestock is generally deductible when paid. The cost of seeds and plants is usually deductible as a current expense unless it has a value lasting over several years. Orchards and timber farms must capitalize seed and plant expense. The full cost of fertilizer and chemicals is deductible in the year paid. Fuel is deductible when used in the farming operation. Insurance to protect farm and ranch property is deductible. Taxes for payroll, farm real estate, and personal property used in the business are all deductible.

Rent paid in cash is deductible in the year paid. Be alert to year-end rent payments. Prepaid rent is not currently deductible, regardless of the farmer's method of accounting.

Wages paid to a farmer's children are deductible even if the children use the money to buy clothes or other necessities that the parent would otherwise be obligated to provide (Rev. Rul. 73-393).

During the initial interview the agent will establish the number of children the farmer has, their ages, whether they are at home or away, the number of vehicles, and who drives them. They will determine if the farmer has hired help other than his children and how their compensation is determined. The fuel and insurance accounts will be scrutinized for personal expenditures.

The cost of repairing and maintaining equipment is deductible. An extensive overhaul is a capital expenditure because it adds value or prolongs the life of the equipment or adapts it to a new or different use.

If the requirements under I.R.C. §119 are met, the employee may exclude meals and lodging furnished to an employee for the employer's benefit from income. The farmer may deduct the expense as a business expense. Lodging furnished to an employee for the convenience of the employer includes the value of any necessary utilities.

During the initial interview the agent will obtain a clear understanding of the farmer's lifestyle, the ages of children, and utilities used and will determine a reasonable allocation for business and personal usage.

XII. Basis and Sales of the Farm and Farm Assets

Tax management begins when a farm is purchased. Decisions made on allocation of the purchase price will affect the amount of income tax paid when the farm is sold. Amounts allocated to depreciable property will be recovered relatively soon in the form of depreciable deductions. The revenue agent will determine whether the value assigned to each asset acquired on the farm is reasonable. The basis of the property is very important in determining current depreciation and gain or loss upon disposition.

XIII. Depreciation, Cost Recovery, and Depletion

Farming is capital intensive, requiring heavy cash outlays for machinery and equipment. The farmer is allowed depreciation on purchased machinery and equipment and on purchased livestock used for dairy, breeding, draft, and sporting purposes. Depreciation on farm property placed in service after 1988 is limited to 150 percent declining balance on property used in a farming business.

The IRS agent will analyze the assets purchased, their cost, and when they were purchased. They will examine all sales to determine whether the proper basis was used and whether the item is reported properly on the return. Reporting items on the wrong forms affects self-employment taxes and can affect the capital gains rates.

44

Colorado Courts and General Procedures: If You Must Resort to the Courts, What Can You Expect?

Nancy S. Greif, *Attorney at Law*

If you and your neighbor have tried to resolve your problem and you just can't work it out, it may be necessary to go to court to get the dispute resolved by a judge or a jury. The first thing you need to decide is whether you will represent yourself or whether you will retain an attorney to represent you. The courts call representing yourself being a *pro se* (for yourself) litigant.

I. *Pro Se* or Attorney Representation

In Small Claims Court in Colorado, you must represent yourself unless the opposing party elects to hire or happens to be an attorney, in which case you may elect to be represented by counsel, and the case is then referred to County Court. In County Court and District Court you may choose either to act *pro se* or to have an attorney. In general, unless you have considerable knowledge of the legal system, it is probably wiser to hire an attorney. Particularly for District Court cases, either criminal or civil, there may be complex procedural and evidentiary issues that you might not know how to handle. In order to put your best foot forward and to be considerate of the judge, whose job is to hear the case, not to teach you the law, it may be best to get a lawyer.

What's a reasonable procedure for finding an attorney who will do a good job for you? First, ask friends and family for referrals. You might also call the local bar association and ask if they have a local legal directory or referral service. The Colorado Bar Association in Denver, (800) 332-6736, will be able to give you a number for the local organization. In the Denver area you can call the Metro Attorney Referral Service at (303) 831-8000. Public and college libraries also have reference volumes, such as Martindale-Hubble, which give information about law firms in specific geographic regions or topical areas of practice. And of course, the yellow pages of any phone book have an attorney section listed under areas of practice (as well as a mediation services section).

For complex cases you may want to interview two or three attorneys before choosing one. You may have to pay for these initial interviews, but it's worth it to find an attorney who is right for the case and whom you can trust. Prepare before the interviews. You should be able to briefly and clearly describe the facts that led up to the dispute. Write out a chronology for reference. Ask the attorney if they have experience with that kind of case in the court that will hear your case. Hire one that is within your budget. Let the lawyer describe his or her experience and general strategy in cases of this sort. Once you've chosen counsel it's a good idea to have a legal representation agreement that specifies what the attorney will be doing for you and the way you will be charged for those services. It is also a good idea to ask the attorneys that you interview whether they routinely use CD-ROM and online legal research services or whether they still use actual books. Frequently, though not always, attorneys who are skilled at computerized legal research can do the job faster and in a more thorough fashion than attorneys who are still leafing through paper copies.

II. Make an Effort to Settle the Case

These days, Rule 16 of the Colorado Rules of Civil Procedure requires that litigants make a genuine good-faith effort to settle the case. In many Colorado jurisdictions, that means that the attorneys for each side have to file a settlement plan, which, if approved by the judge, becomes part of the Case Management Order. If they don't or if the proposal is not specific enough, many jurisdictions require the case to go through a "screening judge," who has the power to mandate a settlement method such as mediation. If either side requests that the judge refer the case to mediation, judges routinely do so. The utility of this system is that even if a neighbor is not inclined to mediate or arbitrate a dispute prior to filing, the current system essentially requires them to make an effort to resolve the dispute prior to going to court.

III. Which Court Will Hear Your Case?

Once you have selected an attorney, the attorney will determine whether your case is considered civil or criminal and which court has the power (jurisdiction) to hear your case. If you are acting *pro se*, you will need to determine the appropriate court to hear your case. Not all courts can hear all cases. The kinds of courts that would probably hear a case between you and your neighbor are: Municipal Courts, Small Claims Court, County Court, District Court, and, if you live in southern Colorado, possibly Tribal Court.

Most, but not all, cases between neighbors are called "civil" cases to distinguish them from "criminal" cases. Certain laws of the state of Colorado are defined by the legislature as "criminal"; if it is alleged that you have violated a criminal statute, then it is a criminal case. Criminal cases reach the courts when a case is filed by government attorneys called district attorneys or, rarely, when an indictment is filed by a grand jury.

Civil law means all law not defined as criminal. A civil case reaches the court when a complaint is filed by a private citizen or their attorney alleging a violation of civil law. Sometimes neighborhood conflicts escalate to the level of criminal charges such as assault and battery or criminal trespass, but most neighborhood problems are heard as noncriminal, or civil, cases.

If the parties or the attorneys in a case have not indicated that they have already sought some form of alternative dispute resolution (ADR) to aid in settling the case, most of the Colorado courts routinely refer cases to mediation or to screening by a person who has the power to refer the case to the form of ADR judged to be most appropriate for that case.

The Southern Ute Indian Tribe and the Ute Mountain Ute Tribe have their own court systems that enforce the Tribal Codes of their respective tribes. Indian court jurisdiction is a specialized subject that will not be addressed in this chapter, but be aware that when you or your neighbors are tribal members, the case may or may not be heard by the Colorado courts. In general, it depends on the type of alleged offense, who committed the offense, where the offense was committed, and who the "victim" of the offense was. If the problem occurred on land under the jurisdiction of the U.S. government or a tribal government or land that belongs to a tribal member, the state courts may not take jurisdiction over a claim when a non-Indian sues a tribal member. As with other neighbors, it is much better to work out differences in person rather than through the court systems.

After you file your complaint with the court, a number of factors determine when you might actually have your day in court. The attorneys will use a process called "discovery" to try to find out the facts that relate to the case, and frequently that process is both long and expensive. The attorneys are likely to file a number of pretrial motions, and that, plus the time it takes the judge to rule on each motion, takes time as well. Then, when a case is finally ready to go to trial, the judge needs to have time on his or her docket. In any case, plan on spending at least three to four months waiting for a simple County Court civil case and possibly years before a District Court civil (not domestic relations) case is heard. Criminal cases are heard faster because of the U.S. constitutional requirement for a speedy trial in criminal matters.

Municipal Courts

Municipal Courts are created by statute to hear cases regarding the violation of city ordinances within the city limits. Many of these cases involve neighborhood civil matters such as trespass, animal control, and zoning matters. Although bringing a case before a Municipal Court is generally fairly informal, it may cost considerable anxiety and some money to bring a case before these courts. Decisions of Municipal Courts may be appealed to a state court.

County Courts and Small Claims Courts

Each county in Colorado has a County Court with one or more judges who serve four-year terms. In some jurisdictions, the County Court judge need not be a licensed lawyer. These judges hear a wide variety of cases, but the type of case involving disagreements between neighbors are usually civil suits in which the debt, damage, or value of personal property claimed does not exceed $10,000 (the maximum for County Court cases). You may be represented by an attorney in County Court, and certain kinds of cases may be heard by a jury.

Most parties choose to be represented by attorneys in County Court cases, and the expense of attorneys, expert witnesses, document preparation, etc. will increase the cost of resolving your dispute. You and your neighbor could figure out what it would cost each of you to take the matter to court and then meet or mediate to work out a settlement that avoids the anxiety, risk, and expense of court. Appeals are heard by the District Court.

Small Claims Courts are divisions of the County Courts. These courts make decisions about civil matters that involve no more than $5,000. Often these cases may be heard by a magistrate of the court. Parties may not be represented by attorneys unless the opposing party also happens to be an attorney. In that case the County Court may take jurisdiction. In most cases, parties to a dispute simply present their own cases. Jury trials are not permitted in Small Claims Court, and the judges or magistrates are not bound by formal rules of evidence and procedure other than the rules specifically adopted by the Colorado Supreme Court for Small Claims Court.

It may be helpful to get some help from an attorney in organizing your case and presenting your evidence. Decisions in County Court may be appealed to the District Court. In Denver, which is both a municipality and a county, the Denver County Court is both a Municipal and a County Court.

District Courts

The District Courts of the state of Colorado hear many kinds of civil and criminal cases. Generally disputes between neighbors are civil in nature and will be heard by a District Court if the value you are arguing over exceeds $10,000. These courts are formal, and knowledge of the rules of civil (as opposed to criminal) procedure and the rules of evidence is important. Although you may represent yourself in these courts, most parties choose to be represented by an attorney. Litigating in a District Court will cost at least $5,000 and possibly much more, and it may take four months to more than a year to be heard by the court.

Like the County and Small Claims Courts, District Courts often refer cases to some form of ADR, so why not do it yourself, voluntarily, before going to the expense of a lawsuit? Appeals are heard by the Colorado Court of Appeals or the Colorado Supreme Court.

Neighborhood disputes frequently involve rights and responsibilities involving water. These cases are heard by one of the seven Water Courts in Colorado. Water Court judges are District Court judges appointed by the chief justice of the Colorado Supreme Court. Appeals involving water appropriations are made to the Colorado Supreme Court.

IV. How Do You Get a Civil Case Started?

If you will be representing yourself, you need to go to the court clerk's office at the local courthouse and confirm which court has jurisdiction to hear your case. If it is Small Claims Court, most clerk's offices will have copies of a simple form that you need to file with the clerk in order to notify the court that you wish to sue your neighbor. And the neighbor will need to be "served" with a copy of the complaint you filed with the court so that they know they're being sued. If you have decided to use an attorney to represent you, the next thing you'll probably need to do is to pay the attorney a particular sum up front; sometimes this sum is referred to as a "retainer." The lawyer will deposit this money in a "trust account" and each month, as work is done for you, will draw the appropriate amount out of the trust account and send you a statement telling you how much work was done and how much money was drawn out of the account.

V. What Happens Between Determining That You Want to Sue and Trial?

If your dispute involves an action that is in progress, for example, building a barn over the lot line, you may seek a temporary restraining order (TRO) or a preliminary injunction that may later become a permanent injunction if granted by the court. The purpose of these actions is to stop whatever's going on and preserve the status quo until a court can hear both sides and make a decision. If none of these actions is sought, the normal procedure is that the person bringing the action to the court, the plaintiff, files a "complaint" at the court clerk's office and the defendant is served with a "summons" and the complaint. The defendant may decide not to do anything, in which case a default judgement is entered against the defendant. Or the defendant has a certain number of days (listed on the summons and complaint papers) to file an "answer." In the answer, the defendant may admit or deny the allegations in the complaint and may file a counterclaim alleging wrongdoing by the plaintiff. If the defendant files a counterclaim, the plaintiff is entitled to file a "reply" to the counterclaim. The defendant may also admit that she or he did what is claimed but that there is a "defense" that may abrogate or limit liability.

Various motions may also be filed rather than answering the complaint immediately. For example, if the complaint is vague or contradictory, a "motion for a more definite statement" may be filed asking for clarification. The defendant may also argue that the action is being brought in a court that does not have the power to hear the case, that is, that the court lacks jurisdiction over the subject matter or over the person of the plaintiff or the defendant. It is also possible to argue that the complaint fails to "state a claim" that may be brought in court or that the defendant was not appropriately notified of the court action.

The process of uncovering information relevant to the legal issues in the case is called "discovery." Unlike criminal trials, in civil trials both sides have the obligation to provide access to everything the other side knows. "Interrogatories" are written questions sent to the other side for answers; these must be answered truthfully and notarized. "Depositions" are testimony taken, under oath, outside the presence of a judge, of any person involved in the case. Both sides may question the person being deposed. There may be requests for documents or admissions and various forms of physical or mental examinations. Discovery can be a lengthy and expensive process. Either during or after discovery, either party may decide that the facts are so clear that all the court has to do to decide the case is to apply the law to the uncontested facts. If that happens, they file a motion for summary judgment, which may or may not be granted by the court. If it is not filed or is not granted, then, after a pretrial conference, the case is set for trial.

If at any time the parties can settle their differences, they simply notify the court and the proceeding is terminated.

VI. What Is a Civil Trial Like?

Unlike criminal trials, in civil trials both sides have the obligation to provide access to everything the other side knows. Many people have some familiarity with civil trials through jury service, television, or the movies.

In many civil actions, such as breach of contract or personal injury, the case may either be heard by a jury or by a judge acting as both the fact-finder and the decision-maker. In other cases, there may be no right to a jury trial. If a jury will hear the case, jury selection is usually the first step. After the jury is seated, both sides present opening statements that summarize what they plan to present. Then the plaintiff presents his or her case. At that point, the defense may file a motion to dismiss that essentially says that the plaintiff failed to prove his or her case based on the evidence presented and that the court should dismiss the case. If that motion is not presented or is denied, then the defense presents the defendant's case.

After all of the evidence has been presented, the lawyers work with the judge to draft the jury instructions (if this is not a bench trial), and the jury retires to decide the verdict. In civil cases the jury decides not only whether the parties have done something wrong but how much the damages should be. Once a jury verdict has been issued, post-trial motions to overturn that verdict may be filed, such as a motion for judgment notwithstanding the verdict or a motion for a new trial. The party may also file an appeal alleging that errors were committed in the trial and that the verdict should not be enforced.

Clearly, the whole litigation process is complex, time consuming, and expensive. It is an anxious and upsetting time for most people. The process is useful and, in fact, essential to settle a few kinds of disputes that can't be resolved any other way. However, most judges will tell you that about 95 percent of the cases filed with the court are settled before trial—and usually only a short time before trial.

From the point of view of the parties involved, a more rational option would be for the parties to stay on top of the process so that they know when they have enough information to realistically assess the legal validity of their claims. That way, at the earliest logical moment the parties can instruct their attorneys to settle the case in a particular way. Simply being able to settle after discovery, rather than after discovery *and* trial preparation, would save a good bit of money for a lot of litigants.

VII. Summary

If you've tried to resolve your dispute with your neighbor and they refuse to talk to you or will not compromise in any way, you may be forced to file a lawsuit. However, even at that late date in the process you can always ask the judge to refer the process to mediation or some other form of ADR. When the case is referred to ADR, both parties must attempt to solve their differences by working in good faith to reach a compromise. That usually resolves the dispute.

However, in the unusual case where good-faith ADR has failed, the case may go to court. Be sure you find an attorney you are comfortable with both personally and in terms of the job he or she is able to do for you. Then make sure the attorney knows that you want to be kept informed of what is going on and that if, at any point, information is produced that indicates an eventual settlement, you'd rather settle sooner rather than later. It may be difficult, but try to remember that the attorney works for you; you don't work for the attorney.

For Additional Information

Call or write the Colorado Judicial Branch, 1301 Pennsylvania, Suite 300, Denver, CO 80203, (303) 837-3658, to request a copy of the most recent edition of the booklets "A Reporter's Guide to Colorado Courts" and "Colorado Courts at a Glance."

David Akers

Water Pollution Protection Section
Colorado Department of Public Health and Environment
4300 Cherry Creek Dr. South
Denver, CO 80246-1530
Phone: (303) 692-3591
Fax: (303) 782-0390

Dave Akers is the manager of the Water Pollution Protection Section in the Water Quality Control Division (WQCD). This section, among other responsibilities, reviews the siting and design for domestic wastewater treatment facilities, including on-site wastewater disposal systems that are designed for a flow of greater than 2,000 gallons per day. The section is also responsible for: all permitting activities (industrial, domestic, and stormwater), field inspections, and engineering reviews for drinking water and wastewater treatment facilities and compliance oversight and data management. Mr. Akers has been employed by the WQCD since 1979. He has experience in wastewater facilities planning and design and spent twelve years supervising permitting and enforcement activities for dischargers of domestic wastewater.

Roger Alexander

BLM—Southwest Center
2465 South Townsend
Montrose, CO 81401
Phone: (970) 240-5335
Fax: (970) 240-5368
E-mail: roger_alexander@co.blm.gov

Roger Alexander is the Public Affairs Specialist for the Bureau of Land Management (BLM) in Montrose, Colorado. He spent his formative years in Gunnison, Colorado, and although his career has taken him all over the southwestern United States, he still considers Gunnison "home." He graduated from New Mexico State University with a B.S. degree in wildlife science in 1977. Mr. Alexander began his career with BLM in New Mexico in 1978 and worked in a variety of different BLM jobs in Colorado, California, and Nevada before returning to Colorado in 1991. He and his wife, Katy, have two grown children, Michael and Tara.

Daniel F. Balsinger

134 Oren Road
Pagosa Springs, CO 81147
Phone: (970) 731-2748
E-mail: balsinger@eudoramail.com

Daniel Balsinger received his higher education at the University of Pittsburgh, Pennsylvania, majoring in geology and law. His career began with Texaco in New Orleans in 1964. Since 1979 he has been employed by various other oil companies, large and small. Most of his career involved exploration management for new oil and natural gas fields in the Gulf of Mexico, onshore along the Gulf Coast states, and the coastal and offshore areas of the Atlantic Seaboard. His international exploration experience includes the countries of Mexico, Peru, Ghana, and Thailand. He retired from British Petroleum in 1992, having held positions of Exploration Manager, Chief Geologist, and most recently Executive Consultant. For the next several years he continued his career with the partnership of Rosen-Balsinger and Associates. Since full retirement in 1997, Mr. Balsinger has lived in Pagosa Springs, Colorado, and Spring, Texas, depending on the season and his many travels with his wife, Georgia.

Jerry C. Biberstine

Drinking Water Specialist
Water Quality Control Division
Colorado Department of Public Health and Environment
4300 Cherry Creek Dr. South
Denver, CO 80246-1530
Phone: (303) 692-3546
Fax: (303) (303) 782-0390
E-mail: jerry.biberstine@state.co.us

Jerry Biberstine has been with the Department of Public Health and Environment for over twenty-five years and in charge of the Drinking Water Program since 1987. He is a professional engineer, having received a B.S. in marine engineering from the U.S. Merchant Marine Academy and an M.S. in sanitary engineering from West Virginia University. He is a past president of the Association of State Drinking Water Administrators. He has sat on the American Water Works Association (AWWA) National Public Advisory Forum and AWWA Small System Policy and Guidance Committees. He is also a faculty member at the University College of the University of Denver.

Kathleen Norris Cook

Kathleen Norris Cook Photography
P.O. Box 1816
300 8th Ave.
Ouray, CO 81427
Phone: (970) 325-0700
Fax: (970) 325-0800
Website: www.kathleennorriscook.com

All photographs used in this book are the work of the world renowned nature photographer Kathleen Norris Cook. Now based in Ouray, Colorado, her most recent book, *Spirit of the San Juans,* displays the spectacular scenery and resplendent colors of the Colorado landscape. Cook's vast experience and love for the mountains of Colorado result in vivid illustrations that allow the viewer to relive their own observations of the state's beauty and majesty.

Cook has completed three other books: a large pictorial book *Yosemite, Valley of Thunder; Exploring Mountain Highways,* a book featuring panoramic photographs; and *The Million Dollar Highway,* about the area between Ouray and Durango. Information about all of her work can be found on the web at www.kathleennorriscook.com.

In over 20 years of freelancing, Kathleen Norris Cook's work has been sought by many international companies including Eastman Kodak, E & J Gallo, Hewlett Packard, and numerous tourism boards around the world. Along with national advertising work for such clients as American Airlines, General Motors, and Ford, she is a major contributor to Sierra Club publications as well as the National Park Service.

Rod Cook

Weed Manager
La Plata County
2500 North Main
Durango, CO 81301
Phone: (970) 247-2308
Fax: (970) 247-2365
E-mail: cookrd@co.laplata.co.us

Rod Cook is a lifelong resident of Colorado who grew up in a family that ranched and provided guiding and outfitting services. One of his hobbies, scenic wildflower photography, sparked an interest in weeds and exotic species invasions. He has been employed as the La Plata County

Weed Technician since the inception of the county weed program in 1992. Mr. Cook has been a member of the Colorado Weed Management Association for ten years and in 1995 received the Award of Innovation for "outstanding effort and creativity in the field of weed management." He continues to be amazed at the rate at which exotic weeds are conquering the land in Colorado and other Western states. Noxious weeds are spreading at an estimated rate of 4,600 acres per day on Western public lands.

Frank C. ("Chuck") Dennis

Wildfire Hazard Mitigation Coordinator
Colorado State Forest Service
9769 West 119th Drive, Suite 12
Broomfield, CO 80021
Phone: (303) 465-9043
Fax: (303) 465-9048
E-mail: cdennis@rmi.net

Frank C. ("Chuck") Dennis graduated in 1973 from Northern Arizona University with a bachelor's degree in forestry. While in college, he worked for the U.S. Forest Service on various range, timber, watershed, and fire projects. Following graduation, he worked at two different sawmill operations in Montrose, Colorado, with an emphasis on wood and wood waste utilization. Mr. Dennis began his career as a forester with the Colorado State Forest Service in 1975. Following various assignments dealing with insects and disease, forest management, land use planning, running a logging and sawmill operation using inmate labor, and fire and timber management, he worked his way to the position of District Forester in 1986 on the Golden District. In 1994 he took a special assignment with Jefferson County to work on land use planning and the development of wildfire-related regulations as well as serving as the county's wildfire coordinator. In January 1997 he assumed responsibility for the state's new position of Wildfire Hazard Mitigation Coordinator. He is one of the cofounders of the Jefferson County Fire Council's Wildfire Committee, the County's Incident Management Group, and the Colorado Wildland Fire Conference. Mr. Dennis is the author of many publications, including *Creating Wildfire Defensible Zones,* and has recently prepared several documents for use within the Colorado State Forest Service. He is a past board member of the Colorado Forestry Association and of the city of Westminster's Open Space Advisory Board. He has been happily married to Melinda for twenty-nine years and is the father of four daughters and a grandfather of two boys. He enjoys bike riding, fishing, and woodworking.

Leslie A. Fields
Faegre and Benson, LLP
370 17th St., 2500 Republic Plaza
Denver, CO 80202-4004
Phone: (303) 592-9000
Fax: (303) 820-0600
E-mail: lfields@faegre.com

Leslie Fields is a partner at Faegre and Benson, LLP, and practices in the area of land use and eminent-domain law, representing both private and governmental entities, including individual landowners, developers, private pipeline companies, counties, municipalities, urban renewal authorities, and special districts. She is a graduate of the University of Denver, College of Law (1981), and the University of Denver (1978).

Randall J. Feuerstein
Dufford and Brown P.C.
1700 Broadway, Suite 1700
Denver, CO 80290-1701
Phone: (303) 861-8013
Fax: (303) 832-3804
E-mail: feuersr@duffordbrown.com

Randall J. Feuerstein is a shareholder and director in the Denver law firm of Dufford and Brown, P.C., where he concentrates his practice in the areas of real estate law, bankruptcy law, and farm and ranch law. An engineering honor graduate of the University of Colorado at Boulder, Mr. Feuerstein received his J.D. degree from the University of Denver, Order of St. Ives. He is the author of "Real Estate Litigation in the Bankruptcy Context," *Real Property Practice and Litigation*, 1990 (Shepard's/McGraw-Hill, Inc., publishers). He coauthored "May the Landlord Unreasonably Withhold Consent to Assignment?" *The Colorado Lawyer*, October, 1983. He has lectured for CLE and other programs in the real estate, bankruptcy, and agricultural law areas upon such topics as contracts, brokers, leases, financing, and various bankruptcy matters involving both real estate and agricultural issues. He is a member of the Denver, Colorado, Bar Association (Real Estate Section, Business Section, Bankruptcy Section, and Agricultural Law Section) and the American Bar Association.

Matt Glasgow
Public Affairs Officer
U.S. Forest Service
2250 Hwy 50
Delta, CO 81416
Phone: (970) 874-6674
Fax: (970) 874-6698

Matt Glasgow is a career officer with the U.S. Forest Service and is a spokesperson for the Grand Mesa, Uncompahgre, and Gunnison National Forests. A former journalist, he has more than one hundred magazine articles and several thousand newspaper news and feature stories to his credit.

Barbara J. B. Green
Otten Johnson Robinson Neff and Ragonetti, P.C.
1600 Colorado National Building
950 Seventeenth Street
Denver, CO 80202
Phone: (303) 825-8400
Fax: (303) 825-6525

Barbara J. B. Green was admitted to the Colorado Bar in 1985 and is an attorney with Otten Johnson Robinson Neff and Ragonetti, P.C., where she practices land use law, environmental law, and municipal law. She is a 1971 graduate of Northwestern University and holds a master's in public administration and a juris doctorate degree from the University of Colorado in Boulder. Ms. Green is an alumna of the Rocky Mountain Program for Public Management, and prior to attending law school, she served as Assistant to the City Manager for Steamboat Springs and Town Administrator and Planner for the towns of Oak Creek and Yampa. Ms. Green represents both private- and public-sector clients on matters involving land use planning, regulation, and litigation, including open lands preservation. She has prepared land use regulations and comprehensive plans for several Colorado municipalities and counties and serves as general counsel to the Northwest Colorado Council of Governments, where she advises local governments on watershed planning. In addition, she serves as Town Attorney for the towns of Silver Plume and Kremmling. Ms. Green acts as a mediator on land use disputes between developers and neighborhood groups and counsels clients on the acquisition, disposal, and development of contaminated property. Her environmental practice includes matters arising under hazardous waste and water quality regulations, NEPA compliance and litigation, and all aspects of local government permitting and enforcement. Ms. Green is a member of the Mined Land Reclamation Board, the University of Colorado Real Estate Council, and the Advisory Board to the Land Exchange Assistance Program. She is a frequent lecturer on environmental and growth management issues.

Daniel A. Gregory

Attorney at Law
1199 Main Ave, Suite 213
Durango, CO 81301
Phone: (970) 247-3123
Fax: (970) 247-8293

Daniel A. Gregory has been practicing law for approximately fifteen years as of the writing of this chapter. He is a member of the Colorado and Florida State Bar Associations, the Colorado and Florida Federal Bars, the Colorado and Florida Construction Law Committees, and the American Bar Association Forum on the Construction Industry. He specializes in real estate and construction litigation and has offices in both Durango and Telluride, Colorado.

Nancy S. Greif

Mediator and Attorney at Law
701 Camino del Rio, Suite 210
Durango, CO 81301
Phone: (970) 382-0023
Fax: (970) 382-9088

Nancy S. Greif holds four advanced degrees, including a Ph.D. in geology and geophysics from Texas A & M University and a juris doctor (including a specialized certificate and award in natural resources law) from the University of New Mexico. After fourteen years of working for the U.S. Geological Survey as a scientist and a manager, Dr. Greif decided she wanted to move to small-town Colorado to practice transactional law and alternative dispute resolution (ADR). She continues to educate and represent clients on numerous issues related to compliance with Colorado water law, land use, and neighborhood conflicts. She considers her law practice an exercise in dispute prevention. Her Durango practice emphasizes the use of mediation and other forms of ADR as a way of resolving conflicts and as a way of ending lawsuits in progress. She is the ADR Coordinator and a mediator for the Sixth Judicial District. She is a member of the American Bar Association, the American Arbitration Association, and the Colorado Bar Association and a past president of the Southwest Colorado Women's Bar Association. Dr. Greif has published numerous articles on law, public policy, and geology.

Victor M. Grimm

Attorney at Law
1027 14th St.
Boulder, CO 80302
Phone: (303) 413-0565
Fax: (303) 413-0681

Victor Grimm and his wife, Denise Grimm, who is a certified paralegal, currently have an office in Boulder with a practice focusing on real estate and commercial transactions and litigation. Mr. Grimm is also a Real Property Instructor at Denver Paralegal Institute. He has been an associate for the real estate practice group in a large international law firm and a solo practitioner in a small mountain town. He has written the *Landlord and Tenant Guide to Colorado Evictions*, published by Bradford Publishing Company. He has also written many articles and chapters for continuing legal education relating to various real estate topics. Mr. Grimm has a B.A. from Syracuse University and a J.D. from Loyola University of Chicago School of Law. Victor has been involved in the real estate business since he was eleven years old, sweeping vacant apartments and serving eviction notices for his family's Chicago real estate business. He and his wife settled into the Rocky Mountain foothills, where they act as landlord to a menagerie of tenants, including horses, heifers, dogs, chickens, and goats.

William Clark Harrell

Center for Constitutional Rights
666 Broadway, 7th Floor
New York, NY 10012
Phone: 212-614-6464
Fax: 212-614-6499
E-mail: CCR@IGC.APC.ORG

William Clark Harrell is the Executive Director of the National Police Accountability Project based at the Center for Constitutional Rights in New York. Mr. Harrell was a staff attorney at Colorado Rural Legal Services, Migrant Farm Worker Division, in 1998. He practiced international human rights law in Central and South America from 1992 to 1997. He is the National Vice President of the National Lawyers Guild. Mr. Harrell has a B.A. in history from the University of Texas, Austin (1987), a juris doctorate from American University, Washington College of Law, Washington, DC (1990), and an L.L.M. in international human rights from American University, Washington College of Law (1997). Mr. Harrell is licensed to practice law in New York and Washington, DC.

Susan W. Hatter

Proprietor
Escrow Services Company
121 East Montezuma Ave.
Cortez, CO 81321
Phone: (970) 565-5404
Fax: (970) 565-2720
E-mail: hatter@notaryoncall.com

Susan W. Hatter is the Owner and Manager of an independent real estate closing company. This company specializes in closings between private parties (no realtors involved), mobile notary services, and intermediary services for 1031 exchanges. Ms. Hatter holds a degree in business administration and has been involved in the business of real estate closings for over twenty-two years. For sixteen of those years she was involved in real estate transactions as the lender. She spent four years as a title examiner and closer for a title company. Three years ago she began Escrow Services Company, providing a service-oriented, insured closing accommodating clients who may or may not use a realtor in their transaction. The company also specializes in the closing of mortgage loan transactions. Ms. Hatter is an affiliate member of the Four Corners Board of Realtors and the Cortez Chamber of Commerce and also currently serves as a Director of the Southwest Health Systems Board of the Southwest Memorial Hospital. She is married to an attorney and enjoys travel whenever the opportunity arises.

Peter A. Holton

Holton Planning Associates
P.O. Box 1508
Durango, CO 81302
Phone: (970) 259-0877
Fax: (970) 382-0185
E-mail: holtonpa@sprynet.com

Peter A. Holton, American Institute of Certified Planners (AICP), is the Principal of Holton Planning Associates, a land use planning firm in Durango, Colorado. Mr. Holton is the former Senior Long Range Planner for La Plata County, Colorado. He is actively involved in rural growth and development issues in the Southwest. Mr. Holton is a member of the American Institute of Certified Planners and holds a master's degree in city and regional planning and a bachelor's of science in natural resource management, both from the University of California.

Kate Jones

Colorado State Board of Land Commissioners
1313 Sherman, Room 620
Denver, CO 80203
Phone: (303) 866-3454, ext. 320
Fax: (303) 866-3152

Kate Jones is the Public Information Officer for the Colorado State Board of Land Commissioners. She has worked for various agencies within the Colorado Department of Natural Resources for more than ten years on projects that have included an energy and water conservation guide for farmers, a booklet on the state's wetlands, and a short guide for landowners in Colorado.

Erin J. Johnson

Attorney at Law, L.L.C.
925 S. Broadway, Suite 206
Cortez, CO 81321
Phone: (970) 565-2628
Fax: (970) 565-2608
E-mail: erin@fone.net

Erin J. Johnson is an attorney and mediator with a law practice and real estate brokerage in Cortez, Colorado. A primary emphasis of her work is acting as a development consultant, and she represents major rural and urban projects throughout Colorado. She is a Colorado Western Slope native with extensive experience in land use, planning, and development issues involving both the public and private sectors. Ms. Johnson received a juris doctor degree in 1994 from the University of Denver College of Law with an emphasis in land use issues and has a bachelor's degree in planning. She is a member of the American Institute of Certified Planners (AICP). Ms. Johnson is a coauthor of *Geologic Hazard Avoidance or Mitigation*, published by the Colorado Geological Survey in 1998. She is one of several authors of *Habitat Protection Planning: Where the Wild Things Are*, published by the American Planning Association Planning Advisory Service (PAS report #470–471) in 1997. She is a coauthor of *Development Agreements: Analysis, Colorado Case Studies and Commentary*, published in 1993 by the Rocky Mountain Land Use Institute. Ms. Johnson is active in several local and regional representative groups, including the Smart Growth Interregional Council. She is an active member and cochair of the BLM Southwest Resource Advisory Council.

Donald H. Kelley

Attorney at Law
9619 South Bexley Drive
Highlands Ranch, CO 80126
Phone: (303) 322-2893
Fax: (303) 470-1557

Donald H. Kelley is a Denver attorney who specializes in estate and business organization planning as well as estate and gift tax appeals. He is the coauthor of *Estate Planning for Farmers and Ranchers* (Clark Boardman Callaghan, 1996), *The Farm and Ranch Industry* (Little, Brown, 1995), *Family Business Organizations* (Clark Boardman Callaghan, 1996), and *Estate Planning Assistant* and *Intuitive Es-*

tate Planner Software (Clark Boardman Callaghan). He received his B.S. and LL.B. from the University of Nebraska and is a member of the bars of Nebraska (Past Chair: Probate Section) and Colorado (Past Chair: Agricultural Law Section). He is a frequent speaker on tax and estate planning topics and has served on the governing boards of the ABA Real Property Probate and Trust Section, the American College of Trust and Estate Counsel, and the American College of Tax Counsel.

Bill Kinney
Out on the Ranch
In the USA

Bill Kinney has a Ph.D. in resource management from the University of California, Davis, where he developed an integrated watershed management plan for public rangelands in California. He has also worked in the states of Washington and New Mexico, where he provided assistance and education to small farmers who were trying to practice more sustainable agriculture and survive in the face of increasing urbanization. After struggling with the traditional academic approaches to resource management for many years, he began exploring the holistic approach in 1992. He has worked with successful practitioners of sustainable agriculture in Colorado, Wyoming, Nebraska, Idaho, Utah, Montana, New Mexico, Nevada, California, and Arizona. Mr. Kinney has diverse experience in resource management, education, and business, including three years of classroom teaching at California Polytechnic State University in San Luis Obispo and consulting to small businesses in marketing and computer systems. He authored a chapter on past rangeland conditions in the Sierra Nevada Ecosystem Project (SNEP) Final Report, a three-year, $7.5 million project involving one hundred scientists.

Craig Larson
La Plata County Assessor's Office
P.O. Box 3339
Durango, CO 81302
Phone: (970) 382-6235
Fax: (970) 382-6299

Craig Larson is a Denver native who has lived in La Plata County, the Durango area, for thirty years. He is married to Jan and has two daughters, Jada and Emily. He is a graduate of Fort Lewis College and majored in geology. He holds a master's degree in public administration from the University of Colorado at Denver. He worked in both the building and the oil and gas industries before becoming an appraiser and then La Plata County Assessor in 1987. He

has been reelected to that position twice and is presently serving his third four-year term. He enjoys tennis, running, skiing, camping, and being involved with education and community issues.

Gail G. Lyons
Boulder Real Estate Services, Ltd.
2541 Spruce St.
Boulder, CO 80302
Phone: (303) 442-3335
Fax: (303) 442-3925
E-mail: HLAGail@ aol.com
Website: http://www.Boulder-RealEstate.com

Gail Lyons is the broker-owner of a small residential firm, Boulder Real Estate Services, Ltd./Realty Executives. The firm specializes in buyer agency and, when selling its own listings, practices dual agency. Gail has been a full-time real estate practitioner for over twenty-six years, all in Boulder, Colorado. During that time she's been president of her local realtor association, the Colorado Association of Realtors, and, nationally, the Council of Residential Specialists. A strong believer in education, she's earned six designations. With her partner, Don Harlan, she's written numerous articles and five books, including *Buyer Agency; Your Competitive Edge in Real Estate;* and *Consensual Dual Agency, a Practical Approach to the In-House Sale.* One of her books has been translated into Spanish: *Como Superar a la Competencia en el Negocio Immobiliario.* Ms. Lyons is recognized throughout the United States as a futurist and expert in agency law and practice, especially buyer agency and dual agency. Together with Mr. Harlan, she has team-taught hundreds of seminars throughout the United States, Canada, and Eastern Europe for local and state associations, large independent firms, and franchises. Their seminars have been so well received that they have been speakers at nearly every National Association of Realtors meeting since 1986 and have taught more than fifty thousand students. In 1994 they received the first annual Agency Educator of the Year award from *Agency Law Quarterly.*

Linda Martin
U.S. Park Service
Mesa Verde National Park
P.O. Box 8
Mesa Verde, CO 81330-0008
Phone: (970) 529-4632
Fax: (970) 529-4637

Born and raised on a Nebraska farm, Linda Martin received a degree in history from Creighton University. She has worked for the National Park Service for twenty-six years, almost twenty-three of those years at Mesa Verde National Park. She helps supervise the Interpretation and Visitor Services staff and works with the public on a regular basis. She is the author of *Mesa Verde: The Story Behind the Scenery.*

Donald E. Moore

Douglas County Planning Dept.
100 Third Street
Castle Rock, CO 80104
Phone: (303) 660-7460
Fax: (303) 660-9550
E-mail: dcpln@douglas.co.us

Don Moore is a county land use planner involved with comprehensive and natural resource planning. Mr. Moore has been with Douglas County, Colorado, since 1984, and has been instrumental in the county's successful open space preservation program and involved in long-range planning. He has been a land use planner for twenty-one years at all levels of government and has worked for Wheat Ridge, Golden, and Jefferson County. Mr. Moore is an active member and cochair of the APA Colorado Legislative Affairs Committee and serves on many local and regional boards, representing a variety of natural resource, environmental, and recreational interests. He has a B.S. from Colorado State University, Fort Collins, and has completed graduate course work in public administration, public policy, and land use planning. He is a member of the American Institute of Certified Planners (AICP).

Patricia K. Murray

M.T., C.P.A.
21 N. 1st Avenue, Suite 290
Brighton, CO 80601
Phone: (303) 659-3951 ext. 23
Fax: (303) 659-4898
E-mail: pkmurraycpa@ibm.net
Website: pkmurraycpa.com

Patricia K. Murray is in public practice as a Certified Public Accountant. She is a shareholder in Patricia K. Murray, P.C. Her practice emphasizes tax matters for farmers and ranchers, individuals, partnerships, corporations, trusts, and LLCs. Her practice also does small business management and planning, estate planning, office automation, and Quick Books® setup and consulting. Ms. Murray received a master's in tax degree from the University of Denver College of Law and her B.S. degree in accounting from Metro State College. She is actively involved with the Agricultural Lawyers section of the Colorado Bar Association.

James M. (Mike) Olguin

Director
Department of Natural Resources
Southern Ute Indian Tribe
P.O. Box 737, 116 Mouache Drive
Ignacio, CO 81137-0737
Phone: (970) 563-0125
Fax: (970) 563-0387

James M. (Mike) Olguin is an enrolled member of the Southern Ute Indian Tribe. He has worked for the Tribe for the last twenty years within the same department but in different divisions. He started work for the Tribe as a Wildlife Conservation Officer in 1978, then was promoted to Wildlife Conservation Director in 1985, then to Director of Natural Resources in 1993. Mr. Olguin has been involved in the reorganization of the Department of Natural Resources and is continuing efforts to ensure that the Tribe employs a well-trained, professional team of laborers, managers, and technical staff. He extends his gratitude and appreciation to the department's Records Manager, Arlene Baker, for her time and effort for this project.

William A. Paddock

Carlson, Hammond and Paddock, L.L.P.
1700 Lincoln St, #3900
Denver, CO 80203-4539
Phone: (303) 861-9000
Fax: (303) 861-9026

Bill Paddock is a trial attorney with a statewide practice representing agricultural, municipal, development, and individual interests in water rights, water quality, federal land law, real property, and environmental issues. He is a 1978 graduate of the University of Colorado School of Law. From 1979 through 1984, Mr. Paddock was an Assistant Attorney General and First Assistant Attorney General for the State of Colorado, involved in all phases of water rights work for the state. He has been in private practice since that time and is the manager of Carlson, Hammond and Paddock, L.L.C., in Denver, Colorado.

Dusty Pierce

P.O. Box 504
Pagosa Springs, CO 81147
Phone: (970) 731-9250
Fax: (970) 731-4466

Dusty Pierce, along with his wife, Beverly, is a nineteen-year resident of Pagosa Springs, Colorado. He has established a statewide reputation of excellence as a General Contractor and Master Carpenter. His thirty years of experience in construction in rural Colorado has been typified by outstanding achievement in a wide variety of successful projects. With a reputation from building local landmarks to numerous nationally advertised and award-winning projects, he has been branded as an innovator who loves a challenge. Mr. Pierce was the State Director of the Colorado Association of Homebuilders' (CAHB) and was the founding president of the Upper San Juan Builders' Association (USJBA). He has been featured in *Builder Architect* magazine as well as many other regional and national books and publications. In his "spare time," his passion is teaching horsemanship to youth, and he is a local volunteer firefighter.

Michael Preston
109 W. Main, Room 302
Cortez, CO 81321
Phone: (970) 565-8525
Fax: (970) 565-3420
E-mail: mpreston@frontier.net

Michael Preston received his M.A. in urban and regional planning from the University of Colorado at Denver. He is the Director of the Office of Community Services at Fort Lewis College, which assists communities and local governments in dealing with growth and change. Preston serves as the Coordinator of the Montezuma County Federal Lands Program and the Southwest Colorado Community–Public Land Partnership, both of which work to build collaborative relationships between local communities and public land management agencies. Projects include a nationally recognized ponderosa pine forest restoration initiative and a community-based approach to revising the San Juan National Forest Plan. Since 1994 Mr. Preston has worked on the development and implementation of the Montezuma County Comprehensive Land Use Plan, which emphasizes citizen involvement and incentive-based approaches to agricultural preservation in a context of population growth and demographic change. Mr. Preston has been invited to speak throughout the West on integrated, community-based approaches to federal and local land use issues.

Anne Rapp
Rapp Guides and Packers
47 Electra Lake
Durango, CO 81301
Phone: (970) 247-8923
Fax: (970) 247-1255

Although a six-time cover girl, Anne Rapp is not just an-other pretty face. Ms. Rapp is an extremely knowledgeable, entrepreneurial horse-industry professional. Her lifetime interest in animals of all kinds led her to work in zoos and as a trail guide at an early age. She has lived in Colorado most of her adult life. She moved to Durango in 1979 to attend Fort Lewis College and worked for an outfitter and as a waitress. A well-respected community member, Ms. Rapp manages Rapp Guide Services (established in 1981 with her husband, Jerry) and raises a family: Barry, fifteen; Ems, thirteen; horses; mules; dogs; goats; cows; cats; chickens; ducks; rabbits; and at times stray deer, beaver, raccoons, and magpies. Over seventeen years in the outfitting business, Ms. Rapp has provided safe, well-operated, successful adventure trips into the San Juan Mountains for well over fifty thousand people. A few of the groups she has worked with are local 4-H clubs, the Backcountry Horseman's Association, Girl and Boy Scout troops, the Women's Resource Center, *Outside* magazine, and *Western Horseman*. After several decades of residing and operating in southwest Colorado, Ms. Rapp is a sought-after authority on "horsing around" subjects from wilderness preservation to helping neighbors figure out amiable ways to share the trails. Her love for the wilderness, animals, and people and bringing them all together in a respectful manner is admirable. "Watch her closely; her star has only begun to rise" (*Guerrilla Adventure Survivor*, 1998). "When Anne Rapp's kids were infants she'd take them into the Colorado wilderness and park them under the stars" (*Cosmopolitan*, March 1993). "On the worst days, I can look at the beauty of the clouds or see the stars coming out and realize how lucky I am" (Anne Rapp interview, *Cowboys and Country*, Winter 1995).

Lauranne P. Rink
Mile High Wetlands Group, L.L.C.
80 S. 27th Ave
Brighton, CO 80601
Phone: (303) 204-4164
Fax: (303) 659-6077
E-mail: laurie@wetlandbank.com

Laurie Rink is a certified professional wetland scientist who has practiced in the field of wetland ecology for fifteen years. She recently founded and is managing one of the first commercial wetland mitigation banks in the Rocky Mountain region. Her prior experience included owning and operating an environmental restoration firm that provided consulting, design, construction, and nursery services throughout the western United States. She holds a bachelor's degree in biology and environmental conservation from the University of Colorado at Boulder.

Thea Rock
Formerly with Colorado State Parks Division Office
1313 Sherman, Room 618
Denver, CO 80203
Phone: (303) 866-3437
Fax: (303) 866-3206

Katharine Roser
P.O. Box 1651
Durango, CO 81302
Phone: (970) 259-3415
Fax: (970) 259-3415
E-mail: lposc@frontier.net

Katharine Roser is a founder and past President of the Colorado Coalition of Land Trusts, a statewide education and service organization for Colorado Land Trusts. She is the Executive Director of the La Plata County Open Space Conservancy, a local land trust organization based in Durango. She was educated at Middlebury College and has a B.A. in geography and experience in land use planning and education.

John R. (Jack) Sperber
Faegre and Benson, L.L.P.
370 17th St, 2500 Republic Plaza
Denver, CO 80202-4004
Phone: (303) 592-9000
Fax: (303) 820-0600
E-mail: jsperber@faegre.com

John R. Sperber is an attorney with Faegre and Benson, L.L.P. Mr. Sperber specializes in eminent domain, land use litigation, and access issues, including the litigation of adverse possession claims, disputes regarding the public or private nature of roadways, the condemnation of private ways of necessity, and takings claims relating to the denial or modification of access rights.

Pat Tucker
Colorado Division of Wildlife, Area 15 Office
151 E. 16th St.
Durango, CO 81301
Phone: (970) 247-0855
Fax: (970) 247-2235

Employed by the Colorado Division of Wildlife since 1986, Pat Tucker is one of nearly 120 District Wildlife Managers in Colorado. Mr. Tucker has an A.A.S. degree in fisheries and wildlife technology and a B.S. degree in wildlife biology. He has been a District Wildlife Manager (DWM) in the Front Range cities of Westminster, Broomfield, and Ar-

vada as well as in his current assignment in Durango. As the local field person, DWMs are the primary public contact for most wildlife-related questions. Their job duties include law enforcement, wildlife and habitat management activities, and information and educational projects.

John F. (Jeff) Welborn
Attorney at Law
Welborn Sullivan Meck and Tooley P.C.
1775 Sherman St, Suite 1800
Denver, CO 80203-4318
Phone: (303) 830-2500
Fax: (303) 832-2366

John F. (Jeff) Welborn graduated from Dartmouth College in 1968 and the University of Colorado Law School in 1972. Mr. Welborn specializes in oil and gas, mining, corporate and partnership matters, regulatory litigation, and mediation. He has served as a Commissioner (1982–1992) and Chairman (1987–1992) of the Oil and Gas Commission for the state of Colorado, and as Chairman (1983) of the Mineral Law Section of the Colorado Bar Association. Mr. Welborn has extensive experience negotiating and drafting natural resource development agreements, financing arrangements, and conveyance documents. Mr. Welborn is an Adjunct Professor, Oil and Gas Law, Natural Resources, Water Law, at the University of Denver Law School. He teaches oil and gas and natural resources law to lawyers and landmen and is a frequent lecturer in continuing education seminars. Mr. Welborn is a member of the Denver, Colorado, and American Bar Associations.

Beth A. Whittier
Whittier, Shupp, and House, L.L.C.
23055 Whispering Woods
Golden, CO 80401
Phone: (888) 640-5010
Fax: (303) 526-5508
E-mail: mgtdbeth@aol.com

Beth Whittier is an attorney and general partner in the law firm Whittier, Shupp and House, located in Colorado Springs and Golden. Ms. Whittier's primary private practice is representing local governments in regulatory takings, land use, environmental, election, and general local governmental law issues. She previously served as El Paso County Attorney (1986–1995), General Legal Counsel to the El Paso and Teller Counties E911 Authority Board (1992–1993), El Paso County Administrative Services Director (1989–1994), and Eagle County Attorney (1979–1986). Ms. Whittier received a bachelor of science degree in business administration from Kansas State University in 1974 and her law degree from Washburn University School of Law in 1978. She recently served on the Colorado Bar Association Real Estate Law Section Council and has previously served as President, Secretary/Treasurer, and Executive Board member of the Colorado County Attorneys' Association; President, Vice-President, and Secretary/Treasurer of the Continental Divide Bar Association; and a member of the Fifth Judicial District Nominating Commission. She has been a speaker on a myriad of local government issues at conferences sponsored by such organizations as Colorado Counties, Inc., the American Planning Association (Colorado), Colorado County Attorneys' Association, Rocky Mountain Land Use Institute, Northwest Colorado Council of Governments, Colorado Association of Stormwater and Floodplain Managers, and the Public Policy Group. She has also represented local governmental agencies as amicus curiae in state appellate proceedings and has successfully handled litigation on behalf of local governments, both at the state appellate and federal levels, in the areas of land use and regulatory takings.

James S. Witwer
Trout and Raley, P.C.
1775 Sherman, #1300
Denver, CO 80203
Phone: (303) 861-1963 ext. 129
Fax: (303) 832-4465

Jim Witwer is a shareholder at the Denver law firm of Trout and Raley, P.C. Mr. Witwer represents municipal, business, and agricultural clients in the areas of water rights, eminent domain, public lands, and environmental law and is a frequent speaker on these topics. Mr. Witwer received his law degree from the University of Colorado School of Law after graduating from Yale College. He is the author of "The Renewal of Authorizations to Divert Water on National Forests," an article that appeared in the October 1995 edition of *The Colorado Lawyer*.

Ed Zink
4166 C.R. 203
Durango, CO 81302
Phone: (970) 259-4621
Fax: (970) 259-6663
E-mail: edzink@frontier.net

Having lived on a ranch in western Colorado for fifty years, Ed Zink has been very involved in many facets of outdoor recreation. In addition to running a bicycle shop and a motorcycle shop, Mr. Zink operates a big-game-hunting outfitting business. Thirty years in the recreation business, coupled with attending hundreds of public meetings concerning recreational use on public land, have qualified him to serve on numerous local, state, and national committees about recreation. Mr. Zink was honored in December 1997 with a lifetime achievement award in supporting the sport of cycling at the fourth annual Korbel Night of Champions at the Eagle's Nest in Vail. He is a 1969 graduate of Fort Lewis College and was honored for his work as the twenty-six-year director of the Iron Horse Bicycle Classic as well as his work in bringing the National Off Road Bicycling Association (NORBA) national championships to Durango in 1986, 1987, and 1992. Perhaps his most highlighted achievement is the first Union Cycliste internationally sanctioned world mountain-bike championships, held at the Purgatory Resort in 1990. All of the events were produced by Mr. Zink and his staff. Mr. Zink has also served on the NORBA board of trustees and is a UCI commissaire.